Theoretical Integration in the Study of Deviance and Crime

SUNY Series in Critical Issues in Criminal Justice
Donald J. Newman, Gilbert Geis, and Terence P. Thornberry, Editors

SUNY Series in Deviance and Social Control
Ronald A. Farrell, Editor

Theoretical Integration in the Study of Deviance and Crime

Problems and Prospects

edited by

STEVEN F. MESSNER
MARVIN D. KROHN
ALLEN E. LISKA

State University of New York Press

Published by
State University of New York Press, Albany

© 1989 State University of New York

All rights reserved

Printed in the United States of America

No part of this book may be used or reproduced
in any manner whatsoever without written permission
except in the case of brief quotations embodied in
critical articles and reviews.

For information, address State University of New York
Press, State University Plaza, Albany, N.Y., 12246

Library of Congress Cataloging in Publication Data

Theoretical integration in the study of deviance and crime: problems
　　and prospects/edited by Steven F. Messner, Marvin D. Krohn, Allen
　　E. Liska.
　　　　p. cm.—(SUNY series in critical issues in criminal
　　Justice) (SUNY series in deviance and social control)
　　　　Includes index.
　　　　ISBN 0–7914–0000–X.　ISBN 0–7914–0001–8 (pbk.)
　　　　1. Deviant behavior—Congresses. 2. Criminal behavior—
　　Congresses.　　I. Messner, Steven F.　　II. Krohn, Marvin D.
　　III. Liska, Allen E.　　IV. Series.　　V. Series: SUNY series in
　　deviance and social control.
　　HM291.T38　1989
　　302.5'42—dc19　　　　　　　　　　　　　　　　　　88–22441
　　　　　　　　　　　　　　　　　　　　　　　　　　　　　　CIP

10 9 8 7 6 5 4 3 2 1

Contents

Preface ix

Strategies and Requisites for Theoretical
    Integration in the Study of Crime and Deviance
    ALLEN E. LISKA, MARVIN D. KROHN,
    AND STEVEN F. MESSNER 1

Part I. Micro-Level Integration

Introduction 21

1. A Social Behaviorist's Perspective on Integration of
Theories of Crime and Deviance
RONALD L. AKERS 23

2. Exploring Alternatives to Integrated Theory
TRAVIS HIRSCHI 37

3. Reflections on the Advantages and Disadvantages of
Theoretical Integration
TERENCE P. THORNBERRY 51

4. A Theory of Mental Illness: An Attempted Integration
of Biological, Psychological and Social Variables
WALTER R. GOVE AND MICHAEL HUGHES 61

5. Cognitive Consistency in Deviance Causation:
A Psychological Elaboration of an Integrated
Systems Model
RONALD A. FARRELL 77

6. Theory Integration Versus Model Building
MARGARET FARNWORTH 93

Part II. Macro-Level Integration

Introduction ... 101

7. Political Decisionmaking and Ecological Models of Delinquency: Conflict and Consensus
   ROBERT J. BURSIK, JR ... 105

8. Towards an Integrated Theory of Criminal Behavior
   CHARLES F. WELLFORD ... 119

9. The Discipline as Data: Resolving the Theoretical Crisis in Criminology
   VICTORIA L. SWIGERT ... 129

10. A Theoretical Approach to Integration
    THOMAS J. BERNARD ... 137

11. Prospects for Synthetic Theory: A Consideration of Macro-Level Criminological Activity
    CHARLES R. TITTLE ... 161

12. Three Perennial Issues in the Sociology of Deviance
    JACK P. GIBBS ... 179

Part III. Cross-Level Integration

Introduction ... 197

13. Deviance and Differentiation
    ROBERT F. MEIER ... 199

14. Micro- and Macro-Structures of Delinquency Causation and a Power-Control Theory of Gender and Delinquency
    JOHN HAGAN ... 213

15. Strategies for Cross-Level Theorizing: Comments on the Meier and Hagan Papers
    CRAIG B. LITTLE ... 229

16. Exploring Integration of Theoretical Levels of Explanation: Notes on Gang Delinquency
    JAMES F. SHORT, JR. ... 243

17. Confronting Control Theory's Negative Cases
    PEGGY C. GIORDANO   261

18. The Challenge and Promise of Theoretical Integration
    in Criminology
    ROLAND CHILTON   279

List of Contributors   287

Notes   293

References   301

Index   339

Preface

This book is the product of a conference held on the Albany campus of the State University of New York in May of 1987. The original idea for the conference was to bring together leading scholars who have grappled with some of the more important issues associated with theoretical integration in the study of crime and deviance. We decided to organize the proceedings around the theme of integration at different levels of analysis—i.e., micro-level integration, macro-level integration, and cross-level integration. However, authors were given leeway as to how they might address these concerns. Within each of these general categories, two sections were organized, each consisting of two presenters and a discussant. The format of this book follows the original format of the conference. The papers contained herein are revised versions prepared specially for inclusion in this edited collection. Also, we have added an introductory chapter, which raises some basic concerns surrounding theoretical integration, and brief introductions to each of the three major sections.

We would like to acknowledge a number of people without whose assistance the conference and subsequent book would not have come to fruition. We are grateful to Vincent O'Leary, President of SUNYA; Judith Ramaley and John Shumaker, past Vice Presidents of SUNYA; John Webb, Dean of Social and Behavioral Sciences; and Jim Garofalo, Director of the Hindelang Criminal Justice Research Center for their financial support of the Conference. We would like to thank Louise Tornatore for her administration of the Conference, Joan Cipperly for her administrative and secretarial support, and Debra Neuls and Eileen Pellegrino for their secretarial support. We would also like to thank various graduate students (Barbara Warner, Jiang Yu, Lisa Bonati, Michael Lieber, and Elizabeth Cass) who assisted with the many incidental tasks in organizing a conference.

Strategies and Requisites for Theoretical Integration in the Study of Crime and Deviance

Allen E. Liska, Marvin D. Krohn, Steven F. Messner

Introduction

The study of deviance and crime has traditionally been characterized by a multitude of seemingly unrelated and competitive theories. Since the 1960s the field has been dominated by the following theories: anomie, social disorganization, differential association, social control, deterrence, labeling, ethnomethodology, and conflict. To many scholars, this large number of theories has made the field seem fragmented, if not in disarray. In response to this seemingly chaotic state of affairs, numerous voices have called for theoretical integration. (Pearson and Weiner, 1985, make one of the latest in the history of such calls.)

What exactly is meant by theoretical integration is rarely made clear. To understand the meaning of the concept "integration," the dictionary may be a useful place to start. Webster defines the infinitive verb form "to integrate" as "to bring parts together into a unified whole." While the term "unified whole" is also not perfectly clear, especially in regard to theory, it tends to mean a relationship or order among parts. Hence, according to Webster, to integrate theories is to formulate relationships among them.

In the pages to follow, we will explore the meaning of this phrase and some of its implications for the study of crime and deviance. We will first consider the rationale for efforts at theoretical integration. What are the ostensible gains to be realized as a consequence of such an enterprise? We will then examine different strategies and directions for integration, paying attention to contrasts between strategies employed in the natural sciences and those commonly employed in the social sciences. Social scientists have used the term "integration" to refer to a much wider range of conceptual enterprises than have natural scientists. Finally, we will conclude with a few remarks on general criteria for evaluating the success of attempts to formulate integrated explanations of crime and deviance.

The Rationale for Theoretical Integration

A useful place to begin our discussion of the rationale for theoretical integration is with a clarification of the nature of the activity under investigation. There is perhaps an intuitively appealing aura surrounding the notion of theoretical integration which derives from the very terms in its name. The central role of theory in the scientific enterprise can hardly be challenged. As Collins (1986, p. 1345) reminds us, "the essence of science is precisely theory." Moreover, a good scientific theory is one that "integrates," or unifies, empirical findings. It offers, in Hempel's words, "a systematically unified account of quite diverse phenomena" (1966, p. 75). Given the positive meanings attached to both "theory" and "integration," the desirability of theoretical integration might appear to be almost self-evident.

It is important to differentiate, however, between theorizing, an activity that inherently integrates empirical findings within a general abstract framework, and theoretical integration, an activity that involves the formulation of linkages among different theoretical arguments. Theoretical integration is best viewed as one means of theorizing—i.e., as one strategy for developing more cogent explanations and for promoting theoretical growth (see especially Wagner and Berger 1985). Thus the key question to raise when considering the rationale for theoretical integration is whether or not it is, in fact, a more useful strategy for theoretical growth and development than are other strategies.

The case for theoretical integration in the field of crime and deviance has been made mainly with reference to the most prevalent alternative strategy, namely that of theory competition. Theory competition has been depicted quite favorably in the literature on the philosophy of science (e.g. Hempel 1966, pp. 25–28; Stinchcombe 1968, pp. 27–28). According to the classical model of the scientific process, theoretical development proceeds by means of the verification of theories, which involves the derivation of test implications and the evaluation of these implications with empirical observations. The acceptability of a theory increases as it successfully survives more and more tests. However, because the number of possible test implications is virtually indefinite, it is often useful to develop "crucial tests"—i.e., to derive test implications that follow from one theory but stand in contradiction to another theory. The value of such "crucial tests" lies in their efficiency and economy: the results of these tests simultaneously lend credibility to one theory while raising doubts about another (Stinchcombe 1968, pp. 27–28).

The strategy of using crucial tests to evaluate competing theories has informed a large number of studies in the literature on crime and deviance. A couple of examples of such research should help illustrate the logic of this strategy (see Elliott 1985, p. 126, for additional citations). Jensen and Brownfield (1983) have recently examined parental attachment and drug use in an effort to assess Hirschi's social control theory in comparison with variants of social learning theory. Jensen and Brownfield argue that Hirschi's theory unambiguously predicts that attachment to parents should reduce children's drug use irrespective of the parents' own drug use. Social learning theory, in contrast, implies different associations for attachment depending on the drug use of parents. Given the contradictory nature of these predictions, the results will necessarily lend credibility to one approach while simultaneously challenging the other. In this particular study, the findings indicate that the inhibiting effect of parental attachment does vary across categories of parental drug use, thereby raising questions about certain elements of the control perspective.

A second illustration of an explicit effort at theory competition in the recent deviance literature is the research on the specific deterrent effect of arrest in cases involving domestic assault (Sherman and Berk 1984). Sherman and Berk argue that two contradictory hypotheses about the consequences of making an arrest in instances of domestic assault logically follow from the deterrence perspective and the labeling perspective. Deterrence theory implies that legal punishment will reduce the probability that the punished behavior will be repeated, whereas labeling theory implies that the stigma associated with legal punishment will actually increase this probability. The results of Sherman and Berk's field experiment reveal decreased recidivism for offenders subject to an arrest, which they interpret as supportive of the deterrence perspective over the labeling approach.

In short, the theory competition strategy has been described in the literature on the philosophy of science as an efficient and economical means of hypothesis testing, and it has informed much research and theorizing on the causes of crime and deviance. Nevertheless, criticisms of the competitive approach to theory building and verification have begun to emerge, along with calls for greater efforts at theoretical integration. Perhaps the most prominent proponent of the strategy of theoretical integration in the field of crime and deviance is Delbert Elliott (Elliott 1985; Elliott et al. 1985; Elliott et al. 1979).

Elliott expresses several reasons for dissatisfaction with the conventional strategy of theory competition. First, despite the general appeal of the notion of a crucial test, classical theories dealing with crime and deviance rarely permit the derivation of unambiguous, truly distinctive hypotheses. In fact, different theories typically predict similar outcomes, and any given set of empirical findings can often be reconciled with various theoretical approaches (Elliott 1985, p. 125). Classical theories thus do not provide a very firm basis for devising crucial tests.

Elliott also contends that the results of allegedly crucial tests are seldom definitive. This is due in part to perennial methodological problems, such as the difficulties in developing adequate measures of key concepts. In addition, there are a number of logical problems in assuming that the acceptance of one theory necessarily entails the rejection of the rival theory (Elliott 1985, pp. 125–6).

Finally, in Elliott's view, the explanatory power associated with theories that manage to survive the so-called crucial tests tends to be extremely weak. Elliott remarks that "the level of explained variance attributable to separate theories is embarrassingly low" (1985, p. 125). The primary reason for the poor performance of classical theories is that these theories typically involve a "single explanatory variable" (1985, p. 127). Hence, insofar as the causes of crime and deviance are multiple in nature (which seems difficult to dispute), it will be necessary to combine different theories to capture the entire range of relevant causal variables. The theory competition strategy discourages this kind of activity by forcing unproductive choices among theories. It is for these reasons, Elliott concludes, that "the competitive hypothesis approach has often seemed to inhibit theory development rather than to enhance it" (1985, p. 126).

In our view, Elliott's arguments on behalf of theoretical integration are not always persuasive. The fact that classical theories rarely permit the derivation of unambiguous hypotheses indicates the need for greater precision in the statement of these theories. Whether or not attempts at integration will promote greater precision is an open question; however, one could reasonably argue that the goal of theoretical precision might be served just as well by further work within any given theoretical tradition.

Elliott's observation that crucial tests of theories of crime and deviance are rarely definitive is undoubtedly accurate. However, similar statements can be made about all fields of inquiry. Indeed, as Hempel cautions in his discussion of crucial tests in the natural sciences, "even the most careful and extensive tests can neither disprove one of two hypotheses nor prove the other" (1966, p. 28). It is unrealistic, in other words, to expect definitive results in any form of hypothesis testing, and hence the lack of definitive results in competitive approaches does not in itself call for the adoption of an alternative strategy for theorizing.

Finally, the suggestion that classical theories of crime and deviance involve a single explanatory variable is somewhat overstated. While distinctive theories do tend to emphasize a certain class of variables (e.g., social controls, reinforcers, and so forth), this in no way prevents theorists from constructing accounts that involve complex interconnections of a number of variables of the type under consideration and that are thus multicausal in nature.

Despite these reservations about some of the specifics of Elliott's arguments in favor of the strategy of theoretical integration, we are sympathetic to his critical assertion that traditional theories of crime and deviance have not been very successful in explaining these phenomena. There is clearly a pressing need for theoretical development, and it seems only prudent to consider new points of departure, including concerted efforts at theoretical integration. In the section that follows, we hope to contribute to integrative theorizing by describing basic types of theoretical integration and identifying some of the critical tasks that must be confronted in order to accomplish successful integration of the various types.

Types of Integration

Some years ago Hirschi (1979) suggested that strategies or types of integration in the study of deviance and crime can be classified as one of three types: up-and-down or deductive integration, side-by-side or parallel integration, and end-to-end or sequential integration. Each type is defined by a principle that links one or more theories together. Up-and-down integration refers to identifying a level of abstraction or generality that encompasses much of the conceptualization of the constituent theories. The classical integration of the natural sciences, which involves deducing the propositions of one theory from the premises of another, is one example of this form of theoretical integration. Side-by-side (horizontal) integration refers to the partitioning of the subject matter of crime and deviance into cases that are explained by different theories. End-to-end (sequential) integration refers to specifying the temporal order between causal variables, so that the dependent variables of some theories constitute the independent variables of others.

These three types of integration can be applied equally well to micro-level, macro-level, or cross-level integration, thereby yielding a nine-cell typology defined by the principles of theoretical integration and by the levels of analysis (Table 1). For example, end-to-end integration may be illustrated at the micro level by Elliott et al.'s (1985) "integrated" theory, at the macro level by Bursik's combination of conflict and social disorganization theories (chapter 7 in this volume), and at the cross-level by Colvin and Pauly's (1983) structural–Marxist theory. Logically, theories could exist to reflect all cells, although in practice some types are prevalent (e.g., micro-level, end-to-end integrations) whereas examples of other types are difficult to identify (e.g., cross-level, side-by-side). The present discussion will be structured around the principles of integration and some special problems posed by cross-level integration.

Table 1   Types of Integration

		Level of Analysis		
		Micro	Macro	Cross-level
Principle of Linkage (Integration)	Side-by-Side			
	End-to-End			
	Up-and-Down			

Side-by-Side (Horizontal) Integration

Depending on how it is done, this type of integration may seem to be the easiest or it may not even be considered theoretical integration at all. The most common form of side-by-side integration is to partition cases of deviance and crime by the theories that best explain them. However, so that we do not end up with as many theories as cases, we must develop general criteria (principles) for partitioning the cases. Should we use characteristics of deviants, such as class, race, and gender; should we use types of crime and deviance, such as drug use, homicide, and alcoholism; or should we use both characteristics of deviants and deviance? The answer to this question can come from both theory and data. The logic of some theories seems particularly applicable to some types of deviants and deviance. For example, rational decision-making, or choice theory, may not be applicable to most homicides, especially homicides between intimates. On the other hand, it may be very applicable to corporate crime. Empirical analyses may also show that some theories do not apply to some situations, to some categories of deviance, and to some types of deviants.

Typology construction of deviance and deviants seems to be one likely strategy of side-by-side integration. Typology construction has been a favorite pastime of criminologists; during the 1940s, 1950s, and 1960s it was somewhat of a growth industry. During that time it became clear to criminologists that crime and criminals are heterogeneous phenomena. Embezzlement may have little in common with homicide, and upper-class white female criminals may have little in common with lower-class black criminals. Throughout the period, numerous typologies were formulated which organized the subject matter of criminology into types of crimes and criminals. In some cases, these types simply reflected commonly used categories (burglary, homicide) and served as a basis for organizing textbooks of deviance and crime. In other cases types were generated by sophisticated conceptual schemes, including a limited number of underlying dimensions that yielded clear and discrete types (for example Clinard and Quinney 1973 and Gibbons 1985).

The construction of typologies became embroiled more with technical considerations than with theory development. Typologies were judged by clarity, parsimony, mutual exclusivity, and inclusivity of the types. A model typology was thought to be one with clear rules for placing cases, with types that do not overlap, and with a limited number of types in which all cases can be placed. While important, emphasis on these concerns yielded theoretically sterile conceptual classifications and detracted attention from the main reason for typology construction: crime and criminals are so heterogeneous that the causes of one type may not be the causes of the other. That is, for typology construction and theory construction to go hand in hand, types must be theoretically relevant. If they are not, it is difficult to determine how the exercise constitutes a form of theoretical integration.

To theoretically partition the subject matter, the partitioning principle should be linked to the scope conditions of theories—that is, it must specify the conditions under which a theory applies. Consider deterrence and labeling theories. Deterrence theory argues that as punishment increases, deviance decreases; labeling theory argues that as labeling increases, deviance increases. The two terms, punishment and labeling, can easily be equated, because most forms of punishment also label and most forms of deviant labeling also punish. Can these two theories be integrated or are they inherently inconsistent? Tittle (1975) argues that there are scope conditions for both theories and these conditions do not necessarily overlap. Deterrence processes may operate where labeling processes may not and vice versa. If the conditions that activate labeling processes outweigh those that activate deterrence processes, then societal reaction that both labels and punishes should increase deviance. Tittle specifies eight such conditions. For example, deterrence processes may operate more for some types of crime and labeling processes may operate more for others. Convicting a woman for prostitution would more likely produce a deviant career than convicting a woman for shoplifting. Being publicly labeled as a prostitute would open opportunities to continue the practice while closing opportunities for conventional relationships with men. To the contrary, being convicted for shoplifting would probably limit opportunities for continuing the practice while not necessarily closing opportunities for conventional employment.

In the above example, integration requires agreement on the criteria that partition the subject matter, thereby allowing the alternative theories to be used to explain different behaviors. A side-by-side approach may also link theories by recognizing that they partially overlap but diverge at some point to account for different behaviors or types of deviants. Hirschi (1979) identifies Elliott et al.'s (1979) integrated theory as a side-by-side approach where cases are initially distinguished on the strength of initial bonds. The process by which those with strong bonds become deviant initially is different than the process for those who never developed such bonds. This form of side-by-side integration has the potential of being transformed into an up-and-down approach, given that the theories share some common assumptions. For example, Hirschi's (1986) recent application of social control theory and rational choice theory are linked by the common assumption of both theories that human beings are self-seeking. Within that common structure, different explanatory variables are used to account for stable differences among the propensity to engage in criminal acts (criminality) and criminal events.

End-to-End (Sequential) Integration

To reiterate, end-to-end integration refers to conceptualizing a dependent variable in one theory as an independent variable in another, an independent variable in one theory as a dependent variable in another, or both. This type of integration would seem to be most applicable when causal conditions can be ordered on a continuum of immediate to remote causes (Jessor and Jessor 1973). By *immediate* we mean those causal conditions that act quickly, and more or less directly, on deviance and crime. The effects are not mediated by other specified conditions. At the individual level of analysis, we tend to think of perceptions and beliefs as immediate causes of behavior. By *remote* we mean those causal conditions that act indirectly, or through other conditions, on deviance and crime. For example, at the individual level of analysis we tend to think of social status or religious affiliation as remote causes of behavior.

Some theories focus on immediate causes, generally psychological states or day-to-day social experiences. Differential association theory, for example, places its emphasis on cognitive states (definitions of right and wrong) and how these states are learned in day-to-day experiences with peers. The extent to which these experiences are embedded in patterns of cultural and social structure that characterize some but not other social units is of minimal concern. Other theories focus on remote causes. Some study complex patterns of social interaction which characterize small scale social units, such as family power structures, or those which characterize large scale social units, such as industrialization. Some study the demographic conditions that characterize small-scale units, such as household density, or those that characterize large-scale social units, such as population change. These conditions are frequently thought to affect deviance and crime, although it is quite unclear how these conditions alter the beliefs, perceptions, and day-to-day experiences that directly affect deviance and crime. Social disorganization theory, for example, purports that population heterogeneity and population change, as indicators or causes of social disorganization, affect deviance and crime, although it is not clear how population heterogeneity or social disorganization enter the day-to-day experiences, beliefs, and perceptions that cause acts of deviance and crime.

Hence, there is considerable opportunity and need to integrate in end-to-end sequences concepts that describe the psychological states and day-to-day experiences of people and those that describe the social and demographic structures of small and large scale social units. Such end-to-end sequences embed the psychological states and day-to-day experiences that directly lead to deviance within the patterns of cultural and social structure which characterize small and large scale social units; such end-to-end sequences also conceptualize these psychological states and day-to-day experiences as mediating the effects of patterns of culture and social structure on deviance.

A prominent form of end-to-end integration in the deviance literature is consideration of concepts from differential association theory as proximate causes and of constructs from social control theory as more remote causes. In a pure form of end-to-end integration, the variables from social control theory do not directly affect deviance but affect the variables from differential association theory, which in turn directly explain deviance. The empirical, if not theoretical, success of "pure" end-to-end integration can be gauged by various path analytic techniques. Quite simply, if the effect of causal variables of one theory on crime (e.g., social control theory) and deviance pass through the causal variables of another theory (e.g., differential association theory), controlling for the latter should reduce the direct effects of the former to zero. However, such a "pure" form is uncommon. In practice, most efforts at end-to-end integration allow for both direct and indirect effects of the variables from both theories (e.g., Elliott et al. 1979; Johnson 1979; Massey and Krohn 1986). By so doing, these models have consistently been able to account for a greater proportion of the variance in deviant behavior than have the constituent theories by themselves.

One of the difficulties with such integrations is that they may not really integrate the constituent theories in any meaningful sense. Hirschi argues that such approaches fail to consider the assumptive differences in the constituent theories. For example, if differential association theory assumes that one must account for the motivation of deviant behavior whereas social control theory explicitly denies that motivational accounts are necessary, the theories can be reconciled only if these assumptions are reconciled. Hence, Hirschi's assertion that Elliott et al. "use the terms and ignore the claims of control theory" (1979, p. 34) is largely accurate.

Both forms of end-to-end integration (i.e., those that stipulate only "intervening" effects and those that also allow for direct effects) might better be labeled theoretical elaboration (Wagner and Berger 1985). While the theoretical product does incorporate empirical insights from research inspired by a second theory, it uses those insights to further specify the causal explanation contained in the first theory (differential association). Wagner and Berger suggest that theoretical elaboration is what most sociologists consider as growth and development.

Up-and-Down Integration

Up-and-down integration, or deductive integration, is the classic form of theoretical integration. It is accomplished by identifying a level of abstraction or generality that will incorporate some of the conceptualization of the constituent theories. This can be done by recognizing that theory A contains more abstract or general assumptions than theory B and, therefore, that key parts of theory B can be accommodated within the structure of theory A. Or it can be done by abstracting more general assumptions from theories A and B, allowing parts of both theories to be incorporated in a new theory C. We will call the former method *theoretical reduction* and the latter method *theoretical synthesis*.

Theoretical reduction is the typical form of integration employed in the natural sciences. This is sometimes easy to do, such as when the two theories use the same terms to describe and explain seemingly different phenomena ("homogeneous integration"). For example, the theory of mechanics was originally developed to explain the motion of point-masses—that is, bodies whose dimensions are small compared to the distances between them—and it was easily extended to similar motions of other bodies, such as rigid bodies which exhibit some forms of motion—rotation—that point-mass bodies do not (Nagel 1961).

Problems of reduction occur when the characteristics of one phenomenon are seemingly very different than the characteristics of another, when the terms of one theory are not among the terms of another, and especially when the terms of one theory appear to obscure the conceptual distinctions of another or to make conceptual distinctions obscured by another ("heterogeneous reduction"). This problem of reduction seems to be even further exacerbated when one theory deals with macro phenomena and another deals with micro phenomena. Such cases have generated the most attention and controversy, possibly because they bring into question the conceptual independence of a discipline of study. A classical case is the reduction of thermal dynamics, the study of thermal phenomena or the thermal behavior of bodies, to statistical mechanics and the kinetic theory of matter. Temperature, for example, a term in thermal dynamics, is used to describe macro phenomena. It has no equivalent in the kinetic theory of gases. Molecules have no temperature; they are neither hot nor cold. How, then, is temperature to be represented in terms of molecules?

Philosophers of science have discussed at some length this problem of heterogeneous reduction. In his classic monograph, Nagel (1961) argues that to reduce one theory to another, the terms of one theory must be embedded in the assumptions of another theory, because to deduce the propositions of one theory from the propositions of another, the terms of the former must be in the premises (assumptions) of the latter. Nagel specifies three general criteria for equating terms in two or more theories. One, the meaning of the terms of one theory are explicated or analyzed in terms of the meanings of another theory (meaning by analysis). Two, the meanings of the terms of one theory are assigned the meanings of the terms of another theory (meaning by convention or fiat). Three, the meanings of the different terms remain distinct and the terms are equated empirically; that is, the phenomena denoted by a term in one theory are assumed to bring about the phenomena denoted by a term in another theory. This assumption, of course, is subject to empirical tests.

Consider the temperature of gases. In the classical reduction it is equated with the mean kinetic energy of gases. Clearly, the meaning of temperature as used in classical mechanics cannot be derived from the meaning of "mean kinetic energy of molecules," as used in the kinetic theory of gases. On one hand, it has been argued that the two terms are equated by definitional fiat, because mean kinetic energy cannot be directly observed. On the other hand, it has been argued that mean kinetic energy *can* be indirectly observed in ways other than the observation of temperature, and that it can thus be empirically linked to temperature (Nagel 1961).

To summarize, in the natural sciences theoretical integration is frequently understood to mean theoretical reduction—that is, the deducing of the propositions of one theory from the premises of another. This requires that the terms in one theory be equated with the terms in another. In some cases this is quite simple and straightforward (homogeneous reduction) and in other cases it is highly problematic and controversial (heterogeneous reduction).

Figure 1

General Theory X	Specific Theory Y
$A \supset C$	$B \supset F$
$C \supset D$	$F \supset$ Deviance
$C \supset F$	$\therefore B \supset$ Deviance
$D \supset$ Deviance	
$F \supset$ Deviance	

Figure 1 illustrates how theoretical reduction might occur in the study of deviance. The proposition F implies deviance is part of both theories X and Y, but the proposition B implies deviance is only part of theory Y. To deduce the proposition B implies deviance from theory X, we must equate the concept B in theory Y with a term (for example, C) in the premises of theory X. For example, if B equals unemployment and C equals status change, we can argue that unemployment is a special case of status change and therefore that the proposition B implies deviance can also be deduced from theory X. Hence, since both propositions about deviance in theory Y are also part of theory X, we can argue that theory Y is reduced to theory X.

With the possible exception of economics, this type of integration is rarely attempted in the social sciences. (See Gibbs 1972 for an exception.) In one attempt at deductive integration, Burgess and Akers (1966) try to subsume Sutherland's differential association theory within social learning theory. Equating concepts contained in differential association theory with those contained in the premises of learning theory, they argue that the learning that takes place in interaction in primary groups is a special case of operant conditioning. Definitions favorable and unfavorable to the violation of the law are reconceptualized as a type of subverbal discriminative stimuli.

Many scholars in the social sciences view deduction as a form of theoretical imperialism because the theory being deduced loses its individual identity. The phrase "theoretical reduction" has a very negative connotation among many social scientists. For example, Burgess and Akers' (1966) modification of Sutherland's differential association theory by introducing (or subsuming it under) behaviorist principles has been characterized as a "revisionist takeover" that is a "travesty of Sutherland's position" (Taylor et al. 1973, pp. 131–132).

Theoretical synthesis is even more difficult to find in the social sciences. It requires that abstract or general principles be postulated that will allow at least parts of both constituent theories to be subsumed and interrelated under them. Effective synthesis usually generates additional predictions not made by the constituent theories. Wagner and Berger (1985) suggest that if the constituent theories are competing theories, synthesis requires a new theoretical language. While this form of integration is difficult to achieve, it may have a dramatic impact on theoretical development.

Cross-Level Integration

Cross-level integration (integrating micro and macro theories) is sometimes thought to be both the most difficult and perhaps the most necessary type of theoretical integration. It is assumed to present unique problems. Some of these can be illustrated with reference to the three principles of integration. Consider side-by-side, micro/macro integration. Are there some types of deviants or deviance that are better suited to micro or macro explanations? Historically, numerous scholars have tried to show that some types of deviance are individual in nature and others are social in nature. Criminal behaviors that are rare and seemingly difficult to understand (for example, exhibitionism) have been thought to be best explained by psychological theories couched at the individual level of analysis. The experiences that lead to the immediate or causal psychological states are assumed to be the products of unique personal biographies not clearly tied to the patterns of culture and interaction which characterize large and small-scale social units. On the other hand, criminal behaviors that are common and seemingly understandable (e.g., burglary), particularly when committed in groups and supported by a subculture, are thought to be best explained at the macro level. The experiences that lead to them are thought to be shared by many and to be tied to the culture and structural patterns of large scale social units.

The problems and simplicity of this historical micro-macro partition were made evident by Durkheim's analysis of suicide—a rare act of deviance seemingly difficult to understand. He showed that suicide variation among macro units is linked to the cultural and structural patterns of these units. Hence, what was thought to be a psychological phenomena turned out to be a social phenomena. Generally, we are not at all sure that side-by-side integration of macro and micro level theories is possible or even desirable.

On the other hand, we feel that end-to-end integration of micro and macro-level theories is both possible and desirable. (We have already discussed this integration as that of remote and immediate variables.) A typical technique of such integration is contextual analysis, in which concepts used in macro level theory (for example, neighborhood disorganization, racial composition of a city, and income inequality) are included in micro theory. For example, people may be described by their own attitudes and race and by the mean attitude and racial composition of their social units such as their school, neighborhood, and city in a theory of crime or deviance. In many cases the contextual condition causes the individual condition, and thus may be thought of as a remote cause in an end-to-end integration. For example, neighborhood integration may affect psychological disorganization, leading to crime and deviance; thus, psychological disorganization may be conceptualized as mediating the effect of neighborhood disorganization on crime.

Contextual analysis, used extensively in many areas of research, has not been used much at all in the study of deviance and crime. Even fewer studies have examined the causal link between contextual and individual concepts in an end-to-end integration. Recently, however, a few studies have looked at the social class of both people and their neighborhood or city in theories of deviance and social control (Sampson 1986). (See also Myers and Talarico's [1987] analysis of the effects of community context on discrimination in sentencing).

To deduce either the propositions of a macro theory from the premises of a micro theory or the propositions of a micro theory from the premises of a macro theory is thought of as theoretical reductionism. As previously stated, such work has been strongly criticized by adherents of the theory whose propositions are being deduced as an infringement of their proper subject matter. Much of this debate—especially the question of whether or not the macro propositions can be deduced from micro premises—has been quite academic and arcane. In the social sciences, particularly in the study of deviance and crime, there is so little deductive theory that even to talk of cross-level deductions seems like an academic exercise.

Directions For Theoretical Integration

Conceptual Integration

Some scholars have argued that if propositional integration is so difficult, one might start with conceptual integration. To conceptually integrate theories, the theorist equates concepts in different theories, arguing that while the words and terms are different, the theoretical meanings and operations of measurement are similar (see Pearson and Weiner 1985). Akers (chapter 1 of this volume), for example, argues that the concepts of many theories (social bonding, strain) can be equated with the concepts of social learning. The concept, "belief" in bonding theory is similar to the concept "definitions" in social learning, and the concept "blocked opportunities" in strain theory is similar to the concept "differential reinforcement" in social learning theory.

The purpose of conceptual integration is not always clear. Is it an end in itself or a means to some form of propositional integration? We feel that as an end in itself, its value is quite limited. It would seem to apply to those theories that use different concepts and measures to represent the same things and that make similar predictions. For example, if theory A states that X increases deviance and if theory B states that Y increases deviance, then conceptually integrating A and B yields conceptual parsimony. But if theory A states that Y increases deviance and theory B states that X decreases deviance, then conceptually integrating X and Y makes no sense and yields inconsistent predictions. However, in an area of study such as deviance and crime, where there are probably more terms, words, and concepts than meaningful distinctions, there is considerable opportunity for fruitful conceptual integration.

Most scholars, however, view conceptual integration as a means to propositional integration. Perhaps without explicitly saying so, they are thinking of deductive integration. But conceptual integration is neither a necessary condition or a means to side-by-side and end-to-end integration. Both forms of propositional integration preserve the conceptual integrity of different theories. Integration is achieved by partitioning the subject matter of study or by conceptualizing the independent variables of one theory as the dependent variables of another. Only in deductive integration is conceptual integration a necessary condition and thus a means to propositional integration. As previously discussed, in deductive integration the concepts of the propositions to be deduced must be included in the premises of the other theory; hence, establishing some conceptual equivalence is necessary for deductive integration.

Theoretical Elaboration

Because of the problems in integrating theories with seemingly inconsistent assumptions, many scholars (Hirschi, Thornberry, and Meier, in chapters 2, 3, and 13 in this volume) argue for a strategy of theoretical elaboration; that is, a strategy of fully developing existing theories. They argue that extant theories of deviance and crime are so underdeveloped that we might better spend our time and energies on developing them rather than on integrating them.

Gibbs (chapter 12 in this volume) further argues that before we can even develop extant theories, three metatheoretical issues or questions must be answered: (1) What questions about deviance should be addressed? (2) How do we construct theories that address these questions? and (3) How do we test theories?

Swigert (chapter 9 in this volume), too, raises questions in this vein. She questions the appropriateness of the dependent variable or the subject matter in the study of crime. She argues that we should not allow lawyers, judges, and legislators to mandate our subject matter, changing it yearly if they so choose. While it is certainly legitimate to study the formulation and enforcement of the law as a social construction, is it useful to study those who violate the law as a distinct category of people? Among those who illegally appropriate others' property, is it useful to distinguish between robbers, burglars, arsonists, and auto thieves as does the contemporary U.S. code? Is it even useful to distinguish between the legal and illegal appropriations of other's property, given that the distinction is not always simple, changes over political units, and changes for the same unit over time?

In sum, these scholars are arguing that before we tackle the problems of theoretical integration, there are prior issues and questions that must be addressed. The search for integrated theory, according to this point of view, is decidedly premature.

"Small" or "Middle Range" Integration

Part of the problem of theoretical integration is that the extant theories are perceived as general theories rather than as *parts* of an emerging theory (Tittle, chapter 11 in this volume). Hence, scholars feel that complete theories must be integrated either propositionally or conceptually. This implicit or hidden assumption has made the task of integration seem monumental. Yet the concepts and propositions of most theories are only loosely linked. We can easily borrow ideas (concepts and propositions) from different theories and explore how they fit. Some propositions of different theories may be incompatible because they are tightly linked to incompatible assumptions. Other propositions, however, may not be so tightly linked to such assumptions, and some propositions of different theories may be deduced from a common set of assumptions, even if they were originally derived from incompatible assumptions.

One classic example of middle-range or small integration is Cloward and Ohlin's (1964) revision of Merton's anomie theory. They borrow from differential association theory the idea that knowledge of illegitimate means must be learned and that opportunities to learn them are differentially available. This idea, traditionally embedded in the general assumptions of Sutherland's differential association theory, is not necessarily incompatible with assumptions of Merton's anomie theory, although many of the assumptions of the general Chicago perspective, in which Sutherland's theory was originally embedded, are incompatible with many of the assumptions of the structural functional perspective, in which Merton's theory was originally embedded. Indeed, the ideas that legitimate and illegitimate opportunities are differentially available seem eminently compatible.

In this book, the papers by Bursik (chapter 7), Farrell (chapter 5), and Gove (chapter 4) illustrate the strategy of middle range integration. Bursik, for example, includes a proposition on political decision making, originally embedded in the conflict perspective, in an ecological theory of crime, which is tied more to the general consensus than the conflict perspective. Following an ecological model, he argues that crime is caused by population instability, which is caused by political decisions on public housing as well as by processes of economic selection.

Summary and Conclusion

As stated at the outset of this essay, the scientific endeavor necessarily includes the goal of integrating or unifying empirical findings under a set of abstract constructs and relational principles. The most efficient means to that goal is clearly more ambiguous and controversial than the agreed-upon goal. We have briefly reviewed some of the requisites and problems inherent in alternative methods for integrating existing theoretical perspectives. We have also identified other strategies for theoretical development, including theory competition and theory elaboration. As our essay suggests and as evidenced by the variety of viewpoints in the essays to follow, it is difficult to determine the best strategy.

Whatever strategy is adopted, the end product must of course be assessed with reference to the general criteria of theory evaluation. As Wagner and Berger (1985, p. 703) note, theoretical growth has often been interpreted in terms of increasing empirical support. We wish to emphasize, however, two additional criteria that are particularly relevant in the assessment of integrated theories. Perhaps of greatest importance is the criterion of logical coherence, a criterion not often satisfied in the deviance literature. Many contemporary efforts that purport to pursue the goal of theoretical integration might be better described as attempts at prediction. Variables from two or more theories are included in the same prediction equation, but there is little concern with relating the various concepts to one another. Instead, attention focuses on the extent to which adding variables to the equation increases the multiple R^2. In this spirit, much contemporary research combines concepts from differential association theory, control theory, anomie theory, and deterrence theory into empirical models to predict all types of crime and deviance.

The problem with this strategy, as we have commented earlier, is that it does not deal with incompatibilities in basic assumptions or premises (cf. Hirschi 1979). It is our strong view that theoretical growth will occur only when theorists seriously attend to the logical structure of their arguments. More specifically, with respect to efforts at theoretical integration, theorists either must be able to show how seemingly contradictory premises can in fact be reconciled, or they must explicitly acknowledge their selection of certain premises in favor of others in those instances where genuine contradictions exist.

A second important criterion for assessing the success of theoretical efforts at integration entails a latent function of theory. As Stephen Cole (1975) has observed, theories serve not only to organize the accumulated body of knowledge and to allow for predictions about empirical phenomena. They also generate "intellectual puzzles" for scientists to work on. It is our suspicion that the growing interest in theoretical integration in the study of deviance and crime derives as much from a sense that the "puzzles" inspired by traditional theories have been exhausted as from dissatisfaction with the predictive power of available empirical models (cf. Cole 1975, pp. 210–214). Accordingly, a clear sign of successful theoretical integration will be the emergence of theoretical statements that will open up new research agendas. These statements should promote, in Merton's (1987, p. 7) apt phrase, new kinds of "specified ignorance"—i.e., novel realizations of the kinds of things that need to be known to foster the advancement of the discipline. Insofar as integrated theories further such developments, they will indeed have been well worth the effort.

Part I

Micro-Level Integration

We begin our exploration of theoretical integration in deviance and crime with essays that deal primarily with micro-level explanations. It is appropriate that we begin with micro-level theories, as they have formed the grist for the integration mill more often than theories at other levels of explanation. However, of the six essays in this section, four are not sanguine about the prospects for successful integration.

Ronald L. Akers ("A Social Behaviorist's Perspective on Integration of Theories of Crime and Deviance"), after exploring some general issues generic to integration efforts, provides a sketch of how social learning theory might serve as a basis for integrating a variety of perspectives across levels of explanations. He recognizes that his argument represents a form of conceptual integration, justifying the primacy of social learning theory on the basis that its concepts are more abstract and empirically validated than those from other perspectives. Akers suggests that previous integration efforts of this kind have either been misunderstood or largely ignored, raising the question of whether such activity is worth the effort.

Travis Hirschi ("Exploring Alternatives to Integrated Theory") is more forceful in his opposition to theoretical integration. In a brief account of theoretical development in criminology, Hirschi argues that there has been a succession of theories generated in opposition to those that were extant at the time. Control theory halted such progression, as it was not a new theory but rather an old theory. This "crisis" generated the push for integrated theories that downplay the significance of fundamentally opposed views of the world. Hirschi views integrated theories as a mistake unless the constituent theories already share assumptions and "for all intents and purposes" are the same theory. He argues, instead, for a fact-based approach to theorizing, and illustrates this approach with his own work on the age–crime relationship.

Terence P. Thornberry ("Reflections on the Advantages and Disadvantages of Theoretical Integration") begins by providing a definition for theoretical integration and identifying the implications of the term. Thornberry asserts that not only is true theoretical integration difficult but that the cost of such efforts in regard to the integrity of theoretical ideas may be too high. Instead, he argues for an alternative, theoretical elaboration. Theoretical elaboration begins with a particular theoretical model and builds to a more comprehensive model by extending its basic propositions.

The papers by Walter R. Gove and Michael Hughes and by Ronald A. Farrell are similar in that they present a theoretical statement anchored in the interactionist tradition while incorporating concepts from other disciplines. Gove and Hughes focus specifically on mental illness. They argue that research on the biological and psychological effects of sleep deprivation can help account for why some distressed people may become mentally disorganized. Importantly, they suggest that such symptoms may interact with personal attributes and with the social expectations of others. Gove and Hughes emphasize the need to incorporate biological and psychological concepts into a sociological understanding of mental illness.

Farrell, in "Cognitive Consistency in Deviance Causation: A Psychological Elaboration of an Integrated Systems Model," introduces the psychological concept of ambiguity tolerance to account for the frequently observed differential response to the labeling process. Those who are unable to tolerate ambiguity are more likely to define their behavior as deviant and act accordingly. The introduction of ambiguity tolerance into an interactionist model suggests additional ways that the labeling process may be explicated by including other psychological influences.

Margaret Farnworth ("Theory Integration versus Model Building") begins her assessment of Farrell's and of Gove and Hughes' papers by generating an operational definition of theoretical integration based on the efforts of Burgess and Akers and of Elliott et al. A central feature of her definition is the combining of two or more preexisting theories into a reformulated model. Based on that definition, Farnworth argues that both Farrell's and Gove and Hughes' essays do not perform theoretical integration. Rather, both efforts can be seen as elaborations of labeling theory with the inclusion of concepts from other disciplines. Theoretical integration should be done only with theories that fit together; conflicting assumptions inhibit successful integration.

1

A Social Behaviorist's Perspective on Integration of Theories of Crime and Deviance

———Ronald L. Akers———

Introduction

I shall not review and comment on the many excellent efforts in the literature to offer integration of deviance theories. Several of these specifically make use of differential association or other social learning concepts. In my estimation, the clearest, although not necessarily the most systematic or elegant, of these other attempts at integrating social learning with a structural or macro-level theory is that of Bernard in his second revision of Vold (1986). However, the most complete, systematic, and carefully crafted integration of all the major deviance theories that use social learning principles as the integrating structure is that of Pearson and Weiner (1985), in which they show the integrative power of learning concepts both at the micro and macro levels and across levels. Although I disagree with their final model, the most thorough integration of social learning and variables from other theories based on empirical data is that by Elliott et al. (1985).

Rather than analyze or compare these other models, I shall first attempt to puzzle through several issues with regard to integration for which no claim for definitive answers is made. What are some of the important problems, difficulties, and objections to integration of theories of crime and deviance? What is to be gained from doing so and is it worthwhile? What form should the integration take? Second, I will present my own past and current efforts at integration from the perspective of social learning. There appears to be some consensus that theoretical integration is desirable and that the only question is how best to do it, but is this the only remaining question? I must admit, as one who has been engaged in theory building and testing, including some integration, a certain amount of ambiguity on the question of how far to take integration of current deviance theories.

On the Question of Whether 'tis Better to be Separate and Unequal or to be Theoretical Mush

Part of my reticence on the issue stems from the fact that I am partially persuaded by Hirschi's (1979) position that while integration sounds fine it is often accomplished by ignoring crucial differences between theories. We might be better off keeping them separate, testing them, and letting the chips fall where they may. Also, the kind of theoretical integration that I have proposed gives centrality to social learning; everything understandably looks and smells like social learning to me. As I have noted elsewhere (Akers and Cochran 1985), my type of integration can be accused of theoretical imperialism and, because it retains such close identity with Sutherland's (1947) theory, could be used as another example by Hirschi and Gottfredson (1980) that differential association theory has too long exercised conceptual hegemony in the study of crime and deviance.

I also have some sympathy for Hirschi's position that integration of theories may possibly result in mixing things that, like gas and water, simply won't mix. There are approaches which have such irreconcilable differences that the only way they can be integrated is to concoct phony parallels, which results in oxymorons. It is also possible to integrate by addition, in the way the old eclectic multiple causation theories did, without regard to conceptual differences, similarities, or congruity among the various causes. This kind of theoretical mush serves no sound purpose.

On the other hand, the insistence on keeping theories separate and competing carries with it its own dangers—namely, pretending that theories are different or saying contradictory things when in fact they are not different. It also carries the risk of ignoring similarities and overlap between two theories even when they are different; the differences may be real but not irreconcilable. Burgess and I were accused of theoretical illiteracy years ago by Taylor et al. (1973) for attempting to integrate the cognitively oriented symbolic interactionism from Sutherland with behaviorism; the two were deemed to have such incompatible domain assumptions that concepts and propositions just could not be fused. We now know that they can be, that psychologists have joined cognitive and behavioral psychology (Bandura 1986) and that Mead, the father of symbolic interactionism, was something of a behaviorist himself (Baldwin 1981). Sometimes, that which at first appears irreconcilable turns out not to be.

If concepts and propositions from two or more theories are essentially the same, why pretend they are different and ignore the similarity merely for the sake of retaining separate theories? Such an attitude results in theories that are different in name only. Further, when there are contradictory propositions from two theories, one is bound to be empirically wrong; thus, it can be dropped in the integration, not in the interest of covering up differences but because it is wrong. What this means is that integration must come from those theories that "fit" together. For instance, sociological theories emphasizing the causal effects of social environments on group members without reference to unconscious motives or abnormalities fit better with a behavioral psychology than with a psychiatrically based psychology. Similarly, at the same level we must start with the most "compatible" theories, those for which there is greater similarity in concept and proposition and less need to reconcile or ignore great differences or contradictions. If integration is not possible without papering over and patching up incompatibilities between theories, then we ought to cease and desist. If instead it moves us toward an integrated, parsimonious explanation of crime and deviance, then it is worthwhile to continue.

On the Question of the Dependent Variable

One way in which theories may be different enough to interfere with or preclude theoretical integration is that they may be attempting to explain different things. We are concerned here with theories of deviant and criminal behavior as the dependent variable, not theories of social control or law. But even when we concentrate on the deviance rather than the control system, there are still questions about whether the dependent variable is the same in different theories.

If the dependent variables are different, how can theories be integrated? The dependent variable may be group rates of deviance or individual behavior. This difference should present no major obstacle, however, because the rates are themselves calculated from individual acts. A basic assumption that Hirschi (1969) stated for control theory is that deviance is taken for granted and conformity is the thing to be explained; universal motivation to deviance is assumed, but motivation to conformity is problematic. He contrasted this with strain theory, which was pictured as assuming conformity in the absence of strong strain toward deviance, and cultural deviance theory, which was pictured as positing positive learning of deviant lifestyles from a deviant subculture. But control theories have not uniformly posited universal motivation to deviance, and Hirschi himself expressed some reservations about it. As Elliott and colleagues (1985) point out, there is no logical necessity for this assumption. Moreover, social learning theory makes this distinction moot, because it addresses both the conformity and deviance questions—How are we to be induced, or fail to be induced, to behave well and how are we to be induced, or fail to be induced, to behave badly, or prevented from doing either? Virtually all of the tests of the various theories, including Hirschi's own, define and measure the dependent variable in basically the same way, usually commission of some form of adolescent deviance. As long as the dependent variable is measured empirically as a dichotomy or a scale in which the absence of deviance is counted conformity and its reciprocal is counted as deviance, then it makes no difference whether one defines the problem as explaining deviance or explaining conformity or both. For these reasons I see no serious barrier to integration caused by differing conceptions of the dependent variable of crime and deviance.

On Conceptual Integration and Integration Across Levels

We have no consensus in the field on how a theory should be constructed or what form it should take, and no consensus on how one should proceed to integrate one or more theories. Should it proceed and remain at the same level of explanation, or tie two or more together? Should we combine propositions or concepts or both? What form should the final product take and when do we know that integration has gone far enough or should be taken to the next step of integrating that integrated theory with yet another one? These questions are difficult enough when talking about integrating theories from one discipline and combining two levels. It becomes even more difficult to do when integrating across disciplinary boundaries and multi-levels of variables.

I have divided theories into either mainly structural or processual levels (Akers 1968; 1985). Although the notion of different levels of theoretical explanation is an old one, there has been a resurgence of interest recently in the interplay between the macro and micro, both in the sociology of deviance (Orcutt 1983; Liska 1986) and in general sociological theory (Alexander et al. 1987). Indeed, this very conference is organized around the idea that some theories are macro- and others are micro-level theories. Actually, there are several levels, which are usually defined by reference to the independent or explanatory variables but can also be defined by reference to the dependent variable: (1) structural/macro (sociocultural); (2) intermediate (group or subcultural); (3) individual/micro (behavioral); (4) psychological/micro (internal, cognitive, psychodynamic); (5) biological/micro (physiological, genetic, neurological).

With the possible exception of the biological level, deviance theories of the sociological variety have a little of each of these. Conflict, Marxist, and anomie theories are most clearly macro-structural, as are some theories of specific deviance such as Gibbs' status integration theory of suicide (Gibbs and Martin 1964; Gibbs 1982). Theories that incorporate intermediate, individual, and psychological dimensions are social psychological; labeling and control theories, while they have more social psychological dimensions, also have structural elements. Social learning theory is the most clearly micro of the major sociological perspectives on deviance, but with intermediate dimensions referring to both interactive and normative aspects. Even the newer physiological theories include references to other levels and are socio-biological rather than purely biological (Mednick and Shoham 1979; Gove and Carpenter 1982).

The original integration across levels in criminology was Sutherland's (1947), which combined social disorganization and conflict with differential association; Cressey (1960) later developed this connection between epidemiology and individual conduct. Integration across levels such as this continues to take the form of causal paths from one set of variables at one level to variables at another level. In this kind of cause–effect model, the variables are conceptually distinct and ideally measured at different levels. The problem is that empirical models with clear, purely societal or community-level indicators of macro variables and with mediating variables measured at the micro level are hard to find.

Another form of integration to which I (Akers and Cochran 1985) and others (Pearson and Weiner 1985) have referred is conceptual integration, which is most likely to implicate theories at the same level—showing not just complementarity but similarity and overlap. Such integration melds two nominal concepts that refer to essentially the same empirical phenomenon into one concept. The social learning integration of differential association and reinforcement principles was essentially a conceptual integration, but the tentative steps I have taken toward additional theoretical integration have involved both cross-level and conceptual integration.

On the Integration of Social Learning with other Theories Across Levels of Explanation

My general views on theoretical integration from a social behaviorist's perspective were first stated more than twenty years ago, and I have not altered them much since. As noted above, the Burgess and Akers (1966) reformulation of differential association theory was presented as an integration with behavioral learning principles, not as an alternative theory. This idea was retained when the differential association–reinforcement (social learning) theory was presented and explicated in the first edition of *Deviant Behavior* (Akers 1973), and the last sentence of that edition expressed the belief that "Social learning is a general processual approach ... which holds some promise as an integrating orientation for the sociology of deviance" (1973, p. 294).

Anomie and conflict theories were seen as more clearly having a structural emphasis, and labeling and control theories as more 'mixed' with both structural and processual features. I argued then, and still believe, that the way in which structural theories and social learning theory could be integrated is to propose that social learning is the basic process by which the structural variables specified in the macro-level theories have an effect on deviant behavior.

> ... [The] burden of these [structural] theories is to indicate what kinds of situations and structures lead to deviant behavior.
>
> But none of them adequately specifies the *process* by which social structure shapes the behavior of individuals.... They propose something about the structure of learning environments likely to produce deviant behavior, but they do not specify *how* they do so. Thus social learning is complementary to, not competing with, the structural theories. By conceptualizing the deviance-producing environments as setting up conditions that have an impact on individual conduct through the operation of the learning mechanisms, we can begin to integrate structural and processual explanations of deviant behavior (Akers, 1973, p. 300).
>
> The general culture and structure of society and the particular groups, subcultures, and social situations in which the individual participates provide learning environments in which the norms define what is approved and disapproved and the reactions of others (for example, in applying social sanctions) attach different reinforcing or punishing consequences to his behavior. In a sense, then, social structure is an arrangement of sets and schedules of reinforcement contingencies.... These social characteristics indicate the individual's location in the structure of society, the particular groups of which he is likely to be a member, with whom he interacts, and how others are apt to respond to him and his behavior. Therefore, they reflect which behavioral and normative patterns the person will be exposed to and which of his behavior is likely to be approved and rewarded or disapproved and punished (Akers, 1973, p. 291).

This general perspective on the impact of social structure on individuals operating through or mediated by social learning is one aspect of theoretical integration across levels which does not need elaboration. It does need more empirical testing. Some empirical support was found in the analysis of the effect of community context on teenage alcohol and drug use, as mediated by social learning and social bonding variables, which I did with Marvin Krohn and Lonn Lanza-Kaduce (Krohn et al. 1984). I have also begun some analysis of community context and social learning variables in regard to elderly alcohol use and abuse.

Although a thorough or systematic integration was never accomplished, the connection between variations in group rates and the reinforcement and definitions of individual behavior has been made quite explicit in several of the chapters in all editions of *Deviant Behavior*, with specific comments on how social learning is compatible with other theories. This compatibility seems clearest with control theory, as a number of others have recognized (Conger 1976; 1980; Johnson 1979; Braukman et al. 1980; Weis and Hawkins 1981; Nettler 1984). I stressed that although direct sanctioning of behavior was not included in all versions of control theory, the central proposition is that conformity is maintained when controls are strong and deviance results when the controls are weak. Social sanctions operate as reinforcing and punishing contingencies. In addition, the breaking or loosening of bonds (which may result from non-rewarding relationships) makes one a candidate for deviance, because the person becomes isolated from those who would continue to approve and reinforce conforming and punish deviant behavior; the person with weakened or broken bonds is less affected by the rewards and punishments of the groups. This is where control theory usually stops—namely, the failure of controls sets the stage for deviance. The social learning process, however, extends to the next steps toward deviance. Failure of conventional social control may be enough by itself for deviant behavior, but:

> [T]he person may also gravitate to other groups or may encounter situations in which the controls operate positively to reinforce his deviant behavior. Thus, the person whose ties with conformity have been broken may remain just a candidate for deviance; whether he becomes deviant depends on further social or other rewards. *Social control is still functioning when the individual's behavior comes under the influence of the sanctions of deviant subcultures or other groups, only the direction of that control is deviant by the standards of the conventional groups with which he has broken* (Akers, 1973, p. 292, emphasis added).

Thus, I was allowing for the fact that it makes a difference to which groups one is bonded. This is counter to Hirschi's (1969) theory, which originally postulated that it does not make a difference. In this sense, I was ignoring an important difference in the theories and possibly making the mistakes referred to above. But Hirschi himself had indicated that this part of the theory was probably overstated, and Elliott et al. (1985, p. 38) argue that such a modification is necessary. Further, empirically it does make a difference, and any theory is incorrect to the extent that it denies this. The deviance-producing conditions stipulated by anomie, labeling, and conflict theories were also seen as operating through behavioral mechanisms.

In the subsequent editions (Akers, 1977, 1985), this integration theme was slightly expanded to include deterrence theory. Deterrence relates to one part (inhibition of behavior by punishment) of the social learning equation which includes facilitation of behavior through positive reinforcement. Also, recent socio-biological perspectives on crime and deviance and their relevance for structural and processual theories were addressed. There is incompatibility between sociological theories and the kind of strict biological determinism that sees deviance as resulting from 'defects' or gross abnormalities in individual physiology, which produce a certain inevitable behavioral outcome largely unaffected by the social environment. Integration of this kind of biological theory with sociological theories would be very difficult. But there is no basic incompatibility of sociological theories with other kinds of biological theorizing. Biological theories which propose to relate the normal physiological and sensory processes to the social and environmental variables in their impact on behavior are consistent with the structural perspectives and with the social learning perspective. Thus, integration could involve yet another level of explanation, that of biological influences. The proper biological perspective may provide a view of the physiological or neurological mechanisms in behavior just as learning mechanisms provide a view of the way structural factors affect behavior, and social behavioral principles may provide the link between the individual's biological makeup and the social environment.

On Conceptual Integration of Social Learning and Social Bonding

I recognized early on, and it became more apparent in developing and testing the theory, that social learning theory was not only compatible with the other theories by virtue of allowing for cross-level integration but that there was also some same-level conceptual compatibility. This was reflected in statements in the text about the conceptual overlap of 'belief' in social bonding theory and 'definitions' in social learning, and later of overlap with other concepts in social learning and social bonding theory (Akers and Cochran 1985). My contention is that such a conceptual integration results essentially in subsuming the concepts of one theory under another, or both under more general concepts. That is what resulted from my own efforts, those of Elliott and colleagues (1985) and those of Pearson and Weiner (1985). There are at least six points of conceptual integration between social bonding (Hirschi 1969) and social learning.

Belief in bonding theory is very close to the concept of *definitions* in social learning theory, as stated above. The individual's adherence to general conventional beliefs, which is a bond making for conformity, is clearly one type of definition unfavorable to deviance; it is subsumable under the definitions concept in social learning theory, which includes not only general but specific positive, neutral, negative, and neutralizing attitudes, beliefs, orientations, and verbalizations.

Commitment, which refers in social bonding theory to the risk of losing conventional rewards and investments of time and energy in conformity and hence a cost of deviant behavior, is essentially a behavioral restraint that is subsumable under one side of the differential reinforcement balance. The concept of refraining from deviance because of the cost in lost stakes in conformity is one example of the more general concept of negative punishment—one refrains from doing something not because of the fear of direct punishment but because of actual or anticipated loss of the reward or investment connected with alternative behavior. The differential reinforcement concept in social learning theory incorporates deterrence, reward–cost balance, positive and negative punishment, positive and negative reinforcement, and other rational and non-rational cognitive and behavioral processes of reward and punishment. The concept of commitment as the potential costs incurred by deviance can legitimately be incorporated into it as well.

The social bonding concept of *involvement,* which is closely related to commitment, is also subsumable under differential reinforcement. One may engage in both conventional and deviant activities, but to the extent that one precludes or conflicts with the other, one interferes with the rewards from the other.

The *attachment* concept overlaps with the concept of differential association. The extent to which one is attached to others may be seen as the intensity of associations, and attachment may be seen as a function of positively reinforced associations.

To the extent that the bonding concept of *attachment* refers to internalizations of norms shared with those with whom one is attached and refers to internal control, it overlaps with the social learning concepts of *norm qualities, definitions,* and *self-reinforcement.*

Attachment is also conceptually intertwined with modeling or *imitation*, since the presence of admired models with whom one identifies (would want to be like) is an empirical referent for attachment used by Hirschi and others.

On Conceptual Integration of Social Learning and Anomie/Strain Concepts

Similarly, there seem to be a number of points of intermingling of social learning concepts, mainly reinforcement, with central social psychological concepts in anomie and strain theory, as found in Cohen (1955), Cloward and Ohlin (1959, 1960) and various empirical tests (Short 1964; Elliott 1966; Liska 1971; Simmons et al. 1980; Elliott et al. 1985).

Perceived *discrepancies between legitimate aspirations and expectations,* and related concepts such as relative deprivation and perceived inaccessibility of legitimate means to success goals (which is the key social psychological component of strain) are conceptually akin to anticipated probability of *reinforcement* for achievement in conforming occupational and educational pursuits.

A closely related concept in anomie theory is that "effective" means to achieve the success goals into which we are all socialized will be utilized: if some of these effective conventional means are blocked or inaccessible, then some people will make use of effective but disapproved means. The blocking of opportunities means that conventional behavior to achieve the approved ends is reduced, while the deviant behavior that does accomplish the goals is enhanced. This is essentially a process of differential reinforcement in which, given two alternative behaviors, conforming and deviant, the one which is rewarded will be strengthened and the one which is not (for whatever reason) is weakened. The behavior that produces the desired outcome (reward) is positively reinforced and the behavior that fails to do so goes unrewarded; the balance of rewards and punishments differentially reinforces one over the other. In neither anomie nor in social learning theory does this have to be a rational or accurate assessment of reinforcement probabilities or opportunities. The innovative or rebellion adaptations in Merton's (1938) scheme are then instances of differential reinforcement through greater positive reinforcement of deviant alternatives, in which the desired cultural ends are general secondary reinforcers able to reinforce whatever behavior is available to secure them.

Those perceiving means–ends discrepancies, normlessness, or relative deprivation are supposed to experience strain, stress, anomie, alienation, powerlessness, or other unpleasant social psychological reactions. This motivates them to commit deviant acts because it resolves, rectifies, or relieves the strain of the anomic experience. Although social learning theory is silent on the issue of the empirical frequency with which this happens, to the extent that it does it can be seen as a process of *negative reinforcement*, in which behavior is reinforced by its removal or lessening of an aversive or unpleasant stimulus.

Negative reinforcement is also the relevant learning concept with regard to the retreatist adaptation or the "double failure" experience in Cloward and Ohlin's theory. The idea that failing to utilize effectively either legitimate or deviant pursuits induces a feeling of despair or failure and induces the person to engage in deviant drug use is conceptually akin to the escape or avoidance behavior that characterizes negative reinforcement. Social learning analysis of both drug addiction and alcoholism utilizes this concept; to the extent that drugs or alcohol alleviate, mitigate, or reduce aversive experiences (which may be those of failure, stress, or anxiety) their ingestion is negatively reinforced. Agnew (1985) argues that while blocked legitimate opportunities may induce strain to utilize deviant alternatives to success, violent deviant acts may represent a lashing out from the frustration of blocked opportunities or inability to get away from the dead ends, either legitimate or illegitimate—in other words, a response alleviating aversive stimuli. Again, while social learning has no specific propositions regarding how often double failure occurs or whether the behavior can be described as retreating from or active involvement in goal-oriented behavior, it seems clear that the concept of retreatism or other responses to means–ends discrepancies or failures is subsumable under the concept of escape and avoidance responses, negatively reinforced.

If anomie theory includes the notion that "unlawful behavior stems from the judgment that the discrepancy between the individual's level of utility acquisition and that of a social model is unjust" (Pearson and Weiner 1985, p. 138) and thus produces a justification for deviance, then we have another instance of definitions favorable to deviance in social learning theory.

Cloward and Ohlin (1959, 1960) described their theory as an integration of anomie and differential association theory, partly because they viewed variations in delinquent subcultures, carried by delinquent gangs (resulting from differences in illegitimate opportunities) in which individuals could become participants, as providing different learning environments. Although social learning theory has no concepts of, and posits nothing about, gang specialization and types of neighborhoods giving rise to different types of delinquent subcultures, the parallels between this part of differential opportunity theory and social learning concepts are fairly obvious. Cloward and Ohlin describe differences in subcultural values to which the deviant behavior conforms, which in social learning concepts is the norm qualities dimension of *differential association*. Differential association also subsumes interaction with gangs, and social approval by peers in the gangs is, in social learning terms, one instance of *positive social reinforcement*. The presence or absence of legitimate or illegitimate role models in the neighborhood contexts on which Cloward and Ohlin place some importance is, of course, conceptually indistinguishable from the observational learning of *modeling* and *imitation*.

Concluding Remarks

One could expand on the conceptual overlap of social learning with social bonding and with anomie and then move on to do the same with other theories. Pearson and Weiner (1985) have done an admirable job of doing this, and I won't attempt to duplicate that effort here. Only the main concepts in social learning theory have been referred to here. The theory includes all the mechanisms of learning, and other aspects of social bonding, anomie, and other theories could be further explicated by reference to discriminative stimuli, schedules of reinforcement, satiation, deprivation, matching function, behavior chains, learning deficits, conditioning, shaping, and so on. These brief remarks, if not persuasive to the skeptical, should at least raise the possibility that the social psychological dimensions of both bonding and anomie and strain theory are compatible with, and may be largely subsumable under, social learning concepts.

My argument is that the social learning concepts are more abstract and more empirically validated than those from bonding and anomie, and that if conceptual absorption is to be done it makes more sense to have the social learning concepts absorb the others. The question that is left unanswered here is whether it is necessary or worthwhile to do so. If after the theoretical integration is done, we are left with essentially the social learning model we started with and have not added any concepts, is it still an integration or have we simply done away with the other theories? What more do we have than that with which we began? We may have expanded somewhat empirical instances or fleshed out some implications of social learning concepts. Further, we may be "making it clear when two or more theories are, in fact, referring to basically the same phenomena, even though different terms are used" (Akers and Cochran, 1985, p. 341). But in the process, bonding and anomie concepts have been changed (distorted?) in ways that are most likely unacceptable to proponents of these theories.

All of this has referred only to conceptual, not propositional integration. As some of my remarks above adumbrate, the fact of conceptual overlap does not necessarily mean similarity in propositions. One can make similar empirical predictions from different concepts and differential empirical predictions from the same or similar concepts. For instance, learning and anomie would not make the same prediction regarding the delinquency-producing effect of discrepancies between means and ends, because learning theory would include balancing and behavioral feedback dimensions absent from anomie theory. Social learning theory would make predictions different from social bonding theory about the effects of attachment. Learning theory would recognize some addictive types of drug behavior as resulting from the negative reinforcement of escape behavior; unlike anomie, however, learning theory would propose that other drug behavior is not escape but is positively reinforced.

Some of the general issues in theoretical integration have been presented, as well as some thoughts on the integration of my social behavioral perspective with certain other perspectives on deviance and crime. I have expressed ambiguity regarding the ultimate value of integrating theories of deviance. There are few who would argue strongly against theoretical integration, and many partial and a few fairly complete integrative efforts have been made. How have these theoretical integrations of the past fared? While some have received some empirical support, I must say that by and large they have not widely replaced the different theories they supposedly integrated. It is as if the integration never took place.

Social learning, on the other hand, is one kind of integration which has been given considerable attention in the criminological and deviance literature. Its connection with Sutherland's original differential association theory has certainly been widely recognized. But more than twenty years after the theory was formulated and described as integrating, not producing an alternative to, differential association, the two continue to be treated and tested by many in the field as separate and even incompatible theories. Differential association is still frequently presented as if nothing has happened to it since Sutherland. Some have presented differential association and social learning as unrelated, or even as offering opposing propositions. Empirical support for differential association is sometimes taken as evidence contrary to social learning! What has happened with other proffered integrations of social bonding, social learning, labeling, or anomie? Not much. They have basically been ignored or have simply taken their places alongside the original theories as either something very different or variations on a common theme. Although we may support a scientific norm of theoretical integration and parsimony, have we really rewarded the effort to conform to it?

2

Exploring Alternatives to Integrated Theory

―――Travis Hirschi―――

Traditional positivistic theories of crime were oppositional in character, simultaneously attacking one view of the phenomenon and aggressively defending another. Thus, Lombroso constructed an image of the criminal that denied the classical image of man as a rational calculator and affirmed the new scientific image of man as a social animal. Thus, Sutherland constructed an image of the white-collar criminal that denied the Lombrosian image of the offender as defective and affirmed the even newer scientific image of humans as always social animals. Thus, Merton and Cloward and Ohlin constructed images of the criminal that denied the Freudian image of defective socialization and affirmed the social sources of the offender's criminal behavior. Thus, too, recent versions of control theory were developed in opposition to purely social theories and as an affirmation of the classical and social disorganization views of the origins of crime.

From the necessity of denying one view while affirming another, oppositional theories tended toward clarity and internal consistency. By simultaneously denying and affirming, oppositional theories gave the impression of strict adherence to requirements of scientific objectivity and disinterestedness, actually identifying, in clear form, their major competitors and sometimes even spelling out sets of alternative hypotheses. By always denying an established perspective and substituting a new one, the oppositional tradition gave the impression that theories of crime were continually getting better, that scientific progress had been the rule in the past and could be expected in the future.

Then came social control theory. In its modern versions, social control theory has followed the pattern of oppositional development, simultaneously attacking strain and cultural deviance theories (Hirschi 1969; Kornhauser 1978) while affirming its own sharply different view of the world. But control theory could not claim to be a confrontation of the new with the old. On the contrary, control theory was itself revisionistic, or, perhaps better, revivalistic, an attempt to bring back to life a theory previously thought to be dead and gone.

With this development, the illusion of inherent progress in the development of crime and delinquency theory was shattered. The circle had been closed, and there was no obvious way to break out of it. Control theory was an old theory; in fact a very old theory, the very theory whose rejection got the evolutionary process going in the first place. Following natural impulses, those in the oppositional tradition would now attack control theory and build a new theory based in large part on its weaknesses. But that had already been done several times, and new theories built in explicit opposition to control theory were certain to look suspiciously like old theories based on the same procedures and assumptions. From this point on, it would be hard to sustain claims to originality or modernity by building a theory of crime on standard oppositional principles.

So the oppositional tradition reached its natural end, and was more or less put to rest. Now, after a decent interval, the Albany conference is convened to celebrate the accomplishments of its replacement. Before joining the celebration, let us pause a moment to consider the strengths and weaknesses of the oppositional tradition, and to think in these terms about what has and perhaps about what could have replaced it.

I have already alluded to one strength of the tradition: its tendency to internal consistency and conceptual clarity. Scholars in the oppositional tradition often felt the need to describe clearly the theory they were rejecting. In so doing, they identified their own theory and automatically described, in a reasonably clear way, its presuppositions and assumptions. Say what we will about them, oppositional theories have names, names that suggest ideas and research programs and social policies. Celebrate as we will their nameless offspring, the originals are capable of concise and meaningful summary, such that each year they can be taught to tens of thousands of college students.

These strengths suggest at the same time the weaknesses of oppositional theories. They tend, in keeping with the rationalist tradition from which they come, to focus on the flaws of their enemies when they could be focusing on their own logical and conceptual problems; they tend, in keeping with the same tradition, to spend much time admiring themselves when they could be applying themselves to the phenomenon they were ostensibly designed to explain. Put another way, oppositional theories have the defects of deductive science: They are overly concerned about methodological and technical issues, about criteria of theory evaluation, about consistency and parsimony and clarity and scope and verification and falsification and all that. And they are too little concerned about the phenomenon that supposedly justifies their existence.

Assuming that this characterization of the history of traditional theories and of their strengths and weaknesses is accurate, at least in terms of actual outcome and general tendency, we are now in position to examine the options available to the field at the time the oppositional tradition was seen as no longer tenable.

Integrated Theory

One option was to abandon the idea that theories of crime should oppose one another in favor of the idea that opposition is itself artifactual, that differences among theories merely reflect differences in focus or emphasis rather than fundamentally opposed views of the world. This conclusion immediately elevates all theories to more or less equal status, leads directly to the idea that they complement one another, and eventually justifies the ultimate conclusion that apparently opposed theories of crime can be brought together in some unified, integrated whole.

Viewed from the perspective of the history of crime theory, however, integration appears to be an unlikely solution to the 'crisis' that developed when the oppositional tradition got itself caught in an endless loop. After all, theories in the oppositional tradition were constructed precisely so as to be incompatible with named enemy theories, so as to affirm what enemy theories denied and to deny what they affirmed. Such attention to the flaws in one's enemies should be conducive neither to conceptual reconciliation nor empirical accuracy.

How, in the face of such difficulties, did the integrationist movement manage to get off the ground? It is easy to show that the integrationists immediately recognized the basic tendency of the oppositional tradition, that they accepted the appearance of competition and incompatibility as something with which they had to deal (Johnson 1979, p. 1; Elliott et al. 1985, p. 18). It is also easy to show that in most cases integrationists seemed to have little trouble combining previously opposed theories into new theories that were in their eyes perfectly compatible with the facts.

Still, I think there is an intellectual puzzle here. If theory A asserts X and theory B asserts not-X, it would seem impossible to bring them together in a way pleasing and satisfactory to both, and also pointless to try. Yet the integrationists did bring such theories together, and they did so with surprisingly little effort. How did they do it?

First, of course, they had to oppose the oppositional tradition. This seeming paradox was resolved by claiming that the competitiveness and incompatibilities of the oppositional tradition do not reside in its theories but in the minds of its theorists. If opposition theorists and researchers could be shown to have made logical or conceptual errors, often for the very reason that they were wedded to the idea that theories should compete with rather than complement one another (Johnson 1979, pp. 1, 60; Elliott et al. 1985, pp. 17 ff.), their theories would be freed of their oppositional character, and could then be modified as needed for the purposes of integration.

The task of showing the illogical character of the oppositional tradition was made easier by limiting attention to the most recent round of oppositional theorizing, by concentrating on control theory as *the* repository of oppositional sentiment. Once control theory was identified as the source of such sentiment, attention immediately shifted to the "attitudes" (Johnson 1979, p. 60) and logic of control theorists. Once their authors were convicted of attitudinal and logical deficiencies, control theories were required to absorb the cuts necessary to eliminate the incompatibilities they had themselves introduced.

Because all theories in the oppositional tradition are built on the assumption of incompatibility, the integrationists' tendency to see control theory as the primary obstacle to integration betrays their own commitment to oppositionalism and to those theories originally constructed in opposition to control theory. Put another way, where integrationists find conflict between theoretical traditions, they ostensibly proceed by first examining the logic of the arguments on both sides. Where defective logic is detected, theories defended by it become fair game for whatever modifications integration requires. Although apparently applied in an evenhanded way to all theorists representing source theories, on inspection it turns out that this ploy is little more than a peculiarly ad hominem form of oppositional theory construction, where the integrationist uncritically accepts the pronouncements of the proponents of one source theory and critically rejects the pronouncements of the proponents of another.

Integrationists also attempted to show that theorists and researchers stressing opposition had misinterpreted the data on crime or delinquency, again apparently because of their undue commitment to theoretical purity. In these cases, too, control theory was the villain, especially because control theory was the only oppositional theory developed after the advent of large-scale quantitative research. Demonstrations of misguided data interpretation are of course themselves straightforward borrowings from the logic of the oppositional tradition, based as it is on the assumption that in some cases "the data" can be construed as providing a crucial test of competing hypotheses. How integrationists are able to use the either/or methods of the oppositional tradition without falling into the errors of this tradition is not clear. In fact, given their disdain for either/or methods, it seems a priori reasonable to expect integrationists to be uncommonly likely to misuse them.

Which brings us to the major device available to integrationists. Once they have cleared the field of conflicting or opposing sentiments, integrationists typically proceed to combine, without further ado, whatever source theories may be at hand. Integrationists somehow conclude that variables appear in nature with opposition theory labels attached to them. This allows them to list variables by the theory that owns them. Social disorganization theory, for example, might own economic status, cultural heterogeneity, and mobility. Social control theory might own time spent with family and time spent playing cards. Biological theory appears to own pulse rate, forceps delivery, and height. Social learning theory owns commitment to delinquent peers. And so on. Each of the many variables is measured and, in an open and fair competition, the theories are ranked in terms of the success of their variables in explaining variation in delinquency. Because in the lists compiled by integrationists there is little or no overlap in the sets of variables claimed by various theories, it is easy to show that the data do not support one theory over another; rather, here the data support one and there support another, such that integration is in effect *required* by the evidence and surprisingly easily accomplished (Johnson 1979, pp. 41–70; Elliott et al. 1985, pp. 43ff.).

Given the ease of integration and the spectacular power and simplicity of the end result, it is not hard to understand the rapid emergence and eventual apparent dominance of integrated theories.

But we must back up a minute. We thought we had incompatible theories. We thought they were incompatible because they were designed to be incompatible. Now along come integrationists who tell us they are not incompatible and we were wrong to think that they should be incompatible. Further, these integrationists tell us they can prove these theories are in fact compatible by actually putting them together. All of which they then proceed to do.

So we now have theories that combine what were once thought to be opposed theories. And what happens in the process to the original theories? Well, where theory A used to assert X and theory B used to assert not-X, we now have an integrated theory that asserts X. How does the assertion of X and the denial of not-X within the context of an integrated theory differ from the assertion of X and the denial of not-X within the context of an oppositional theory? The answer is, obviously it does not. Integrated theories are merely oppositional theories in disguise, theories that pretend to open-mindedness while in fact taking sides in theoretical disputes. I reached this conclusion some time ago (Hirschi 1979).

By concealing its oppositional stance under the guise of scientific open-mindedness, integrated theory inherits the defects or limitations of the oppositional tradition without gaining much in the way of recompense. The oppositional and integrative traditions are similar in that they are both derivative and deductive, starting from some combination of, or stance toward, existing theories and going from there to the data. The appearance in integrated theory of concern for the facts is largely misleading. The facts of interest are those defined as interesting by one or another of the source theories. Integrated theories themselves appear to be indifferent to empirical outcomes (what difference do they make to integrated theories?) and they have added little or nothing to the lists of causes of crime (although they have added many lists of causes to the literature). They appear also to have added little to the conceptualization of crime, being again content to accept a view derived from one of their source theories (presumably the favorite).

Being free of prejudice or bias, lacking defined boundaries and credible enemies, integrated theories end up with identity problems of some magnitude. After spelling out one of the more thoughtful integrated theories of delinquency, Richard E. Johnson faces the problem of what to call it:

> It can be characterized as an 'attachment' brand of control theory, but it also includes an appreciation for the roles in generating delinquent behavior of class, strain, peers, values, and perceived risks. It could also be tagged as a brand of differential association theory that includes a place for social controls and so forth. Indeed, perhaps one of its greatest assets is the difficulty in naming it (1979, p. 70).

Johnson's problem is not unique to his theory. Apparently, it is very hard to come up with names for integrated theories that capture their unique contribution and distinguish them from *other* integrated theories of crime. This is so, apparently, because the factors influencing the construction of integrated theories are so complex and numerous that the end product can only be described as a more or less idiosyncratic list of variables potentially important in crime causation. Integrated theories are, in effect, shopping lists prepared by others. Integrated theorists take the list to the store and bring back what it has in stock, but they often cannot seem to decide on their own how and when the list should be modified, and it is very hard to say whether one list is better than another. Shopping lists do of course have a function. They remind us of some of the things we need. When they are prepared by others, however, they often produce disappointing results. Further, I am sorry to say, they will tend to be found toward the bottom of ranked lists of contributions to our understanding of crime. I therefore conclude that the integrated theory response to the crisis in oppositional theory was a mistake, and that we should look elsewhere for valuable and potentially valuable developments in crime theory.

Classical Theories

One place to look for ideas is in the classical theories themselves. Few of these theories appear to have been exploited to their full potential. Given the character of the oppositional tradition, theorists in it often did little more than note the obvious defects in opposing views and display a few examples of the power of their own perspective. This was enough, as noted, to provide a reasonable understanding of the basic assumptions of these theories. It was not enough, however, to show their scope or limits, the settings in which they might be effectively applied, the range of variables whose correlation with crime they might predict or explain, or the extent of their compatibility with existing theories other than the theories they were constructed to oppose.

Take, for example, my version of social control theory. This theory was developed in explicit opposition to strain theory and cultural deviance theory. One more or less obvious purpose of my oppositional stance was to make room for control theory within sociology, to establish its essential credibility as a sociological perspective. Given this goal, I could not emphasize its connections to the Chicago tradition of Thrasher and Shaw and McKay (at the time, social disorganization as a concept was in bad repute), I certainly could not note its potential consistency with the discovery of biological correlates of crime, and I did not have the time, the energy, or the skill to extend the theory beyond delinquency to other forms of crime and deviance or to link it to such cognate if not identical theories as socialization, rational choice, and deterrence.

As is evident, I was only partially successful in establishing a beachhead in sociology, and by the time Ruth Kornhauser (1978) published her brilliant defense of control theory, again vis-a-vis strain and cultural deviance theories, the theory was already on the verge of becoming just another list of variables somewhere near the middle of integrated models. For that matter, Kornhauser's convincing demonstration of the identity of social control and social disorganization theory itself seemed merely to add one more list of variables to be absorbed by integrated theories. Today, social disorganization sublists are beginning to appear at the beginning of lists of crime causal variables claimed by integrated theories, or at the left side of integrated lists when these are arranged to represent causal models.

Still, I think there is much life in the complex of theories that concentrate on variation in restraint and ignore or deny variation in criminal motivation. Indeed, it seems to me that the complementarities of the routine activities (Cohen and Felson 1979), rational choice (Cornish and Clarke 1986), and social control perspectives are such that they must be considered the same theory (Hirschi 1986; Felson 1986). Michael Gottfredson and I have begun to develop a general theory of crime that we feel is sufficiently compatible with this perspective; there is no need to think of integration as a separate problem, and no need to acknowledge in some explicit fashion its debt to these source theories (Hirschi and Gottfredson 1987; Gottfredson and Hirschi 1987). For that matter, the free (i.e., unintegrated) version of social control theory continues to fare reasonably well, recently producing an explanation of white collar crime that ranks in my judgment among the better efforts in that regard (Lasley 1987).

Put another way, I share Charles Tittle's optimistic view of the field and I specifically agree with him that we [may] already possess "many powerful theories, the potentials of which have not yet been realized" (1985, p. 112). The difference between us is in how this potential should be developed. I do not favor efforts to link theories together unless it can be shown that they are for all intents and purposes the same theory. Instead, I think we should take individual theories as far as we can before we abandon them or try to save what is left of them by adding them to some integrated stew. Seen in this light, the oppositional tradition has performed a useful service. It established the distinctiveness and enhanced the clarity of several theories of crime. This task having been accomplished, we may indeed wish to rid the surviving theories of their oppositional or polemical element, but integration is not necessary for this purpose. In fact, the best way to cure a theory of excessive concern for its enemies is to put it to work doing what it is supposed to do—i.e., explaining crime.

If control theory is alive and well, social learning theory is thriving. This theoretical perspective is the darling of the integrationists, perhaps largely because it focuses on the process thought to account for all or at least most of the other variables on their lists, perhaps also because it by tradition owns the peer group (Wilson and Herrnstein 1985; Elliott et al. 1985). The theory continues to receive much attention from scholars who do not necessarily share the integrationist impulse (as I define it—see, e.g., Akers and Cochran 1985), and certainly does not require a vote of confidence from me. I have for a long time thought that reconciliation of social learning and social control theory was just a minor concession away, but the true believers in the theory remain obstinate, and I suspect the most direct route to "integration" remains independent development of the two perspectives. Control theorists have, I think, good reason for not being first to make these concessions. A major mistake in my original oppositional comparison of social control and social learning theory was to grant a gap in control theory that might possibly be filled by social learning theory. Almost immediately, hordes of integrationists and social learning theorists began to pour through the hole I had pointed out to them, and control theory was to that extent subsequently ignored. It was there I learned the lesson mentioned above: the first purpose of oppositional theory construction is to make the world safe for a theory contrary to currently accepted views. Unless this task is accomplished, there will be little hope for the survival of the theory and less hope for its development. Therefore, oppositional theorists should not make life easy for those interested in preserving the status quo. They should instead remain at all times blind to the weaknesses of their own position and stubborn in its defense. Finally, they should never smile.

Strain theory too remains alive, in spite of decades of pounding by research and general neglect by those who might make something more of it. It could be said with justification that the apparent failure of strain theory was the major motive behind the integrationist movement. With strain theory gone, those who accepted the idea that crime has its own motives were left with no place to begin. They therefore revived strain theory and placed it to the extreme left of their models, where it appears to remain today. Put another way, integrationists have patronized strain theory, but they have not contributed to its development. It may deserve more attention than it is now getting.

Crucial Facts

If concentration on the positive contributions of individual theories was a legitimate response to the exhaustion of the oppositional tradition, another was to reduce our interest in abstract, deductive theory and pay more attention to the facts. Several arguments favor this approach, some mentioned already. For one thing, as long as theorists are debating among themselves, the terms of the debate are likely to be defined by traditional theoretical concepts, and opportunities for empirical input will be limited. For another, as long as existing theories are the primary concern, the favored mode of research will tend to be the large-scale survey whose systematic data allow direct test of theory-derived hypotheses. This too is all well and good, but it is not conducive to the discovery of ideas, and it is strangely lacking in ability to introduce empirical tension into theoretical systems. Finally, the inductive mode can be justified as the typical response of a scientific discipline when it finally breaks with the rationalism of its formative period.

Once again, of course, the proof is not in the argument but in the result. And the evidence, it seems to me, speaks well for an inductive or fact-oriented research strategy as opposed to the much favored deductive or theory-oriented strategy. A hard and fast line is hard to draw between the two traditions, but we should have no trouble placing *Unraveling Juvenile Delinquency* (Glueck and Glueck 1950) and *Delinquency in a Birth Cohort* (Wolfgang et al. 1972) near the inductive end of the continuum; I think most of the important gang research (e.g., Short and Strodtbeck 1965; Klein 1971; Suttles 1968) belongs on the inductive side as well.

These examples should be sufficient to make the point that an inductive orientation has much to offer, that at the moment we may have too much theory and too few *facts* to guide theory construction. In this connection, it may be worthwhile to reveal the true story behind the age and crime debate as seen from the Hirschi–Gottfredson side. Gottfredson and I reached the conclusion that the age–crime relation is invariant across social conditions after (1) looking at all the data we could find and (2) trying as best we could to explain the relation using standard theories of crime. Once we decided this relation was invariant and therefore beyond the reach of current theory, it became in our minds a "crucial fact," a fact capable of critically reorienting our own thinking about crime and delinquency. Given this conclusion, we were no longer free to entertain with an open mind all of the many theories that might be advanced to explain the age–crime relation, nor were we any longer willing to entertain with an open mind all of the findings apparently contrary to our invariance thesis. In other words, we decided to defend a fact against theory and research.

I can testify that this is not an easy task. Theorists, we soon learned, can get along on very little sleep. And researchers, we soon learned, are more interested in the idiosyncrasies of their data than in their consistency with previous research. Still, we managed to remain firm in our conviction, to knock down to our satisfaction the many efforts to undermine the age–crime relation with theory or to contradict it with evidence.

At last we came up with a conceptual scheme that could account for an invariant relation between age and crime—i.e., a conceptual scheme that could account for the relation without destroying it. This scheme could also accommodate differences among people in the likelihood of crime at any given age. The starting point was a distinction between crime and criminality. "Crimes are short term, circumscribed events that presuppose a peculiar set of necessary conditions (e.g., activity, opportunity, adversaries, victims, goods). Criminality, in contrast, refers to stable differences across individuals in the propensity to commit criminal or theoretically equivalent acts" (Gottfredson and Hirschi 1988, p. 4).

Our 'crime' theory, therefore, now had two dependent variables, one that could vary with age and another that could remain reasonably stable over much if not the bulk of the life course. The likelihood of criminal acts may vary with age (as it does), but this no longer required us to assume that differences in the propensity to commit criminal acts also vary with age. By remaining faithful to one crucial fact, we were eventually led to another fact often ignored by crime theorists, the basic stability of crime-relevant individual differences over much of the life course. Combining these two facts leads to a distinction that, once made, is hard to ignore. Thus freed of the restrictions imposed by a single concept of crime, we have come to see many issues in the field in a new light. For example, this conceptual scheme led us to doubt the usefulness of the career criminal concept before we looked at the literature on the topic; this doubt was intensified by subsequent investigation (Gottfredson and Hirschi 1986). Similarly, the distinction between crime and criminality led us to doubt the necessity or utility of longitudinal research designs before we examined their results, a doubt also justified in our view by subsequent inspection of the data (Gottfredson and Hirschi 1987). And our conceptual scheme has, we think, allowed us to show that white-collar crime need no longer be treated as a special topic in criminology (Hirschi and Gottfredson 1987).

The distinction between crime and criminality obviously puts many questions about such things as specialization in a new light. It also has the potential to restructure our thinking about the causes or correlation of crime. Is gang membership a cause of crime or a cause of criminality? Does a muscular body build affect the likelihood of criminal events directly by altering the individual's perception of the immediate situation, or does it indirectly affect the long-term probability of involvement in criminal events through its impact on propensities? To what extent does parental supervision affect crime without altering crime propensity?

These examples should be enough to illustrate the potential value of a conceptual scheme based ultimately on facts rather than data—that is, on the results of research oriented more to the phenomenon and less to a priori theoretical explanations of it. Such conceptual schemes have the virtue, in the present context, of being non-oppositional (although they may of course be controversial) and they require no commitment one way or another to such extraneous and irrelevant considerations as integration.

Conclusion

Although we may not always agree on what theories of crime and deviance are, we have less difficulty agreeing on the qualities they should possess, on what they should be able to do. For one thing, we appear to agree that theories should somehow organize available data, telling us which of our current findings are important and which are not. For another, we appear to agree that theories should serve as guides to research design, data collection, and analysis, telling us what our samples should look like, advising us on appropriate measures and measurement techniques, and even helping structure the models we use to inform our statistical decisions. We agree that theories should actually define or at least help define crime itself. Finally, we seem to agree that theories should explain the correlates of crime either by predicting them from more general concepts or by identifying the mechanisms that connect them to crime.

Theories able to do these things, we assume, probably also possess the formal virtues often ascribed to good theories, such things as internal consistency, falsifiability, broad scope, and policy relevance. Whether they do or do not, the informal virtues should, I believe, have priority. Concern for formal or philosophical correctness often does more harm than good, leading at times to spurious rejection of perfectly useful general theories of crime and at times to the invention of theories that do none of the things theories are supposed to do.

I am afraid I consider integration one of these formal virtues, and an especially problematic formal virtue at that. It is something to be thankful for if one's theory happens to combine the major insights of theories previously thought to be different (as has happened with social learning theory), but it is something else again to *set out* to combine theories previously designed to be different. The evidence, it seems to me, suggests that theories constructed with this tiny formal virtue in mind are likely to be lacking in the informal virtues just described.

The search for a better way thus led to existing theories of crime and to inductive theorizing, where, in my view, we found a good stock of theories capable of doing well many of the things we want theories to do, a stock of theories therefore worthy of careful, individual attention.

3

Reflections on the Advantages and Disadvantages of Theoretical Integration

────*Terence P. Thornberry*────

Introduction

The value of theoretical integration is an intriguing and controversial issue in contemporary criminology. Some, such as Elliott and his colleagues (1979, 1985) and Pearson and Weiner (1985) argue forcefully for the integration of existing theoretical models, while others, such as Hirschi (1979) and Short (1979), either argue against or at least raise serious questions about the propriety of such efforts. The present paper examines the question of whether theoretical integration is an efficient method to advance the understanding of delinquent and criminal behavior. In large part it reflects my own views concerning the advantages and disadvantages of theoretical integration; however, since it is also a reactive piece, it is influenced by the issues raised in the companion papers by Akers and Hirschi.

Akers rightfully points to the pitfalls of extreme solutions with respect to this issue; if integration is pushed too far we run the risk of generating theoretical mush, while if integration is ignored we miss important commonalities in seemingly competing theories. After identifying this dilemma, Akers presents a fairly supportive treatment of integration, especially what he refers to as "conceptual integration." He identifies considerable conceptual overlap in the major theories of delinquency, but that should hardly be surprising since they derive from the same general sociological perspective. But it does raise an interesting question: is the identification of conceptual overlap or absorption enough to claim that *theoretical* integration has occurred? This issue will be addressed directly in the discussion that follows.

Hirschi also begins by pointing to the pitfalls of extreme solutions with respect to integration—and then sides with extremity. Pointing out that most classical theories of crime are by design oppositional, he raises serious questions about the logical ability to integrate such theories and concludes that "... the integrated theory response to the crisis in oppositional theory was a mistake."

In its place Hirschi proposes that classical theories can be developed to their full potential. While this view is in substantial accord with the one elaborated below, the extremity of his contention that theorists should remain—"... at all times blind to the weaknesses of their own position and stubborn in its defense"—must be questioned. We are after all theorists, not defense attorneys. Moreover, opposition to this view parallels precisely the weaknesses that Hirschi identifies with oppositional theories: they tend "... to focus on the flaws of their enemies when they could be focusing on their own logical and conceptual problems." Indeed, one could go a step further and suggest that they might even learn a thing or two from their presumed enemies in an effort to improve theoretical explanation, without incurring the attendant pitfalls of theoretical integration.

Definitional Issues

It would be appropriate at the outset of this discussion to define theoretical integration. Surprisingly, no clear definition of this term can be found in the criminological literature. Elliott (1985) comes closest to offering a formal definition, but still uses the term as a sensitizing concept. So let us begin by offering a more formal definition.

In the social sciences, a theory is generally defined as "a set of logically interrelated propositions designed to explain a particular phenomenon" (see Blalock, 1969). From this perspective, therefore, the two most fundamental characteristics of a theory are its *propositional* form and its *explanatory* purpose.

The second term, *integration*, is defined by the Random House Dictionary (Second Edition) as "the act or an instance of combining into an integral whole." It is essentially the combination of separable parts to form a larger unit with an integrity or completeness that is missing in the separable parts.

Theoretical integration can be defined as *the act of combining two or more sets of logically interrelated propositions into one larger set of interrelated propositions, in order to provide a more comprehensive explanation of a particular phenomenon*. This definition maintains the two primary characteristics of a theory; it is still propositional in form and it is still explanatory in purpose.

Defining theoretical integration in this more formal fashion moves beyond the use of the term simply as a sensitizing concept and makes explicit what theoretical integration entails and what it implies as a theoretical tool. Four of its implications can be identified; the first two derive from the propositional form of theories and the second two from their explanatory purpose.

Theoretical integration does not refer to the simple identification of conceptual overlap between two or more theories, nor to the absorption of the less abstract concepts of one theory by the more abstract concepts of another. In other words, the requirements of theoretical integration are not met when *concepts* from differing theories are integrated, precisely because propositions, not concepts, are the building blocks of theories.

Since what is being integrated are sets of propositions, theoretical integration entails more than the simple addition to one theory of an isolated proposition or two from a second theory. Such limited integration lacks the melding together of previously separable parts to form an integral whole which is an essential quality of the definition of integration. This does not imply that all the propositions of the original theories have to be incorporated in the integrated model; such an expectation is unreasonable. But it does mean that the basic claims of each of the theories—i.e., their propositional structure—should be incorporated.

The definition implies that the earlier theories, the objects of integration, are fundamentally altered by the process of integration. Since the integrated theory offers a more comprehensive explanation of the phenomenon of interest, the old theories are to some substantial extent rendered obsolete. Like the objects of corporate takeover bids, be they friendly or hostile, the objects of theoretical integration bids are fundamentally altered if the integration is successful.

Finally, the primary criteria for evaluating the success of theoretical integration do not center on the demonstration of an increase in predictive power or in the magnitude of the coefficient of determination. Since the basic purpose of any theory is to explain something—in our case, delinquency—it is not appropriate to claim that an integrated model is better than the original ones solely because it offers better predictions of delinquency; there are more expedient ways of improving predictions than theoretical integration. But it is important for the integrated model to offer a better explanation or understanding of the processes that cause delinquency than do the earlier models. The question before us now is whether there are also more expedient ways than integration to accomplish improved explanation.

The Process of Integration

Before that question can be answered, more detail about the process of theoretical integration is required. Although not an exhaustive list, any theory contains at least these four general elements:

1. A set of basic assumptions upon which the propositions and concepts are based.
2. A statement as to the level or levels of explanation at which it operates, e.g., macro, micro or individual levels.
3. A set of logically interrelated propositions.
4. An underlying structure that determines the manner in which the propositions are interrelated; there are, for example, recursive and non-recursive structures.

At a minimum, the exercise of theoretical integration requires the theorist to attend to each of these four theoretical elements in forging a more comprehensive theory. The process followed appears to have three basic stages. First, the original theories are described in terms of these elements; second, all conflicts or competing claims among the theories are identified; and third, those conflicts are resolved in a manner internally consistent with the framework of the integrated model.

It is important to note that substantial conflicts among the original theories with respect to some, if not all, of these basic elements is assumed. For if there were few differences among the original theories they would in essence be the same theory, and their integration would be rendered trivial.

Clearly, the reconciliation of differences at this level of abstraction is no easy task. The difficulties encountered can be illustrated by a brief examination of attempts to reconcile assumptive differences and to move across levels of explanation.

Elliott has identified the assumptive conflict with respect to social control and social learning theories. "The motivation for crime is either a constant (control theory) or it is a variable (social learning theory)" (1985, p.131).

Now it seems that the integrationist has one of two options in reconciling this conflict; the theorist can choose one or the other of these assumptions about human nature, or he can adopt both. Clearly the latter is logically contradictory and inappropriate.

But the former option is also fraught with difficulties. For if one abandons such a fundamental point of a delinquency theory as its assumption about the motivation for deviance, it is not at all clear that one has integrated that theory, as a theory, with another one. As Hirschi put it, such a " . . . solution is to use the terms and ignore the claims of [the] theory" (1979, p. 22).

The difficulty of adequately integrating theories with conflicting theoretical elements can also be seen with respect to the level of explanation. If the theories operate at different explanatory levels, two options are available for reconciliation.

The first is to accept the difference and integrate across the levels. Such an outcome is viewed as one of the primary advantages of theoretical integration and has been identified by Short as the "penultimate integration" (1979). Although a worthy goal, even such an undaunted integrationist as Elliott appears to concede the difficulty of this effort: " . . . it is clear that integration efforts to date are much more modest and remain primarily at the individual level of explanation" (1985, p. 130).

A second, and at least for now more common option is to 'translate' the theoretical concepts—or, more commonly, their measurement—to a common level. Akers points to this type of solution with respect to the integration of control and learning theories (see chapter 1 above). Yet the difficulty with this approach should be obvious. What has been achieved is a common measurement strategy, but the theoretical concepts—and, probably, the propositions in which they are embedded—have neither been integrated nor tested.

In general, the resolution of conflicts as abstract as these are clearly difficult to achieve, but they are by no means impossible. Indeed, there are a number of theoretical models in the criminological literature that have, with varying degrees of success, integrated previous theories; the works of Cloward and Ohlin (1960), Akers (1977), and Elliott et al. (1979; 1985) come readily to mind.

It should also be noted that these integrated models play an important role in the development of criminological thought, precisely because they point to the commonalities in theories and break down petty differences that impede rather than advance understanding. Like Sztompka, these theorists argue " . . . against closed, dogmatic 'schools,' and for the mutual cross-fertilization of theories" (1979, p. i). This is a major advantage of theoretical integration and one of its great contributions to theory construction. But these advantages and contributions do not come for free; there is a cost entailed, and the question is whether that cost is excessive.

The Cost of Integration

The previous section began by asking if theoretical integration is the most efficient way to improve theoretical understanding. To assess its relative efficiency, the costs associated with theoretical integration have to be enumerated.

The previous discussion, concerning the inherent difficulty of reconciling contradictory assumptions and differing levels of explanation, identified and illustrated the most important cost. In essence, theoretical integration diverts attention from matters of substance to matters of form, from the fundamental purpose of theory construction—the explanation of a particular phenomenon—to a secondary purpose—the reconciliation of differences found in previous theories in the hope that such reconciliation improves explanatory power.

Theoretical integration incurs this cost by forcing the theorist into a set of compromises rather than affirmative statements about the substantive issues at hand. If the earlier assumption, that the theories to be integrated invariably differ on one or more fundamental dimensions, is accepted, then the reconciliation of these differences seems to lead ineluctably to compromise.

For example, one can choose between one of the two assumptions about the motivation for deviance, and that choice compromises the integrity of one or another of the theories. Or one can translate across levels of explanation, but again that choice tends to compromise the integrity of one or more of the original theories. The very effort of reconciliation—of melding together conflicting demands—increases the risk of watering down the clarity and strength of the theoretical statements. While this is not the inevitable consequence of theoretical integration, the very nature of the enterprise increases its risk. If this assessment is correct, this is indeed a high cost to pay for the reconciliation of differing theoretical perspectives, especially if there is a viable alternative.

Theoretical Elaboration

What is proposed in place of theoretical integration is the process of elaboration. Rather than starting with multiple theories and attempting to reconcile their differences to generate a comprehensive model, theoretical elaboration explicitly starts with a particular theoretical model. Accepting its assumptions, level of explanation, and causal structure, it attempts to build a more and more comprehensive model by the logical extention of the basic propositions contained in the model.

The process can be illustrated by examining the elaboration of control or bonding theory. Control theory is a consequential theory; it identifies the mechanisms by which people are bonded to conventional society and then explicates the behavioral consequences of those bonds. Essentially, it uses the observed variation in the strength of the bonds to explain deviance and conformity.

Beginning with this basic perspective, a more comprehensive and accurate model of delinquency can be generated. First, rather than using variation in the bonding elements as the theoretical starting point, one can examine the sources of variation in such factors as attachment to parents, commitment to school, and belief in conventional values and so forth. Variation in factors such as these should be systematically related to temporally prior conditions such as family structure, social class, and area of residence.

Second, one can examine in more detail the consequences of weak bonds. Do they have a direct effect on delinquency, as proposed by Hirschi (1969), or can intervening variables be identified that further explicate our understanding of the factors that lead to delinquency?

Third, one could examine the adequacy of the recursive and rather static causal structure adopted in the original theory. Indeed, recent theoretical and empirical work suggests that this structure is limiting and that a richer understanding of delinquency is afforded by examining the consequences of delinquency on the bonding elements as well as the consequences of the bonds on delinquency (Thornberry and Christenson, 1984; Thornberry, 1987; Liska and Reed, 1985). In elaborating control theory in this fashion, the fundamental premises of a model (or what Hirschi calls the "claims of control theory") are not necessarily violated.

This brief diversion to control theory identifies two issues concerning the process of elaboration that need to be addressed. First, what are the sources of theoretical elaboration, and second, how does this process differ from theoretical integration?

Sources of Theoretical Elaboration

The basic sources of theoretical elaboration are the same as those used in any theory construction effort. First and foremost is the imagination of the theorist. This entails the logical evaluation and extension of the theoretical model to make sense of the observational world and to state more accurately the propositions of the theory. Clearly, any one presentation of a theory is not all-encompassing; it can inevitably be altered to offer better explanations of the phenomenon of interest. The elaboration could entail the reformulation of existing propositions, the addition of new ones, a reduction in the number of propositions as old ones are deleted or combined in the interest of parsimony, or any combination of these steps.

Second, empirical observations inevitably lead to theoretical elaboration. Despite our best theoretical efforts, people occasionally do not behave as they are supposed to. When they are attached to others when they should not be or persist in behaviors that have not been properly reinforced, it is, alas, we who have to pay the price by returning to the theoretical drafting board. Clearly, such outcomes are both common and the source of much theoretical refinement.

Finally, propositions contained in other theoretical models, especially propositions which have received empirical support, are a rich source of information for theoretical elaboration. There is no logical objection to improving a particular theory by borrowing from others, provided the borrowed material can be logically incorporated into the focal theory.

But it is clear that many propositions from other theories, including empirically supported ones, cannot simply be incorporated into the focal theory—they are logically inconsistent with the theory's assumptions, other propositions, or level of explanation. Nevertheless, these propositions play an important role in the process of elaboration. In essence, they constitute a set of challenges to the focal theory that allow, but do not require, the theorist to revise the theory's assumptions, propositions, and structure in an effort to improve its explanation of delinquency. In the end, some of those propositions will remain outside the theory's purview, but others, because of their explanatory importance, will be incorporated and will force fundamental revisions of the original theory. For example, our increasing understanding of, and the empirical support for, the importance of delinquent peers seems to be bringing about such fundamental revisions of control theory, including a reconsideration of its basic assumption about the motivation for human behavior. Some may argue against this as Hirschi has in chapter 2, since the resulting model is not a 'pure' control theory. However, if the resulting model offers a better, more powerful explanation of delinquency, then the pure control model should give way to its replacement.

Indeed, this is the desired outcome of the process of elaboration. A theoretical model is revised and expanded in light of new theoretical and empirical information to provide better explanations of delinquency. There is no overt attempt to reconcile the theory's statements with those of other models at the outset; as theory construction develops, such reconciliation forces itself on the process, unless we are completely blind to the work of our colleagues. In the end, therefore, the resolution of the conflicting issues turns neither on the value of integration nor on the value of protecting the purity of a theoretical tradition but on the much more pragmatic value of whether or not the resolution offers an improved explanation of delinquent behavior.

The end result of elaboration is a theoretical model that differs from the one with which we began in a number of important ways. Among them are the following:

1. It is likely that propositions have been added, deleted, combined and re-ordered to offer a better explanation of delinquency.
2. The basic assumptions have probably been re-evaluated and possibly altered to allow for the inclusion of propositions from differing perspectives.
3. The structure of the theory, including the temporal ordering of concepts and the types of relationships permitted, may well have changed.
4. It is likely that when this process is played out over time from the point of view of a number of different focal theories, the overall result will be the blending together of originally different and competing theoretical models into a more general body of explanatory principles. In turn, this will require fundamental changes in the theories of origin as the elaborated models replace them.

Integration vs. Elaboration

Clearly the outcome of this process is similar to the outcome of theoretical integration. Yet there is a profound difference between the two approaches. That difference lies in the basic orientation of the theorist towards the effort of theory construction.

In the process of integration, the theorist is primarily concerned with the reconciliation of conflicting theoretical elements. In that process some theoretical compromises will be made if the competing demands of the original theories are to be addressed. Moreover, the outcome of the process is, in some sense, pre-ordained; substantial portions of each of the original theories have to be incorporated into the integrated theory. If not, there is no integration.

In the process of elaboration, on the other hand, the theorist is concerned with maximizing the explanatory power of a particular theory without the attendant concern of reconciling differences across theories.

Some of those differences may well be reconciled, but that is clearly a secondary issue. Also, the theorist is free to borrow or not borrow from competing theories, and there is certainly no obligation to represent all, or even substantial portions, of the competing theories in the elaborated model. The use of propositions from other theories can be quite limited or quite extensive, depending entirely on the explanatory value they offer. Finally, the outcome of theoretical elaboration is always in doubt; the melding together of differing theories may or may not occur.

In the end, the two processes may lead to the same outcome. Nevertheless, the process of elaboration is theoretically more defensible. Like integration, it breaks down the artificial barriers that have grown up between differing theoretical traditions. Unlike integration, however, it does not value the melding together of differing theories as an end in itself; it values the incorporation of differing perspectives only selectively, and only if they offer a clear increment to our efforts to explain delinquency.

4

A Theory of Mental Illness: An Attempted Integration of Biological, Psychological, and Social Variables[1]

Walter R. Gove
Michael Hughes

Introduction

The following discussion proposes a general theory of mental illness, one which combines biological, psychological and social variables and which focuses on both etiology and process. We have long seen the need for such a theory—not a precise theory of a particular disorder or disorders, but a discussion of general causes and processes.

In the past few decades there have been marked changes in what is known about mental illness and its treatment; four clearly stand out. First, with the publication of The Diagnostic and Statistical Manual of Mental Disorders (DMS-III) (American Psychiatric Association 1980), psychiatry and psychology have a classification scheme which, with most but not all disorders, has a reasonable degree of reliability (Klerman 1982). Second, it is becoming increasingly clear that psychotherapy is effective—even though there are occasions when it is not and there are times when it has negative effects (e.g., Smith and Glass 1977). Third, the efficacy of drug therapy in the control of symptoms is well established (e.g., Berger 1978). Fourth, there have been marked advances in the understanding of the biological underpinning of mental illness (Klerman 1982). These advances occurred after the efficacy of tranquilizers and antidepressants was established, and are closely linked to the study of how these medications work.

In spite of these advances, our ignorance about mental illness is pervasive. We not only lack a theory of mental illness, we do not even have any serious contenders. The new diagnostic manual, while evidencing a substantial increase in rigorousness and reliability, is not only atheoretical but pointedly so. The absence of theory in the manual reflects the fact that the advances in understanding the biological aspects of mental illness have not been accompanied by comparable developments in the social and psychological domains. In fact, as biological psychiatry has begun to flourish, the social and psychological aspects of the psychiatric image of mental illness have tended to atrophy. Further, as even the strongest proponents of a biological approach would acknowledge, our understanding of the biological aspects of mental illness is still in a very early stage of development, and from a practical perspective it is more promise than fact.

One of the fundamental requirements of scientific inquiry is the development of a means of identifying the phenomenon to be investigated. In the area of mental illness, such an identification should be reflected in the patient's diagnosis. Ideally, the diagnosis a patient receives would not only appropriately categorize the patient's disorder but would also suggest the treatment that would be most suitable and would be a good prognostic indicator. The present psychiatric classification system does not do this, largely because of its atheoretical nature. DSM-III can, in fact, be viewed as an attempt to develop a classification scheme for *all* persons in treatment so that they can reliably be placed into particular categories without the diagnostician ever seriously confronting the questions of (1) whether or not they are mentally ill, (2) the cause of the disorder, (3) the appropriate treatment and (4) the positive and negative consequences of particular forms of treatment.

One of the major difficulties in developing a theory of mental illness is that American society has treated mental illness as a residual category into which an array of troublesome persons, with very different problems, are grouped. In order to develop an empirically valid theory of mental illness, we must therefore differentiate between persons who are properly viewed as mentally ill and those who are not mentally ill but who nonetheless are patients in mental institutions simply because they are aggressive, impulsive, willing to violate social norms, and unconcerned about the long-term consequences of their acts.

Our proposed theory holds that mental illness is best viewed as a process involving the interaction of three general variables: symptoms, social expectations, and personal attributes. Three types of symptoms are discussed: distress, disorganization, and overt disruptive behavior. These symptoms can be used to classify mentally ill patients into three types, representing a progressive development toward increasing severity of illness.

The Development of Psychotic Disorganization

It is probably the symptoms of the mentally ill, particularly bizarre ideation and behavior, that make mental disorders appear incomprehensible and abnormal. Certain key symptoms, however, such as being upset, depressed, or anxious, to which we will refer under the general terms of distress, are *not* generally perceived as incomprehensible reactions. This is probably because everyone is regularly subject to such feelings, and most persons, at least at some time in their lives, are acutely distressed. The consequence is that such affective states are generally perceived as normal reactions. They are only viewed as abnormal when they are extremely persistent, are not congruent with reality (typically as perceived by both others *and* by the person in question), and when they create trouble for the person experiencing them. Even then the person is typically viewed as someone who is "nervous," "tense," "anxious," or "depressed" and not as someone who is "mentally ill."

Psychotic symptoms, such as hallucinations or delusions, which are generally thought to be peculiar or abnormal, are in actuality also common reactions under certain conditions. Elsewhere the first author (Gove 1968, 1970) has shown at some length that these conditions include physical exhaustion, sensory deprivation, a state of heightened attention, isolation, monotony, reaction to certain drugs, and the transition zone between sleeping and waking. The vast majority of persons who experience thought disorders under such conditions do not become mentally ill. They probably avoid mental illness largely because the experience is of brief duration, because there are not other compounding factors such as being emotionally disturbed, and because they and others see the experience as a normal, although unreal, response to unusual circumstances. For our purpose, the most important link may be the one between sleep deprivation and psychotic disorganization.

It is very common for individuals who are in the transition zone between sleep and wakefulness to experience auditory and visual images, images which they perceive as distinct from dreams. These images are generally referred to as "hypnagogic hallucinations," a term first coined by Maury in 1848. People reporting hypnagogic hallucinations report that they were awake at the time of the experience, and they frequently indicate that they were up and moving around. They generally report that the hypnagogic hallucinations, whether auditory or visual, intrude into their stream of thought in an obtrusive and irrelevant manner. An additional characteristic of auditory hypnagogic hallucinations is that a voice frequently refers to the subject, commonly by name, and it appears to be a voice of someone familiar.

A number of systematic studies of sleep deprivation have consistently produced hallucinations and other disorders of thought and speech commonly associated with psychosis. Sleep-deprived subjects have transitory episodes of sleepiness during which they function poorly, but they are generally able to maintain what appears to be a reasonably alert state. Most subjects experience a general rise in irritability, and tend to avoid activities requiring intellectual effort. Disturbance of thinking is difficult to detect during formal psychological testing, but it is very obvious in more unstructured situations. Rambling speech with repetition and mispronunciation is common; frequently there is a complete break in a train of thought or in an action. Tyler (1955) also reports a cataleptic-like maintenance of uncomfortable sitting positions. The development of depersonalization is particularly common. For example, Morris, Williams, and Lubin (1960) report a subject who felt so changed that he became concerned that he might be somebody else and had to be reassured that he was still himself. Similarly, Bliss, Clark, and West (1960) mention that all subjects felt "apart from others" and had other feelings of depersonalization. In addition, their subjects reported abnormal bodily sensations, such as peculiar electric shocks running up the leg, numbness, and flushing of the skin.

Almost all the subjects in sleep deprivation studies report some perceptual changes, ranging from relatively minor disturbances to complex hallucinations. Changes in the perception of time, size of self, space, weight, and speed of movement are very common, as is the illusion that stationary objects are moving. In almost all of the studies, some subjects report elaborate hallucinations. By far the largest study was the one by Tyler (1955), who studied psychological aberrations in 350 male subjects who went without sleep for periods up to 112 hours. As in other studies, Tyler found that sleep deprivation produced psychotic-like reactions in practically all of his subjects, seventy percent of whom reported auditory or visual hallucinations. What lends particular significance to his study is that seven of his subjects spontaneously developed states completely analogous to acute paranoid psychosis. They carried on completely irrational conversations, became aggressive and combative, and accepted their hallucinations and delusions as real. Furthermore, these states were not transitory, and the subjects manifested no insight into their conditions.

The most common cause of insomnia is anxiety. The literature consistently indicates that persons who are acutely disturbed are often seriously sleep-deprived. The sleep deprivation studies have demonstrated that anxiety substantially increases the degree of psychotic disorganization and affects its nature. The evidence, which admittedly is based on relatively few studies, also indicates that at the time of hospitalization people who are acutely distressed or experiencing an acute psychotic episode have a very serious sleep deficit.

The evidence from the sensory deprivation and sleep deprivation studies, as well as from the autobiographic accounts, suggests that such experiences as depersonalization, disordered thought, hallucinations, and delusions are normal, given a particular set of circumstances. Furthermore, the extremely similar, if not identical, character of these experiences to those of the psychotic suggests that the physiological processes are basically identical. The fact that persons who are sleep-deprived frequently have psychotic-like experiences, in combination with the fact that anxiety and agitation tend to both inhibit sleep and heighten selective attention, provides a basis for developing a model of mental disorganization in the mentally ill.

A Proposed Model of the Development of Symptoms

We propose that the original development of psychotic thought in the mentally ill typically occurs in the following sequence. A person becomes acutely disturbed or distressed for some reason. Although the reasons for the distress will vary, they generally will involve some sort of crisis or disruption in the person's life, although it may simply be produced by an acute dissatisfaction with his or her situation or reflect other intrapsychic difficulties. Because the person is anxious and agitated, he or she will have difficulty sleeping, and is likely to approach the physical state found in sleep-deprived subjects. In the case of a distressed person, however, the effects of sleep deprivation will be magnified, for: (1) anxiety may interact with the lack of sleep, thereby increasing the likelihood of psychotic experiences, (2) what sleep the person does have is apt to be of poor quality, lacking both REM sleep and deep sleep, and (3) the person is in an environment which, instead of promoting relaxation, is apt to exacerbate the effects of sleep deprivation. Such a person is apt to be not only acutely distressed and sleep-deprived but is also likely to be highly emotional, unsure of him or herself and others, and extremely concerned about particular events or relationships. A person in this frame of mind will be especially attentive to information that bears upon the situation, but will have poor judgment and tend to misperceive and even fabricate clues.

As noted above, persons who are acutely distressed and sleep-deprived will have a poor attention span, loose and unconnected associations, frequent thought blockages, and feelings of depersonalization. If the disorder is severe, they will probably experience hallucinations and delusions, and these psychotic experiences will probably focus on their immediate personal difficulties. We would not expect people having these experiences who are already very unhappy with themselves and their situation to function effectively. Their behavior is therefore likely to increasingly alienate those about them, disrupting their interpersonal relations and increasing their isolation. It would appear that this process, once well underway, would have a snowballing effect.

Persons who become disorganized due to acute distress are likely to accept their psychotic experiences as real. Their experiences are apt to occur when they are up and apparently awake, and there is no ready explanation for these experiences such as an experimental study or on the border line of sleep. The psychotic experience of persons who are distressed is generally sufficiently unusual and powerful that they must in some way come to grips with it. They may feel that they are "losing their minds," but unlike experimental subjects they cannot "leave the experiment." Their mental processes are already impaired, and they are anxious, puzzled, and unsure of themselves and their situation. They are therefore suggestible and may accept their experiences as real, particularly if the experiences provide an "explanation" for, or a relief from, a difficult situation (Gove 1968; pp. 48–49). Probably much of the peculiar, idiosyncratic, and even "delusional" life organization of the chronically mentally ill can be attributed to their attempt to assimilate and explain their psychotic experiences. For example, a person may recognize that he or she is having unusual and uncomfortable experiences, but—lacking another explanation of them—may attribute them to someone with whom he or she is having difficulties, particularly if depersonalization has led the person to feel as if some other self was controlling his or her behavior. Probably a major determinant of how persons define their psychotic experiences is the interpretation of these experiences they receive from others. If others can convince them that their experiences are normal, although "unreal," responses to their mental condition and present situation, they probably would not incorporate their psychotic experiences into their life organization. On the other hand, if they do not receive an acceptable interpretation from others, they will develop their own, one that may lead to an idiosyncratic, "delusional" life organization.

We suspect, as do others (West 1967), that the persistence of an active psychotic disorder over a prolonged period of time results in physiological changes that increase that person's susceptibility to further psychotic experiences. Elsewhere, the first author has presented case histories that suggest that persons who chronically experience hallucinations can identify and ignore them in much the same manner that persons who are on hallucinogenic drugs learn to ignore the drug-induced illusions when they function in society (Gove 1968, pp. 55–56). In these cases, the correct interpretation of the hallucinatory experiences appeared to depend upon the orientation and information provided by others.

If persons accept their psychotic experiences as real and act accordingly, their behavior will be very disruptive and their actions will pointedly disavow the world as others understand it. They will thus produce what Goffman (1971) has referred to as "insanity of place," and their actions will create "havoc." In suggesting that as psychotic reaction is a normal experience, given certain conditions, and that those conditions include acute distress and lack of sleep, we do not mean to imply that all persons are equally susceptible to mental disorganization. Individuals clearly differ in their ability to function effectively in society and, thus, some are more adept at avoiding stressful situations. Persons also differ in the way they react to situations and in their ability to control their emotions. It is therefore very likely that a person's social experience affects his or her ability for organized thought. For example, the double bind theory of Bateson et al. (1956) should be interpreted as saying that a person who experiences a continuing and severe double bind will be predisposed toward confusion and disorganization. In addition, the literature on schizophrenia and manic depression clearly indicates that individuals have different biological propensities for disorganization. Thus, inherited characteristics, level of social integration or isolation, and the social environment will all be strong predictors of the development of psychotic disorganization.

It also seems very likely that there is substantial variation in the tendency of persons to accept their psychotic symptoms as real and to incorporate the symptoms into their behavior. Similarly, the social situation of the individual will have a strong effect on the interpretation of the psychotic symptoms and the degree to which they affect the behavior. In short, the likelihood that persons will act in a disruptive fashion as a consequence of their psychotic experience is strongly affected by the attributes of the individual and the situation.

Social Expectations

According to symbolic interactionists, most characteristics of an individual take on a socially viable meaning only within a particular social framework. It is through the actions of others that individuals are able to develop an image of how they are perceived by others. The actions of others, to use Cooley's (1902) term, provide one with a "looking-glass self." Because a person's situation vis-a-vis others is the primary source of evidence about his or her identity, the actions of others play a major role in the development and maintenance of a self-image, and all individuals continually orient themselves by observing the behavior of others.

The way one person acts toward others is largely determined by the person's perception of who the others are and how they expect him or her to behave. One's expectations regarding others depend, of course, on a number of factors, such as the behavior of the others, the nature of the relationship, the setting, and past history. The self-image of an individual reflects, of course, far more than the immediate social expectations with which he or she is confronted; in most cases it is probably primarily determined by one's societal roles and life history. It is from the full range of experience that an individual develops a set of expectations regarding himself or herself. At any particular time, a person's self-image may be either in agreement or in conflict with the expectations of other persons with whom the individual is involved.

There are certain circumstances, however, in which it is very hard for a person to avoid acting to the expectations of others and incorporating their expectations into his or her self-image. One such circumstance occurs when the person is involved in close and continuing primary interaction with other persons. This primary interaction is what one's self-concept is typically based on. Another such circumstance is the situation in which the others have almost total control over all aspects of the person's life. Generalizing from experimental findings about the processes of conformity, resistance to influence, and conversion, Blake and Mouton (1961) state:

> An individual requires a stable framework, including salient and firm reference points, in order to orient himself and to regulate his interactions with others.... In the absence of a stable framework he actively seeks to establish one through his own strivings by making use of significant and relevant information provided within the context of interaction. By controlling the amount and kind of information available for orientation, he can be led to embrace conforming attitudes which are entirely foreign to his earlier ways of thinking. (pp. 1–2)

Situations where others are close to having total control over a person's life exists for inmates of what Goffman (1961) has called total institutions; a mental hospital is such an institution. In his book *Persuasion and Healing*, Jerome Frank (1961) not only delineates the similarity between psychiatric treatment and thought reform (brainwashing) but also cites considerable evidence that the very ambiguity of the patient's situation encourages the patient to pick up cues from the environment and from the therapist about how to behave and to act upon them. Patients, particularly if they have been hospitalized, are apt to accept the role of someone who is mentally ill, due to (1) the unsettling nature of their psychiatric symptoms; (2) the critical state of their societal position; (3) the actions of persons close to them; and (4) the characteristics of the patient role. Whether accepting this role has a positive or negative effect depends largely on the nature of the setting and the treatment provided. As the labeling theorists forcefully and correctly assert, becoming a mental patient redefines who one is, and this definition may lead to substantial isolation and discrimination (Scheff 1984). At the same time, such a redefinition may result in others viewing one as ill instead of as one who is purposely disruptive and troublesome (Gove 1968).

In this section, we have indicated that the expectations of others play the primary role in determining the actions of an individual and in the development of a person's self-image. It is this phenomenon that theorists such as Scheff have been discussing when talking about the problems of labeling and the role of the mentally ill. Henceforth, when we refer to social expectations as a factor in mental illness, it is this concept, with all its elaborations, to which we will be referring. It is important to remember, however, that social expectations typically presume normality and not abnormality.

Personal Attributes

Personality attributes of the individual comprise one of our basic variables of the proposed theory. *Personality attributes*, as the term is used here, refers to individuals' social and instrumental skills, their aspirations and expectations, and their general orientation to the social system. Included would be such things as the individuals' ability to act in an appropriate fashion, their willingness to accept responsibility for their actions, their ability to organize their activities in a coherent fashion, and their desire and ability to operate in accord with the norms of the social system. We assume that one's personal attributes are a reflection of inherited capabilities, the location of one's parents in society, one's childhood experiences, and experiences as adults.

People who occupy normal societal roles will, on the average, be more skilled in the performance of these roles than those who do not occupy such roles and who are only tenuously tied to society. As the previous discussion of social expectations suggests, the personal attributes reflect an entire life history. It would follow from this that persons who become acutely disturbed after having had a long history of effective participation in normal societal roles would, although perhaps shaken by their present emotional state, desire to return to normal societal roles, believe that they could do so, and retain the necessary skills. For most, the emotional state would be transitory. If, however, they continued to experience pervasive and incapacitating difficulties, they would eventually settle into roles where they were expected to behave in a symptomatic and ineffectual fashion. If this happens, their personality attributes would change. Their self-images would gradually become that of someone who is incompetent (or mentally ill), and there will be a loss of both aspirations for normal roles and the ability to perform effectively in such roles.

A Problem of Definitions

The concept of mental illness, as it is being used here, refers to a more precise and limited process than the traditional definition, and clearly does not encompass all the states and behaviors covered by DSM-III. For example, we would exclude from the category of 'mentally ill' those who have been disruptive but who are not disorganized; such persons we have labeled the *Disruptives*.

Some characteristics of the Disruptives can be inferred from the fact that they create serious problems for others, and that although they are not disorganized, their behavior is seen as either incomprehensible or 'sick.' We suggest that the Disruptives generally tend to be asocial and that they will readily ignore the norms of society. It is likely that Disruptives characteristically have limited social skills, being largely unaware of how others perceive them and unable to take the role of the others. We would also suggest that the Disruptives tend to be concerned with immediate gratification and that their actions are almost entirely controlled by their immediate environments. Thus, they probably typically act in an aggressive, nonreflective manner and do not take into account the long-term consequences of their actions. Further, many of the Disruptives are apt to use drugs or to have serious drinking problems. In terms of traditional psychiatric categories, many of these persons would be seen as having character or personality disorders.

A Sketch of a Theory

One way of conceptualizing mental illness is to think of it as a career, composed of a number of important contingency points at which different paths may be taken, some of which lead the person out of the condition of mental illness while others maintain or even aggravate the condition. It has been suggested that three basic parameters are involved in mental illness—symptoms, social expectations, and personal attributes. Each of these parameters may be placed on a continuum depicting the severity of mental illness, as has been done in Figure 4.1. These parameters, however, should not be viewed as acting in isolation, for they are in constant interaction. In a sense, the parameters can be simultaneously viewed as both independent and dependent variables. For example, the social expectations persons encounter to a large degree determine how they think of themselves, and in the long run determine their capabilities, skills and aspirations—that is, their personal attributes. At the same time, the personal attributes of an individual to a large degree determine the social expectations others have for that person.

The process by which mental illness develops may be conceived of as a continuum that can be divided into three stages, as outlined in Figure 4.1. The first stage involves the development of acute distress in persons who otherwise have fairly average personal attributes and whom others expect to act in a normal and reasonably competent fashion. The second stage involves the development of mental disorganization or psychosis in persons who occupy normal societal roles but who have limited skills and aspirations and whom others expect to perform in a marginal fashion. The third stage involves persons who have accepted, at least to some extent, their psychotic experiences as real and who have incorporated those experiences into their comprehension of the world and into their behavior. Persons in this stage will have very limited skills, and will tend to lead fairly isolated existences. Although they may be viewed as 'peculiar' or 'ill,' they will generally be left alone unless they start acting in a manner that is overtly disruptive to others.

In terms of our theory, the causes of distress, which may vary widely, are not as important as the intensity and persistence of distress. Of particular importance is the degree to which the distress interferes with the person's ability to function effectively and whether or not distress promotes a thought disorder. The likelihood that things will eventually improve will depend, in part, on whether the person takes direct action to change the situation. The reaction to distress thus is a very critical issue. The more competent and knowledgeable a person is, the more likely he or she is to take positive and realistic action. Another important factor is how others respond to the distress—do they aggravate it, do they ignore it, or do they encourage the person to take some positive action? The way others react depends on (1) how aware they are of the distress, (2) the types of problems the distress creates for them,

	LOW			MODERATE, SEVERITY OF DISORDER		HIGH
(1) Symptoms	Acute distress, anxiety, and heightened concern	Development of lack of sleep and tendency to misperceive	Thought disorder	Persistence of thought disorder and other problems over time		Incorporation of psychotic experiences into life organization
(2) Social expectations (community)	Perceived as capable of occupying normal societal roles and acting in an appropriate fashion	Development of a history of poor performance	Expected to perform poorly	Continued poor performance combined with bizarre behavior		Perceived as incompetent and peculiar (or mentally ill)
(3) Personal attributes	Capable of performing normal societal roles and both wants and expects to do so	Development of a history of poor performance	Limited skills; becomes concerned with acting appropriately and maintaining societal roles	Loss of roles and development of bizarre life organization		Little skill for or interest in normal societal roles; wants a secure existence where he is left alone to live in his own "peculiar world"

Figure 4.1. Progressive development of mental illness.

and (3) whether they are involved in some sort of "pathological game" with the person. The reaction of others is thus largely determined by the type of interpersonal relationships the individual has, which is, in turn, related to the individual's personal attributes.

Persons who are distressed arrive at another critical juncture if the distress continues to the point of evolving into a thought disorder. In addition to being severely distressed, they may now also feel that they are 'losing their minds.' By this time, not only is their judgment impaired but they may be experiencing hallucinations and delusions and having difficulty distinguishing between fantasy and reality. Their condition thus causes ineffectual behavior, which in turn may substantially increase the difficulties they experience. In this condition, although they may recognize that they need help, their ineffectiveness and confusion will make them increasingly dependent upon the actions of others, and they are unlikely to seek help on their own initiative.

If disorganization is allowed to persist for a prolonged period, there will be two important additional developments. First, the disorganization, by causing ineffective behavior, will force others to adapt to the incapacity of the mentally ill, who then will gradually lose their societal roles. Once the roles are lost and expectations of incompetency are developed, it will be hard to reverse the process. Second, if people continue to have psychotic experiences, they must in some manner come to terms with those experiences. They may do this either by interpreting the experiences as real, in which case they will develop a very peculiar conception of themselves and the world, or they may come to think of themselves as mentally ill. Most likely the solution will involve some combination of these two explanations.

The persistence of the mental disorganization is closely tied to whether others will intervene in an effort to see that the disorganization is controlled. The likelihood that others will intervene depends upon the attributes of persons, their social roles, and the expectations others have. If persons have little interest and little skill in normal societal activities, they are likely to be fairly isolated when they become disorganized. This is also true of persons who play roles in which they have transitory or rigidly structured relations with others that insulate their individualized behavior from view. In such cases; the disorganization will probably be allowed to unfold and develop. As the disorganized experiences become more acute and elaborate, the individuals will start to incorporate the experiences into their perception of themselves and the world. Eventually, the actions of these persons will come to reflect their hallucinations and their delusional system. If this occurs, they will become disruptive to others with whom they are relatively uninvolved. At this point, treatment may be initiated against their will. If, on the other hand, persons developing thought disorders are closely involved with others, the others are likely to intervene before the disorganization becomes very elaborate, and they may help obtain professional treatment. It is our position that to prevent chronic mental illness, it is very important that disorganization be brought under control rapidly. In most instances, drug therapy is the most effective and efficient method of controlling such disorganization.

The relationship between social expectations and the development and maintenance of mental illness has already been discussed, but two points warrant emphasis. First, by entering treatment, especially if one is hospitalized, one is identified as mentally ill and confronts the processes pointed to by labeling theorists. At the same time, when someone becomes a mental patient, behaviors that previously alienated others and caused serious trouble may be recast as the acts of someone who is ill and who needs understanding and help. Second, once a person has developed a well-established role in a group, it is very difficult to change that role, especially if the role is that of an ineffectual, incompetent person.

With regard to personal attributes, we would emphasize that persons who are competent in their social and instrumental roles are less likely to develop symptoms of severe distress and mental disorganization. Among persons who do develop such symptoms, an effective response to both the symptoms and their cause is more likely to occur with those who have a high level of competence.

Patient Types and Some Predictions

It is possible to classify mental patients according to their stage of mental illness at the time they enter treatment by using the three types of symptoms that have been discussed, namely acute distress, disorganized thought, and overt disruptive behavior.

Patients who are acutely distressed at the time they enter treatment but who are not disorganized and who have not acted in an overtly disruptive manner should have the other characteristics (personal attributes, social expectations) of persons in the first stage of mental illness. Patients identified by these symptoms may be referred to as the *Distressed*. The Distressed patients would generally occupy normal societal roles. They would be fairly competent, and they would typically be very focused on their personal problems.

Patients who are disorganized at the time of admission but who have not been disruptive should fit into the second stage of mental illness—the *Disorganized*. These patients presumably occupy normal societal roles but are not as competent as the Distressed. Although these patients would characteristically have realized that something was the matter with them, they would, due to their limited capabilities and their disorganization, act typically in an ineffectual fashion.

Patients who are disorganized at the time of admission and who have acted in a manner that has been overtly disruptive to others should have the characteristics of persons in the third stage of mental illness. Persons identified by these symptoms may be referred to as the *Disorganized-Disruptives*. Unlike acute distress and disorganization, which are apparent at the time a person is admitted to the hospital, disruptive behavior refers to actions that occurred just prior to hospitalization and concrete overt acts that interfere with the activities and concerns of others. It is presumed, in the case of the Disorganized-Disruptives, that their disruptive behavior would be a consequence of their actions reflecting their psychotic experiences, and that their disorganization would be fairly developed. The Disorganized-Disruptives would have generally occupied marginal positions in the community.

In discussing these three patient types, it should be emphasized that although they are being treated as distinct stages or types, they are being created by establishing arbitrary, although highly pragmatic, cutting points along a developmental continuum. Thus, in terms of their characteristics, we would actually expect some patients to be on the borderline between two stages.

In discussing the dynamics of mental illness, we have suggested that it is possible for a person to shift progressively along the continuum we have outlined. Although some persons may eventually shift across the full range of the continuum, this is not the experience of most who become mentally ill. Most persons who have normal personal attributes who experience an emotional crisis will return to their previous lifestyles after the crisis is over. Most persons at the other end of the continuum probably never possessed normal levels of personal attributes. It is also probable that the progressive development (or improvement) of a person's mental disorder does not usually occur in a single unilateral shift but is a cyclical process involving a number of ups and downs, and that it takes time before movement in a particular direction is clearly manifest.

The major theoretical contribution of the present theory are propositions regarding the developmental process of mental illness. Of special importance are the propositions about how acute distress may lead to mental disorganization and how the person's symptoms and experiences interact with his or her attributes and with the social expectations of others. The three patient types, although labeled in terms of the symptoms that brought the patients to treatment, reflect a wide range of characteristics, including social and instrumental skills, aspirations, and societal roles. Just because a person in the community has a particular symptom, one cannot simply transfer the patient category reflecting that symptom to that person. Thus, an individual who is distressed will not necessarily enter the hospital as a Distressed patient. The person may, for example, have very limited personal attributes, and might not enter treatment unless he or she became disorganized and acted in a disruptive manner. We can say that a person has the characteristics that we would generally associate with a particular patient type and that thus we could predict the type of patient the person would be if he or she did enter the hospital, but we should not say that a person is a Distressed or a Disorganized-Disruptive if the person is maintaining himself or herself in the community.

The importance of treating biology as a critical component of mental illness is, we hope, obvious. To a substantial degree, who we are is genetically determined. More important, it appears that we have genetic predispositions with regard to psychotic disorganization. Even more fundamental is the fact that distress and disorganization have a clear physiological base, a fact which is clearly demonstrated by their reactivity to medication. This means that the affective and cognitive symptoms of the mentally ill have a clear biological reality, and are not something that is simply in "their heads."

It is possible to test the theory of mental illness that has been proposed by investigating these patient types to see if the total configuration of symptoms, skills, aspirations, and roles conforms to what the theory would predict. Because of the simplicity of the proposed classification scheme, which involves only three elementary and apparently comprehensive variables—the two psychiatric variables of acute distress and disorganized thought, and the largely sociological variable of disruptive behavior—it should be possible to identify the patient types quickly and reliably at the time they enter treatment. We would end by noting that the theory we have outlined depends on our society's ability to view mental illness as a biological, psychological, and social phenomenon.

5

Cognitive Consistency in Deviance Causation: A Psychological Elaboration of an Integrated Systems Model[1]

Ronald A. Farrell

Abstract

Efforts to address the complementarity of sociological perspectives on deviance have given rise to several integrated theories. Although these theories have contributed to an appreciation of the complex nature of deviance causation, they have provided little understanding of individual differences in response to the social forces that are said to shape the behavior. The purpose of this paper is to develop a psychological elaboration of one such integrated model that draws on interactionist, strain, and social and cultural support theories. The model is elaborated by incorporating the personality attribute of *ambiguity tolerance* into its major assumptions. A central supposition of the model is that conflicting cognitive elements regarding deviation produce stress and the need for its reduction. The mechanisms for such tension reduction are often the redefinition and eventual reorganization of one's overall situation in terms of the more salient attribute of the deviation. That is, the deviation becomes the overriding basis of social perceptions, role identity, associations, and behavior. Because those unable to tolerate ambiguity are more sensitive to the stresses of incongruent situations, it is argued that they are more likely to perceive stereotypical imputations of deviance, to incorporate those imputations into their identity, to feel the need to validate their identity through association with others similarly labeled, and to respond intensely to definitions that emanate from such associations.

Introduction

Few areas of social scientific inquiry have displayed as much diversity of explanation as that of the study of deviant behavior. Accompanying this situation has been the adherence of scholars to singular theories and the treatment of alternative ones as contradictory and conflicting. While these commitments to independent theories have contributed substantially to an understanding of deviance, they have also diverted attention from consideration of the multidimensional nature of the phenomenon. At the same time, because the various theories often address different aspects of deviance, they lend themselves to an integration of their assumptions. In this manner a more holistic understanding may be achieved, one that reflects the different dimensions of deviance and the causal influences operative at different levels of analysis.

Previous efforts toward theoretical integration have dealt almost exclusively with sociological explanations of deviance. Few have attempted to include the concepts of the more person-oriented theories of psychology. As a result, these sociological efforts provide little understanding of individual differences in response to the various social forces that are said to shape behavior. The question of the part that basic personality attributes, for example, play in mediating the social causes of deviance thus go unanswered. Yet consideration of these attributes is essential to a comprehensive theory of deviance, and to an understanding of causal influences at both individual and group levels of analysis. The purpose of this paper is to explore such an elaboration of an integrated systems model of deviance and, by implication, to expand upon the theories from which it has drawn.[2]

Toward An Integrated Theory

The search for explanations of deviance has given rise to several sociological theories. The more social-psychological explanations among these are: the interactionist perspective, with its emphasis on the effects of stigmatization and social isolation in nonconformity (Cooley 1902; Tannenbaum 1938; Lemert 1951, 1962, 1967; Garfinkel 1956; Becker 1963; Goffman 1963; Scott and Lyman 1968; Schur 1971; Scheff 1984); strain theory, with its focus on deviance as an adaptation to the status frustration that results from an inability to comply with conventional group norms (Merton 1938; Parsons 1951; Cohen 1959); and social and cultural support theory, with its emphasis on differential exposure to deviant versus conventional behavioral definitions as they give rise to nonconformity (Sutherland 1947; Glaser 1956; Sykes and Matza 1957; Cloward and Ohlin 1960; Jeffrey 1965; Burgess and Akers 1968; Hirschi 1969; Linden and Hackler 1973; Akers, Krohn, Lanza-Kaduce, and Radosevich 1979; Scully and Morolla 1984).

Several integrated theories have been constructed from assumptions contained in these three general approaches to deviance (Wilkins 1965; Quinney 1970; Hackler 1971; Elliott, Ageton, and Canter 1979). Because these integrated theories are derived from the same general approaches, they share common themes. They emphasize the combined forces of the social response, adaptation to stressful relationships, and socialization to deviant subcultures as explanations for deviant behavior. Efforts to link the major assumptions of the different approaches have also resulted in a processual orientation to the theories, one that emphasizes that deviant behavior develops in a sequential manner.

The following model is an elaboration of one such effort toward theoretical integration. The model assumes that any particular case of deviance is the outcome of an interrelated system of social forces. An individual's progression through each stage of the system depends on the outcomes of the previous stages (Farrell and Swigert 1982, 1988). With its emphasis on previous outcomes as determinants of subsequent events, the approach lends itself to consideration of the predisposing influences of personality on the social causes of deviance.

According to the general argument of the model, society defines deviance as a salient and discrediting position prescribed in terms of a stereotype. Such a definition and the social responses that ensue restrict alternative roles that the individual may assume, thereby limiting the nature and boundaries of his subsequent interaction. As a result, the individual becomes engulfed in the deviant role and defines himself in terms of its expectations.

An important mediating influence in this labeling process is how the individual's initial reference groups define and respond to the deviation. Association with those from whom he perceives acceptance in terms of his legitimate attributes and behavior will provide insulation from the larger society's definition and response and ultimately from secondary involvement with the deviation; association with those from whom he perceives either acceptance or rejection in terms of his deviant attributes or behavior will reinforce the societal definition and response and move him toward secondary deviation. Because the acceptance and support found within the latter context tends to be guided by the popular stereotype of the deviation (although often reinterpreted in more positive terms), the individual will incorporate the stereotype into his role identity and behavior.

The model further suggests that when support is withheld by initial reference groups, individuals often shift reference association to groups from whom they can obtain acceptance and reward. This adaptive mechanism is an attempt to ease the stress caused by the labeling process; it represents an effort to achieve status and to maintain a positive identity in light of rejection and stigmatization. Also critical at this stage of the process is the basis on which the individual is accepted into the new group. A shift of association to groups from whom he perceives acceptance in terms of legitimate attributes and behavior will minimize the effects of the labeling process, while a shift of association to groups from whom he perceives acceptance in terms of the deviation will produce further movement toward secondary deviance.

Individuals often adapt by shifting their reference associations to a group whose members have experienced similar difficulties. As the individual receives input from the new associates and attaches meaning to it, he redefines his situation. The result is a form of behavior that depends on his and other group members' conceptions of the deviant role. Because those who form these groups are likely to have come to view themselves in terms of the stereotype, it is these stereotypical role conceptions that serve as the basis for secondary deviance. However, given that the group norms validate the role, a more positive identity is likely to evolve from the interaction.

The following propositions are derived from these assumptions. These interrelated statements are diagrammed in Figure 5.1.

PROPOSITION 1: If the individual perceives a stereotypical social response to his primary deviation, he will incorporate a stereotypical role identity.

A. Perceived reference group acceptance on the basis of his nondeviant attributes and behavior will insulate the individual from a stereotypical role identity.

PROPOSITION 2: If the individual perceives rejection and incorporates the stereotype into his identity, he will adapt to the attendant stigma by shifting reference association to groups from which he may obtain acceptance and a more positive identity.

PROPOSITION 3: If the individual perceives that the new reference group accepts him in terms of his deviation, he will come to define both himself and the deviation in more positive terms and enculturate to secondary deviance.

A. If the individual perceives that the new reference group accepts him in terms of his nondeviant attributes and behavior, he will come to define himself in more positive terms and his primary deviation will stabilize or subside.

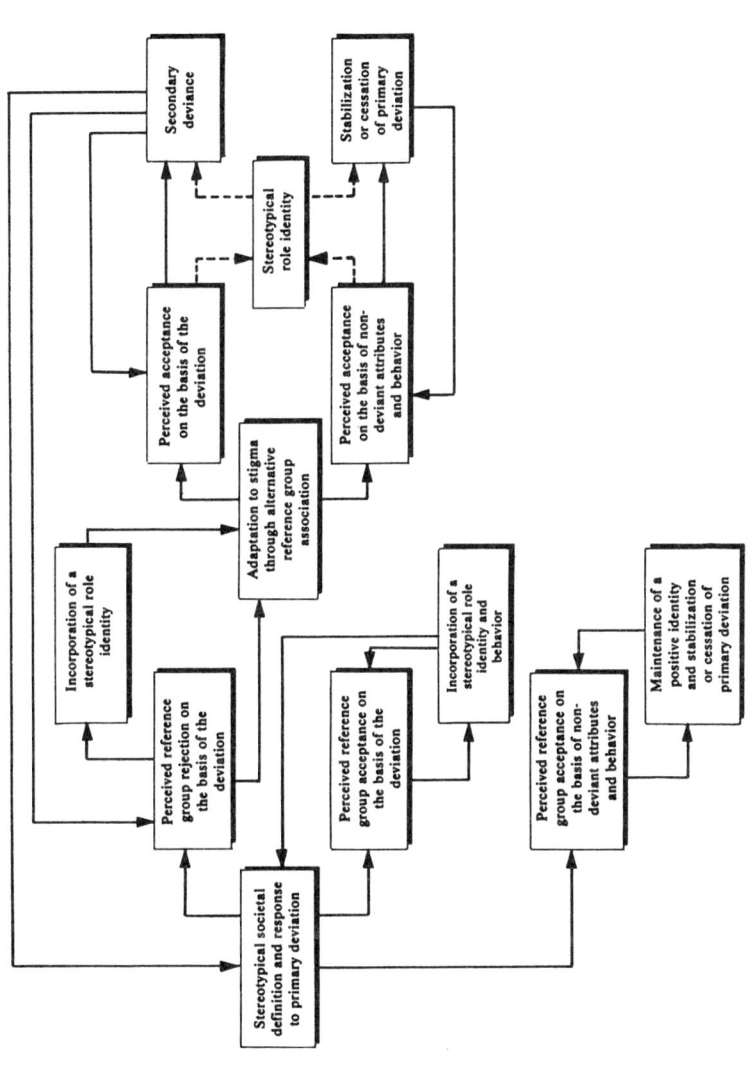

Figure 5.1. An integrated systems model of deviance.

PROPOSITION 4: As the individual enacts either deviant or nondeviant roles, he reaffirms societal and reference group definitions and responses.[3]

The Psychological Dimension

The remainder of this work elaborates the preceding model by incorporating into its major assumptions the personality attribute of ambiguity tolerance. The concept of ambiguity tolerance has been developed within personality theory (Frenkel-Brunswick 1949; Adorno, Frenkel-Brunswick, Levinson, and Sandford 1950). It refers to the degree to which persons accept uncertainty and the subjectivity of meaning (Frenkel-Brunswick 1949). Persons intolerant of ambiguity need structure and are absolute in their interpretation of social experience. They have fixed cognitive categories and tend to avoid situations that contradict their beliefs. These latter tendencies are said to be based on interpretations of unfamiliar and complex situations as threatening, while those tolerant of ambiguity find comfort in such situations and may even come to see them as desirable (Budner 1962).

Numerous studies have explored the relationship of ambiguity tolerance to social and psychological differences in individuals. The results of these efforts have shown the attribute to be associated with various factors related to the underlying conceptual structure of the model. The inability to tolerate ambiguity is positively related to cognitive rigidity (MacDonald and Games 1974; Tatzel 1980), role inflexibility (MacDonald and Games 1974), conventionality (Budner 1962), stereotyping (Ilardo 1973), and more negative attitudes toward deviance (English 1971; Galbreath and Feinberg 1973; MacDonald and Games 1974). It is also positively related to status frustration (Trow 1977), anxiety (Hassan and Khalique 1981), psychological strain (Keenan and McBain 1979), the need for structure (Budner 1962; Chabassol and Thomas 1975), role conflict (Posner and Randolph 1980), and role ambiguity (Posner and Randolph 1980). Those who cannot tolerate ambiguity, furthermore, tend to shield themselves from information through withdrawal (Ilardo 1973), to make strong commitments to groups and to group ideologies (Ilardo 1973), to have low critical ability (Feather 1967), and to select interaction partners on the basis of perceived similarity (Ball-Rokeach 1973). Conversely, the attribute is negatively related to fewer needs for social approval (English 1971), a more positive self (English 1971; Goldsmith 1984), mental flexibility (Tatzel 1980), role flexibility (Matthijssen 1973), and psychological androgyny (Rotter and O'Connell 1982). Because these factors are related to the underlying structure of the model and because individuals differ significantly in terms of ambiguity tolerance, consideration of the attribute may further our understanding of the individual's response to the proposed causes of secondary deviance.

Incorporation of Ambiguity Tolerance into the Model

A major determinant of responses to deviance is the inability of individuals to tolerate information that is incongruent with the deviation (Tannenbaum 1938; Garfinkel 1956; Kitsuse 1962; Matza 1969; Schur 1971; Farrell 1984). Conflicting cognitive elements produce stress and a need for its reduction (Festinger 1957, 1964). In an effort to reduce the stress, individuals may redefine and eventually reorganize their overall situation to correspond with the more salient aspects of their life. Since the deviation is usually the most salient aspect of one's life, the tendency is for individuals to define and reorganize the other aspects in its terms (Farrell 1984). The result is to diminish the significance of other bases of identification and to give increased meaning to the deviation. The deviation becomes the overriding basis of social perceptions, role identity, associations, and behavior.

At the same time, we have seen that individuals do not react uniformly to incongruent situations; they vary in their tolerance of such ambiguity. It might thus be inferred that those who are high in ambiguity tolerance would not be as likely to perceive stereotypical imputations of deviance, to incorporate these imputations into their identity, to feel the need to validate their identity through association with others similarly labeled, or to respond as intensely to definitions that emanate from such associations. The influence of the attribute as it mediates the effects of these social causes of deviance deserves explication.

The Labeling Process. The model argues that movement from primary to secondary deviance involves a number of factors central to the labeling process: the relative saliency of the deviant status (Lemert 1962; Becker 1963; Scott and Lyman 1968), attribution of a stereotypically defined role to that status (Goffman 1963; Simmons 1965; Scott 1969; Scheff 1984), and the redefinition of other statuses and identifications of the individual in terms of the deviance (Garfinkel 1956; Kitsuse 1962; Schur 1971). These factors allow both the individual and reacting others to deal with the ambiguous and dissonance-producing reality of deviance by introducing continuity into the situation. By attributing overriding significance to the attribute or behavior, assigning auxiliary role expectations to it, and reinterpreting other aspects of identity in terms of the deviation, homogeneity is introduced into the otherwise heterogenous configuration of elements that comprise the lives of most deviants, and ultimately into the interaction that occurs between them and nondeviants.

The cognitive needs upon which the labeling process is based vary, however, in terms of the personality differences of those labeled as deviant.[4] Recalling that intolerance of ambiguity is positively related to such cognitive attributes as mental rigidity (MacDonald and Games 1974; Tatzel 1980), role inflexibility (MacDonald and Games 1974), conventionality (Budner 1962), and stereotyping (Ilardo 1973), and further that it is negatively related to role flexibility (Matthijssen 1973) and psychological androgyny (Rotter and O'Connell 1982), we would expect intolerant individuals to rely more heavily on the dissonance-reduction mechanisms of the labeling process. The result would be for such individuals to experience a greater effect of the process on their role identity. For those capable of tolerating ambiguity, on the other hand, the need for such dissonance reduction, and consequently its social-psychological effect, would be low. The result would be for them to maintain a more positive identity and for their primary deviation to stabilize or subside.[5]

More specifically, we would expect ambiguity tolerance to mediate the saliency of the deviant position and the subsequent sensitivity of the individual to the cultural definitions and responses of others. In this regard, it may be inferred from research in the area that the inability to tolerate ambiguity may lead to anxiety in social relationships (Hassan and Kahlique 1981). This would seem to be especially so in new and more complex relationships, and particularly in secondary encounters in which the individual has limited familiarity with relevant actors. Given the ambiguity of these encounters, the intolerant individual might tend toward a heightened sensitivity to and need to make sense of the cues and gestures that ensue. As a result, he may more readily accept the stereotypical definitions and responses that ordinarily characterize such encounters (Farrell and Morrione 1974).

The effects of ambiguity tolerance are even more apparent with regard to the processes of retrospective and concurrent interpretation. Labeling theorists (Tannenbaum 1938; Garfinkel 1956; Kitsuse 1962; Schur 1971) argue that the individual's more general social identity may lose validity when others attempt to neutralize their conflicting information about the deviant by reinterpreting other aspects of his situation to fit with the deviation. While such reinterpretation allows others to act toward the individual without ambivalence, a result of this process is also to invalidate other bases of the individual's identity and to give increased meaning to the deviation.

The individual psychological processes that occur as one perceives this collective response to the deviation may be elaborated by drawing from the more psychologically oriented equilibrium models (see Festinger 1957, 1964). These theories provide explanations similar to those contained in labeling theory regarding the collective response. They suggest that individuals also tend to attribute continuity to their own situation in an attempt to avoid the stress associated with conflicting cognitive elements. In the case of the deviant, given that the deviation may be perceived by the individual to be his most salient attribute or behavior, the tendency would be for him to define other aspects of his identity in terms of the deviation. This would be true for elements over time (retrospective interpretation) as well as for the range of elements involved at particular points in time (concurrent interpretation). Proposing that there is a selective quality in personal recollections, Adlerians suggest that even the earliest memories of individuals reflect this effort toward equilibrium, one that involves in this instance the reconstruction of their past in light of their present situation (Adler 1937, 1956; Ansbacher 1973; Schrecker 1973). Although labeling theory does not address these individual interpretive processes, it may be inferred that they are shaped by those occurring in the collective response. Through a looking glass process (Cooley 1902), individuals may reconstruct their situation to fit with their interpretations of the meanings that others assign to it.[6] In this way, they affirm their identity and prepare themselves for action relative to the behavior or attributes in question.

Relating this aspect of the labeling process to basic personality structure, it may be argued that the relative need to reconstruct one's situation in accordance with the social response is determined by the individual's ability to tolerate ambiguity. Those unable to tolerate ambiguity are more likely to unequivocally define their behavior or attributes as stereotypically deviant, to interpret more literally the definitions and responses of others, and to experience the dissonance and need to resolve the conflicting cognitive elements surrounding the deviation. Through retrospective and concurrent interpretation, the intolerant individual is able to avoid or reduce conflicting elements and thereby maintain the consistency of identity so essential to his cognitive equilibrium.

Adaptation to Strain. The attribute of ambiguity tolerance may also aid in the explanation of the stress and subsequent adaptations that result from the labeling process. It has been argued that exclusion of individuals from legitimate statuses leads to frustration, ambivalence toward conformity, and the need to equilibrate. Especially relevant is the relationship of ambiguity tolerance to the problem of ambivalence—the uncertainty that arises from status frustration and prompts the individual to explore alternative reference associations. This exploration is an effort to reequilibrate, and often involves shifting one's reference associations away from legitimate society to others who are more accepting of the deviation, especially to individuals who have themselves experienced difficulties in relationships within the larger society.

The empirical literature has demonstrated that those unable to tolerate ambiguity are especially prone to status frustration (Trow 1977) and to the anxiety (Hassan and Khalique 1981) and psychological strain (Keenan and McBain 1979) that accompany this frustration. They are also more inclined to experience the personal conflict associated with ambivalence (Posner and Randolph 1980) and the need for its resolution (Budner 1962; Chabassol and Thomas 1975). It would follow, therefore, that intolerant individuals would experience greater necessity of adaptation and would more likely change their reference associations by withdrawing from conventional relations (Ilardo 1973) and establishing ties within deviant groups. Through the latter associations, such individuals would obtain not only the collective support required to reduce stress but would also be provided with the structure and consistency of role identification necessary to resolve ambivalence (Budner 1962; Chabassol and Thomas 1975).

In deviant groups, conventional criteria for social differentiation are deemphasized and more readily accessible criteria are established. This serves both to define the deviant position more positively for the individual and to clarify his role in the larger society. Association with others of similar background also affirms the individual's identity, thus further crystallizing his position relative to conventional others. Deviant groups thus ultimately provide for the human need for consistency, a need, however, which seems to vary in terms of the basic personality structure of individuals.

For some, the establishment of alternative reference associations will mean the assumption of legitimate statuses and roles within the newly adopted groups. Opportunities for legitimate positions would appear to be available through deviant as well as conventional group ties. The response to such opportunities, however, may vary according to the individual's ability to tolerate ambiguity. Acceptance as legitimate by the new group would be greatly at variance with the more salient societal views and reactions regarding the deviation. Receptivity to the acceptance as legitimate would, therefore, be facilitated by a personality that could tolerate the contradictions, one with a high tolerance for ambiguity.

Learning the Deviant Role

Ambiguity tolerance also appears to be related to the processes of enculturation to the deviant role. Research suggests that intolerant individuals are more likely to seek relationships with persons of perceived similarity (Ball-Rokeach 1973), to establish commitments to such relationships (Ilardo 1973), and to be subject to their control (Feather 1967). The social and cultural support of deviant groups would, therefore, have greater meaning for those who are less tolerant of ambiguity. The intolerant individual would more likely establish deviant group ties, embrace such relationships and their values, and succumb to their influence.

Because the inability to tolerate ambiguity is related to greater need for approval (English 1971), the intolerant individual would also be more subject to the deviance-reinforcing effects of the rewards that emanate from relationships within deviant groups. Additionally, the more simple and concrete orientation of the individual might predispose him to a more conditioned response to the reinforcements.

One would also expect intolerant individuals to strictly adhere to the deviant role because of their relative inflexibility (Matthijssen 1973; Tatzel 1980). They would tend to become engulfed in their role relationships and to excessively imitate group behavior (Ilardo 1973). Their stereotypical views of the deviation (Ilardo 1973; Tatzel 1980) would incline them to perceive the behavior of group members in stereotypical terms and to adopt a role based on the stereotype.

As the individual enacts the deviant role, it becomes increasingly necessary for him to legitimize his behavior. The deviant group provides the rationalizations required to satisfy this need. Such rationalizations are necessary to protect the self in light of the person's inability to fully escape societal condemnation and demands for conformity, no matter how encompassing his involvement in the deviant group (Sykes and Matza 1957). Only through rationalizations can one neutralize the societal definitions and responses encountered during efforts to satisfy needs that may be met only in the larger society (e.g., employment, education, goods and services). Thus, while the labeling process may result in the development of a stereotypical role identity, association within deviant groups provides the social and cultural support necessary for the individual to become committed to the deviant position and to redefine its role in more positive terms.

As in any other group, then, the belief system of the deviant group serves to legitimize the behavior of group members. We have seen from research, however, that the tendency toward acceptance of belief systems is related to intolerance of ambiguity (Ilardo 1973). Thus, the intolerant individual would be expected to subscribe more strongly to the new group's beliefs regarding the deviation. He would also feel a greater need to rationalize and would more likely accept such rationalizations. This conclusion is based on inferences from empirical observations that intolerant individuals are more likely to experience threat to the self as they enact the deviant role (English 1971) and are less capable of tolerating the opposing views toward the deviation (Matthijssen 1973; Rotter and O'Connell 1982) that they encounter as they necessarily move between the deviant group and legitimate society. Rationalizations allow one to resolve such conflicts and to establish a more positive identity. The result is to reduce the internal and external demands for conformity that might otherwise inhibit enactment of the deviant role.

Finally, among individuals who are able to establish alternative reference associations on the basis of their nondeviant attributes and behavior, those who are more capable of tolerating ambiguity would tend toward greater acceptance of the contradictory definitions of themselves that emanate from such associations. Their greater receptivity to these definitions would allow them to maintain access to legitimate statuses and roles as well as to obtain the group support necessary for the development of a more positive identity. These associations would thus provide tolerant individuals greater insulation from secondary involvement with the deviation; their primary deviation would stabilize if not subside.

The influence of the psychological dimension as it operates in the overall process of deviance causation is illustrated in Figure 5.2.

Toward a Synthesis and Further Elaboration of the Model

Intolerance of ambiguity would appear to be a psychological dimension that operates at each stage of the model. Because of the anxiety associated with the inability to tolerate ambiguity, the intolerant individual may respond more sensitively to the cultural definitions of the deviant position and to the social responses that the position elicits. This would be especially so in secondary encounters, where both ambiguity and stereotypical responses predominate. In an effort to resolve the dissonance of conflicting input from such encounters, the intolerant individual may tend to accept the cultural stereotype as the appropriate definition of his situation. In his further efforts to deal with the ambiguity of conflicting cognitions, the intolerant individual might also be more likely to reinterpret other aspects of his life in terms of the more salient aspect of the deviation. This is likely to involve a reflective process

Figure 5.2. Psychological elaborations of the model.

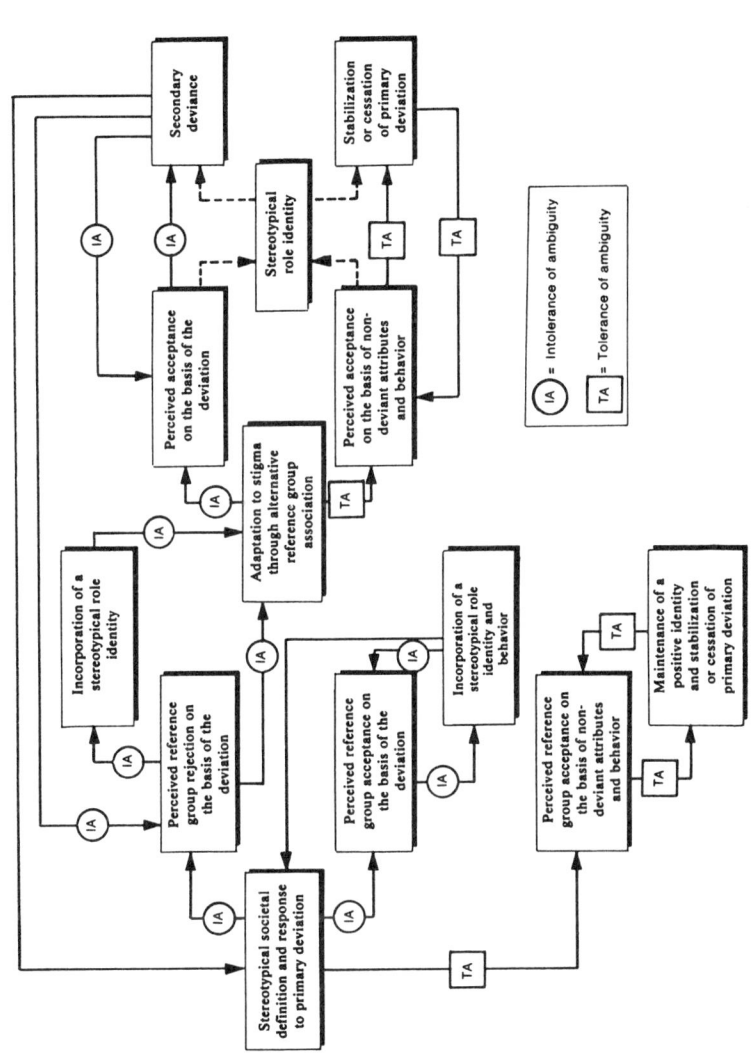

wherein he assigns overall meaning to his situation on the basis of his interpretations of the meanings that others assign to it.

We have also seen that the intolerant individual is more likely to experience the strain of disequilibriated relationships and to feel the need to adapt to them by developing alternative social ties. The problem is one of his greater difficulty in coping with the ambivalence and frustration that arise from his inability to conform to the expectations of conventional society. The tendency under these circumstances is for him to shift his reference associations to others of perceived similarity, to a group that is supportive of the deviation. Such groups provide the consistent definition of the situation so essential to the individual, and have role expectations to which he can conform.

Tolerance of ambiguity may also mediate the influences of deviant associations. Intolerant individuals are more likely to establish ties to deviant groups and would more readily subscribe to the group norms and behavior. This is likely a function of their greater need for cognitive equilibrium and their more literal interpretations of social life. Adoption of the group norms and behavior may also be attributed to their greater receptivity to group sanctions, as ambiguity intolerant individuals have a greater need for approval and may tend toward more conditioned responses. Finally, the deviant role of intolerant individuals may be reinforced by their tendency to accept group rationalizations. This seems to be a result of their lower self-esteem and their inability to deal with the conflicting views toward the deviation that they encounter as they of necessity move between relationships in the deviant group and larger society.

Locus of Control and Self-Monitoring

This effort toward theoretical integration points to the value of considering personality attributes in sociological explanations of deviance and, by implication, to the importance of including such variables in empirical explorations in the area.[7] The work also suggests the importance of identifying other dimensions of personality that might interact with the social forces that shape deviance. Future theory development and research might address, for example, the effects of *locus of control* (Rotter 1966) and *self-monitoring* (Snyder 1974, 1979a, 1979b), as these personality attributes interact in the overall process of deviance causation.

Developing out of social learning theory, locus of control refers to the relative extent to which individuals see themselves as internally or externally influenced. The attribute has particular significance for individual receptivity to social reinforcements for behavior. The behavioral effects of rewards and punishments are viewed as dependent on the individual's perception of such reinforcement, as influenced by his own actions. Reinforcements are thus said to have greater effect on behavior when they are viewed as having been elicited by some prior conduct.

Conceptually grounded in the interactionist tradition, self-monitoring involves a similar, if not overlapping, attribute. It refers to the extent to which individuals are attuned to their public presentation of self. High self-monitors are more sensitive to the cues and gestures of social situations and pragmatically adjust their behavior accordingly. Those low in self-monitoring are, as a matter of principle, more inner-directed and concerned primarily with maintaining congruence between their personal identity and social behavior.

Locus of control and self-monitoring have been shown to be related to social perception (Jellison and Green 1981^{lc}; Snyder and Monson 1975^{sm}), to various aspects of personal identity (Clayson and Frost 1984^{lc}; Sampson 1978^{sm}), to susceptibility to stress and anxiety (Clayson and Frost 1984^{lc}; Schmitt and Kurdeck 1984^{lc}; Lippa 1978^{sm}), and to peer orientation and receptivity to social support (di Cindio, Floyd, Wilcox, and McSeveney 1983^{lc}; Sandler and Lakey 1982^{lc}; Berscheid, Graziano, Monson and Dermer 1976^{sm}; Ickes and Barnes 1977^{sm}).* The relevance of these attributes at the several stages of the model is therefore readily apparent. Explanations of individual differences in receptivity to the labeling process, to problems of strain associated with disequilibrated relationships, and to influences that emanate from alternative reference associations are likely to lie in these and related dimensions of personality.

Conclusion

The literature on the sociology of deviance has a long tradition of treating theories as competing and contradictory, and is replete with references to the preeminence of the sociological approach. While this tradition has broadened our perspective in sensitizing us to the various social causes of deviance, it has also led to the fragmentation of the field and to the overriding tendency to regard alternative explanations as ill-founded in their emphasis on individual differences. The result has been

---

*sm refers to research on the relationship of self-monitoring to the variable, and lc refers to the relationship of locus of control to the variable.

for sociologists to minimize the significance of psychological influences in deviance causation. Because the various theories often address different aspects of deviance, however, it is important that we consider the points at which they might be complementary. Based on this assumption, this paper has argued for the introduction of personality attributes in sociological analyses of deviance. Until the much-needed interdisciplinary science of deviance has developed, such efforts will have at least recognized the interaction of social and psychological causes of deviant behavior.

6

Theory Integration Versus Model Building

———Margaret Farnworth———

Introduction

Theory integration in criminology usually implies the combination of two or more pre-existing theories on the basis of their perceived commonalities. The overarching purpose of the integration exercise is the development of new theory that improves upon any one of the single constituent theories from which the reformulated theory derives. In other words, the goal of theory integration, as in traditional theory development, is the advancement of our understanding and explanation of crime and deviance (Elliott et al. 1979; 1985).

The purpose of this paper is to assess the contributions to theory integration in the preceding papers by Walter R. Gove and Michael Hughes, and by Ronald A. Farrell. Since integration may be viewed as one approach to theory development, the comments that follow address a two-tiered question: first, what are the contributions of each of the reviewed papers to theory integration; and second, how do they contribute to the development of better theory, the broader goal of theory integration?

Evaluative criteria for assessing the contributions of the papers to theory development are drawn from the traditional literature on the conduct of theoretically-guided research. The characteristics of good theory have been described in that literature as a high level of generality, internal integrity and logical consistency, testability, and grounding in empirical reality (Hanson 1958; Kaplan 1964; Kuhn 1970; Popper 1959). To the extent that the authors' new theories reflect these traits, their works represent significant contributions to theory development.

Integration is an approach to theory development still in its embryonic stages. As a result, theory integration lacks both a clear definition and formal criteria for its assessment. In the section that follows, I draw on recent comments and research in criminology as a basis for proposing a definition of theory integration and evaluative standards.

Defining Theory Integration

Despite the recent attention directed toward theory integration in criminology, the concept is not defined in a standard way. In practice, theory integration has been associated with a variety of exercises characterized by empirical tests of hybrid research models. Those models have sometimes included rather motley arrays of concepts or variables abstracted from different perspectives (e.g., Cernkovich 1978; Johnson 1979; Pearson and Weiner 1985; Simons et al. 1980).

In the strictest sense, those exercises fall short of *theory* integration, since they involved the disintegration of separate theories into their component parts (propositions, concepts, or variables), and their recombination in models for research. The research models that typically result consist of inventories of concepts or variables useful for predicting delinquency or crime. Since theory is essentially aimed toward explanation and understanding rather than prediction (Kaplan 1964), the relevance of such exercises for *theory* integration is questionable.[1]

Two noteworthy exceptions to the practice of integration on the concept or variable level are evident in the works of Elliott and his colleagues (1985) and Burgess and Akers (1966). As a basis for definition and evaluation, therefore, we turn to those works.[2]

Elliott and his colleagues (1985) began their integration attempt by selecting three existing sociological theories of crime (social strain, social control, and social learning) with apparent potential for synthesis. Burgess and Akers (1966), on the other hand, combined the sociological principles of social learning implicit in Sutherland's (1939) theory of differential association with behavioral learning theory described in the writings of Skinner and other psychologists (Akers 1973).

An operational definition of theory integration is implicit in these works, particularly in the step-by-step procedures followed by Elliott et al. (1985, p. 12). First, the authors selected three pre-existing theories and argued for their integration potential. Next, they attempted to reconcile the basic assumptions of the theories. Following a modification of the "pure" forms of the beginning theories for purposes of parsimony, Elliott et al. combined the truncated versions of each in a single theoretical model.

The cross-disciplinary integration in Burgess and Akers (1966) paralleled Elliott et al.'s effort in that it involved the combination of more than one previously-developed perspective on deviance. Unlike the integration attempted by Elliott et al., that accomplished by Burgess and Akers was enhanced in two ways. First, the beginning assumptions intrinsic to each of the combined perspectives were not contradictory.

Second, the two theories that were combined shared a common underlying concept (social learning) which provided logical consistency in the reformulated theory.

Despite these differences in the two integration efforts, both seem to fulfill the expectation of *theory* integration. The intended integrations were of complete theories rather than of concepts or variables devoid of theoretical context. Abstracting from these attempts, and with sensitivity for traditional definitions of theory itself, the following operational definition of theory integration is proposed. Theory integration is defined as the combination of two or more pre-existing theories, selected on the basis of their perceived commonalities, into a single reformulated theoretical model with greater comprehensiveness and explanatory value than any one of its component theories. What follows is an assessment of Farrell's and of Gove and Hughes' works in the context of this definition.

Comments on the Preceding Papers

Overview and Summary

Farrell's work began with a theoretical model developed in his earlier studies of homosexuality and delinquency (Farrell and Nelson 1976; 1978). On the basis of the empirical findings from those studies, Farrell concluded a need to develop that part of the theory concerning an individual's ability to resist a socially-applied label. The author presented a logical, empirically-supported argument for introducing the concept of *ambiguity tolerance* as an intervening factor that modifies the effect of self-concept on internalization of the deviant label. The addition of the new concept promises to advance our understanding of the interactive process leading to deviance, particularly as that process involves association with delinquent peers, commitment to delinquent values, and derogated self-concept.

Gove and Hughes focused on general causes and processes in the development of mental illness. The authors specified in their "sketch of a theory" that "three basic parameters are involved in mental illness—symptoms, social expectations, and personal attributes." Like Farrell, Gove and Hughes were more concerned with secondary then primary deviance. In their words, " . . . the causes of distress, which may vary widely, are not as important as the intensity and persistence of distress" (p. 14).

Theory integration was implied in both papers on the basis of the inclusion of concepts from more than one academic discipline. Farrell began with a theoretical model consistent with the social-psychological and social structural assumptions of the interactionist perspective. While citing past integration attempts in the literature, the only integration apparent in his own paper involved the addition to the model of a single concept drawn from the literature on personality theory. In a more ambitious manner, Gove and Hughes began by proposing the need for "a general theory of mental illness which combines biological, psychological, and social variables and which focuses on both etiology and process."

Integration in the Reviewed Papers

Both of the papers reviewed here reflect the spirit of Burgess and Akers' cross-disciplinary integration. The interactionist perspective that seems to underlie the integration attempts in both papers, however, is itself cross-disciplinary: it includes both psychological and sociological concepts. On this basis alone, then, the theoretical elaborations by these authors are not particularly innovative and hardly need justification as integration. Moreover, neither work attempted to merge two or more complete, pre-existing, independent theories or perspectives as in the integration attempted by Elliott et al. (1985) or Burgess and Akers (1966). What, then, was accomplished?

Rather than demonstrating theoretical integration, Farrell's addition of a single concept from the psychological literature to a pre-existing interactionist perspective illustrates the value of theory construction through "model building": (1) beginning with a simple model that is less than adequate to "mirror the real world" and (2) introducing complexity through the addition of a concept or concepts to elaborate the beginning model (Blalock 1969, pp. 3–4). In this instance, the beginning model seems to be based on a social interactionism perspective. Even proponents of that perspective have conceded its need for further theoretical development (e.g., Schur 1971). Farrell's introduction of a new concept addressed that need. Ambiguity tolerance specified an intervening path toward secondary deviance consistent with the beginning assumptions of the original theoretical model. In this way, the concept added complexity to an interactionist perspective on the development of a deviant identity.

An evaluation of the theoretical integration intended by Gove and Hughes is handicapped by the authors' neglect to identify the specific theories they propose to combine. Since the paper seems to emphasize the importance of secondary rather than primary deviance, their model too is consistent with an interactionist perspective on deviance.[3] If we accept this premise, and begin our review with the section entitled "A Sketch of a Theory", the authors present an interesting reciprocal model of secondary deviance processes. The theoretical model reflects such labeling concepts as social interaction, social reaction, and individual perceptions of self and reality.

The verbal description differs in some ways, however, from the diagram of Gove and Hughes' theory in Figure 4.1. The figure describes three side-by-side process models with three different dependent variables. But the text directs that "These parameters... should not be viewed as acting in isolation, for they are in constant interaction. In a sense, the parameters can be simultaneously viewed as both independent and dependent variables." This seems to imply two-way arrows across the three independent processes in the diagram, but the figure does not link the three seemingly-independent models. The "integration" of the three process models that are diagrammed remains unaddressed.

In short, neither of the works reviewed here represents theory integration within the operational definition I proposed.[4] On the other hand, the presumed underlying goal of theory integration is the development of better theory for the study of crime and deviance. The more important question, then, concerns the success of the authors in developing better theory quite aside from their success or failure as "integrationists."

Theory Development in the Reviewed Papers

As elaborations of the interactionist perspective, both reviewed works represent significant theoretical advances. Farrell's addition of a new variable promises to advance our understanding of the labeling process as it involves association with delinquent peers, commitment to delinquent values, and derogated self-concept. The theoretical model that results enjoys logical consistency. All of the concepts and propositions it combines are derived or derivable from the assumptions of traditional interactionist theory. Moreover, the new propositions follow logically within a labeling perspective. The final model lends itself to empirical analysis using standard analytical techniques. The final challenge lies in the author's acquisition of data adequate to operationalize his concepts and estimate the revised model.

In my view, Farrell's greatest contribution lies in the potential of his elaborated model to address an important question neglected in labeling theory: why do some individuals socially labeled as deviant resist internalization of the label, while others adjust their self-images and lifestyles to accord with society's expectations of continued deviance? The concept of *ambiguity tolerance* promises to fill this void.

In regard to Gove and Hughes' paper, my final critical comment concerns the place that biology plays in the theory that Gove and Hughes proposed. The first two sentences of their paper promise to outline a "general theory of mental illness which combines biological, psychological and social variables . . . " At the end of their paper, they once more emphasize the importance of biology as a component in mental illness. While in no way impugning either (1) the importance of biological theory in the study of mental illness; or (2) the insights in Goves and Hughes' sketch of a theory, I submit that biological theory has *not* been integrated into the model described in Figure 4.1.

But Gove and Hughes' failure to achieve the herculean task they describe—combining biological, psychological, and social variables in a single theory of mental health involving both etiology and process—should not detract from their accomplishments. Later sections in the text provided a logical, internally-integrated elaboration of an interactional process model of immersion in the mentally ill role. The centrality in the model of the concept "personal attributes" suggests its considerable potential for specifying the process of secondary deviance. The incorporation of this concept into a model of societal reaction introduces an element of individual determinism to social interactionism. This is not a trivial contribution since interactionism has been roundly criticized in the past for its apparent tendency toward *social* determinism.

Good theory is also testable, and provides a guide to research. The complexity of Gove and Hughes' implied model presents a challenge for analysis. The three parts of the theory outlined in Figure 4.1 are each amenable to research addressing the propositions of the verbal theory. The nonrecursive nature of the model linking the three separate propositions (its "snowballing" feature and two-way effects) suggests a need for longitudinal data, longterm followup study of individuals subject to severe stress, and rather sophisticated statistical procedures.

Thus the theory sketched by Gove and Hughes meets most standards for "good theory." Its distinctions among levels of mental illness are particularly insightful. The authors' hope to integrate biology into the theoretical model suggests an interesting direction for further development.

Implications

Within the stringent operational definition of theoretical integration I proposed, neither of the papers reviewed here confronted or resolved the central issues surrounding theory integration. In contrast, the theory *development* described in these papers represents in each case a contribution to the study of deviance and crime. Thus the procedures employed and the theories produced illustrated the usefulness of traditional approaches to the development of better theory. In effect, these approaches to theory development illustrated a salutary *alternative* to theory integration, and demonstrated how theory can be improved with traditional model-building principles. The prudence of this alternative is underscored when we consider the formidable obstacles to successful integration that were avoided in this way.

Concluding Comments On Theory Integration

In view of the emphasis placed on quantitative analysis and hypothesis-testing in current-day criminology, the appeal of theoretical integration is perhaps not surprising. In a discipline that emphasizes "variance explained" as a primary standard for good research, the most unsophisticated researcher can grasp the basic arithmetic principle that a large number of variables from different theories is more likely explain variance than is a smaller subset of variables from one theory. But the efficient prediction of outcomes (hefty R^2's) is not synonymous with understanding and explanation, the real goal of theory (Kaplan 1964).

This is not a denial that theory should be grounded in empirical reality. Reasonable predictive efficiency is therefore a necessary part of good theory. But prediction in itself is not a *sufficient* standard for good theory, or a convincing argument for theory integration. As Elliott et al. (1985) noted, successful theory integration should also produce a reformulated model that (1) can be justified on logical grounds, and (2) preserves the major causal arguments of the beginning theories. Clearly, the accomplishment of these goals is a more stringent criterion for successful integration than is predictive efficiency alone.

In addition, a major logical obstacle to integration involves the combination of propositions from different theories with beginning assumptions that are logically incompatible (Hirschi 1969). The irreconcilable nature of theories that flow from opposing *a priori* assumptions is particularly evident in a Kuhnian perspective, which holds that the theorist's world view permeates all that follows in the logical development of a theory and theory-driven research (Kuhn 1970).

A second problem in theory integration involves the disintegration of the beginning theories in the name of parsimonious model-building. When the proposed integration involves as many as four or even thirteen different theoretical perspectives (as in Simons et al. 1980; and Pearson and Weiner 1986), theory "modification" is often replaced by a selective sampling of theoretically-unrelated variables. Fidelity to the essential causal arguments of each beginning theory is virtually impossible when so many diverse theories are subjected to the integrative attempt.

On a more positive note, the possibility of logically-tenable theory integration has been demonstrated in criminology (see, e.g., Akers 1973; 1987). Following the precedent in successful integration attempts, aspiring integrationists might heed Akers' simple suggestion that integration is best suited to theories that "fit" together (1987). With this logic, the most promising candidates for integration are those perspectives that are least restrictive in their beginning assumptions and least developed in their propositional formality.

In closing, it is tempting to speculate on the broader implications of integration attempts across disciplines, as endorsed in the papers reviewed here. Cross-disciplinary integration could undoubtedly improve the comprehensiveness of theories, as Burgess and Akers (1966) have demonstrated. But the challenge of reconciling the opposing paradigms that prevail in psychology, sociology, or biology are formidable indeed (Kuhn 1970). Further experiments in theory integration across disciplines, in the absence of greater rigor and method in the practice of theory integration, may well involve the familiar hazards of within-discipline integration, writ large.

Part II

Macro-Level Integration

In this section, the focus of attention shifts from individuals to social collectivities—i.e., from the micro to the macro level. The papers contained herein encompass both discussions of the requisites for macro-level integration and efforts at constructing integrated explanations based on macro theories. As in the previous essays, there are profound disagreements between some of the authors about the prospects for successful integration given the current state of sociological and criminological theory.

The first paper in this section, Bursik's "Political Decisionmaking and Ecological Models of Delinquency: Conflict and Consensus," represents an effort at macro-level end-to-end integration (see the editors' introductory chapter). Bursik proposes that insights from conflict theories can be incorporated into social disorganization theories, even though the latter theories are typically identified with a 'consensus' perspective on crimes and delinquency. The key to integrating these approaches is to recognize that the internal dynamics of neighborhoods, which are regarded solely as 'independent variables' in conventional social disorganization models, are themselves affected by political decisionmaking. Bursik illustrates the utility of expanding the social disorganization perspective in this way by conducting an empirical analysis of the effects of the construction of new public housing units on the residential stability of Chicago neighborhoods.

Wellford's paper, "Towards an Integrated Theory of Criminal Behavior," addresses some of the preconditions for the formulation of powerful integrated theories. He proposes that three categories of explanations have dominated the field of criminology at different historical moments—limited factor reductionism, multiple factor approaches, and systemic reductionism—and argues that each of these types of explanations is incomplete. The major task for the future, Wellford contends, is to develop explanations of crime that are truly interdisciplinary. To facilitate such an agenda, Wellford proposes fundamental metatheoretical principles that should underlie integrated theories and outlines the content of an interdisciplinary theory of criminal behavior.

Swigert ("The Discipline as Data: Resolving the Theoretical Crisis in Criminology") offers commentary on the first two papers in this section and discusses the importance of definitional issues in the study of crime. She summarizes the contributions of Bursik's empirical analysis and endorses in principle Wellford's plea for pooling the insights of different approaches. She expresses skepticism, however, about the prospects for interdisciplinary theory before more interdisciplinary (and disciplinary) work has been done. In addition, Swigert expands on the point raised in Wellford's paper that the dependent variable in criminology—"crime"—is defined from outside the discipline. In Swigert's view, future theoretical development will require a serious rethinking of the very concept of crime.

Bernard's essay ("A Theoretical Approach to Integration") represents an effort to develop an integrated macro-level theory based upon five major theories in criminology. It basically involves the "up-and-down" approach to integration. Bernard's strategy is to identify causal arguments that are common to each of the component theories—i.e., arguments that make the same predictions for the same reasons. In addition, Bernard considers explicitly the logical implications of points of divergence between the component theories. He concludes that the areas of divergence do not preclude meaningful integration, and he proceeds to construct a more abstract, general theory of action that encompasses the causal arguments of the constituent theories. Bernard's theory of action is intended to explain both criminal acts and official reactions to crime.

Tittle ("Prospects for Synthetic Theory: A Consideration of Macro-Level Criminological Activity") argues that theoretical integration—or, more precisely, theoretical synthesis—is an indispensable element in the scientific enterprise. He discusses the practical benefits of synthetic theories (products of up-and-down integration) and identifies the technical operations required for effective synthesis. To illustrate the possibilities for formulating synthetic theories, Tittle reviews three macro-level explanations in criminology and observes that each of these theories employs similar concepts. Hence, by abstracting more general concepts from these explanations (in a manner similar to Bernard's efforts) and by unifying these abstract concepts around certain principles, a synthetic theoretical argument can be constructed. Tittle concludes with a discussion of two of the more important impediments to theoretical science: disagreement about how to conduct theoretical science and dissension over the ultimate desirability of such activity.

Gibbs ("Three Perennial Issues in the Sociology of Deviance") develops a critique of the papers by Bernard and Tittle by relating their arguments to three perennial issues in the study of deviance: the criteria for assessing theories, the kinds of questions that should be asked, and the desirable modes of theory construction. While recognizing the extent to which both authors pursue important ideas, Gibbs contends that neither satisfactorily addresses the above-mentioned issues. Gibbs' position is that genuine theoretical growth in the sociology of deviance must await the following developments: the widespread acceptance of the use of predictive power as the appropriate criterion for theory assessment; the formulation of clear definitions of deviance and the specification of the kinds of data relevant to these definitions; and the adoption of formal rather than discursive modes of theory construction.

7

Political Decisionmaking and Ecological Models of Delinquency: Conflict and Consensus[1]

——Robert J. Bursik, Jr.——

Introduction

The central set of dynamics underlying the traditional ecological approach to the spatial distribution of delinquency reflects the movement of population groups among the local areas of a city. Shaw and McKay, who introduced this perspective into American criminology (1929, 1942), assumed that a competitive, open housing market naturally made certain areas of the city more attractive for settlement and, in turn, more residentially stable than others. They argued that this process led to variation in the ability of neighborhoods to regulate themselves, which in turn led to variation in rates of delinquency.

Although this 'social disorganization' approach has been generally shown to be robust (see, for example, Bursik 1986), it provides a model of delinquency rates which is incompletely specified, for the processes of invasion and succession in which it is grounded are far from totally 'natural' phenomena. Rather, there has been a dramatic increase in the degree to which local urban communities are consciously planned, especially since World War II. Suttles (1972, p. 41), for example, has noted that modern neighborhoods not only reflect the economic processes considered by Shaw and McKay but also "politics and some cultural image of what the city ought to be like" (see the criticism of their model by Snodgrass 1976). Thus, as Finestone (1976) has shown, the primary thrust of Shaw and McKay's model gives the impression that the composition and internal organization of local communities are relatively independent of the broader political dynamics of the city.

Given its assumptions concerning the existence of shared goals within a community, social disorganization is clearly a normative concept with consensual overtones. However, political decisionmaking often involves the resolution of conflicts concerning the protection and acquisition of scarce resources. Therefore, for a fuller understanding of the urban dynamics that give rise to the spatial distribution of delinquency rates, it is necessary that our models incorporate processes reflecting both consensus and conflict in a theoretically parsimonious manner.

In this paper, we will present an initial attempt at such an integration by focusing on the effects of a single type of political decision that can have a dramatic effect on the internal dynamics of a local community: the decision to locate a public housing project within its boundaries.

The Consensual Aspects of Ecological Models

Although they are generally considered to be the fathers of the ecological approach to crime, Shaw and McKay have been criticized for not seriously pursuing the implications of Park and Burgess' (1924) model of urban dynamics, in which they have grounded their work (Allihan 1938; Baldwin 1979). However, they cannot be totally faulted for this neglect, for the ecological dynamics most likely to be characterized by conflict-based processes—the articulation and accomodation of the 'moral order' which provides the arena for the struggle for status—were not really developed by Park and Burgess. Rather, they primarily concentrated on the "biotic order" of human ecology, which reflected the "natural" dynamics of the competitive market system that resulted in the existing pattern of land usage and the spatial location of population groups. In such a "natural market," the price of housing reflects the relative demand for a particular property or area in the city; consumers in such a market may change residences as often as they wish if their income and credit-worthiness makes such a move affordable (see the discussion of Bottoms and Wiles, 1986).

This orientation is best reflected in Burgess' concentric zone theory of urban structure (1925). As immigrant groups became more fully integrated into the economic structure, they were assumed to progressively move outward from the central city into more attractive and more expensive housing units. Areas that were least attractive (i.e., close to the central business district) tended to be characterized by high rates of population turnover, as residents moved out of them as soon as economically feasible. In addition, since this rapid transition made it difficult to form strong formal and informal linkages between the residents, the organization of a concerted resistence against the influx of unwanted new residents was highly problematic. Therefore, these neighborhoods also were characterized by relatively high levels of population heterogeneity. As one moved into areas of increasing housing values and socioeconomic status, there was a progressive decline in the extent of instability and heterogeneity.

These arguments strongly influenced the development of the Shaw and McKay model. They noted a fairly stable areal distribution over time in the distribution of delinquency rates in Chicago; high rates were primarily found in areas characterized by low socioeconomic status, rapid turnover, and population heterogeneity. Drawing from Thomas and Znaniecki's (1920) notion of social disorganization, they argued that such high rates reflected the inability of unstable and heterogenous communities to regulate themselves sufficiently enough to realize the common values and solve the common problems of their residents (see Kornhauser, 1978, p. 63).

In one respect, this shared value aspect of social disorganization is not as restrictive an assumption as it may appear. As Janowitz argues (1976, pp. 9–10), the normative basis of social control (i.e., community self-regulation) does not necessarily mean rigid control and social repression. Rather, nonconformity in an area can be tolerated as long as it does not interfere with the attainment of a commonly accepted goal. In this regard, all that needs to be demonstrated is that the residents of an area value an existence relatively free of crime; it is not necessary to accept the assumptions of the other "universal human needs" that Kornhauser detects in the work of Shaw and McKay, such as economic sufficiency, education, and family stability (p. 63). The widely replicated findings of the body of research concerning the perceived seriousness of crime (Sellin and Wolfgang 1964; Rossi et al. 1974) indicate that it is a reasonable assumption that residents desire a lifestyle at least free from the threat of serious crimes (such as index offenses).

However, there is a second normative assumption of the traditional ecological and social disorganization framework, one which has limited its ability to characterize the modern urban dynamics related to crime and delinquency. The ecological framework of Shaw and McKay at least implicitly assumes that the distribution and movement of populations within an urban area reflect the 'natural' market of housing demand; they did not discuss in any detail the political decisions that may have accelerated (or decelerated) population turnover and heterogeneity in Chicago's neighborhoods. The work of Liska et al. (1985), for example, suggests that it might be in the best interest of political decisionmakers to keep certain neighborhoods relatively disorganized, so that concerted attacks on existing power bases are difficult to maintain. Therefore, there may be exogenous determinants of social disorganization in addition to the traditionally considered economic forces, ones that reflect the outcome of negotiated political conflicts. In the next section, we examine the nature of some of these processes and propose a method for integrating them into more traditional models of social disorganization.

Conflict-Based Exogenous Sources of Social Disorganization

Many writers have observed that the effect of non-natural market mechanisms on the spatial location of population groups has been especially pronounced since World War II (see Schuerman and Kobrin 1983; Bursik 1986; Suttles 1972). Hirsch (1983), for example, has presented strong evidence that the activities of slumlords in Chicago's traditional Black Belt may have accelerated movement out of that area over what might have been expected given the economic status of the residents.

Such market manipulation has not been solely determined by private initiative. As Guest notes (1984, p. 293), the large bureaucracies that have arisen since World War II "undoubtedly have important influences over the political processes in determining the allocation of land." One of the reasons for the increase of such bureaucracies is that with the rise of suburbanization and the resulting decline in the population of the central cities, local governments are finding themselves facing extreme fiscal strain—i.e., an imbalance between government spending or debt and the resources of the private sector (such as reflected in the median family income, tax base, and property values; see Clark 1981). A common response to this crisis has been the creation of zoning regulations that attempt to simultaneously maximize the tax yield from the properties in an area and minimize the public dollars necessary to service the community (Foley, 1973, p. 111).

In addition, as Suttles (1972, pp. 82–86) has indicated, incentives have been offered to potential builders and developers that were not necessary in the past. As he argues, current decisions to develop are not simply based on an economical use of land but also on expectations concerning the future potential of adjacent property (p. 86). Since few developers or realtors are large enough to control such a large block of land and since many private firms are reluctant to risk a major investment in an area in which the future is problematic, the local government is forced to provide inducements to such developments, such as the financing of construction, the clearance and sale of land, and the establishment of standards for builders (p. 82).

Such incentives have also been used to influence the amount of internal residential mobility within a community. Clarke and Moore (1980, pp. 14–15) note that these may include the provision of grants to increase the perceived benefits of moving to or remaining in a particular neighborhood (such as for the rehabilitation of older dwelling and housing allowances), the direct control of the relative costs of alternate dwellings (through rent control and the manipulation of interest rates), and attempts to influence the cost of moving (through subsidies, capital gains tax rates, and the allocation of public housing).

Since these programs have a direct effect on the immediate future of local neighborhoods, residents have a vested interest in the protection of resources that they already control and the maximization of future potential benefits. For example, one of the most controversial types of "planned" community change—the decision to locate a public housing project within the boundaries of a community—has resulted in pronounced conflicts between residents and the local government. This conflict to a large extent reflects the general public image that such housing projects are primarily designed for slum clearance and are usually designated for location in run-down areas (see Foley, 1973). Therefore, residents may feel either that they have been abandoned by the local government or may perceive that the future of the community has been greatly jeopardized. Reactions to the possibility of such housing being located in one's neighborhood have been dramatic; Hirsch (1977) has documented the violent reaction to the creation of public housing projects which characterized many areas of Chicago (see also Berry and Kasarda 1977).

One of the outcomes of such political planning is that neighborhoods may undergo rapid and unexpected compositional changes. As Bursik and Webb (1982) have shown, such changes can be associated with dramatic increases in the rates of delinquency in these areas because (1) many former residents abandon existing local institutions and they must essentially be created anew and (2) the linkages between residents that are essential for community self-regulation are difficult to create and maintain during periods of rapid change. Therefore, the extent to which a community can regulate itself for the control of crime and delinquency reflects not only the traditional economically based process of invasion and succession considered by Shaw and McKay but also the way that "resources are allocated in the larger society" (Spergel and Korbelik 1979, p. 109).

The effects of such non-market mechanisms on the spatial distribution of crime and delinquency have received very little attention in the literature, and yet the integration of political decisionmaking into the social disorganization framework can be accomplished in two straightforward ways. First, it is possible that political decisions may *directly* affect the delinquency rate of a neighborhood. For example, the city may decide to locate a residential treatment center for serious delinquents within the boundaries of a community. If, in fact, these youths continue to engage in delinquency, the delinquency rate of that area may rise.

Second, and of more interest from the ecological perspective, political decisions may have an effect on the level of social disorganization in the area, thereby *indirectly* affecting the delinquency rates. This indirect effect can be of two types. First, and most obviously, the outcome of the political decision may increase the level of economic deprivation, population heterogeneity, or residential stability in an area, thereby leading to an increase in the delinquency rate. However, decisions that *increase* the level of organization in an area may also be associated with increases in delinquency. Heitgerd and Bursik (1987), for example, have presented evidence suggesting that when neighborhoods perceive themselves as threatened from external sources, they may use the delinquent activities of their youths as a form of protection of life and property, in a manner implied by Suttle's notion of the "defended community" (1972, p. 199). Heitgerd and Bursik, for example, find that increases in delinquent activities associated with potential threat in adjacent neighborhoods were most pronounced in stable, blue collar areas (see also Bursik's 1984 discussion of Burnside).

In this paper, we have limited ourselves to the examination of the indirect effects that political decisions may have on the delinquency rates of the local communities of Chicago. In particular, due to the conflict that has often characterized such decisions, we have focused on the degree to which changes in local delinquency rates between 1970 and 1980 reflect the construction of new public housing units that were built with funds provided by Section 8 of the 1974 Federal Housing and Community Development Act.

The 1974 Housing and Community Development Act

Three programs were developed under this act to provide subsidized housing for those families in Chicago who earned up to 80 percent of the median income of the city. One of these provided subsidies for existing dwelling units that required extensive rehabilitation, while another subsidized the costs of living in existing units that required no such work; more than half of these units were single family units. In this paper we concentrate on the third part of this program: the construction of new public housing (for a detailed description of these three programs, see Weicher 1980).

In the new construction program, subsidies were given to particular projects, rather than to individual families. Each city eligible for this program (which included Chicago) was asked to evaluate its own housing market to determine its priorities concerning the mix of new, existing, or rehabilitated dwelling units that might best supplement the current housing market; the distribution of funds to each city was determined by this local evaluation. It is important to emphasize that the cities incurred *no cost* for new or rehabilitated dwelling units, even though the cost per unit rates were significantly higher than for the subsidy of existing units. In light of the fiscal crisis of cities that was noted earlier in this paper, the potential benefits that might incur from new construction are obvious: the channeling of funds to local developers, the employment of large numbers of construction workers, and an increase in the local tax base. In fact, Weicher notes that the response to this program was so great that HUD began to put pressure on local municipalities to focus primarily on the use of existing units (p. 66).

Decisions have to be made concerning the placement of such projects. If a strictly open market housing mechanism prevailed, one would expect that these units would be built in areas in which the costs to the program were minimal, in terms of both the value of the land that had to be purchased and the fair market rents that the federal government would be willing to subsidize. On the other hand, if in fact these locational decisions reflected the outcome of conflict-based political negotiations, one would expect that neighborhoods least able to organize an effective resistance to their construction would be the primary targets for construction, since public housing projects are not typically a valued community resource.

In the research to be reported in the following sections, we examine first the degree to which open market considerations were apparently related to the locational decisions of the municipal government. We then turn our attention to the effect of new public housing on the levels of social disorganization in the targeted communities and, in turn, the ensuing effects on the delinquency rates.

The Measurement of Change

Our central concern is the extent to which the ecological and delinquency rate changes characterizing Chicago's local community areas between 1970 and 1980 can be attributed to the construction of new public housing units. As has been argued by Bursik (1986), the operationalization of change is not straightforward in an ecological context.

First, the ecological argument of Park and Burgess (and, by extension, of Shaw and McKay) assumes that certain areas of a city are continually characterized by change because of their role in the ecological system. Therefore, it is necessary to differentiate changes that are expected on the basis of long term trends in a neighborhood from those that represent a restructuring of a neighborhood's dynamics. Second, from an ecological perspective, changes in local communities can only be understood in terms of the processes characterizing the system as a whole. For example, assume that all of the local communities of a city experience a 10 percent increase in their delinquency rates. Since this change maintains the relative distribution of delinquency in that city, then in fact no significant ecological redefinition has occurred. Therefore, what is needed is a measure of change that can separate both components of change while controlling for the overall dynamics of the ecological system.

The approach we have used to operationalize all indicators of change is the residual change score (see Bursik and Webb 1982; Bursik 1986). In our analysis, the level of the variable of interest in 1980 is regressed on the 1970 level of the same variable. The residual from this model represents the difference between the 1980 level and that which would be expected on the basis of the 1970 level (which would represent an ongoing trend) after controlling for the dynamics of the ecological system as a whole (since all of the communities in a city are used to estimate the equation). For example, a residual change score of 10 for the delinquency rate would indicate that a given community had ten more offenses per thousand than one would expect on the basis of its 1970 rate, after controlling for changes characterizing the entire city; a negative score would reflect the opposite.

It is important to emphasize that it is possible for a community to exhibit an increase in its raw delinquency rate but have a zero (or negative) residual change score. A zero score would indicate that despite these increases, the relative ecological position of the community in the city had remained the same; a negative score would indicate that it was moving downward in its relative position as a delinquency area.

The Data

The delinquency change scores (DELCH) used in the analysis are based on the rates of referral of male juveniles ages 10–17 to the Cook County, Illinois juvenile court on delinquency petitions in 1970 and 1980 for each of the 75 recognized local community areas of Chicago. As in our previous analyses of these data, the Loop (Chicago's central business district—area 32) has been eliminated due to the very small number of males in this age category. The indicator of public housing construction is designated as PHOUSE; due to the small number of communities in which new construction took place between 1970 and 1980 (16), the distribution of PHOUSE is extremely skewed. Therefore, it has been recoded as 1 = construction, 0 = no construction.

The effects of three constructs on the location of new public housing are considered in our analysis. The first (VALUE70) is a factor score reflecting the combination of the median value of owner-occupied dwelling units and the median rent for non-owner-occupied units (see Table 7.1). It is assumed that this scale represents an indirect measurement of the competitive market considerations that might be reflected in the decision to locate public housing: the greater the market value of the dwelling units in an area, the more expensive should be the purchase of land or the demolition of existing housing units. One Chicago community (the near South side—area 33) had no owner-occupied dwelling units at all in either 1970 and 1980, and was therefore eliminated from this analysis.

The second construct (COMP70) reflects the racial and economic composition of the local communities (see Table 7.1). The final variable

Table 7.1
Measurement Model For Scaled Constructs:
Factor Loadings

	COMP70
Percent Nonwhite	.773
Percent Owner-Occupied	−.652
Percent Unemployed	.849
	VALUE70
Median Value Owner-Occupied	.863
Median Rent	.863
	COMP80
Percent Nonwhite	.838
Percent Owner-Occupied	−.549
Percent Unemployed	.888

is a single indicator measure of the percentage of residents in the community who had lived in the same house for less than 5 years (MOVE70). Changes in these last two variables, which represent ecological change in the composition and stability of the area, are represented as COMPCH and MOVECH respectively (the factor structure for COMP80, on the basis of which the residual change scores were computed, is presented in Table 7.1).

It must be noted that we have no direct measurement of social disorganization per se; both COMP70 and MOVE70 were assumed by Shaw and McKay to be determinants of that process. This is a major deficiency of studies that have used the population of all local community areas within a given ecological system as the unit of analysis. Usually, census boundaries (or some rearrangement of these boundaries) are used to demarcate the local communities. The collection of data that would provide representative data concerning the local formal and informal networks of a community—the spans of control, identification with the community, and so forth—would entail a very intensive series of interviews, surveys, and field work within each of the local neighborhoods. The logistic and economic problems of such an approach are obvious in large metropolitan areas that may have over a hundred locally recognized communities. Therefore, given the assumed theoretical connection between composition, stability, and social disorganization, we have used these variables as proxies. However, the analysis does not provide a definitive test of the causal mechanisms that exist between social disorganization and delinquency.

Findings

The first step of the analysis was the determination of the extent to which the construction of new public housing units reflected the dynamics of an open, competitive market. An initial examination of the model indicated that two communities were extreme outliers to the overall pattern that characterized Chicago during this period—Grand Boulevard (area 38) and Washington Park (area 40). The models presented below were estimated after their elimination from the analysis. Although a full examination of the source of discrepancy for these two communities is beyond the scope of this paper, it is interesting to note that not only did they exhibit extremely high delinquency change scores between 1970 and 1980, but they are also characterized by some of the densest public housing projects found in Chicago. Although these developments were built prior to 1970, it is possible that the effects of their placement continue to affect the dynamics of these areas.

Table 7.2 presents the results of a stepwise discriminant analysis in which the construction of new housing is predicted on the basis of the composition and stability of the community, as well as the market value of the occupied dwelling units. As can be seen by the zero order statistics, while the likelihood of construction is significantly associated with the measures of composition and stability, the market value of the occupied units is independent of the locational decision. The stepwise analysis indicates that such housing is most likely to be constructed in areas characterized by high rates of instability; after controlling for this effect, the composition of the neighborhood adds no predictive power. Most importantly, VALUE70 continues to be a poor predictor of the location of new public housing units. This is an extremely significant finding, for it indicates that the dynamics typically associated with the existence of an open, competitive housing market were not related to the location of public housing in Chicago during this period. Rather, neighborhoods characterized by such construction tended to be those least able to organize an effective resistance.

Table 7.2
Prediction of Public Housing Construction:
Stepwise Discriminant Analysis

	Univariate Statistics		
Variable	R^2	F	p
COMP70	.07	5.24	0.03
VALUE70	.00	0.02	0.90
MOVE70	.09	6.52	0.01
	Entered on Step 1		
Variable	R^2	Lambda	F
MOVE70	.09	.914	6.52
	Statistics For Entry		
Variable	R^2	F	p
VALUE70	.00	0.02	0.89
COMP70	.02	1.74	0.19

The effects of this construction are examined in Table 7.3. While public housing is not associated with any significant change in the composition of these neighborhoods, there is a marked relationship with the subsequent degree of instability in an area: on the average, neighborhoods experiencing construction were characterized by an eight percent increase in instability over what would have been expected on the basis of the 1970 patterns. Thus, the construction of public housing dramatically accelerated the patterns of instability that existed in Chicago's neighborhoods.

Table 7.3
Effect of Public Housing Construction On
Local Community Change 1970–1980

Independent Variable	Beta	S.E.	B	T	p
Dependent Variable: COMPCH					
PHOUSE	−0.138	0.120	−.137	−1.15	0.255
Dependent Variable: MOVECH					
PHOUSE	8.060	2.657	0.343	3.033	0.003
Dependent Variable: DELCH					
COMPCH	4.991	6.719	0.091	0.743	0.460
MOVECH	0.685	0.303	0.292	2.258	0.027
PHOUSE	6.523	6.775	0.118	0.963	0.339

Table 7.3 also indicates that PHOUSE had no direct effect on changes in local delinquency rates. However, given the significant effect of MOVECH on these rates and the significant direct effect of PHOUSE on MOVECH, it is apparent that increases in delinquency rates are partially a function of the indirect effect of the construction of new public housing projects. Therefore, the redefinition of delinquency areas in Chicago is not a simple reflection of a competitive market mechanism. Rather, processes of political decisionmaking are able to indirectly shape the direction of these changes.

Conclusions

In this paper, we have examined the traditional assumption of ecological models of delinquency that the dynamics of a competitive open market housing system underlie the spatial distribution of delinquency. Evidence has been provided that political dynamics can directly affect the level of social disorganization in a community, thereby indirectly affecting the level of delinquency. In particular, the politically planned construction of new public housing projects has been shown to affect the residential instability of Chicago's local neighborhoods. In addition, as shown in Table 7.2, the planned location of these projects does not appear to be a function of the market value of the potential sites. Rather, they were most likely to be located in neighborhoods that were already unstable and presumably unable to organize and negotiate an effective defense against their construction.

One implication of the analysis is worth emphasizing. The model provides no support for the assumption that such housing projects might attract "problems populations" that are more crime prone than the existing residents. As was shown in Table 7.3, the construction of new housing did not have any significant effect on the compositional characteristics of Chicago's neighborhoods. Therefore, the primary effect of this construction was not to introduce new "kinds" of people into a neighborhood that might change its delinquency character. Rather, in a manner that can be directly predicted from a social disorganization approach, it introduced a new source of instability into the neighborhood that decreased the community's ability to regulate itself.

It must also be pointed out that this is not a necessary consequence of subsidized housing. As noted above, the Section 8 directive under which the new housing was constructed also contained provisions for the rehabilitation or direct subsidization of the existing housing stock. Although the symbolic differences in these types of subsidized housing can only be a matter of conjecture at this point, it is reasonable to assume that such programs are not as likely to be viewed by residents as a sign that their neighborhood has been abandoned by the city government. Rather, the government has provided funds to maintain the housing in that area as part of a viable community.

Such conjecture receives support when the effects of these two other plans on the structure of Chicago's communities are considered. Neither the rehabilitation nor existing unit programs were associated with compositional change, change in instability, or change in the delinquency rates during this ten year period. Such findings indicate that the existence of subsidized housing per se need not have an effect on the ecological position of a community. Rather, it appears that only when the placement of such housing is a disvalued outcome of political decision-making that the ecological dynamics of a community may be fundamentally altered.

8

Towards an Integrated Theory of Criminal Behavior

———Charles F. Wellford———

Introduction

Recently, numerous commentators have noticed that there have been few significant developments in theories of criminal behavior in the last 10 to 15 years.[1] After reviewing the modern history of criminological theory, Williams (1984, p. 92) concludes that "the 1970's, while certainly not sterile, represent one of the least creative periods in criminological history." Wilson and Herrnstein (1985) lament the failure of theories of criminal behavior to move beyond the traditional sociological perspectives of labeling, conflict, opportunity, social control, social learning, and so forth, which were promulgated mainly during the 1950s, 1960s, and 1970s. Existing theoretical paradigms in criminology have received limited support from empirical research, and have failed to facilitate the prediction or control of criminal behavior. This paper reviews one possible explanation of the absence of significant theoretical breakthroughs in recent years, and proposes an agenda for theory development. In so doing, I do not claim to be providing new theoretical insights for our discipline, but rather hope to define a path that, if followed, will move us out of our theoretical paralysis.

Models of Criminological Thought

The history of criminological theory can be described in terms of three major categories of explanation: limited factor reductionism, multiple factor approaches, and systemic reductionism. It is not necessary at this time to review the specific theories within these general categories of theory. However, assuming our past is a guide to avoiding some failures in the future, it may be helpful to remind ourselves of the path criminological thought has taken since the late 1800s.

Most of the early work on theories of criminal behavior is best described as single factor or limited factor reductionism. The early theories of crime tended to focus on one aspect of the criminal (e.g., family heritage, IQ, level of biological development, and so on) as an explanation of law-violating behavior. This is not uncharacteristic of other disciplines where early attempts to develop theory resulted in the identification of concepts that might later be included in a more general theory but seldom resulted in the specification of those elements that proved to be central to a mature scientific theory. Shortly after a single factor or limited factor reductionistic approach emerges, friends and critics alike note its limitations by identifying other factors obviously related to the occurrence of crime. For example, in later editions of Lombrosos's *Criminal Man* we find hundreds of potential explanations of crime that are given importance equal to atavism. Still, in criminology, limited factor reductionism dominated until the early 1900s.

A second stage in the development of theories of criminal behavior involved the identification of a variety of factors that were believed to be related to criminal behavior. As noted above, by the fourth edition of *Criminal Man* Lombroso had added over 100 explanations of criminal behavior to the concept of atavism. The book itself grew from 252 pages in the first edition to 1903 pages in the fourth and final edition (Vold 1979). Garofalo (1914) and Ferri (1917) recognized variation in types of criminals and in the explanations of criminal behavior. The tendency to expand the list of explanatory variables and to emphasize empirical relations over theory development is most usually identified with the work of Sheldon and Eleanor Glueck and their emphasis on prediction (1950). While clearly atheoretical, this approach contributed to the emergence of criminological theory by encouraging us to recognize the importance of social, psychological, and biological factors—and by emphasizing the relationship between explanation and empirical research.

The third approach to explaining criminal behavior, one in which we still find ourselves, is systemic reductionism. By systemic reductionism I mean the attempt to explain criminal behavior in terms of a particular system of knowledge. In criminology, particularly in the United States, the dominant discipline has been sociology. Therefore, it is not surprising to find that most current explanations of criminal behavior are sociologically based and are attempts to explain variations in the rates of criminal behavior as opposed to individual instances of that behavior. These explanations tend to emphasize certain characteristics of societies or cultures and their transmission. Even when the effort is to explain individual behavior, the attempt is to use exposure to or belief in cultural or social factors to explain individual instances or patterns of criminal behavior.

Since it is unlikely that behavior is understood from the point of view of any particular academic discipline (disciplines that were created for academic, historical and political reasons), systemic efforts fail to explain substantial amounts of the variation in behavior that is not systemically defined. In those sciences (e.g., economics) where the behavior studied can be defined by the discipline or system of knowledge, systemic explanations are more powerful. When this does not occur, as in criminology, where the basic dependent variable is defined external to the discipline, systemic reductionistic explanations have proven to be relatively weak. We find ourselves at the stage of development in criminology where a variety of sociological, systemic, reductionistic explanations dominate, all of which have proven to be relatively inadequate (to the standard of total explanation, prediction, or control) in explaining the individual occurrence or the distribution of crime through time or space. The less developed systemic models that have been proposed from psychiatric, psychological, and biophysical perspectives have also proven inadequate in explaining criminal behavior.

The above very brief description of the development and status of criminological theory is not unique to this paper. For example, a similar though less complete discussion of this problem was offered by Ferdinand (1967) when he described what he referred to as a jurisdictional dispute between the purists, that is "those who insist that delinquency in both substance and cause is basically social and therefore not amenable to other forms of explanation," and the empiricists, who maintain that delinquency is in "the last analysis an empirical problem that any factor—whether social, psychological, or physiological—can be utilized in explaining delinquency, so long as it is demonstrably related to the problem" (p. 3). In his analysis of this basic dichotomy in criminology, Ferdinand observed that both approaches recognize the existence of multiple levels of analysis. Multiple factor or empirical approaches draw upon sociology, psychology, and biology to identify the variables used to account for variation in behavior. Systemic reductionistic approaches acknowledge other levels but treat them as explainable by reference to the level of analysis emphasized by the theory (e.g., when sociologists define personality as the sum total of an individual's roles). While it is somewhat arbitrary to determine how these multiple levels of analysis should be classified, it is convenient for our purposes to follow the distinctions made by Talcott Parsons (e.g., 1961, pp. 30–79) between four levels of analysis: cultural, social, personality, and biophysical.

Systemic reductionism involves developing explanations of criminal behavior from any *one* of the multiple levels of analysis. Multifactor approaches involve selecting factors from any level, provided they have an independent effect on the dependent variable in question. Thus, the history of criminological theory can be seen as a movement from single factor through multiple factor to systemic explanations. While the emphasis in criminology has been on sociological approaches, we have consistently moved towards the recognition that limited factor reductionism and systemic reductionism are conceptually and empirically inadequate, and that multiple factor approaches are atheoretical and logically incomplete (see, for example, Cohen 1951, for such a critique). In my judgment, jurisdictional dispute between disciplines (i.e. competing systemic reductionistic theories) and the continued tension between theory and empirical research account for the current stagnation in theory development. To advance theories of criminal behavior, we must determine how best to structure a meta-theoretical position that allows us to move out of the inadequacies inherent in current approaches to explanation. The remainder of this paper considers how this might be achieved and what we must do to move out of our current theoretical paralysis.

Interdisciplinary Theory

The journal of the American Society of Criminology is called *Criminology: An Interdisciplinary Journal*. The preambles to the constitutions of the American Society of Criminology and the Academy of Criminal Justice Sciences speak of the need to bring together multiple disciplines and multiple perspectives to explain a phenomenon that is not subject to explanation from any one perspective or level of analysis. Ferdinand (1967), in his attempt to resolve the jurisdictional dispute between purists and empiricists, recognized the need to relate different levels of analysis to advance the understanding of criminal behavior. These declarations and presumptions reflect the fact that increasingly we have come to understand that as a science of nondiscipline-defined behavior, we need to move towards an interdisciplinary theory. The history of criminological thought makes clear the movement towards such multiple systems theory.

In order to develop an interdisciplinary behavioral theory we must better understand the concept of an interdisciplinary approach.[2] Frequently, we find in the literature recognition of the limitations of systemic reductionism, but an apparent inability to develop an interdisciplinary perspective. For example, Wilson and Herrnstein (1985), who clearly recognize the limits of sociological explanation and the need for multiple levels of analysis, offer an explanation of criminal behavior that is essentially systemic reductionistic (Cohen 1987). While numerous authors have understood that the problem facing our discipline in the advancement of theories of criminal behavior is our tendency toward systemic reductionism, none has been able to avoid it in theoretical work.

If we accept the notion of multiple levels of analysis, then in order to define an interdisciplinary theory we need to accept the following meta-theoretical principles. First, we must accept the independence of each of these levels of analysis. That is, no level of analysis can be totally explained, nor can its effects be totally explained solely by the operation of any other level of analysis. Hence, we must develop theories of criminal behavior that take seriously the notion that there are biophysical effects on criminal behavior, psychological effects, social effects, and cultural effects (or any other organized effects that we wish to identify through our specification of the appropriate categories or levels of analysis). However, if we stop only at that point and focus on independent levels of analysis, we have essentially created a multiple factor approach. Therefore, in addition to the notion of independent levels of analysis, a second meta-theoretical principle must be accepted, concerning the inter-relationships between levels of analysis. We must accept the proposition that these independent levels interact, affecting but not determining each other.

Philip Rieff articulated such a model for the development of a general theory of society. Rieff identified as the essential elements of a general theory: multiple levels of analysis; the concept of internalities, that is, those elements at each level of analysis that could not be explained by any other level; and the concept of externalities,—that is, the way in which each level impacted on and was influenced by all other levels of analysis. In Rieff's meta-theory, the explanation of any social behavior involves the interaction of multiple levels of analysis. While Rieff has not developed this model, it remains an instructive guide to those who attempt to develop interdisciplinary theories of criminal behavior.

One of the early and still useful expositions of the characteristics of interdisciplinary theory was offered by Abraham Edel (in Gross 1959). Edel notes that:

> Within contemporary social theory, we find that many of the fundamental controversies about the nature of the field itself are cast in terms reminiscent of levels disputes. There are accusations of reduction of the social to the psychological, occasional insistence on the autonomy of the cultural and the reality of the superorganic.... (p. 172)

The concept of levels (the first meta-theoretical position noted above) was identified by Edel as a powerful analytical tool to avoid the tendency towards reductionism. Edel argued that the concept of emergent levels could help advance all social and behavioral sciences:

> It has helped the social sciences resist the reductive tendencies to impose upon them the concepts and methods of the physical and biological sciences in apriori fashion. It has also, in the reverse direction, helped them oppose the attempts to isolate the study of man from the sciences, in the interests of non-naturalistic conceptions of man. Again, it has helped them avoid falling into the seductive metaphysical trap of seeing whatever order they discover in a partial segment of human history as the permanent nature or essence of man and society. For the levels concept brings, methodologically, a constant historical perspective to social description and explanation. It can become a sensitive alertness to the possible emergence of stable new forms, to their interaction, both in their rise and their maturity, with the milieu in which they emerge, to the conditions that make for continued stability or change, and to the way in which interaction at any given point may produce further incipient transitions.[3] (p. 170)

However, Edel is also quite explicit on what the meta-theory of emergent levels, or interdisciplinary theory, cannot achieve:

> It cannot supply out of itself the specific hypotheses.... It cannot specify in advance even which of the components within itself will be found applicable in the various domains of human phenomena. (p. 170)

Edel's outline of interdisciplinary theory is clear, but it does not lead us to the substantive elements to be included in an interdisciplinary theory. Rather, it sets the minimal requirements that must be met by a non-reductionistic theory. It sets the parameters for the development of theories of criminal behavior that continue the trend in criminology from single factor to interdisciplinary theory.

Towards an Interdisciplinary Theory of Criminal Behavior

Using Rieff and Edel as guides, it is clear that in order to develop an interdisciplinary theory of criminal behavior we must take four preliminary steps. First, we must end the useless debate between various systemic positions. While we may discard certain variables, concepts, or theories because they prove to be empirically inadequate, to continue the debate between the major sociological perspectives or between biological and sociological positions is at best foolish. Second, we must develop a language for understanding the requirements of interdisciplinary theory. The above discussion of levels, internalities, externalities and emergent levels is a first step in developing a meta-theory of interdisciplinary theory. Third, we must recognize and encourage our students to recognize the importance of psychological and biophysical approaches as essential elements in explanations of criminal behavior. These are the most underdeveloped areas in our field; areas that need considerable development—areas that must be incorporated into more general theoretical models. Finally, we must begin to identify some of the correlates of interdisciplinary theory. For example, such theories assume simultaneous causation; imply a developmental perspective that requires internally reciprocal effects; make no assumptions about the relative importance of any level or concept within or between levels; and, usually, assume a cybernetic system in which energy flows up (from biophysical to cultural) the model and control flows down, but neither flow is completely unidirectional. The more we explore the concept of interdisciplinary theory, the more we will understand the requirements of a fully developed, scientific, interdisciplinary theory of criminal behavior.

Figure 8.1 depicts a very preliminary attempt to outline the content of an interdisciplinary theory of criminal behavior.

Figure 8.1

Level	*Internalities*	*Externalities*
Cultural	Values	Institutionalization
Social	Social Facts	Economic, Demographic, Political and Technological Change
		Socialization
		Social Learning
		Social Control
Personality	Self Mind	Super Ego
		Ego
Biophysical	Genetic Structure	Biophysical limits or demands
	Biochemical Structure	

This model suggests that the internalities of the theory would be values, social facts or social organization, self or mind, and genetic and biophysical structure. It is assumed that those elements (which obviously need refinement and operationalization) can be influenced by but not determined by each other. The internalities are related by certain externalities. Institutionalization describes the impact of culture on social levels; socialization, social learning, social control, and super ego refer to the externalities between social and psychological levels, and so on. If an interdisciplinary theory such as this organized criminological thought, we could begin to move out of the theoretical stagnation that currently characterizes our field. This first step at outlining the integration suggests the overwhelming nature of our task. While the development of system specific theories and research must continue, the development of the kind of "grand theory" so briefly noted here must organize our discipline if we are to move beyond the current state of theory.

Future criminological theory must move in a direction similar to that suggested by Figure 8.1 if we are to avoid systemic reductionism. If criminology is more than the sum of the basic sciences on which it stands, we must take seriously the development of interdisciplinary theory. It is no longer satisfactory to call ourselves interdisciplinary while clinging to our disciplinary heritages or preferences.

Alternative Models of Theory Development

The above is obviously premised on a particular approach to theory development. I have used the terms "behavioral theory" and "empirically based theory" throughout this paper, and would like to close by making my position on the nature of theory more explicit. It has been said that theory consists of statements about unobservables. I take this to be true. We are not likely to see a useful theory that consists of simple restatements (no matter how complex) of empirical observations. While theory does attempt, as we all know, to interpret and summarize empirical observations, theory that is worth worrying about is basically statements about unobservables (concepts). We then establish relationships between these unobservables and the real world by specifying how some of the concepts in a theory are related to the observable world. The theory itself is a structure that cannot be *directly* tested. This is characteristic of all sciences, not just social sciences and certainly not just criminology. Once we have enough knowledge to develop a theory, it is important that we establish the rules of correspondence between elements of our theory and elements of the observable world. Hence, we must continue in our theoretical work to give special consideration to the problems of measurement. (For an excellent statement of this position, see Torgerson 1958.)

Some reviewers of criminological theory continue to emphasize the tension between theory and research. For example, Williams' (1984) position is that criminological theory has been slow to develop because we have become too empirical. He suggests that theory will develop if people are taught how to be creative. Both of these positions are seriously flawed. Theory will progress as we develop better models of what adequate theory should be and as we pay close attention to the relationship between empirical results, theoretical concepts, and the measurements that are required by the theories we develop. While some may reject this approach as simply mimicking the physical sciences and those social sciences that have achieved some degree of theory advancement, such dismissals show a basic misunderstanding of the philosophy of social science. We are not able to step back and decide that we will follow a different path because our dependent variables seem more difficult or are more subject to variation. We are required to apply to our own work the same standards of proof and the same standards of development applied to all sciences. This is required so we will have standards by which to judge our own development; it is also required because of the role science plays in modern society.

Almost four hundred years ago, Sir Francis Bacon observed that knowledge is power. Increasingly, scientific knowledge, real and imagined, influences social policy. Criminological sciences can be a major contributor to the understanding and improvement of society, provided we are able to demonstrate, in ways sciences for two centuries have demonstrated, that our theories have value—by developing theories that "work", theories that are concise and explain reality in ways that are understandable and testable. If we move in this direction and out of discipline disputes and disputes between research and theory, we will begin to take the necessary steps toward the development of a more mature discipline—a discipline that can more rightfully take its place among the sciences that are contributing to the improvement of mankind.

9

The Discipline as Data: Resolving the Theoretical Crisis in Criminology

———Victoria L. Swigert———

Criminological theory has, it seems, come hard upon infertile ground. For at least a decade nothing new has been said about the causes of crime and none of the old appears to have validated our claim that we have a handle on the problem. Gone are the days of heated debates between functionalists and conflict theorists, or among labeling, anomie, and differential association theorists. Conflict turned out to be functional; labeling, anomie, and differential association theories were right and wrong in equal measure. Besides, they were all asking different questions. While these intra-disciplinary debates were, as Wellford points out, futile, they were also exciting. There's not much excitement in criminology these days. In fact the most interesting material I have read in recent years has been conceptual histories of the discipline (e.g., Rennie 1978; Jones 1986).

Reading about criminology or writing about it is, however, as bit disconcerting; it has the ring of an obituary. Has criminology died? Does the proof of its demise lie in crime rates that rise and fall with full disregard for the criminologist's predictions or policy recommendations? Perhaps it is not dead but enfeebled; in need of transfusion or paradigmatic revitalization or revolution. Although knowing where to find the remedy is at least as problematic as explaining crime, that is among the purposes of this conference. The strategy we will pursue is integrating theory, within and between levels of analysis, within and between disciplines.

Wellford notes that sociology has been a predominant contributor to criminology. The discipline has produced a library full of facts about crime. Many of these are not embedded in theory; they were generated by the single- and multi-factor approaches of earlier years. Many others were born of hypotheses derived from the major sociological perspectives on crime, including anomie, differential association, labeling, conflict, and political economic theories. Lots of very smart, talented, and dedicated people have reported what they have seen, as trained observers, regarding crime. These observations are facts just as surely as are burglaries, robberies, and homicides. This mass of data suggests that perhaps it is not that we know too little about crime, but that we know too much. All this information begs inductive organization, a piece at a time, so that we may make statements that subsume these facts.

The strategy of taking what is known and explaining it is illustrated in Bursik's paper. He begins with Shaw and McKay's (1942) observations regarding the spatial distribution of delinquency as a correlate of neighborhood disorganization. These are the facts with which Bursik works. Making theoretical sense of them requires that he separate observations from the unexamined assumptions and interpretations within which they are embedded. Shaw and McKay assumed that natural market processes motivated the patterns of dominance and succession that left communities unable to organize in their own defense. Bursik replaces this assumption with facts about the interest-group politics and conflict that alter the structure and organization of neighborhoods and, correlatively, their delinquency rates.

From these data Bursik induces an empirical generalization which, in turn, predicts the hypothesis that he tests in the paper. We learn from his own observations that the sites of public housing construction were neighborhoods which, for lack of competitive resources, lost a political contest; that this construction exacerbated instability in those neighborhoods; and that delinquency rates followed accordingly. We have learned something from Bursik, who learned something from conflict and disorganization theory.

Bursik also provides us with ports to which we might add other facts. He tells us directly that his measures of disorganization—variations in the racial and economic composition of the neighborhoods and patterns in residential stability—are proxies derived from assumed theoretical connections between composition, stability, and social disorganization. There's room for fact finding here.

There is also, implicitly, lots of room to think about contributions from functionalist notions of boundary maintenance. Communities are organized insofar as they can assert the limits of behavior and belief required of members. Crime and deviance are a necessary part of social organization; they are both cause and effect of organization. Crime is the consequence of community solidarity; the social response to crime revitalizes that solidarity. There is a wealth of data generated by tests of functional hypotheses in laboratories and small groups as well as in historical and comparative contexts. We have learned from Bursik that planned change can affect a community's ability to regulate itself—to maintain and draw from its boudaries. What additional hypothetical deductions might we derive from the observations made by Durkheim (1904), Mead (1918), Dentler and Erikson (1959), Lauderdale (1976), Davies (1982), and Ben-Yehuda (1985)?

These are ways in which disciplinary data might be used to derive explanations of aggregate rates. Aggregates are, of course, comprised of individuals who behave in terms of the meanings they use to make sense of the world around them and their place in it. Once again we know a great deal about the causes of criminal behavior, here at the individual level. We know that people are bonded to one another; that they share attachments, commitments, involvements, and beliefs (Hirschi 1969). We know that these bonds are more or less strong; that the content of the learning that occurs through attachment to others varies from class to class, culture to culture, subcultural to subculture, reference group to reference group. We know about general learning processes and how people respond to rewards and punishments (Burgess and Akers 1968). We know something about relative deprivation (Merton 1938) and differential opportunities for conformity and nonconformity (Merton 1938; Cloward and Ohlin 1960). We know about labels and stereotypes (Schur 1971) and situated transactions (Luckenbill 1977). Out of all these data there are generalizations to be derived, generalizations that cumulate the bits and pieces of some larger variance we would explain.

Thus, we have the sociology of crime where scholars have approached an issue from several *intra*-disciplinary levels of analysis: structural, interpersonal, and psychological. Each of these levels within this one discipline has its as yet unspecified internalities and externalities. As important, each has an integrity that is inherent to its own angle of vision. At this point it is difficult not to recall the tactile explorations of the elephant by those who could not see the whole. Had they pooled their information by first acknowledging the limitations in the terrain each had mapped, they would have had a pretty good picture of the beast with which they were dealing. Structuralists, inter- and intrapersonal specialists, along with those at each of these levels who adopt conflict, political economic, learning, labeling, and anomie perspectives, see crime from their particular vantages. We stop learning when we presume that there is one vantage.

Getting the discipline's act together seems to me to be a precondition for developing an interdisciplinary model. Before we can talk about the internalities and externalities of culture and society and psychology and biology, we have to have some confidence in the nature of the contribution to be made by each. We can not yet articulate a sociology or sociologies of crime. An interdisciplinary *theory* of crime, at least at this stage of our own understanding, is a proposal which, while visionary, may also be premature.

Many criminologists may feel an urgency about understanding what we have not yet been able to explain. This urgency may tempt us to look beyond our own store of knowledge before we have fully mined it. If we have been unable to identify the causes of crime, perhaps they (the psychologists and biologists) can. Here I am reminded of two volumes on homosexuality published within two years of one another. The first, *Homosexuality in Perspective* (Masters and Johnson 1979), was authored by natural scientists. Masters and Johnson concluded that the failure of biology to explain homosexuality indicated social causation. Two years later three social scientists, Bell, Weinberg, and Hammersmith, in their book, *Sexual Preference* (1981), concluded that the failure of sociology to explain homosexuality pointed to the relevance of biology. Haste may make for waste.

This does not deny the value of looking to other disciplines. I too am convinced that there is a great deal to be learned from them. There was a paper earlier in this conference, Farrell's "Psychological Dimensions to an Elaboration of Labeling Theory," that demonstrated the utility of interdisciplinary work. Research done by psychologists on personality, in particular their concepts of intolerance of ambiguity and locus of control, can be used to predict the social effects of labels. This is very exciting to discover a link between inter-subjective and intra-subjective worlds. And it is a link that can only be made by reaching across disciplinary lines. By doing so, we not only add to the angles of visions from which to view a phenomenon, we acquire more conceptual tools—more hands, if you will—to map the whole. However, as with the job we have to do in sociology, we must approach our disciplinary neighbors one observation at a time. They have their facts to offer as we do. There is as little agreement within psychology on what constitutes the overall disciplinary vision as there is here at home.

Wellford's hierarchical model of levels, externalities, and internalities is the unified theory to which we aspire. Before interdisciplinary theory, however, must come a great deal more disciplinary and interdisciplinary work, making sense of the libraries full of data already at hand. This work can not be a mere restatement of facts, as Wellford cautions, but work that builds generalizations to subsume those facts.

There is another issue, also raised by Wellford, which I think goes a long way in explaining why criminology seems so stuck. We have not satisfactorily dealt with out dependent variable. We are trying to explain a phenomenon whose definition comes from outside the discipline. It is not just an inconvenience that lawyers tell us what crime is. It is not just a situation that complicates the problem of prediction. It is a serious violation of the scientific process and its basic requirement that scientists be clear about the concepts they formulate and the categories of events to which these concepts refer. The dependent variable as we know it—legal crime—and the substantive categories of that variable as we have studied them—robbery, burglary, homicide, prostitution—beg different questions than the ones we have been asking.

The causes of legal crime are to be found in law. Here it is appropriate to ask questions about the formulation of the legal codes and their enforcement. Law as a social construction is amenable to sociological analysis, and much has been done to analyze it. We know things about the history of law and crime, the politics of lawmaking and law enforcement, the organization and function of police, prosecutors, courts, juries, jails and prisons. We need to know much more about this dependent variable, and we need to explain what we have learned. One fact, however, does seem to me to be clear: along a range of human activities, brackets are imposed which distinguish good from bad, right from wrong, criminal from noncriminal. That range of behaviors is bisected by people using whatever tools they have at their disposal for exercising social control. Among the tools available in state societies are laws.

Once the continuum is bisected, we spend a tremendous amount of energy behaving as if there really were categorical distinctions between behaviors on either side of the official norm. Legislatures devote many hours drawing the line, courts many more deciding precisely which activities are beyond this law, judges and juries make the same determinations of specific individuals, and criminologists dedicate careers to predicting who will end up where, as if there really were us and them. Criminology becomes an apology for social control as long as our dependent variable *is* social control—that is, as long as we act as if there is a categorical distinction between street brawlers and all others who inflict physical harm on human beings, or between bank robbery and all the alternative ways that people appropriate other people's money. Legal distinctions between robbery and not-robbery may not produce a whole lot of variation in need of explanation. Within the control group of non-robbers there are many, many people who steal.

This does not mean that there are not really bank robbers, nor does it mean that most people convicted of robbery did not rob. This is not an argument for the unreliability of official statistics. It is not even and argument to categorically reject legal definitions of crime in favor of "antisocial behavior" or "violations of conduct norms." In this latter regard, however, I do believe that there is much to be learned by studying aggression and cupidity, in addition to assault and theft, in order to understand why people physically injure and steal from others. And let me add that I think that the study of aggression and cupidity points the way to the interdisciplinary work we need to do.

The facts therefore, that legal crime is a social construction does not preclude its appropriateness as an object of study. If it did, any student of any social institution—family, education, corporations—would be in serious trouble. People break legal rules. Why do they do that? This is an important and valid question. But what exactly is the behavior we want to explain? The answer to that question becomes our dependent variable, and that decision guides us to the population from which samples will be drawn and to which generalizations will be made.

I might want to know why people *illegally* inflict lethal or potentially lethal physical harm on human beings. The population to be studied includes those who inflict unlawful harm and those who do not. To select my sample, I must choose across legal distinctions of kinds of physical harms: assault and battery, spouse abuse, violators of health and safety regulations, willful producers of dangerous products. It would be critical in such an investigation to find representative samples of offenders, including the unconvicted, unreported, and undetected, since we have learned that the causes of legal treatment are different than the causes of criminal behavior. Similarly, a study of unlawful acquisition of property would include robbers and larcenists as well as tax evaders and inside traders. Thus do we take charge of the dependent variable, defining the concept in terms of social behaviors among which lawyers make legal distinctions. These legal distinctions may be appropriate ones for lawyers and ultimately for social control, but they may not be meaningful distinctions for social scientists.

We gain more than the integrity of our conceptual scheme by rethinking the dependent variable. By attending to a definition of the behavior we want to explain—by constructing, that is, an abstract term which summarizes discipline-relevant commonalities among legally distinct events—we get beyond the point of mistaking the correlates of social class for the causes of crime. Our comparison, whether implicitly or explicitly made, of conventional crimes and criminals with those activities and actors which are legally but not substantively distinct inevitably leave us with social class as a major predictor. Lower-class people commit lower-class crimes. Middle-class people commit middle-class crimes. Social class predicts which events shall be legally known as conventional crime and which shall be legally known as nonconventional crime; it may not predict who steals or kills. It is interesting to know that class (or race, or IQ, or divorce rates) specifies types of crime; class (or race, or IQ, or divorce rates) may, however, not tell us what we want to know about the causes of crime.

There is no doubt that reconstructing the concept of crime will be a difficult task. We will disagree about which behaviors and which consequences comprise which categories of our dependent variable. The effort and the disagreement are necessary, as necessary as they have been in the development of any conceptual schemes in any discipline that claims the scientific method.

The two papers presented in this panel have given us much to think about and point to all the work we have to do. More, they tell us and show us the directions our efforts might take. They are proof that the discipline is vital, in spite of what the obituaries might tell us.

10

A Theoretical Approach to Integration

Thomas J. Bernard

In this paper, integration is achieved on the basis of a convergence among the causal arguments in various criminology theories.[1] The resulting integrated theory can only be as valid as the *least valid* of the theories from which it is derived.[2]

Why integrate theories at all if the integration minimizes validity? The reason is to clarify the situation for criminologists and allow criminology itself to advance. The validity and methodological adequacy of one integrated theory can be assessed more readily than that of a variety of competing theories. If the integrated theory is determined to be invalid or inadequate for meaningful theory construction, then criminologists can abandon all the theories containing it and construct more valid and adequate theories. If the integrated theory is determined to be valid and adequate, then criminologists can abandon competitive testing of the theories that contain it and develop a general theory of crime based on its arguments. Either way, criminology is freed from unproductive controversy and allowed to develop as a discipline.

Preliminary Distinctions

Prediction vs. Explanation

The usefulness of a theory is determined by its predictive ability, but the theory itself lies in its explanation. That is, theory inheres in the *reasons* for a prediction, not in the prediction itself. Competing theories, while they may make the same prediction for different reasons, cannot be integrated on that basis. Integration can take place only when theories make the same predictions *for the same reasons*. Theories cannot be integrated by placing predictions 'side-by-side' to see if explained variance is increased (Hirschi 1979). If explained variance were increased by such a procedure, then (as with factor and cluster analysis) one could seek a coherent and logical explanation for this result. The explanation would then be a new theory.

A theory can be false even if its predictions are quite accurate—e.g., the Ptolemaic system of the universe (Kuhn 1970, p. 68). At the same time, the falsification of a prediction does not falsify a theory unless the prediction plays an essential role within the explanation the theory provides. If the prediction plays only an incidental role, then the proper response is to modify the theory to incorporate the discrepant finding. The terms 'essential' and 'incidental' imply a dichotomy where in fact there is a continuum. The impact of a falsified prediction can only be assessed by examining its logical role in the theory's explanation.

Theory vs. Causal Image

Criminology theories are discursive and complex (Gibbs 1985), making them difficult to test (cf. Blalock 1984). Criminologists at times categorize theories (e.g., strain, control, and cultural deviance theories) and attach simple 'causal images' to the category (e.g., variation in drives, variation in restraints, and variation in cultural beliefs). They then competitively test the causal images and attribute the results to all theories they had placed in that category.

These causal images maximize differences among the theories and make it easier to test them against each other; they also distort and oversimplify the original theories. They must be abandoned in serious discussions of the theories and of efforts to integrate them.

Macro vs. Micro

Micro[3] theories have individual actions as the dependent variable, while macro theories have as the dependent variable the rates and distribution of actions in societies. Each type of theory can be assessed in relation to the other type of theory.

Micro predictions tied to structural characteristics (as opposed to those tied to purely individual characteristics) can be aggregated into macro predictions about rates and distributions. I include macro predictions derived from micro theories in this paper; it is thus an integration of macro and micro theories at the macro level.

Some macro theories imply probabilistic predictions about individuals: if an individual is a member of a group with a given rate or distribution of activity, then that individual has a certain probability of engaging in the activity. This prediction can be conceptualized as one factor in a multiple factor micro theory and included in an integration of macro and micro theories at the micro level.

But aggregate predictions disaggregated to the individual level are normally quite weak. For example, Merton's (1968) aggregate predictions, when disaggregated to the individual level, imply neither a necessary nor a sufficient relation between the actions of individuals and their structural situation (Bernard 1987a). The temptation when moving from macro to micro is to derive strong micro predictions from macro theories and thus commit the ecological fallacy (Robinson 1950).

Other macro theories explain the rates or distributions of group phenomenon—e.g., Cohen's (1955) and Cloward and Ohlin's (1960) theories explain rates and distributions of juvenile gangs. Probabilistic predictions about individuals cannot be derived from these theories at all (Bernard 1987a, 1987b). Despite many attempts (see Elliott et al. 1985), I do not believe it is possible to integrate micro and macro theories in criminology at the micro level.

Definitions and Methods

Causal Arguments in Component Theories

Merton's (1968), Cohen's (1955), Cloward and Ohlin's (1960), Hirschi's (1969), and Akers' (1985) theories are referred to as the "component theories." Each component theory makes a variety of "causal arguments"—i.e., empirical predictions and theoretical explanations of those predictions. Many of the causal arguments in any one theory contradict causal arguments in other theories.

Explaining Criminal Action

First, I identify two causal arguments common to the five component theories. These are points at which the five theories make the same predictions for the same reasons.

Second, I isolate points at which two or more of the theories use contradictory reasons to make contradictory predictions and determine the consequences for each theory if research were to determine that the prediction of the competing theory is correct. That is, rather than speculate on which prediction is actually correct, I take each theory and 'plug in' the contradictory prediction. In effect, I assume that each theory is wrong on this particular point and examine the logical implications of the error. This clarifies the nature of the integrated product and identifies those elements of present theories that must be set aside pending the outcome of future research.

This method supplements but does not contradict the traditional method of seeking differences in empirical predictions. Researchers traditionally control for similarities and focus on points where different theories make different predictions for different reasons. They then test those different predictions with data. I control for differences and focus on points where different theories make the same predictions for the same reasons. I then use those common points to determine the relationships among the various theories.

A Theory of Action

I join the two causal arguments into a single 'theory of action.' The theory of action, while necessarily simpler than each component theory, is used by those theories as part of their explanation of criminal actions. Integration of the component theories can be achieved by determining the relation each theory has to the theory of action, establishing the relation each has to the others.

Explaining the Official Reaction

Vold and Bernard (1986) use the same theory of action to explain the actions of legislators, criminal justice agents, and the public in constructing official reactions to crime. Vold and Bernard's theory therefore can be integrated with the five component theories if the theory of action is an appropriate explanation for both criminal actions and official reactions. This would use the same theory to explain the actions of two different sets of people, thus generating two different dependent variables.[4]

Explaining Official Crime Rates

Official rates of deviance require a separate explanation from the explanation of the deviance itself (Kitsuse and Cicourel 1963). In the present case, official crime rates arise from the interaction of criminal actions and official reactions, those being the two dependent variables of the theory of action. If both criminal actions and official reactions are consistent with the theory of action, then the predicted distribution of official crime rates turns out to be the distribution actually found in most societies at most times. This is a third dependent variable derived from the theory of action.

A Theory of Crime

The coordinated explanation of criminal actions, official reactions, and official crime rates is described as a theory of crime (cf. Vold and Bernard, 1986, pp. 286–87).[5] It involves using the same theory of action to explain two different sets of actions (criminal actions and official reactions), and then analyzing the implications of the interaction of those sets of actions. Integration of a wider variety of criminology theories can be achieved by determining the relation of those theories to the theory of crime, rather than to the theory of action.

The First Causal Argument: Structure, Interests, and Actions[6]

I first state a causal argument in the form of two axioms linking three constructs. Then I discuss the relation between the causal argument and Hirschi's (1969), Merton's (1968), and Akers' (1985) theories.

$$\text{Social Structure} \xrightarrow[\text{Axiom 1}]{(+)} \text{Interests} \xrightarrow[\text{Axiom 2}]{(+)} \text{Actions}$$

Social structure is defined in terms of the different social positions and the social relations among those different social position (cf. Blau 1977). Interests are defined in terms of the range of choices available to individuals as possible courses of action, and the relative costs and benefits of those possible courses of action (cf. Dahrendorf 1959, 1979). Axiom 1 states that interests vary directly with social structure. This is interpreted to mean that available choices and the relative costs and benefits of those choices are influenced by structural location, and that individuals in "higher" structural locations tend to have a greater range of available choices with more benefits and fewer costs than individuals in "lower" structural locations.[7]

The term "action" is defined in terms of voluntary choice within the context of a socially structured situation (Parsons 1937, 1951). Axiom 2 states that actions vary directly with interests. This is interpreted to mean that individuals tend to act in ways that maximize benefits and minimize costs within the context of available courses of action.[8] Interests are not said to be the sole determinant of human action—they are said to be one such determinant, and a positive relation exists between interests and action.

Merton, Hirschi, and Akers all include this causal argument within their broader theories. I now discuss similarities and differences between the three theories and the causal argument.

Similarities

Merton's theory can be interpreted as making the following argument:

Social	(+)	Means to	(+)	
Structure	-----	Monetary	-------	Actions
	Class	Success	Culture	

The means to monetary success are those courses of action realistically available to the person by which he or she might acquire money. Thus they are a subset of interests, as defined above. Monetary success influences actions through the intervening variable of culture, which proposes monetary success as a cultural goal. The relation between social structure and the means to monetary success is mediated by class. Merton focused on the class-related distribution of legitimate means, while Cloward (1959) and Cloward and Ohlin (1960) later expanded this to include the class-related distribution of illegitimate means.

A comparable argument occurs in the context of Hirschi's discussion of commitment. Hirschi (1969, pp. 20–21) defines commitment as "the rational component in conformity," where an individual decides not to engage in deviant behavior because a rational calculation leads him to the conclusion that the costs are greater than the benefits. This concept includes but is not limited to[9] what might be called 'objective' interests, which Hirschi links directly to the organization of society (1969, see also p. 162):

> The concept of commitment assumes that the organization of society is such that the interests of most persons would be endangered if they were to engage in criminal acts. Most people, simply by the process of living in an organized society, acquire goods, reputations, prospects that they do not want to risk losing. These accumulations are society's insurance that they will abide by the rules. (p. 21)

In this passage, Hirschi describes legal behavior as purely rational and calculating and in that sense as motivated by objective interests. He also describes criminal behavior in the same way:

> In the sociological control theory, it can be and is generally assumed that the decision to commit a criminal act may well be rationally determined—that the actor's decision was not irrational given the risks and costs he faces. (pp. 20–21)

In these two quotations, the difference between legal and criminal behavior is explained through differences in what is rational and calculating for the person—i.e., differences in objective interests. Hirschi (1969, pp. 20–21) describes interests in terms of the relative costs and benefits of the different "lines of action" open to the individual, which is quite similar to the definition of interests proposed above. He ties the distribution of interests directly to the organization of society, and in that sense includes a macro argument in the context of his micro theory.

The mediating variable between interests and actions in Hirschi's theory is human nature: the natural human tendency to fulfill wants and needs without regard for the wants and needs of other individuals (Hirschi 1969, pp. 31–34). Thus individuals are assumed to naturally act in ways that are consistent with their interests. Since he presents a micro-level theory, Hirschi does not explore at length the exact connection between structure and interests. However, it would be consistent with his research (1969, pp. 173–78, especially Table 63), his later work (Hirschi and Hindelang 1977), as well as earlier work cited by Hirschi (Toby 1957; Briar and Piliavan 1965) to argue that academic competence is such a mediating variable. That is, those with more academic competence find that it is in their interests to obey the law (i.e., have high commitment), while those with less academic competence find that it is in their interests to break the law (i.e., have low commitment). Thus, the following argument is contained in Hirschi's theory:

Social Structure $\xrightarrow{(+)}$ Academic Competence Interests $\xrightarrow{(+)}$ Human Nature Actions

Finally, Akers (1985) presents a comparable argument in his structure–process model. Differential reinforcements operate when an individual chooses between two or more alternate actions in a given situation and concerns the relative reinforcements vs. punishments associated with the alternate actions. Simply put, differential reinforcements define which behaviors are more successful in obtaining the desired payoff (Akers 1985, p. 47). In that sense, they are comparable to what is defined above as 'interests' except that the concept is broader and more scientific.

Individuals naturally choose actions that are more highly reinforced and less highly punished, but similar stimuli can be experienced differently because of variations in biological or psychological makeup. Thus, the connection between differential reinforcements and actions is mediated by biology and psychology. Akers identifies several mediating variables between structure and reinforcements which he derives from the major structural theories of deviance, including control and strain theories (Akers 1985, pp. 62–70). The following argument is therefore contained in Akers' theory:

Social Structure $\xrightarrow[\substack{\text{Controls}\\\text{Anomie}\\\text{Conflict}\\\text{Labeling}}]{(+)}$ Differential Reinforcements $\xrightarrow[\substack{\text{Biology}\\\text{Psychology}}]{(+)}$ Actions

Differences

Criminologists might agree that Merton, Hirschi, and Akers make a common prediction but argue that they do so for different reasons: Merton because of the presence of a driving force, Hirschi because of the absence of a restraining force, and Akers because of a difference in cultural beliefs. if that were true, there would be no basis for integration among the theories. In contrast, I argue that the three theories provide *the same explanation* for this prediction.

The causal argument explains the distribution of crime among social structural locations within a given society. if Merton's theory explains this in terms of a 'drive,' then it must describe a variable driving force in the theory and link it to the distribution of crime in a society. There is a 'drive' to crime in Merton's theory—the American cultural value of monetary success. But that drive is said to be uniform throughout society, so that criminals do not experience it more strongly than noncriminals (Merton 1957, pp. 132–39). This variable drive explains the overall *rate* of crime in American society, but not the *distribution* of crime within that society (Bernard 1987a). The distribution of crime is explained by the distribution of legitimate opportunities in the social structure. This structures the individual's choices but does not drive him or her to crime (Cullen 1983, pp. 83–87; Stinchcombe 1975, p. 12). Individuals in some social locations are likely to choose crime because, given the lack of legitimate opportunities, crime is more efficient at achieving the cultural goal of monetary success.

Merton's theory therefore explains the relation between structure, interests, and actions in terms of the relative costs and benefits of available courses of actions and the tendency to choose actions that are more beneficial and less costly. Hirschi's theory explains that relation the same way.

Attachment operates in Hirschi's theory at Axiom 2 as a mediating variable between interests and actions: it causes the individual to consider other interests besides his or her own in choosing actions. This is the same place in which human nature operates in Hirschi's theory, so that attachments 'restrain' the individual from pursuing the 'natural' course of pure self-interest. Commitment, however, operates at Axiom 1 between social structure and interests: after weighing all the costs and benefits of available courses of action, people with high commitment find that their interests are best pursued through legal acts, while people with low commitment find that their interests are best pursued through criminal acts. Both sets of people then pursue their pure self-interest.

Commitment therefore operates through the structuring of interests—i.e., it assumes a constant tendency to seek self-interest and variation in the structural distribution of interests (Bernard 1987c). This is the same explanation found in Merton's theory.

Finally, in Akers' (1985) theory, individuals are neither driven nor restrained—they merely respond to the contingencies of socially structured reinforcements and punishments. This is a more scientific way of saying that people tend to act in ways that are consistent with their socially structured interests, which is the same explanation found in Merton's and Hirschi's theories.

There are three additional disagreements between Hirschi's and Merton's theories: (1) Merton's definition of interests in narrow, Hirschi's broad; (2) Hirschi's mediating variable between interests and actions is human nature, while Merton's is culture; and (3) the mediating variable between structure and interests in Hirschi's theory is academic competence, while in Merton's it is social class. Akers' theory is not discussed here, since his arguments are broad enough to encompass both Hirschi's and Merton's arguments on these three points.

The first difference is straightforward: Merton's narrower argument about monetary success is a special case within Hirschi's broader argument about commitment. Hirschi argues that people who find it in their interests to pursue monetary success by legitimate means (high commitment) will tend to do so, while Merton argues that those who find it in their interest to pursue monetary success by illegitimate means (i.e., low commitment) will also tend to do so.

The second difference is more substantive and concerns the mediating variable between interests and actions. At that point the two theories make contrasting theoretical arguments that can be resolved only through empirical research. The present methodology, however, is to assume that each theory is wrong on the issue and examine the logical consequences for the rest of the theory. That is, I examine the consequences for Merton's theory of replacing his cultural argument with hirschi's view of human nature and the consequences for Hirschi's theory of replacing his view of human nature with Merton's culture argument.

The difference between these two theories is sometimes described in terms of a variable vs. a constant drive to crime (e.g., Kornhauser 1978).

However, within any given culture, the cultural drive to crime in Merton's theory is a constant, because of cultural uniformity. Both theories therefore propose constant drives to crime within a given culture. The difference is that Merton proposes cross-cultural variation in this drive because the drive is rooted in culture, while Hirschi's proposes cross-cultural uniformity because the drive is rooted in nature. That question can be settled by cross-cultural research on whether there is variation in the valuation of monetary success and, if so, whether that variation is correlated with variations in overall crime rates (Bernard 1987a).

If Merton's theory were supported, then Hirschi's theory about human nature would be falsified. However, that would not affect any of Hirschi's predictions about how attachments, involvements, commitments, or beliefs operate *within cultures*. That is, Hirschi's entire control theory would stand as an explanation of the distribution of crime within cultures, but an additional source of variation would have to be introduced to account for differences in the overall rate of crime between cultures. If, on the other hand, research demonstrated cross-cultural uniformity in the drive to crime, Merton's cultural argument would be falsified. However, the structural argument linking the distribution of crime to the distribution of legitimate opportunities within cultures would be unaffected.

The culture–nature controversy affects only cross-cultural predictions, not within-cultural predictions. Within cultures, both theories propose a constant drive to crime, and each constant drive can replace the other without affecting the rest of the theory. Both theories therefore can incorporate discrepant empirical findings on this issue without being totally falsified. To that extent, the culture–nature controversy does not prevent theoretical integration and can be set aside pending the outcome of empirical research.

The third disagreement is whether the mediating variable between structure and interests is socioeconomic class or academic competence. As mentioned above, academic competence is not explicitly contained in Hirschi's theory as a mediating variable, although it is generally consistent with Hirschi's work. Socioeconomic class, on the other hand, is not inconsistent with Hirschi's theory at this point—in fact, Hirschi cites earlier theorists who explicitly describe commitment as related to class position. The relation for Hirschi is empirical rather than theoretical—his theory does not exclude class, he simply fails to find it in his research. If future research did find such a relationship, it could be incorporated into Hirschi's theory. Thus, the prediction about academic competence is incidental rather than essential to Hirschi's theory.

The prediction about class in Merton's theory is also incidental, not essential, since class does not have a direct causal role in Merton's explanation of crime (see Bernard 1987a). The causal mechanism in Merton's theory lies in the distribution of legitimate opportunities. Class is said to be directly related to the distribution of legitimate opportunities, but there is no causal role for class itself. If research showed the distribution of legitimate opportunities to be related to academic competence but not to class, Merton's theory could incorporate this finding and retain all its causal arguments about the relationship between crime and the distribution of legitimate opportunities. Thus, both theories can incorporate discrepant empirical findings on this issue without being completely falsified. The class vs. academic competence disagreement does not prevent integration, and can be set aside pending the results of empirical research.

Finally, one can ask how people experience what Hirschi calls lack of commitment and what Merton calls the absence of legitimate opportunities. Do they experience it as freedom, as suggested by Hirschi's theory, or as stress, as (possibly) implied by Merton's? Merton's theory actually makes no predictions about this question (Bernard 1987b). Hirschi's theory does not make an essential prediction (i.e., one that, if proved wrong, would falsify the theory). This is an interesting question but it has no implications for falsifying either theory. On the other hand, both theories spring from Durkheim's (1951) argument that individuals who are free from social controls tend to commit suicide. Freedom is not necessarily a happy state—perhaps freedom and stress are experienced at the same time.

The Second Causal Argument: The Role of Values

In addition to a direct link from structure to interests to actions in criminology theories, there is a second link, mediated through values. The term 'values' is *not* used in Kornhauser's (1978, p. 6) sense, to refer only to "those symbols by means of which a people apprehend and endow experience with ultimate human significance." Rather, it is used more generally to refer to shared ideas, attitudes, orientations, and beliefs that contain moral evaluations of actions in the context of situations—in these circumstances, those acts are good, right, appropriate, justified, or at least excusable, or they are bad, wrong, inappropriate, unjustified, and inexcusable. Values, as defined here, encompass a wide set of diverse ideas in any social group, whereas in Kornhauser's definition they are restricted to a much narrower and more uniform set of ideas.

The second causal argument is as follows:

```
Social     (+)            (+)         (+)
         ─────── Interests ─────── Values ─────── Actions
Structure  Axiom 1         Axiom 3     Axiom 4
```

Axiom 3 states that values vary directly with interests. This is interpreted to mean that there is a tendency for people to believe that actions that benefit them personally are good, right, appropriate, justified, or at least excusable under the circumstances, and also for them to believe that actions that harm them personally are bad, wrong, inappropriate, unjustified, and inexcusable under the circumstances.[10] Interests are not the sole determinant of values, but a positive relation is said to exist between the two constructs. Axiom 4 then states that values achieve an independent effect on actions—people's actions are influenced by what they *think* is good, right, appropriate, and so forth, as well as by what benefits or harms them personally.

This second causal argument is consistent with Hirschi's (1969), Akers' (1985), Cohen's (1955) and Cloward and Ohlin's (1960) theories. However, it is not found in Merton's (1968) theory, where cultural values are said to be uniform and independent of structure.

The second causal argument is most easily found in Akers' theory, where evaluative beliefs are said to be a product of differential reinforcements (1985, pp. 48–51). Those beliefs then are said to independently affect action:

```
Social     (+)                   (+)               (+)
         ─────── Differential   ─────── Evaluative ─────── Actions
Structure         Reinforcements         Beliefs
```

The second causal argument is also found in Cohen's (1955) and Cloward and Ohlin's (1960) theories, since both describes a causal sequence that moves from a structural situation to some aspect of objective interests to some aspect of evaluative beliefs to actions. In Cohen's theory, the "culture" of the gang is a set of shared evaluative beliefs that evolves in response to problems of low status youth. Gang youths adopt these beliefs because it is in their *interests* to do so[11]—they can then endow each other with status that is unavailable to them in the context of conventional values. The beliefs then affect actions independent of the direct effects of social structure:

Social   (+)   No access to   (+)   Inverted   (+)
Structure ─────   legitimate   ──────   status   ─────   Actions
            class   status   reaction criteria
                                 formation

Cloward and Ohlin's theory has a similar organization. In their theory, structural situation limits access to legitimate means to acquire money and provides access to illegitimate means. Subcultural delinquents respond by withdrawing legitimacy from conventional norms and by acquiring norms that justify criminal actions. Those beliefs then affect their actions independent of the direct effect of structure:

                                         criminal,
Social   (+)   differential   (+)   conflict, or (+)
Structure ─────   opportunity   ─────   retreatist ─────   Actions
                                          values

Statements consistent with the second causal argument also appear throughout Hirschi's discussion of beliefs. Conventional beliefs are said to be differentially reinforced by parents, but "whether these definitions are accepted depends upon the extent to which they are congruent with the person's attitudes and experience vis-a-vis conventional society" (1969, p. 200). Thus, beliefs are linked to the structural location of the youth, although this may not be the same as that of the parent (cf. Hirschi 1969, p. 82). Belief in the moral validity of law is consistently related to measures of commitment (p. 203) but commitment, as discussed above, is defined by interests. Thus Hirschi's data on conventional beliefs is consistent with the second causal argument. Definitions favorable to violation of the law "often reflect the absence of stakes in conformity," and those definitions "affect delinquency in their own right" (p. 203). That is consistent with the above model in that interests (i.e., absence of stakes in conformity) affect behavior directly while beliefs derived from interests have an independent effect. In Hirschi's (1969, p. 208) opinion, delinquent acts come before "neutralizing" beliefs rather than after, as proposed by Sykes and Matza (1957). Again, this position is consistent with the second causal argument, since it is in the youth's *interests* to develop and hold these beliefs. Hirschi (1969) also provides a "noncultural explanation" for lower class beliefs:

> The issue is whether acceptance of (lower class) beliefs is rooted in culture or social structure, whether the feeling that one is powerless

arises from objective powerlessness or is transmitted by one's culture, regardless of one's power in some objective sense. (p. 219)

Hirschi finds that the lack of academic competence, rather than class position, determines adherence to lower class beliefs. Thus he concludes that these beliefs are not "cultural" (1969):

> The ease with which middle class children absorb "lower-class" beliefs, and the ease with which they are discarded or ignored by lower-class children forces us to conclude that if "lower-class" culture is "many centuries old," it is only because powerlessness and deprivation are older. If they were to disappear, lower-class culture would quickly die. And there would be no one to mourn its passing. (p. 223)

All of this is consistent with the second causal argument:

$$\text{Social Structure} \xrightarrow[\text{Low Adademic Competence}]{(+)} \text{Interests} \xrightarrow{(+)} \text{Lower class values} \xrightarrow{(+)} \text{Actions}$$

Various criminology theories therefore make the same prediction for the same reason. As with the first causal argument, there remain differences among the component theories. The second causal argument is inconsistent with Merton's view that cultural values are uniform and unrelated to structural position. Cultural uniformity has been regarded as a weak point in Merton's theory (e.g., Lemert 1964), so this inconsistency may not compromise the utility of the model for integration. In a related difference, the second causal argument is inconsistent with a pure 'cultural deviance' theory in which criminal acts are said to represent conformity to criminal values in a deviant subculture, where the subculture is independent of structure (Kornhauser 1978). However, the concept of 'cultural deviance' distorts the theories placed in this category, and I believe that there are no 'cultural deviance' theories in criminology with the possible exception of Sellin's (1938) culture conflict theory (see Vold and Bernard, 1986, pp. 214–19, 227–29). Thus, I do not believe this inconsistency is relevant to the integration of criminology theories.[12]

Second, assuming structural sources for beliefs, there is a related issue about the length of time for which beliefs can persist after the structural conditions generating those beliefs have disappeared. Hirschi appears to hold that the beliefs have virtually no persistence if the structural conditions disappear, Curtis (1975) suggests a somewhat longer persistence, Shaw and McKay's (1942) work could be interpreted as suggesting a transition period of two generations, and Wolfgang and Ferracuti (1981) suggest an even longer historical persistence. This controversy does not challenge the assertion that all of the theories contain the second causal argument. Thus the controversy does not prevent integration and can be set aside pending the outcome of future research.

Third, the second causal argument does not incorporate the role of associates in forming or transmitting values. Hirschi suggests that there is no transmission of criminal values. Curtis (1975) and Liebow (1967) suggest that individuals in similar structural locations derive similar beliefs from their similar experiences and mutually support and reinforce the beliefs among themselves. Cohen (1955) and Cloward and Ohlin (1960) add that individuals in other structural situations can be socialized into criminal or delinquent values under some circumstances. Sutherland and Cressey (1978, pp. 77–97) emphasize the role of associates but acknowledge the structural sources of the beliefs in question (1978, pp. 99–116). Again, this controversy does not challenge the assertion that each theory contains the second causal argument, and thus the controversy does not prevent integration and can be set aside pending the results of future research.

A Theory of Action

Two causal arguments have been derived from the five component theories and can be combined in a single 'theory of action':

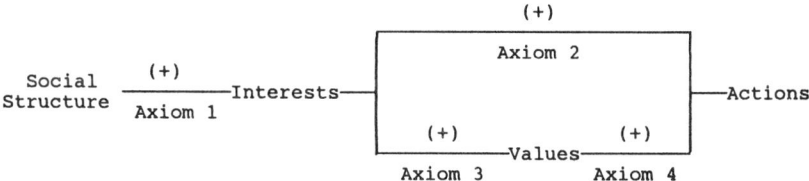

Although the specifics in the component theories differ, in general the theory of action holds that people in some structural situations find it in their interests to break the law, while people in other structural situations find it in their interests to obey the law (Axiom 1). Both sets of people tend to act in ways that are consistent with their interests (Axiom 2). Both sets of people also tend to believe that their actions are good, right, appropriate, justified, or at least excusable under the circumstances, as part of the general tendency for people's evaluative beliefs to conform to their interests (Axiom 3). The values have an independent effect on actions (Axiom 4).

Simply put, the theory of action states that *people tend to think and act in ways that are consistent with their socially structured interests.* As a macro theory, the theory of action asserts an aggregate relation between structural characteristics and the rates and distributions of actions and beliefs, and does not assert a strong relation between the actions of individuals and their structural situations. The five component theories from which the theory of action is derived use it to explain criminal actions. An integrated theory of criminal action can be achieved by determining the relation each component theory has to the theory of action, thereby establishing the relation each theory has to each other.

Integrating Conflict Criminology

As phrased above, the theory of action is not limited to the explanation of criminal actions but can also be used to explain other types of actions by socially situated people. Vold and Bernard (1986, pp. 286–97) use the same theory of action to explain the actions by which the criminal law is enacted and enforced. Specifically, the theory of action is used to explain the actions of legislators who enact criminal laws, criminal justice agents who enforce those laws, and individuals and groups who influence the enactment and enforcement of criminal laws through the political process. Vold and Bernard's theory can be integrated with the five component theories if the theory of action is appropriate for explaining these actions as well as criminal actions.

The Social or Public Reaction to Crime

There are conflicts of interests in every society, some of which are resolved by enacting and enforcing criminal laws. Some conflicts are resolved in ways that increase overall benefits, but the resolution inevitably apportions more benefits to some people and more costs to others. Other solutions are zero-sum, in which benefits for some are achieved only at equal costs to others.

The theory of action predicts that people in different structural situations have different personal interests in relation to criminal law. It also predicts that when they attempt to influence the enactment and enforcement of criminal laws, people tend to do so in ways that maximize their personal benefits and minimize their personal costs, even when broader societal costs and benefits differ from their own personal costs and benefits. As a macro theory, the theory of action predicts that this tendency is sufficient to produce aggregate rates and distributions of actions, although it may be a weak predictor of individual action.

The theory also predicts that individuals and groups tend to develop values consistent with their interests that independently affect actions. In this instance the values concern beliefs about crime: which actions are appropriately considered serious crimes, which trivial crimes, and which legal behaviors. People should tend to view as serious crimes those actions that decrease personal benefits or increase personal costs, and should tend to view as legal or as only trivial crimes those actions that increase personal benefits or decrease personal costs. This tendency should be sufficient to produce rates and distributions of values, although it may be a weak predictor of individual values.

The Enactment of Criminal Laws

In all political systems, legislators who enact criminal laws have personal interests—they are dependent on people in society in proportion to the political and economic power those people have. In general, the benefits of supporting and the costs of opposing a set of values and interests are proportional to the political and economic power of the people who hold those values and interests. The theory of action predicts that these personal interests of legislators directly affect their actions, and that legislators also tend to develop values consistent with those interests that independently affect their actions. This influence should be measurable in various legislative outcomes, including the content of criminal law.

There is controversy about the extent of consensus or conflict on the content of criminal law—i.e., which actions are appropriately viewed as serious crimes, which as trivial crimes, and which as legal. The extent of this disagreement is a matter for empirical investigation. To the extent that people with different amounts of power hold different views on the content of criminal law, the theory of action predicts that legislators should tend to agree with the views of more powerful people and to develop values about criminal law that endorse and support those views. As a result, the criminal law should reflect the views of the more powerful when their views differ from the views of other groups, and exclude the views of the less powerful when their views differ from the views of other groups.

A final prediction can be inferred from the theory of action as applied to the public and to legislators. As applied to the public, the theory of action predicts that people tend to act in ways that are consistent with their personal interests and that they also tend to hold views on the content of criminal law consistent with those same interests. As applied to legislators, the theory of action predicts that criminal law tends to be consistent with the views of people in proportion to their political and economic power. Taken together, these predictions imply that, all other things being equal, there should be an inverse relation between power and the likelihood of violating the criminal law. Assuming everyone acts according to their interests, more powerful people would be expected to violate the criminal law less frequently because more of their interests are represented in the criminal law, while less powerful people would violate the criminal law more frequently because fewer of their interests are represented in the criminal law (Bernard, 1987c, pp. 418–20).

The Enforcement of Criminal Laws

Individuals who work in the criminal justice system have personal interests at stake when they make decisions about whether and how to process people who are thought to have violated criminal law. There often are clear personal and organizational costs and few and uncertain benefits to processing those who have large amounts of political or economic power. At the same time, there often are clear personal and organizational benefits and only few and uncertain costs for processing relatively powerless people (e.g., Wilson 1978). This means that it often is in the interests of criminal justice agents to process the relatively powerless and to avoid processing the relatively powerful.

The extent of differential processing in justice systems is a matter for empirical investigations. To the extent that differential processing exists, the theory of action predicts that criminal justice personnel will tend to process relatively powerless people and to avoid processing relatively powerful people. These agents will also tend to develop values consistent with their interests. That is, they will tend to view the types of offenses they most frequently process as more serious and thus more deserving of official action. They will also tend to view the types of offenses they do not process as less serious and not warranting official action. These values will independently affect their actions. As a macro prediction, this tendency should be sufficient to produce aggregate rates and distributions of actions, although it may be a weak predictor of individual action.[13]

Explaining Official Crime Rates

Official rates of deviance require separate explanation from the explanation of deviant actions (Kitsuse and Cicourel, 1963). If legislators, criminal justice agents, and individuals and groups in society all act in ways consistent with the theory of action, then an inverse relation exists between the distribution of power and the distribution of official crime rates. This inverse relation is predicted to exist after controlling for all other factors that might influence the distribution of official crime rates. The extent of this inverse relation can only be determined by empirical research.

No assertion is made that the distribution of power is the only factor influencing the distribution of official crime rates. Other factors, such as behavioral differences among the different social groups, may also affect that distribution. The theory of action predicts such differences since it argues that people in different structural situations respond to different interests. For example, it is consistent with the theory of action to predict that powerless people have high rates of individual violence (Bernard 1984). In general, powerlessness can be considered an antecedent variable in most criminology theories (Vold and Bernard 1986, pp. 294–95). Since the theory of action is derived from those theories, it is consistent with it to argue that crime (as defined in criminal law) is concentrated in low power groups.

Despite the controversy about whether poor people actually commit more crime (e.g., Tittle et al. 1978), the inverse relation between power and official crime rates is probably the most stable and widespread pattern known in the field of criminology. Nettler (1984, pp. 111–31), for example, reviewed a large number of studies and concluded:

> In every country that provides information about its crimes, official statistics of arrests, convictions, and imprisonment indicate a *negative* association, with varying degree, between these measures of crime and indicators of social position, like income and occupational prestige. Within each jurisdiction, people with less money, lower occupational status, and, note, less schooling and lower measured intelligence are disproportionately represented in official statistics on the serious crimes. These correlations have been consistent for at least this century. (p. 111)

The prediction of the theory therefore matches empirical reality. Although one cannot infer from this that the theory is valid (see above discussion of prediction vs. explanation), it is worth noting that the theory is quite parsimonious and the prediction extremely broad. The theory therefore may be a potentially fruitful area for future research.

If the theory of action were ultimately determined to be valid, then the inverse relation between power and official crime rates would be the expected distribution of official crime rates in all societies at all times. Deviations from the expected distribution would be explained by specific causal factors associated with the particular time, place, or group in question (Bernard, 1985). Thus, the relation between power and official crime rates would function as a constant (like the speed of light in relativity theory) on which other theory and research would be based.

A Theory of Crime

The coordinated explanation of criminal actions, official reactions, and official crime rates is described as a "theory of crime" (cf. Vold and Bernard 1986, pp. 286–87):

The theory of crime provides a framework within which the arguments of various criminology theories can be arranged in order to systematically examine the controversies among them. It also makes various aggregate predictions derived from those theories, although it does not make individual-level predictions. In general, the theory argues that socially structured interests are an antecedent variable in explanations of criminal actions and official reactions (see Bernard 1987c, pp. 421–23). If this argument is invalid or inadequate for meaningful theory construction, then so are the various criminology theories from which it has been derived.

Integrating Other Criminology Theories

Other types of criminology theories can be integrated by considering their relation to the theory of action and the theory of crime, thus establishing their relations to each other. Classical criminology, for example, assumes a direct link between interests to actions via human nature, much like the argument in Hirschi's theory at Axiom 2. It then focuses on Axiom 1 linking structure to interests, arguing that interests can be affected by criminal justice policies such as the certainty, severity, and swiftness of punishments. Because of the direct link at Axiom 2, these policies are supposed to result in changes in people's acts.

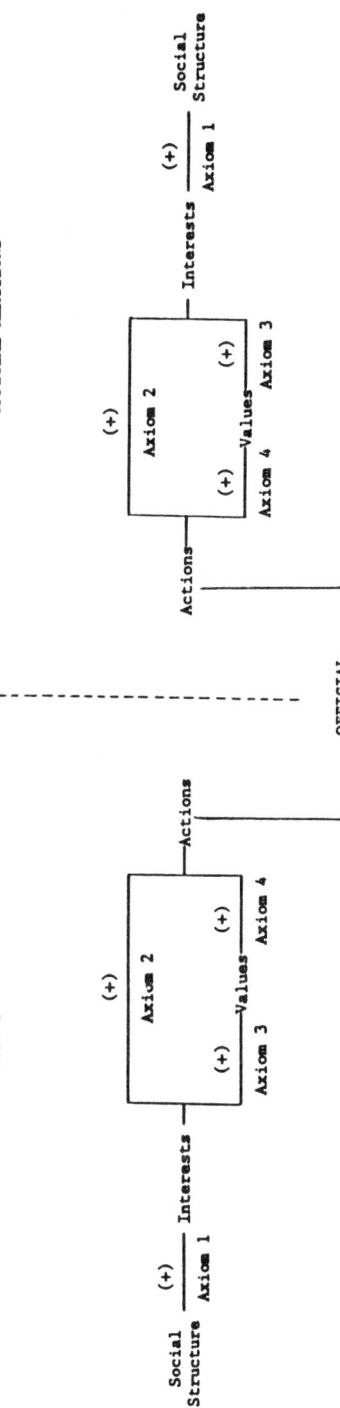

Figure 10.1. A theory of crime

Biological and psychological theories describe variations in the way individuals respond to socially structured interests—i.e., they mediate the link between interests and actions at Axiom 2, where they are placed by Akers. Those who question the relevance of biological and psychological variables essentially assert an invariant 'human nature' at this point, as described by Hirschi.

At least some Marxist theories view criminal behavior as the rational actions of rational individuals in situations structured by the social relations of capitalism. The theory of action is consistent with this view if structure is defined in terms of capitalist social relations. The theory of action is also consistent with Marxist views of the criminal law enactment and enforcement process if interests are defined in terms of economic interests and power in terms of ownership of the means of production. Finally, the idea that values tend to be consistent with structured interests was originally proposed by Marx. This basic argument can be combined with a historical view of the evolution of criminal law to reach a Marxist argument about the role of ideology.

The theory of action is also consistent with the three components of labeling theory (Gibbs 1985). First, it is consistent with a reactive conception of deviance as a theoretical argument, but only as applied to official rates (cf. Gibbs 1981, pp. 31–32). Second, it makes an empirical assertion that societal reaction is determined in part by an extralegal characteristic (power). Third, the model can be interpreted in a way that is consistent with a theory of secondary deviance. A person develops a deviant self-concept in order to reevaluate behaviors that the person both engages in and disvalues. That is, the function of the deviant self-concept is to embody a new set of values where the old set was out of line with the person's actions. In that sense, the tendency to develop a deviant self-concept is one aspect of the more general tendency for values to come into line with interests. That new self-concept then achieves an independent effect on actions in secondary deviation.

Finally, the recent 'routine activities' (Cohen and Felson 1979) and 'rational choice' theories (e.g., Cornish and Clarke 1986, 1987) both assume that people act in accordance with their interests, as described by Axiom 2. The rational choice theorists introduce various modifications such as limited rationality and cognitive ability, and then focus on the various properties of offenses that structure the offender's choices. The routine activities theorists argue that recent structural characteristics of modern societies, combined with the tendency toward self-interested action, are sufficient to explain recent changes in crime rates without reference to other factors. Neither approach includes a value component, but both appear to be compatible with the first causal argument that links structure to interests to actions.

Conclusion

The theory of action is somewhat insulting because it depicts people as pursuing their own interests and as holding values that, consciously or not, are a cover for those interests. We describe criminals in this way in various criminology theories, but in this paper the same insulting theory is applied to the rest of us.

Do we law-abiding folks really tend to rationally pursue our self-interest in everyday life, much as we describe criminals when they commit crime? Evidence on that issue is extensive and contradictory, but there is at least some merit in the argument (Etzioni 1987; Frank 1987). Do we, like the criminals we describe in our theories, have a tendency to think that the actions that benefit us personally are good and right and just and appropriate or at least excusable under the circumstances? Less evidence is available on that direct question, but it is consistent with several bodies of theory and research. In general, the sociology of knowledge links ideas to their social context, and related historical analyses have demonstrated the relation between crime-related values and the personal interests of socially situated people (e.g., Foucault 1977).

Historical analysis provides a distance that makes this relation more visible. Much harder to see would be the same relation in ourselves, if it perchance existed. However, a tendency to bring values into line with interests would be consistent with research on cognitive dissonance, since, when values and interest conflict, values can be readily changed because they are ideas. Interests, in contrast, often are determined by structural situations that are beyond the control of the individual.

By sticking to the macro level, I avoid making predictions about individual actions. That reduces the pressure to explain everything that can drive theories towards tautology. The point at which the theory would be most susceptible to tautology is the linkage between structure and interests, since that linkage is described as "objective" rather than subjective. Nevertheless, the widespread utilization of this linkage in existing criminology theories suggests that, with care in operational definitions, tautology can be avoided (cf. Burgess and Akers, 1966).

11

Prospects for Synthetic Theory: A Consideration of Macro-Level Criminological Activity

Charles R. Tittle

The feasibility of theoretical integration depends largely upon how criminologists define and carry out their task. There is disagreement about an appropriate philosophy of the enterprise of criminology, with many embracing approaches that contradict efforts at synthetic theory building. Even among those who endorse a favorable philosophy, diversity in operating principles hinders development of integrated theories.

A Favorable Philosophy of the Enterprise

Criminologists are guided by four more or less distinct philosophies of work. One of those philosophies gives a central place to theory building and conceives of theoretical integration as the main means to that end, while the other three either deny the relevance of general theory, recognize such relevance but disparage its achievement, or ignore theory completely.

The philosophy I call 'theoretical science' mandates synthetic theory (cf. Braithwaite 1960). Its goal is to account for the phenomena within its domain in a way that is intellectually satisfying to a critical audience of fellow theoretical scientists. 'Account for' means that an intellectual structure has been constructed which contains the necessary ideas, concepts, and specifications of interconnections among them to provide explanations for the phenomena of interest. That is, theories permit understanding of how things within given domains 'work.' They are the ultimate objective of scholarship because they answer questions about how and why.

Theories are constructed so as to permit derivation of predictions about the phenomena of interest and about other phenomena that may not be of immediate concern but can nevertheless be subsumed under the general premises of the theory. A good theory permits specification of expected interconnections among variables in a concrete situation by applying the reasoning or premises of the general, abstract scheme. Such predictions are of the form "if A, then B"; e.g., if some variable changes in a particular way, one expects corresponding variations in some other variable(s) under specified conditions. The ideal expression of "if, then" predictions are causal statements: A causes B; if A changes, so will B, even when all other potential antecedent influences are controlled; under stipulated conditions an X change in A leads to Y amounts of B within a time period of Z, etc. Deriving potentially negatable predictions enables scholars to empirically test the adequacy of a theory. Without such capability, ideas cannot be reconciled with the real world (Gibbs 1985).

Since theories are composed of constructs and abstractions (Willer and Webster 1970) they are necessarily general. Explanations, on the other hand, are specific; they answer the questions of why and how for a limited phenomenon using concrete, empirically observable variables. Theories are stated abstractly because they must encompass many explanations of different phenomena. The process of theoretical science involves eight steps: (1) observing and identifying empirical regularities; (2) tying observations of empirical regularities together into explanations; (3) deriving specific predictions (hypotheses) from the explanations so developed, and putting them to empirical test; feeding the results back to evaluate and modify the explanations; (4) tying various explanations of different phenomena together into abstract theories; (5) deducing explanations of various phenomena from the general theories so formed; (6) deriving predictions that can be stated in empirical terms (hypotheses) from these derived explanations; (7) testing the empirical fit of the derived hypotheses and using the results to evaluate and modify the derived revised explanations; and finally (8) modifying the theory to take account of the revised explanations. This process goes on until as many phenomena as possible have been incorporated under one theoretical umbrella and scholars have convinced themselves through empirical test that the structure is consistent with reality.

The main objective of the enterprise, then, is to build general theories; i.e., to encompass observations of specific phenomena into explanatory schemes subsumed within larger, more general theories that satisfactorily answer questions of how and why posed by critical scholars and can be shown to yield empirically correct predictions (Freese 1972a,b). Hence, theoretical science *requires* integration (Glaser 1980). And since the enterprise is based on interplay between theory and research, it follows that general theory cumulates from the theoretical and empirical work of all criminologists.

Synthetic theories have many practical advantages over explanations of specific phenomena and over theory fragments. They account for more phenomena; they are more complete, thereby providing greater satisfaction that we understand things; and they are more flexible and revealing, since things can be explained that may not even have been imagined by those who set forth the specific explanations or theory fragments of which general theories are composed. Moreover, theories are more efficient, because newcomers who get interested in some phenomenon do not have to begin from scratch to achieve explanation, and they are more readily testable since generality permits use of data from many contexts.

An Illustration

So far, few attempts at theoretical synthesis have been undertaken (for exceptions see Elliott 1985), especially at the macro level (Bennett 1980). In fact, despite the strong Durkheimian tradition in criminology (Liska 1987; Vold and Bernard 1986), efforts to account for crime-relevant system or group features using system or group concepts or variables are relatively uncommon. Nevertheless, there are some macro explanations that we could begin to synthesize.

Synthesis requires three technical operations: (1) conceiving of concepts in existing theories or theory fragments as instances of more encompassing abstract constructs (Hage 1972; Wagner and Berger 1985; Willer and Webster 1970); (2) organizing abstract concepts around unifying explanatory principles (Braithwaite 1960; Glaser 1980; Wagner and Berger 1985); and (3) conceptualizing variations or deviations from the main patterns as contingencies (scope conditions—Walker and Cohen 1985) to be covered by specifying conditions (higher order theories—Gibbs 1972) under which the unifying principles apply with greater or less force (Bennett 1980; Cullen 1984). With these operations, seemingly disparate theory fragments can be subsumed, or integrated, within a general theory.

These procedures can be illustrated using three explanations, or theory fragments, originally designed to explain why particular social groupings display unusually high deviance and crime rates: (1) Shaw and McKay's community/ecological explanation of delinquency (1969), (2) Wirth's theory of urbanism as it applies to crime and deviance (1938; Clinard and Meier 1979), and (3) Friday and Hage's explanation of youth crime in industrial societies (1976). This example of how to begin a synthetic theory is not complete or refined and is intended only to show the operations to be used.

The Community/Ecological Explanation. The ideas of the Chicago ecological tradition are not fully and coherently articulated, but one version, the statement by Shaw and McKay in *Juvenile Delinquency and Urban Areas* (1969), does present a meaningful account of why low-income inner-city areas in the United States have high rates of delinquency. The main argument is that economic and environmental factors combine to produce two features of social life conducive to criminal or delinquent behavior—poor social integration (resulting in unconventional role modeling and the absence or ineffectiveness of social control) and a large number of people with a strong motive to commit crime (stemming from economic deprivation).

Physical deterioration and economic depression in an area are said to produce low-rent incentives that attract poorer people. These two preexisting conditions cause population instability, because residents remain only until they acquire the means to move. Population instability, in turn, causes heterogeneity, making community integration difficult. Weak community integration precludes effective social control and makes it difficult to exclude individuals, organizations, or activities that represent alternative (unconventional or law-violating) lifestyles. Along with this, the economic deprivation of the residents of such areas produces strong incentives for illegal or unconventional behavior. Absence of social control and the influences of successful criminal or unconventional role models, therefore, lead to high rates of deviance.

While this account is often referred to as a "theory," it is really an explanation. It attempts to answer the question of "why" (are the delinquency rates high) in a specific situation with concrete variables. But it could be conceived as a more general account, applying to whole societies or other social groupings. Thus: *any* society or social grouping with a heterogeneous population and high residential instability will be poorly integrated. Members of such societies will have difficulty developing a sense of common destiny, a spirit of collective identity, and a feeling of social responsibility toward each other. It will be hard for them to cooperate to solve common problems and to agree about appropriate conduct. These conditions, will, in turn, prevent mutual surveillance, community action, and collective reaction to misbehavior.

Urbanism. While Shaw and McKay focused on features of a specific social situation with poor integration, linking them to environmental and economic factors, another scholar in the same tradition (Wirth 1938—but see also Park 1969 and Simmel 1969), formulated a more comprehensive account of why deviance (like other "pathological" conditions) varies by size, density, and heterogeneity of the population. Wirth explains the general effects of urban living on crime and deviance regardless of the degree of deterioration and economic depression (Fischer 1985; Shevky and Bell 1955).

Since cities bring large numbers of unlike people together in a small space, interaction produces social relationships characterized by extensive normative conflict, high mobility, emphasis on material or symbolic phenomena, weakened intimate communication, and release from social controls (especially informal ones). The reasons for these outcomes are succinctly summarized in the Shevky/Bell description, but the focus here is on the main ideas. Urban dwellers are motivated to crime by the need to acquire symbols of status, they are shown how to pursue such ends by the plethora of deviant role models attracted to and generated by cities, and they are free to deviate because social control is weak. In other words, urban living, like deterioration and economic depression, makes social integration unlikely, and low social integration leads to the other features. In addition, city life presumably motivates crime and deviance by creating a need for individuals to acquire and display status symbols.

This specific explanation of high deviance rates in urban areas can also be reconceived as a general theory accounting for differences in rates of crime or deviance *across* societies or other social groupings. Perhaps any collectivity with large concentrations of unlike people in limited space will experience poor social integraton. That is, the members of such societies will not easily develop a "we" feeling, they will readily change residence and break whatever tenuous ties they have to each other, they will be insensitive to personal or collective opinions, and the resulting lack of cohesion will permit an abundance of deviant role models. Moreover, this pervasive condition of social "looseness" will add a premium to symbolically oriented relationships and give incentives to the pursuit of status criteria through deviant behavior.

Hence the theory resulting from a larger conceptualization of the urbanism explanation is similar to the theory arising from a larger conceptualization of the community/ecological explanation of high deviancy rates in inner city areas—both focus on the same key idea. Each portrays a set of interrelated phenomena, collectively constituting the concept of "social integration," which is linked to crime/deviance because poor integration permits deviant behavior to occur. However, the theories differ in two important ways: (1) they specify different conditions that affect the degree of social integration, with the ecological scheme stressing physical deterioration and economic depression and the urbanism formulation stressing size, density, and heterogeneity; and (2) they differ in specification of the sources of enhanced deviant motivation, with the ecological/community explanation favoring economic deprivation and the urbanism account touting pursuit of symbols.

Youth Crime in Modern Societies. Friday and Hage's explanation of delinquency in industrialized societies (1976) also involves the key concept of social integration, but with a slightly different meaning. They contend that conformity will be greatest among youth drawn into intermeshed role relationships across five institutional spheres: kin, neighborhood or community, school, work, and peers. The more that activities and time are dispersed across the five spheres, the more likely the youth is to avoid deviant behavior, and the greater the proportion of youth in a society so immersed, the lower the rate of youth crime. Youth who are involved in one or another sphere to the exclusion of the others are more likely to deviate than integrated youth, because intimacy in many spheres promotes commitment to societal values and norms by exposing the youth to larger numbers of conforming definitions and by imbuing him or her with a sense of being part of the whole. No one sphere, even if deviant, can become too important, because the other spheres counterbalance (cf. Lyerly and Skipper 1981).

Further, Friday and Hage contend that the degree of social integration, so conceived, is affected by the level of modernization and urbanization. The more modernized and urbanized a society, the more are youth isolated from active participation in at least some of the five institutional spheres, due to extension of the period of training for adult roles. Most modern youth spend no time and have no involvement in the institutional sphere of work; partly as a result of that, they are limited in kin and community relationships. Since youth must rely upon role relationships in school or among peers, they are inherently less constrained by overlapping role relationships, and they are more subject to peer pressures for fun and status seeking, which often involve deviant or criminal behavior. Therefore, the greater the modernization and urbanization, the less the overall integration of youth, and the freer they are to commit criminal acts.

Generalizing this explanation, we would state that the greater the degree to which *any* population is integrated (involved in overlapping role relationships), the lower will be the rates of crime (because people will be exposed to more conforming definitions, will have a greater sense of being part of the whole, and will be more constrained by mutually reinforcing social controls). In addition, the degree of integration is determined by levels of modernization and urbanization which separate and disperse the institutional spheres geographically, socially, and temporally, thereby reducing aggregate numbers of overlapping role sets that can be participated in simultaneously.

Synthesis. All three theories emphasize social integration and related effectiveness of social controls. All place importance on population instability, movement, or dispersal as generators of social integration. Yet they differ in the specific generative concepts that drive the causal systems implied by the theories and they differ in the motive elements postulated. For Shaw and McKay the driving forces are economic (the chief motive element being deprivation), for Wirth they are demographic (motive is status seeking), and for Friday and Hage they are technological (at least this is one interpretation of modernization and urbanization), producing situational motives stemming from peer group pursuit of fun or status. And, of course, the three theories differ somewhat in the specified or implied interconnections of concepts. Nevertheless, it is possible to imagine a general formulation that subsumes the ideas and arguments of all three.

Abstraction. A synthetic theory of social integration could be begun by abstracting the concepts of the three theories to form seven more general ones: (1) social fluidity, (2) heterogeneity, (3) social integration, (4) tokenism, (5) social control, (6) exemplarism, and (7) deviation.

We could first abstract the concept of *social fluidity*, which would incorporate the ideas of change, movement, or dispersal. So conceived, it would refer to permanent realignments of individuals or population elements (such as rates of residential mobility or social mobility from one age or social category to another) or to continuous dynamics (such as commuting to work, taking shopping trips, or visiting recreational centers). Since it is abstract, it incorporates more limited ideas such as Shaw and McKay's residential turnover and Wirth's within-city daily movement, but it conveys more. In addition, it is quantitative: a social grouping can then be characterized by more or less social fluidity.

A second concept, *heterogeneity*, could be taken to mean differences in socially relevant characteristics, such as race, occupation, religion, age, language, attitudes, values, and income. It too could be regarded as quantitative, since any set of social groupings can be differentiated from each other by the various degrees of heterogeneity exhibited by each.

All three theories center on *social integration*, and although each conceives of it somewhat differently, all seem to convey the core idea of people in a collectivity feeling, or in fact being, part of a stable, larger, meaningful whole. Using the specific ideas of the three theories, integration might be thought of as having three separate aspects that might be quantified into one index: the extent to which people in a social grouping (1) base personal identity on psychological involvement in a coherent network of people (Wirth), (2) are, in fact, behaviorally involved and time-connected across all the various institutional spheres (Friday and Hage), and (3) are capable of collective action (Shaw and McKay).

A fourth concept, which we might call *tokenism*, could refer to the extent to which patterns of interaction in a social grouping or collectivity are so transitory that individuals must predict behavior and plan their responses mainly from clues provided by material symbols such as clothing, modes of transportation, uniforms, titles, jewelry, or other tangible factors. It is, of course, quantitative, since any social grouping will probably display at least some degree of tokenism while some will display a lot. Although this concept is associated with Wirth's formulation, it is potentially relevant to the other two as well, at least if they are thought of as variations of an integrated theme.

All three theories stress *social control*—the ability and willingness of the members of a social collectivity to influence other's conduct through actual or implied positive and negative sanctions. Social groupings can display different degrees of constraint due to mutual fear of sanctions.

The ideas of Shaw and McKay, as well as those of Wirth, implying that social contexts can be described by the degree to which important people engage in continuous deviant activities that benefit them without loss of prestige, suggest a concept to be called *exemplarism*.

Finally, *deviation* is a general construct referring to rates of behavior disapproved by most people in a social context or prohibited by legal authorities with jurisdiction or power in that context. It encompasses delinquency (behavior by youth disapproved by adults—Shaw and McKay), youth crime (illegal acts by young people—Friday and Hage), and social pathology (behavior that harms or shows indifference to the plight of other, bizarre or disoriented behavior, hedonism, and illegalities—Wirth), as well as other disapproved behavior.

Unification. The next step in theoretical synthesis is to unify abstract constructs around central explanatory principles (Hage 1972, pp. 148–155). This is done by identifying key processes suggested by the three theories. The general scheme might begin by stating that social integration and tokenism are fundamental characteristics of social systems that mutually but inversely affect each other. With sustained interaction, a social system will move toward integration and away from tokenism, unless other influences prevent such development. The potential preventive elements are social fluidity and heterogeneity. Social fluidity inhibits the process of interactive stabilization by constantly producing new interactants and new responses, thereby making tokenism necessary. In like manner, heterogeneity establishes barriers to identification and mutual trust, and it too hampers personal or intimate knowledge, rendering symbolic relationships more practical.

Hence, social integration is affected by social fluidity and heterogeneity (see Angell 1974; Crutchfield et al. 1982 for similar syntheses) and it in turn directly affects social control and indirectly influences exemplarism, because effective sanctioning is dependent upon how concerned the members of a collectivity are about the potential reactions of others and upon the ability of the collectivity to act in concert in imposing sanctions. Social integration, because it implies mutual feelings of identity and concern, becomes a major factor in determining whether potential sanctions can control behavior, and social integration itself determines whether people can act collectively to impose formal sanctions. The ability to control behavior through social control influences, in turn, the extent to which important people can continue to engage in and benefit from deviant behavior, just as it influences overall deviation. Logically, of course, exemplarism directly affects deviation.

Social integration also inversely affects tokenism. The less that people in a social collectivity feel a part of a whole and the less they are actually bound together in recurrent behavioral networks, the less they know about each other and the more they relate symbolically. By the same mechanisms, as tokenism increases in response to factors such as social fluidity or heterogeneity, the more it causes a reduction in social integration. This is because patterns of behavior built around anticipation of and response to external symbols reduce the probability that people will become intimate enough to take into account the character and history of potential interactants. That is, they will have difficulty establishing and maintaining mutual trust or in cooperating in collective action.

But just as social integration ripples out to influence other variables, ultimately including deviation, so does tokenism. It is likely to influence exemplarism directly because of the strong incentive it gives to status seeking through symbol acquisition and manipulation, thereby encouraging and making possible continued prestige and benefit to repeat offenders, and indirectly to influence deviation through exemplarism. It also is likely to generate deviation directly, for the same reasons.

These processes all imply causal effects. Figure 11.1 summarizes the internal causal structure of the synthetic theory.

Specifying Contingencies. The process presumably operating as the internal part of the theory could be conceived as quite general, applying to all social groupings. Any social collectivity can be characterized by the degree to which it is socially fluid or heterogeneous, and given varied degrees of these two factors we should expect corresponding amounts of social integration and so forth. But the general theory also encompasses specific explanations of high or low rates of deviance in any given collectivity, and provides explanations of rate variations across collectivities of a similar type. To use the theory for such explanation, one need only designate a set of 'social groupings' to which it applies.

If we, like Shaw and McKay, wanted to explain different delinquency rates among areas within cities, we would designate them as our

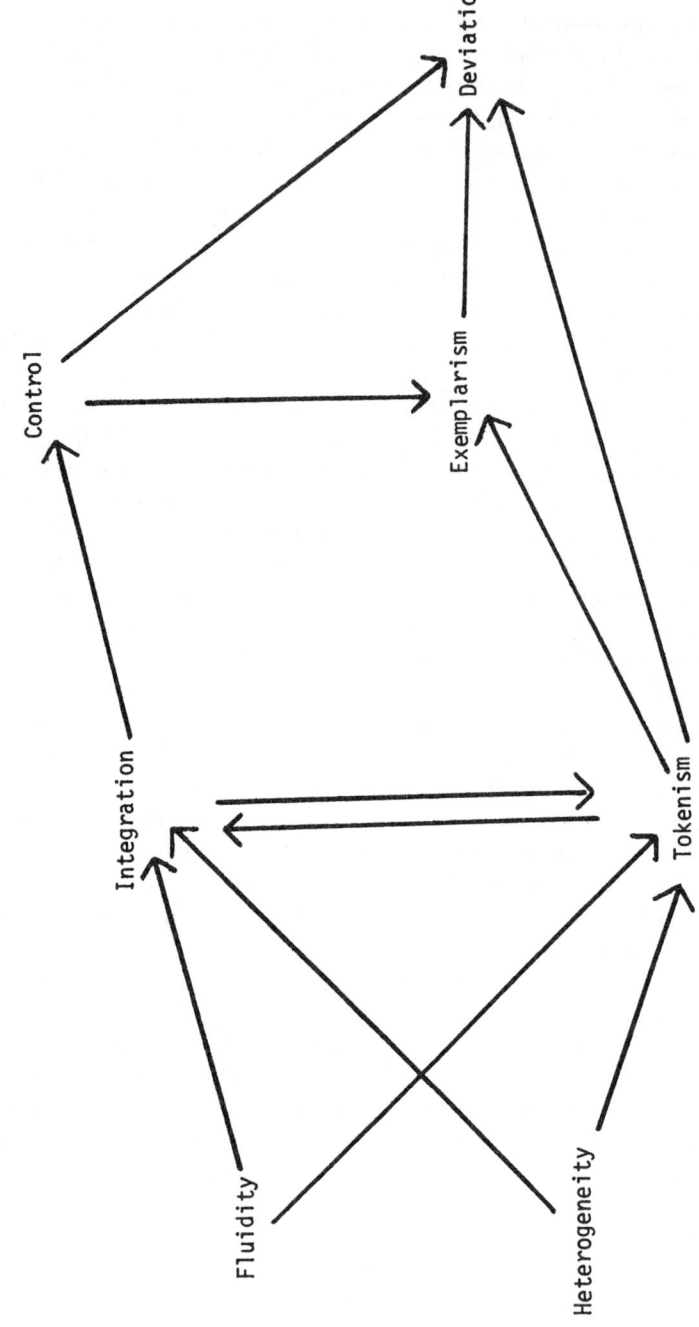

Figure 11.1. Internal structure of illustrative synthetic theory of social integration.

units, postulate that under certain conditions (such as economic stagnation) there will be extensive heterogeneity and social fluidity, and follow the flow of the theory to the outcome. If we were interested in rates of deviance across political entities in a specific society, or across societies, we would designate those as our social groupings and postulate that under certain conditions (size and density) these units will have different degrees of social fluidity and heterogeneity. And so on to explain youth crime rates among societies (like Friday and Hage) or even to account for variations in rates of deviance among other social groupings not envisioned by any of the original formulations. For instance, since the theory is general, it should apply as well to student misbehavior rates among schools.

Although the internal structure of the theory portrayed in Figure 11.1 applies to all social groupings, various ones may differ in the specific conditions that affect social fluidity and/or heterogeneity. The internal processes are predicated on particular contingencies characterizing different social groupings (Bennett 1980; Gibbs 1972; Walker and Cohen 1985). Those contingencies are not incorporated into this synthetic structure, although they might later be.

Testing. This illustrative synthetic theory and the explanations derived from it are, of course, purely intellectual products. They may be completely wrong as accounts of how the real world works. For theoretical science to be successful, intellectual products must be squared with reality. To do that, we translate the concepts into variables (measurement), state some predictions (hypotheses) suggested by the theory, and then check them out empirically. An advantage of a general formulation over a collection of specific explanations is that it permits numerous contexts to be used for testing. While there are only a limited number of whole societies, there are many cities, areas of cities, and schools.

For instance, we might focus on the theory's implication that social control affects deviation. We could derive numerous specific hypotheses such as: (1) the greater the percent of a school population that fears loss of reputation among peers for cheating, the lower will be the rate of cheating, or (2) the higher the probability of arrest in municipalities, the lower the rate of auto theft. Or we might look at the implication that social fluidity affects social integration and derive a multitude of specific hypotheses such as: (1) the greater the proportion of a city population that changes residence within a five year period, the less the likelihood that the city will provide for its poor, or (2) variations among areas in a city in the average distance travelled per day by its residents will affect rates of residential burglary (cf. Cohen and Felson 1979). And, of course, one could consider several of the postulates simultaneously, spelling out hypotheses about the interconnections of specific variables for specific kinds of social groupings, even perhaps empirically specifying the entire model portrayed in Figure 11.1.

Testing these single hypotheses, collections of hypotheses, or models will reveal the quality of the theory at any given time and will suggest how it needs to be modified for improvement. The greater the number of hypotheses upheld and the greater the strength of evidence in those cases where it is upheld, the more confidence we will have in the theory. But we will never completely prove its correctness, nor will we completely negate it. We will simply gain greater or less assurance as the evidence piles up and as we assess it in light of the logic of hypothesis derivation and the adequacy of empirical referents (Blalock 1969, pp. 151–154; Gibbs 1985). Meanwhile, the results of testing numerous hypotheses in many contexts will guide us in modifying the general theory to more accurately portray reality or in specifying the circumstances where the theory applies. Reciprocation between theory and research, therefore, must be continuous.

Continuing Synthesis. Even as hypothesis derivation, testing, and theoretical modification proceed, the business of synthesis must proceed as well if the goals of theoretical science are to be achieved. Clearly, this example of a synthetic theory does not encompass all ideas about why rates of deviance vary from social group to social group. Differential routine activities (Cohen and Felson 1979), subcultural formation stemming from achievement of "critical mass" (Fischer 1975), anomie (Merton 1968), and economic organization (Bonger 1969; Greenberg 1981) are but four lines of thought that provide alternative possibilities, yet it may be possible to synthesize them as well. The illustration does not even encompass all theory fragments about social integration per se (examples: Durkheim 1933, 1951; Gibbs 1964; Hirschi 1969), although, again, a larger synthesis might incorporate them. And it does not attempt to deal with other theory fragments about the effects of heterogeneity or fluidity (see Wolfgang 1968, for example). Moreover, this formulation may itself be subsumable within a still more general theory about social organization.

Theoretical science requires continual synthesis and integration. How far it can go is influenced by the collective skills, commitments, and organizational features of the criminological community (Tittle 1985). But it may also be influenced by the nature of the subject matter. Perhaps general, synthetic theories can only be developed within narrow domains. And it is conceivable that the social world will, in the final analysis, turn out to be so fragmented or incoherent that general theory, even within narrow domains, is impossible. But this cannot be judged until genuine efforts at theoretical science have proceeded for some time. Unfortunately, such work is rare. There appear to be two general reasons for this: (1) disagreement about operating principles of theoretical science and (2) dissension about the desirability of theoretical science for criminology.

Impediments to Theoretical Science

Disagreements about Operating Principles

Many social scientists and criminologists are committed to theoretical science, but they disagree about its essential features and/or how to do it. Two differences of opinion about operating principles are particularly important to the question of integration. One concerns the immutability of original ideas and the other has to do with empirical testing.

Immutability

Some believe that theories are essentially products of individual thought, and that they are to be preserved as sacred entities credited to their originators. To such theorists, a theory or explanation must be applied and evaluated in its own terms (Bernard 1986). For example, if Sutherland claimed that his theory of differential social organization ultimately explained rates of criminal behavior, then it would be a corruption to use it to explain non-criminal deviant behavior. Similarly, if he used the words "motives and drives" to describe some of the things that individuals learn from differentially associating with an excess of definitions favorable to crime, purists would regard attempts to operationalize the concept in terms of 'desires' to commit crime as wholly inappropriate. Moreover, if, in building theories, somebody borrows one element or idea from Sutherland while discarding the rest, critics will view it as vulgarization.

As admirable as it is to respect original ideas and to honor those who actually tried to make theories, immutability violates the spirit of theoretical science and almost guarantees that no synthesis will occur. The end result is a collection of incomplete, limited theory fragments or explanations. This is because more general, comprehensive, and accurate theories require abstraction and unification. One must grasp the underlying similarity of disparate-appearing ideas and express them in more generic terms, which are then unified by general explanatory principles. Successful theory building also rests upon a willingness to apply and test broader theoretical schemes in a variety of contexts not necessarily envisioned by the individual thinkers. Finally, the spirit of theoretical science mandates altering theories in light of the evidence. All of these processes directly contradict the idea of preserving original formulations.

As long as criminologists waste their time arguing about what Durkheim *really said* or meant, or whether a given piece of research is really consistent or inconsistent with what Merton *actually implied*, or if cases of "real" socialism exist to permit tests of Marxian ideas, then little progress will be made. It is only when we get beyond Durkheim, Merton, or Marx that we can truly begin to build theories. This does not mean we should ignore their ideas—integrated theories will most assuredly incorporate ideas of the masters, but the final product will not be identifiable as Merton's theory, Marx's formulation, or Durkheim's statement. It will be an amalgamation, indebted to the masters but not beholden to them. They will be credited, but will not be personally and directly accountable. Just as an automobile is more than a collection of parts separately invented or stimulated by individual engineers or scientists, so is a synthetic theory more than a bunch of separate parts. And it does no violence to the memory or integrity of Thomas Edison to use improved versions of several of his inventions in building automobiles.

Theory Testing. A second common practice destructive to theoretical synthesis is assuming that theories must be either wholly true or false. Standard procedure is to derive one or more hypotheses from a theory or explanation, collect data, test the hypothesis(es), and declare the theory right or wrong (see Elliott 1985). The weight of evidence over time will presumably allow one or more theories to 'win' while the others 'lose.' The putative ideal is to derive the hypothesis so carefully that a particular test will be crucial; that is, the hypothesis will capture the essence of the theory so thoroughly that the empirical outcome will prove the theory to be completely correct or incorrect. Actually, those who explore the implications of this approach usually maintain that a crucial test can never verify a theory, only falsify one (Vold and Bernard 1986).

This style of work is inappropriate except at the most advanced stages of theoretical development, where synthetic theories have been so tightly formulated that one can realistically imagine that they could be utterly true or false. Except for that most advanced synthetic product (which is yet to be developed), any theoretical formulation is best regarded as tentative. Empirical research is to test a current account and to guide *modification*, especially in pointing up the contingencies under which it applies (Cullen 1984). Theories must be deliberately adapted; 'natural' evolution won't work. In fact, a 'survival of the fittest' assumption inhibits creative theoretical work. It induces would-be theorists to qualify their arguments to the point of uselessness, to express their ideas in ambiguous terms so that they (or their followers) can escape criticism or negative evidence by claiming such and such was not really what they said or meant, or to set forth only limited explanations to avoid being wrong. This win or lose mentality intimidates most from theorizing at all, while fostering a disciplinary climate that regards theoretical adaptation in response to evidence as somehow 'fudging.'

Perhaps most important of all, the strategy cannot succeed. No actual theory or explanation, whether individually formulated or collectively built, is likely to be fully true or false (Walker and Cohen 1985). Almost all thinkers start with some grasp of reality, but none is likely to have the perspicacity to see it all. As long as we continue to test the several theory fragments now existing, or even those that might be invented, as if they were completely right or wrong, we will be trapped in a research game of "gotcha," and the goal will forever elude us.

Unfavorable Philosophies of the Enterprise

While many scholars regard theoretical science as the exemplar of good work, relatively few actually practice it. This may be partly because the philosophy and what it entails are widely misunderstood, and partly because of the prevalence of contrary operating principles. In addition, however, a substantial number of criminologists reject theoretical science altogether, embracing instead other philosophies of the enterprise which deny the relevance or possibility of synthetic theory. There are at least three such unfavorable philosophies, all of which contend for our loyalties and energies.

Evangelism. One of these rival positions rejects the goal of building general theory, as well as the idea of reciprocation between empirical test and theoretical verification or modification. Its adherents believe in a general theory that explains all important or interesting criminological phenomena. While the evangelists acknowledge that this master theory may not be fully articulated, they view any attempt to incorporate other ideas or insights as corrupting. Moreover, within that philosophical framework there is no need to derive hypotheses or to empirically test predictions drawn from the general theory. Rather, the task of 'theorists' is to show how the master scheme applies to different situations or aspects of crime, and the job of researchers is to compile persuasive evidence of the truth of the master theory or to demonstrate exactly how, in specific historical circumstances, the premises of the theory are played out.

Whereas theoretical science relies upon an interplay of research and abstract thinking to arrive at explanation and theoretical accounting, evangelism begins with what its practitioners regard as completely adequate explanation; the task is simply to translate the premises into specific descriptions of concrete situations and to ferret out evidence consistent with the prescribed explanation and the master theory from which it is drawn. Theoretical integration is not only unnecessary, it is ludicrous. Since any contending theories are obviously false or, at best, blind to reality, attempts at synthesis would be silly. Moreover, efforts to test hypotheses derived from the master theory would be counterproductive because they would inevitably be confirmed, and efforts so directed would waste energy needed to persuade others and to implement the truth.

While it would be inaccurate to describe any particular set of criminologists as being exclusively evangelistic, there are clear strains of evangelism evident among some radical Marxian conflict criminologists (Bohm 1982) and some conservative economists interested in crime and criminology (McGahey 1980), as well as among many otherwise careful scholars who become too enamored with a specific view of the world or of policy (cf. Kitsuse 1980; Wilson and Herrnstein 1985). In short, the effort to build good synthetic theory faces a potent barrier in the widespread tendency toward premature closure and zealous crusading. This is not to say that the products of evangelical scholars are of no value. In fact, it is possible, despite the objections of true believers, to borrow and synthesize some of the explanatory elements of the evangelists' master theories. While evangelism contradicts the idea of theoretical science, it at least has the virtue of recognizing the conceivability and uses of general theory.

Particularism. Unlike theoretical scientists, who strive for general theory through synthesizing partial explanations and less general theories, and unlike evangelists, who recognize the possibility of general theory but believe it has already been achieved, particularists deny the orderliness or coherence of the social world or of crime-relevant phenomena and decry efforts to express social reality in general, abstract formulations. Particularists believe some or all of the following: the subject matter of criminology is hopelessly ambiguous; crime-relevant phenomena are unique, or so specific that theory is impossible; social processes are so disorderly and situationally problematic that generalization is precluded, or the causal processes of crime-relevant phenomena are too complex or diverse for synthesis (see Tittle 1985). Consequently, some would build only narrow explanations of limited phenomena in specific situations; others would only *describe* various crime-relevant behaviors or situations; and still others would attempt only to understand folk interpretations.

All versions of particularism view theoretical integration as either impossible or unthinkable, and in some versions it is thought to be dangerous or naive. Since theory assumes regularity and generality, it is clear that particularism has no place for theory, much less theoretical integration. Therefore, to the extent that criminologists embrace this philosophy, as many have, the effort to achieve synthetic theory will suffer from limited personnel and from a shortage of empirical materials that might contribute to general theories.

Pragmatism. A third anti-integration approach concerns itself mainly, or perhaps completely, with crime control. The objective of those who embrace this philosophy is to discover specific variables, the manipulation of which will enable controllers to reduce criminal behavior as it is defined in a given society or to solve practical problems in the operation of criminal justice systems. Discovery of such variables may occur by trial and error, by evaluating particular applications of policy, or sometimes by taking advantage of theories or explanations current in the literature. But pragmatic scholars are not concerned with building general theories through integrating specific explanations or by reciprocation between theory and research. In fact, they are interested in theory only if it can yield programs that "work." Research is not to document regularities to be explained or to test hypotheses for evaluating and modifying theory; rather, it is to determine if particular ideas have immediate application. For such criminologists, theoretical science is ivory tower nonsense, the products of which are largely irrelevant to the task at hand.

There are three types of pragmatists. The first are bureaucrats employed by public or private agencies, whose job it is to serve the interests of their employers. There are the thousands who work as administrators of criminal justice agencies, or who occupy staff positions as researchers or consultants, as well as employees of the countless government departments directly or indirectly concerned with crime, law making, or government policy that might involve rule violation. There are also bureaucrats who work for private foundations, businesses, or agencies that have an interest in one or another aspect of law making or breaking. The second type are entrepreneurs who consciously formulate their interests in practical terms in order to obtain grant monies, to build public recognition exchangeable for consulting income, or to enhance their own standing in the eyes of power holders. They are traders in the criminological commodity market, thriving on faddish concerns, announcing their work and results at press conferences, and cultivating the 'right' people. Finally, there are the moralists, who are genuinely concerned about the welfare of their societies. Some endorse and support the particular political structures that currently define and enforce the law, viewing law violation as dangerous and harmful. Others think current systems are immoral and want to modify practice or structure to prevent crime control efforts from harming people. The moralists of both stripe are civic-minded and are inspired by the urge to improve the human condition.

No matter how noble (or disgusting) a particular form of pragmatism might appear, they all have the common consequence of diverting collective energies from theory building. Worse, pragmatists conspire with those who control the financial means for our work to define worthy criminological activity in extremely narrow, time and place-bound terms, resulting in the impoverishment and starvation of theoretical science.

Conclusion

Criminologists disagree about the objectives of their work and about how to go about it. Of four identifiable philosophies of the enterprise, only two recognize the value of general theory, and only one of them is oriented toward theoretical integration. Even those who embrace theoretical science disagree about operating principles, many espousing positions that make theoretical integration unlikely if not impossible. Therefore, any discussion of the problems and pitfalls of synthetic theorizing must recognize that disunity in criminology is itself the major drawback.

To be sure, the skills and technologies of synthesis are not widely dispersed, and the task is especially difficult when one is attempting to account for macro-level phenomena. Nevertheless, the possibility of synthetic theory is real enough, as I hope I have demonstrated with my simple example. The major impediment is simply a shortage of scholars committed to the enterprise of theory building and to sharing workable operating principles. Since synthesis is a process ultimately dependent upon collectively practiced reciprocation between theory and research, it follows that success may largely be a product of the size of the work force, which, in turn, is directly linked to the absence of agreement about our mission.

12

Three Perennial Issues in the Sociology of Deviance[1]

―――― Jack P. Gibbs ――――

Since an all-inclusive theory is supposedly the ultimate objective in any scientific field, it may appear that Bernard and Tittle (this volume) have pursued a commendable goal. Unfortunately, the goal is a distant prospect at best, and its pursuit is a questionable enterprise without the prior resolution of three perennial issues in the sociology of deviance. Their resolution would not end the debates, such as that between Hirschi (1979) and Elliott (1985), over strategies for integrating deviance theories, but any successful strategy will require a resolution.

The First Issue: Criteria for Assessing Theories

What should be the primary criteria for assessing theories? There is currently no real prospect of even effective consensus in answers by sociologists, and their seeming indifference to the subject suggests the belief that a field can make genuine progress without such consensus. Yet an integration of theories is likely to entail acceptance of some theories and rejection of others. Bernard and Tittle did not make their acceptance-rejection criteria explicit and clear, nor did they otherwise confront the issue; the same is true of other integrative efforts (see, e.g., Elliott 1985). Perhaps they refrained because the issue is not peculiar to the sociology of deviance, but that consideration in no way lessens the issue's importance.

A Grand Tradition

For more than a decade, during the 1960s and 1970s, many sociologists employed ideological criteria to judge the merits of theories. The question of a theory's empirical validity became strictly secondary to this question: What value judgment about capitalism, racism, or sexism is implied by the theory? The argument that theories do not necessarily imply such value judgments came to be regarded as naive, and ideologues reserved a special contempt for expressions of concern with testability or even empirical validity.

Of course, few sociologists made their commitment to an ideological criterion truly explicit, and what with the dimming of collective memory, the present argument may appear vastly exaggerated. One example must suffice. Contemplate Quinney's (1976, p. 415) characterization of deterrence research: "we are given a defense of punishment applied in order to protect a late capitalist order." Never mind that many findings raised doubts about the empirical validity of the deterrence doctrine, or that Marxists implicitly attribute efficacy to legal punishments (otherwise, the implication would be that capitalists control dissidents through an ineffective means). Logic is commonly the first victim in ideological assessments of scientific work.

The Immediate Danger. Ideologues did not eliminate consensus in sociology as to appropriate criteria for assessing theories. Discord was rampant long before sabbatical revolutionaries became fashionable. As a case in point, Talcott Parsons did more to create discord than the shrillest Marxist.

The subject is relevant in assessing Tittle's thoughtful analysis of philosophies unfavorable to the integration of theories. Those philosophies may be even more widespread than Tittle suggests; unfortunately, it does not follow that advocates of theory integration agree as to the appropriate criteria for assessing candidates for integration. Discord on that subject is not just an impediment to theoretical integration; it is crippling.

Although Gouldner appeared unbothered by it, he argued (1970, p. 30) that sociologists are especially prone to assess theories in light of background assumptions. Those assumptions are not ideological in the political sense; rather, they are preconceptions of the nature of human nature and social life. Hence, if a theory appears inconsistent with those preconceptions, so much the worse for the theory. Since few sociological theories are testable, preconceptions are commonly the only basis for assessing them; all too many sociologists, however, pay mere lip service to tests of theories.

The Necessity of Effective Consensus.

Why oppose ideological criteria for assessing theories? Because the values of sociologists are so diverse that reliance on ideological criteria would insure perpetual anarchy. Those sociologists who abhor anything akin to orthodoxy may ask: But why be obsessed with realizing effective consensus? The question is less than candid. Those who pose it surely would balk at the prospect of their own theories being judged by whimsical, idiosyncratic criteria.

Needless to say, the argument runs contrary to the wave of antipositivism that engulfed the philosophy of science some 20 years ago. Kuhn's work (1970) is especially relevant because of its enormous following in sociology. That following is remarkable if only because Kuhn expressed doubt that his argument applies to the social sciences; however, given the variety of ways that Kuhn used the term 'paradigm' (see Masterman 1970), it is not clear why his arguments supposedly hold only for the advanced sciences. Be that as it may, in suggesting that scientists accept or reject theories for reasons that have nothing to do with tests or empirical evidence, Kuhn supplied ammunition for three camps of sociologists: (1) incorrigible ideologues, (2) those who deny the very idea of value-free sociology, and (3) those who warn against taking physics as a model of science but do not offer a coherent alternative.

Predictive Power as the Only Realistic Hope

Predictive power is the appropriate criterion for judging theories of deviance. The rationale is not that science is supported because humans are concerned with realizing a predictable world and think of predictability and control as related. After all, there is no scientific reason for science. However, it is hardly radical to describe the purpose of all scientific work as the cognitive creation or discernment of an order in the universe; accepting that, one can state that a theory's predictive power is the gauge of the amount of order it creates or discerns.

Some Contenders. The present emphasis on predictive power does not extend to a denial of contenders. To the contrary, sociologists entertain numerous contenders, all distinct from ideological criteria.

According to *verstehen* sociology, a theory is acceptable if and only if it promotes understanding. No one is genuinely puzzled by the *verstehen* criterion. Imagine someone proclaiming that a theory should promote misunderstanding. Nonetheless, it is hardly less obvious that a given theory may promote the understanding of some sociologists but not others. Weber's theory of capitalism and the Protestant ethic is a case in point, and the sociology of deviance often appears to be engaged in a vast debate as to whether one theory or another promotes understanding. Bernard's work will perpetuate that debate because he offers no prospect of any alternative to the *verstehen* criterion when assessing his integrated theory.

Whereas the *verstehen* criterion is largely peculiar to the social and behavioral sciences, another criterion is widely endorsed in all sciences. Briefly, a theory is acceptable if and only if it explains the phenomena to which it pertains. Although conventional, the explanatory criterion is conducive to discord among sociologists in assessments of theories. For one thing, a generation of philosophers of sciences have voiced misgivings about Hempel's conception of the form of an explanation (1965) but have yet to formulate a truly coherent alternative (see, e.g., Salmon and Salmon 1979). One of many objections is to Hempel's insistence that at least one premise in the *explanans* must be a "covering law." Many sociologists endorse that objection because of doubts that their field will ever have anything like ostensibly valid laws. As for sociologists who agree that a covering law is essential, some reject Hempel's suggestion that the covering law need not assert causation. Finally, whereas Hempel's conception of explanation calls for the deduction of statements about the *explanandum* through conventional rules of logic, most sociologists appear indifferent to the need for explicit rules of deduction. Even Homans' (1974) emphasis on the deductive character of explanation is misleading. In stating his own theories, Homans never bothered to identify rules of deduction, and one of his requirements for an adequate explanation—that the premises be psychological principles—has nothing to do with deduction.

Thus one can only conclude that the notion of explanation does not promote consensus in assessments of sociological theories, whether about deviance or otherwise. The problem is not just that sociologists have quite divergent conceptions of an adequate explanation. The notion of an adequate explanation also suggests a qualitative, categorical distinction: a theory either does or does not provide an adequate explanation. Stated otherwise, the notion is not conducive to a *doubly* relative criterion of assessment, meaning that a theory's merits should be judged quantitatively *and* with reference to contenders. The qualitative, categorical character of an explanatory assessment is all the more pronounced when causal explanations are demanded. Thus, the assertion that X causes Y admits *only* four conventional interpretations, one being a denial: (1) X is necessary and sufficient for Y, (2) it is necessary but not sufficient, (3) it is sufficient but not necessary, or (4) it is neither necessary nor sufficient. The problem is exacerbated by the persistent refusal of sociologists to make their criteria of causal evidence explicit, perhaps because the subject is a thicket of issues (see Gibbs 1982).

By contrast, when a theory is assessed in terms of predictive power, its merits are relative to contenders; predictive power, however, can be construed as having some bearing on explanation or causation. Imagine someone saying: such-and-such theory offers an adequate explanation of crime, but there is no way that one can deduce any predictions from the theory. Now suppose that someone asserts a causal relation between the unemployment rate and the robbery rate but then denies that any prediction about a statistical association between the rates can be made. Surely the denial would make the notion of causation meaningless. Finally, it is ludicrous to suggest, as Dubin does (1978), that one can make all manner of accurate predictions about a phenomenon and yet not understand the phenomenon. Savor this illustrative statement: I can accurately predict who will and who will not commit robbery, and I can accurately predict differences between the robbery rates of any two social units, but I understand nothing about robbery.

The Stance of Bernard and Tittle.

The suggestion is not that Bernard and Tittle are totally insensitive to criteria for assessing theories. One way or another, they allude often to explanation, understanding, and causation. Yet Bernard and Tittle do not face the possibility that such notions are conducive to dissent in assessments of theories.

Because of Tittle's much greater emphasis on testing theories, his position on the issue may appear much clearer than that of Bernard. Nonetheless, he scarcely speaks to this question: What is the bearing of tests on explanation, understanding, or causation?

The Second Issue: Questions about Deviance

Debates in the sociology of deviance are often sterile because the protagonists ostensibly presume that there is only one defensible question, and then disagree as to what that question is. In particular, the labeling perspective was fueled by the rejection of etiological questions about deviance in preference for two 'reactive' questions. First, what are the causes or antecedent correlates of reactions to deviance? Second, what are the consequences or postcedent correlates of reactions to deviance? But there is no basis whatever for an exclusive concern with reactive questions, even granting that the emphasis on etiological questions was once inordinate. For that matter, those who pursue the etiology of deviance commonly fail to grant that there are really two defensible questions. First, what are the causes or antecedent correlates of variation in the rate of particular types of deviance? Second, what are the causes or antecedent correlates of individual differences as regards deviance?

Related Strategy Issues

Neither Bernard nor Tittle argue that there is only one defensible question about deviance; nonetheless, they scarcely recognize that alternative questions pose a special problem when integrating theories. Tittle appears concerned exclusively with integrating theories pertaining to the rates question, but the rationale is left unstated. By contrast, Bernard indicates that reactive and etiological theories can be integrated, but he seems to argue that the integration of a macro theory and a micro theory can result only in a synthetic macro theory. The criticism is not just that Tittle and Bernard should have devoted more attention to the kinds of strategy issues raised in the debate between Hirschi (1979) and Elliott (1985). No less important, Tittle and Bernard ignored what are here identified as special strategy issues, special in that they stem from alternative questions about deviance.

The Initial Special Strategy. Many sociologists use the term 'labeling perspective' to denote one or more of three distinct things: (1) the reactive conception of deviance; (2) a theory or some loose arguments about the consequences of reactions to deviance; and (3) a line of work, commonly designated as societal reaction theory, pertaining to causes or antecedent correlates of reactions (for elaboration, see Gibbs 1981a, 1981b). Such uncritical use of the term 'labeling perspective' confounds several distinct issues, one of which can be resolved by simply recognizing that the sociology of deviance is not limited to etiological questions. By contrast, the issue raised by the reactive conception of deviance appears intractable. Suppose a deviant act is defined this way: an act is deviant if and only if it is reacted to punitively. There is no way to demonstrate that the definition is false or even inferior to the once conventional normative definition of deviance. So it is an illusion to assume that after more than twenty years the conceptual issue has been resolved or will go away if ignored. That assumption is now fashionable, and Bernard and Tittle should have treated it at length.

There is an alternative assumption, but it is also dubious. One can argue that a definition of deviance or related terms is not needed. After all, so the argument could go, theories about robbery, suicide, and homosexuality, to mention only three types of behavior, need not identify the behavior as deviant. The argument is correct, but there can be no integration of deviance theories without a conception of deviance.

Two Proposals. Scientists, sociologists in particular, are reluctant to confront conceptual issues because they recognize that no definition is true or false. Yet who would deny that empirical applicability is a relevant criterion in assessing definitions? Similarly, who would deny that a theory's predictive accuracy is contingent on definitions of its constituent terms?

So there are two proposals. First, in stating what the theorist describes as a theory about deviance, he or she must formulate a definition of deviance, deviant behavior, and a deviant. Second, researchers should be concerned not just with tests of the theory but also with systematic assessments of the definition. If those assessments indicate negligible empirical applicability, the definition is not suited for the sociology of deviance, and certainly not to the integration of deviance theories.

It may well be that the two proposals are alien to Bernard and Tittle's thinking. Be that as it may, they should have confronted the conceptual issue and arrived at some proposal.

The Other Special Strategy Issue. Tests of a theory will be idiosyncratic unless the theorist speaks to this question: Exactly what kinds of data are to be used in expressing the dependent variables? There is no necessary connection between the question and any previous subject, and a definition of deviance does not necessarily imply the use of a particular kind of data to express the dependent variables of a deviance theory. Thus, a theorist may adopt a purely normative definition of deviance but prescribe clearly reactive data, in which case he or she assumes some relation between true rates or instances of deviance and rates or instances based on labeling actions by social unit members, officials or not.

There is no defensible a priori basis for stipulating the appropriate kind of data to express the dependent variable in deviance theories, and the point is not just that appropriateness depends on the questions pursued by the theorist. Just as a definition's ultimate defense lies in the predictive power of theories, the same is true for the stipulation of data. The argument extends to specifications of data for the expression of both independent and dependent variables, but specification of the dependent variable is especially controversial and a fountain of misunderstandings. The most common misunderstanding: the reactive conception of deviance implies that official data on deviance, especially those on crime, are grossly unreliable. To the contrary, according to a strictly reactive conception, there can be no crimes undetected by legal officials; and the crime rate cannot be other than what legal officials report it to be.

A forcible argument can be made for deviance theories in which the dependent variables are to be expressed by reactive data, official or unofficial, legal or extralegal. The argument would commence with a detailed description of seemingly insoluble problems with the notion of a norm (see Gibbs 1981a), the essential notion in a normative definition of deviant behavior (briefly, deviant behavior is behavior contrary to some norm). However, even if there were no such problems, it is difficult to imagine rates of deviance based on direct observations. Theorists should therefore stipulate the use of reactive data to express dependent variables, whatever the question about deviance.

Despite what has been advocated, deviance is not necessarily a purely reactive phenomenon. A theorist can argue that even when a deviance rate is based on reactive data, the rate's primary determinant is the incidence or prevalence of some designated type of behavior, and that when an individual is somehow labeled as deviant by social unit members that action commonly has something to do with that individual's actual behavior. In the case of self-reported deviance, as when an individual identifies himself or herself as a homosexual, criminal, or delinquent, the datum is reactive; however, it does not follow that the identification had nothing to do with that individual's actual behavior. The same argument applies when an individual reports having shoplifted or having been raped.

Since there may be several alternative kinds of reactive data, even alternative official data, there is a difficult question: Which kind is appropriate for expressing the dependent variable in a deviance theory? A brief answer must suffice: the most appropriate kind of data is the kind that maximizes the theory's predictive accuracy.

If the argument is accepted, then the integration of deviance theories is even more essential than suggested by Bernard or Tittle. Every theory should be such that its independent variables considered together imply answers to two questions. First, what are the causes or antecedent correlates of the behavior type under consideration? Second, given an instance of that behavior type, what determines whether that act will be reacted to by social unit members such as to label it some particular way? A theory that combines etiological and reactive independent variables is, therefore, not merely desirable; it is necessary in order to realize impressive predictive accuracy, especially when reactive data are used to express the dependent variable (for elaboration, see Gibbs, 1981a, 1981b, 1985). Unfortunately, Tittle takes no step toward the integration of etiological and reactive theories of deviance. Bernard clearly advocates such integration, but he leaves the rationale obscure.

Questions About Deviance and Their Bearing on Predictive Power

Sociologists may reject predictive power as the primary criterion for assessing theories, because they are prone to confuse predictive power and predictive accuracy or "explained variance" (see, e.g., Elliott 1985, p. 124). Even if they recognize that a theory's predictive accuracy should be judged in terms of ordinal predictions and always as relative to that of contending theories, there are six other dimensions of predictive power (see Gibbs 1972), and only one—testability—has a real connection with predictive accuracy. The connection between tests and predictive accuracy is rarely recognized by sociologists. They often speak of the desirability of tests but without stressing this point: a theory is testable only insofar as it implies possibly false statements about *particular* events or things, data or otherwise. Regardless of temporal considerations, those statements are predictions; positive tests are simply accurate predictions.

Space limitations make it necessary to consider only two dimensions of predictive power other than accuracy and the testability. They are range and scope, and both are particularly relevant for a critique of Bernard and Tittle.

The Range of a Theory. Any scientific theory makes assertions about properties of at least one class of events or things, and the term that denotes such a class is here identified as a unit term. The variety of possible unit terms for sociological theories, including deviance theories, is suggested by this illustrative list: organizations, groups, families, age groups, status categories, cities, countries, and individuals. If only because of such variety, a sociological theory without an explicit unit term is ambiguous, and it is most improbable that any empirical generalization about sociocultural variables holds regardless of the unit term. Nonetheless, sociologists are commonly careless in their use of unit terms, whether in connection with deviance theories or otherwise.

One illustration must suffice to indicate the sense in which range is a dimension of predictive power. Suppose that a theory about the suicide rate explicitly applies only to variation in the rate among countries, while another theory about the suicide rate explicitly applies to variation in the rate among metropolitan areas and age groups as well as countries. As such, the latter theory has greater range; if there are no other contrasts (e.g., testability, predictive accuracy), it has greater predictive power.

Sociologists often assess theories as if totally oblivious to range as a dimension of predictive power. However, although ignored by Bernard and Tittle, range is relevant in contemplating opportunities for integrating theories. Suppose two theories make identical assertions about the relations among the same three variables, X, Y, and Z; and also suppose that the unit term is "metropolitan areas" for one theory but "countries" for the other. The two theories should be integrated, but the integration would demand considerable imagination. The integrator must devise a third unit term and define it so that there are *at least* two subclasses—countries and metropolitan areas. In defining the new unit term, the integrator should confront two questions. First, given the assertions made about X, Y, and Z, for which types of conventionally recognized units do those assertions imply correct predictions? Second, if the claims imply correct predictions for some types of units but not for others, why the contrast?

A demonstration that a particular generalization does not hold for some types of units should be informative and perhaps sobering. To illustrate, social scientists who attempt to explain variation in the homicide rate by reference to variation in aggregate income measures (for a brief survey, see Messner and Tardiff 1986) should examine sexual differences in the homicide rate and variation in the rate among age groups or marital statuses. Those examinations would raise doubts about the relevance of income, and it would end the astonishing preoccupation of sociologists with population density and race in the etiology of homicide.

There is a major controversy concerning the range of deviance theories. Tittle and many other sociologists display no interest in deviance theories about individual differences, while Bernard is content to suggest that micro theories may have implications for macro theories but not the reverse, thereby unwittingly identifying macro theories as inferior. However, to ignore or belittle the individual differences question is an intolerable price to pay for anti-reductionism and fidelity to Durkheim. Why should sociologists surrend the question to psychologists or biologists? Indeed, if they do surrender it, why then battle furiously against the contention that criminal behavior has a genetic basis (see Jenck's commentary, 1987)? Even granting that a genetic theory about the rate question is not testable, the most effective refutation of a genetic theory about individual differences in criminality is a contending theory of greater predictive accuracy and/or range.

The Scope of a Theory. The assertions made by a scientific theory always pertain to designated properties of events or things. In a conventional deviance theory, such properties are designated as variables, and it must suffice to say that a theory's scope is largely a matter of the number of its constituent dependent variables.

Sociologists are likely to grant that scope is a dimension of predictive power, and that greater scope may be a goal or at least an unanticipated consequence when integrating theories. However, several related issues are ignored in the sociological literature, and the present treatment must be limited to the most relevant issue for this critique.

Bernard and Tittle write as though interested only in deviance theories in which the rate of deviant behavior or the crime rate is the dependent variable. Yet no one even thinks of computing a *total* crime rate, much less a total deviance rate; the rate's reliability would also be extremely dubious. True, a theory about variation in the total deviance rate could be tested by making predictions about rates for particular types of deviance, but that strategy is virtually pointless. Although no longer traditional, researchers once commonly computed the correlation among territorial units between rates for different types of crimes. Regardless of the territorial units—census tracts, cities, or states—there were numerous instances of a negligible correlation between the rate for one type of crime and the rate for another type (for some references, see Gibbons 1982, p. 29, notes 11–13). There were even instances of substantial negative correlation coefficients, homicide and suicide being cases in point. Such findings clearly suggest that the causes or antecedent correlates of variation in deviance rates are markedly different for the various types of deviance. Hence, even if it were possible to compute reliable total deviance rates, the pursuit of a theory about such rates is likely to be a feckless enterprise. The sheer number of independent variables required for accurate predictions would make the theory incomprehensible.

There is an alternative to the pursuit of a theory about variation in the total deviance rate; it is the integration of theories about rates for particular types of deviance. To oversimplify, assume impressive test results for three theories, each pertaining to variation in some type of crime rate among, say, metropolitan areas. Think of the independent variable in the burglary theory as X, that in the robbery theory as Y, and that in the auto theft theory as Z. Now suppose that someone conceptualizes a fourth variable, W, such that it is logically identical with and/ or positively correlated with X, Y, and Z. If so, the stage would be set for integrating the three theories, but integration would require an answer to this question: How can some analytical type of crime be defined such that the rate is highly correlated with variable W? Features of burglary, robbery, and auto theft might be suggestive, but the analytical type must include more that those three subtypes. Indeed, the rate for the analytical type of crime should be much more correlated with variable W than are the combined rates of burglary, robbery, and auto theft.

Neither Bernard nor Tittle entertain the integration strategy just explicated, perhaps because well-known theories purport to explain deviance or crime in general. Even if those theories could be tested systematically, for the reason previously indicated those theories would not imply even remotely correct predictions about variation in the rates of each of the various types of crimes (e.g., burglary, robbery). So despite the fact that the pursuit of inclusive theories rather than theories about particular types of crimes has impeded the integration of theories, Bernard and Tittle evidently believe that constructive attempts at integration do not require theories about particular types of deviance.

The Third Issue: Modes of Theory Construction

Any theory is stated in accordance with particular rules or conventions, be they explicit or implicit. If nothing more than the conventions of a natural language, such as German or English, the theorist has employed the discursive mode of theory construction. If there are explicit rules and some or all of them transcend the conventions of a natural language, then the theorist has employed a formal mode. Sociologists appear committed to the discursive mode, even though more than a century of experience indicates that the mode virtually assures an obscure logical structure and idiosyncratic tests of a theory, if any at all. That argument is especially relevant when contemplating the integration of well-known deviance theories. Because those theories were stated discursively (see Gibbs 1985), the outcome of an integration attempt will be inherently debatable; and if the synthetic theory is also discursive, it will be even less comprehensible than the original theories.

Some Essential Distinctions

There are various contending formal modes of theory construction (for several references, see Turner and Beeghley 1981). Nonetheless, a mode will not promote testable theories unless it encompasses rules pertaining to types of terms, types of statements, and deduction.

Types of Terms. A scientific field's vocabulary inevitably encompasses some terms that denote purely theoretical notions. Those terms cannot be defined precisely or clearly because they pertain to phenomena that cannot be observed, experienced, or measured in any direct sense. The sociology of deviance, including criminology, is no exception; but many of the field's terms defy a complete and clear definition, not just because they denote unobservable phenomena but also because each term denotes extremely diverse phenomena. Contrary to the tradition of operationalism and unbridled empiricism, the type of term in question is evidently essential for impressive theories, but unless the distinction between those terms and others is maintained, untestable theories are inevitable. The distinction can be maintained by identifying the terms in question as *constructs*. A construct is a property term used in stating a theory; if it is defined at all, the theorist does not regard the definition as complete, clear, and empirically applicable. More specifically, when a construct pertains to a quantitative phenomenon, no statement in the theory links the construct to a symbol that designates a formula and intrucions for its application, including a description of requisite data and their acquisition. Some illustrative candidates for constructs are: anomie, differential association, social integration, class conflict, differential reinforcement of deviant behavior, and commitment to conformity.

By contrast, a concept is a term that must be defined when used, and the theorist regards the definition as complete, clear, and empirically applicable. If the concept pertains to quantitative phenomena, a statement in the theory links the concept *directly* with a symbol that denotes a formula and instruction for its empirical application, including a description of requisite data and the procedure for data acquisition. Some illustrative candidates for concepts are: official burglary rate, residential population density, objective certainty of imprisonment, per capita income, unemployment rate, and median years of education completed.

Types of Statements. . Although sociologists often use the words axioms, postulate, proposition, theorems, and hypotheses, they rarely clarify the meaning of those words or even confront crucial questions. If axioms, postulates, and propositions are premises, how do they differ? If a theorem is one of a theory's conclusions, how does it differ from the premises other than being derived from them? If that is the only difference, why derive theorems? If theorems are derived because they are the only statements in the theory that are considered testable, why are they so considered? Since a test of a theory requires predictive statements about particular events or things, what is the appropriate designation of those statements?

Coherent answers require recognition that the property terms in an empirical statement determine the statement's typification in the context of a theory. Some illustrative definitions: an axiom is a premise that links constructs; a postulate is a premise that links a construct and a concept; a proposition is a premise that links concepts; and a theorem is a derived statement that links referentials, symbols that designate empirically applicable formulas (only theorems enter directly into tests).

Rules of Deduction or Derivation. . Systematic tests of a theory require the deduction of theorems and the subsequent deduction of predictions, designated as hypotheses, from the theorems. Hence, whatever the mode of theory construction, it must stipulate deduction rules.

Anyone who denies the need for explicit deduction rules must be unfamiliar with deviance theories and sociological theories in general. There we find theorists using phrases something like "it follows that" without even identifying either the premises or the rules of deduction (see examples gathered by Gibbs 1972; pp. 102–106). Explicit deduction rules are needed all the more if one grants the desirability of a rigorous verbal statement of a theory *before* using the language of mathematics, the most formal of all modes.

Bernard and Tittle as Illustrative Cases

Bernard and Tittle appear more indifferent to the issue of theory construction modes than they are to the two major issues previously considered, and that indifference may well be the most serious. An integrated deviance theory does not require agreement as to the field's central questions, nor need it speak to all of those questions, whatever they may be. As for the argument that predictive power is the appropriate criterion for assessing a theory, it is extremely difficult to assess a discursive theory's scope, range, parsimony, intensity, and discriminatory power (see Gibbs 1972).

Tittle's Seeming Indifference. . More than Bernard, Tittle emphasizes the need for testable theories; however, he does not recognize that a formal statement of a deviance theory is necessary for defensible tests. Further, unless the original theories are stated formally, an integration of them will prove debatable at best and is likely to border on the incomprehensible.

Tittle never acknowledges the necessity of recognizing types of property terms; indeed, he appears to treat the labels 'construct' and 'concept' as interchangeable. Yet his abstracting the concepts of three theories to form seven 'more general ones' was an imaginative creation of ostensible constructs. The suggestion is not that Tittle should have formulated clear, complete, and empirically applicable definitions of the seven ostensible constructs; such definitions are not feasible. However, if what Tittle identified as "ideas" in the original theories are constructs, he made no effort to link those ideas to concepts.

If only because the premises of Tittle's synthetic theory's are limited to postulates, the theory is grossly incomplete. Each line in Tittle's Figure 11.1 represents a postulate, one of which Tittle speaks of as 'yielding' numerous specific hypotheses. Hence, Tittle evidently uses the label 'hypothesis' to denote a theorem or conclusion as well as a prediction. In any case, there is no indication of how Tittle's illustrative hypotheses were derived from the postulates, and it is inconceivable that they can be derived by any conventional logic without additional statements. Finally, Tittle speaks of testing hypotheses as though the procedure has nothing to do with the theory; such statements are the traditional road to idiosyncratic tests or none at all.

Bernard's Selective Use of Formal Theory Construction. Bernard appears sensitive to the distinction between the formal and the discursive modes of theory construction and he is clearly aware of the need to recognize types of property terms, constructs in particular. Yet he appears insensitive to this argument: If there is no ostensible connection between even a partial definition of a construct and the way the construct is used in stating a theory, the construct has not facilitated the theorist's thinking and the audience's comprehension of the theory is jeopardized. In that connection, critics are likely to regard several of Bernard's axioms as incomprehensible, largely because he does not justify treating social structure, interests, values, and actions as *quantitative* properties or variables. Consider Bernard's articulations of some of his axioms: interests vary directly with social structure, actions vary directly with interests, and values vary directly with interests. One of the many questions left unanswered is this: How can actions or values vary among social units in any quantitative sense? The intensity of some particular value, such as the desirability of material possessions, may vary; and so may the per capita frequency of some type of action, such as armed robbery. But Bernard's integrated theory is not couched in terms of types of anything, and for that reason alone his axioms are empty formulas. The criticism is not the usual and misinformed complaint about tautologies; rather, it is simply difficult to imagine how any predictions can be derived from Bernard's theory.

Bernard can reply rightly that a theorist enjoys a license in defining and using constructs, but his use of formal theory construction is highly selective. He uses constructs with abandon but makes no systematic use whatever of concepts. Consequently, his theory comprises only axioms, which makes the theory nugatory; his use of the currently fashionable word 'model' obscures rather than mitigates. It is not just that Bernard failed to deduce testable theorems; additionally, there is no way to deduce them from the axioms. Testable theorems are precluded not because Bernard failed to stipulate a procedure for measuring social structure, interests, values, and actions. Sociological tradition notwithstanding, those terms denote phenomena that cannot be measured in any sense of the word, not even if thought of as quantitative. Insofar as the terms can be said to have empirical referents, it is only through concepts that are linked to empirically applicable formulas; and those connections require types of statements completely ignored by Bernard.

The Blind Spot. To describe Bernard's or Tittle's effort as a failure would suggest that someone of greater ingenuity could have succeeded. To the contrary, for nearly a century deviance theories have been stated such as to preclude integration; even that argument, however, does not convey the awful state of deviance theories.

That awful state can be summarized this way: the well-known theories never have been subjected to a defensible test, nor will they without a radical formal restatement (for elaboration, see Gibbs 1985). Consider two brief illustrations. Many purported tests of Sutherland's theory (Sutherland and Cressey 1974) have focused on generalizations something like this: the greater a juvenile's number of delinquent friends, the more that juvenile has committed or will commit delinquent acts. If anyone can show how that generalization is deducible by some conventional logic from the premises of Sutherland's theory, they should share that knowledge at once. Now contemplate Lander's report of an inverse relation among subareas of Baltimore between the official delinquency rates and the percentage of owner-occupied homes (see Clinard, 1964, p. 33). Lander and others depicted that finding as bearing on Merton's anomie theory (1957), but even assuming that the theory's premises can be identified, there are no rules of logic by which those premises imply Lander's finding. The truth is that purported tests of most deviance theories are studies in ad hoc decisions, idiosyncratic procedures, and unbridled opinions. The findings are published because journal referees do not recognize that recourse to the ambiguous language of operational definitions and indicators is the premature termination of theory construction.

No apology is made for emphasizing tests and preditive accuracy. Imagine someone declaring that untestable theories or testable theories with no predictive accuracy whatever are prime candidates for integration. Yet let us assume that the emphasis on tests and predictive accuracy is merely a deplorable legacy of positivism. Suppose we are content to select theories for integration because we regard them as intuitively plausible or ideologically comforting. Even so, only the premises of Sutherland's theory and the Akers-Burgess theory can be identified with confidence, and no predictive statements can be deduced from those premises by any conventional logic (see Gibb 1985). Yet Bernard writes as though the premises of deviance theories are obvious; and, Tittle notwithstanding, it is doubtful that independent critics can agree when identifying the key ideas of well-known deviance theories.

Conclusion

Although Bernard and Tittle have taken steps toward the integration of various deviance theories, the direction taken is not promising. Tittle evidently sees no need for a formal mode of theory construction, and Bernard's use of that mode is all too limited; hence, they have added to the mountain of untestable deviance theories. That outcome was inevitable. Since well-known deviance theories are discursive and untestable, it is difficult to see how their integration could be formal and testable.

Had Bernard and Tittle described their work as the pursuit of important ideas in the sociology of deviance, it would be more defensible. Who would deny that Tittle's abstraction of ostensible constructs required imagination? As for Bernard, surely the ultimate goal is an integration of deviance theories with a general theory about human behavior and sociocultural phenomena. Consequently, Bernard's concern with the notions of social structure, interests, values, and actions is understandable and defensible.

The issue is not the supremacy of ideas over all else in science, including methods, modes of theory construction, and even research. That supremacy is admitted, but that admission does not negate this argument: Having an idea is one thing; expressing it is quite another.

Part III

Cross-Level Integration

Cross-level integration (integrating micro and macro theories) is sometimes thought to be the most difficult type of integration and perhaps the most necessary type. Of the four major papers in this section, two (Hagan and Short) attempt end-to-end integration (see the editors' introduction) and two (Meier and Giordano) discuss issues of theoretical development that must precede theoretical integration. The two comments (Little and Chilton) critically discuss and compare the respective papers, raising additional issues of cross-level integration.

Robert F. Meier, "Deviance and Differentiation," argues that before we achieve micro-macro integration in the sociology of deviance, we must first resolve some preliminary issues. We must develop metatheory and unit theory at both the macro and micro levels; we must link deviance to the concept of social order, such as to processes of differentiation, integration, and stratification; and we must develop conceptual linkages between deviance and related concepts, such as social problems and social control.

John Hagan, "Micro and Macro-Structures of Delinquency Causation and a Power-Control Theory of Gender and Delinquency," attempts an end-to-end integration. Generally, he examines how the social organization of the workplace, a dependent variable in Marxian theory, affects the organization of the family, an independent variable in many theories of deviance and crime, and how the organization of the family (family control structures) affects juvenile delinquency.

Craig B. Little, "Strategies for Cross-Level Theorizing: Comments on the Meier and Hagan Papers," generally discusses cross-level integration as a mode of theorizing and what each of these papers contributes to cross-level integration. He then relates the papers to one another and scrutinizes their contributions.

James F. Short, Jr., "Exploring Integration of Theoretical Levels of Explanation: Notes on Gang Delinquency," discusses different levels of explanation (individual, microsocial, and macrosocial) in the study of deviance and the problems and prospects of developing cross-level explanations of juvenile delinquency. He suggests a rationale for integrating levels of explanation; he specifies alternatives to simplifying assumptions which ignore well established knowledge; and he identifies relationships between levels of explanation which may foster cross-level integration. He then illustrates these points, drawing on studies of collective juvenile delinquency.

Peggy C. Giordano, "Confronting Control Theory's Negative Cases," emphasizes the necessity of theoretical development before theoretical integration, especially cross-level integration, can be successful, and she explicates the role of negative cases in theoretical development, using control theory. She focuses on control theory's negative cases as a way of critically evaluating the theory, conceptually broadening the theory, and integrating the theory with other theories. For example, cases of low attachment to parents and low delinquency suggest ways of conceptually broadening control theory to include a wide range of deviance.

Roland Chilton, "The Challenge and Promise of Theoretical Integration in Criminology," discusses linguistic and ideological impediments to theoretical integration, especially cross-level integration, while commenting on papers by James Short and Peggy Giordano. He points out that researchers frequently cannot communicate among themselves because major concepts, such as social structure, are not clearly defined or are defined differently within different theoretical perspectives. He also points out that ideologies inhibit many theorists and researchers from reviewing work that falls within theoretical perspectives thought to be either too liberal or too conservative.

13

Deviance and Differentiation

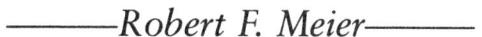

Introduction

One of the significant issues in sociological criminology is reflected in the continuing debate regarding the relationship between micro and macro analyses of crime. The relationship may be complementary, with each approach representing a level of explanation addressing features not covered by the other (e.g., Short 1985), or the relationship may be so close that micro and macro analyses can be combined in some integrative analysis that maintains the logical integrity of each approach (Elliott, Ageton, and Canter, 1979). The idea of integration is so appealing that the topic seems to reside at the top of the theoretical agenda of criminologists today. In the last few years, work on this subject has included actual integrative theoretical efforts (e.g., Colvin and Pauley 1983; Pearson and Weiner 1985) as well as examinations of the more general issue of whether integrations are possible and desirable (e.g., Hirschi 1979; Short 1979; Elliott 1985). Even the larger discipline of sociology has seen major efforts during the past decade at bringing together macro and micro analysis (Collins 1975; Giddens 1984; Alexander, 1982–1984).

This paper examines the issue of micro and macro analyses of deviance and suggests preliminary work that is necessary before efforts are made to integrate these different analyses.[1]

Micro and Macro Analyses.

Micro analyses find the meaning of crime in social psychological properties of individual actors. Concepts such as socialization, social learning, commitment, motivation, identification, attachment, subculture, primary and secondary deviation, and motivation have been integral to micro understandings of criminality. Macro analyses of crime, on the other hand, concentrate on features of social structure that influence crime among individual and collective actors. Concepts such as class, power, elite interests, social disorganization, anomie, value conflict, and normative structure have been important to macro level theories of crime.

The goal of a micro theory of crime is to identify the social psychological properties under which individual and group criminality is generated. The goal of a macro theory of crime is to specify the conditions under which crime is socially structured—in time, space, and among groups in the social structure. There are many examples of each kind of analysis. Social learning and labeling traditions are clearly within the micro, while the anomie and conflict or Marxist traditions are decidedly macro.

It is debatable whether a macro understanding of crime requires theoretical development at the micro level. I do not think it is possible to obtain a macro understanding of crime with even very well developed micro theory, if only because micro analysis of deviance cannot address fully the basic fact of crime--the fact that crime is not random; it is patterned and socially structured in society. As Durkheim pointed out nearly a century ago, even a highly individualistic form of deviance such as suicide cannot be fully understood knowing only the psychological or social psychological state of the individual (if further confirmation is needed, see Breault 1986).

Criminologists have not resolved the issue of whether criminological theory should be micro, macro, or some combination of the two, and for the time being, it might be more prudent to ignore the entire question and concentrate instead on constructing more adequate macro and micro theories. If we are then satisfied with the state of theoretical development, we can worry about integrating macro and micro perspectives. At that time, we might find that reconciliation is not possible, is unwise, or is unfruitful. One major reason to delay integrative efforts is that such efforts to date have not been satisfactory. Only with adequate theories to begin with can integrations succeed. Another reason to delay such efforts is that they are likely to be unsuccessful, even with fully adequate micro and macro theories. Some have argued that macro and micro theories cannot be reconciled and that such efforts are always and everywhere condemned to fail (Kornhauser 1978). Whether that is, in fact, correct, nearly all criminologists would agree that present theories of crime are not where they should be in terms of theoretical development and empirical support.

Yet, it is hard to deny the lure of integration—taking the best, most workable parts of alternative theories and putting them together to eliminate the respective weaknesses of those theories.[2] But integrative efforts seem more likely to occur under certain conditions. Consider the following hypothesis: theoretical integrations are most popular (1) when individual micro and macro theories are seen as inadequate and (2) when alternative micro and macro theories have not been developed to replace earlier theories. If correct, integrations are most pursued when there is little else to do theoretically. In much the same ways that typologies usually signal the failure of theory, so too does the appearance of theoretical integrations.

The Nature of Social Theory

Wagner (1984) makes a distinction between two kinds of theory, unit theory and metatheory. Metatheory serves as a general orientation, a framework from which unit theories can develop. Functionalism, phenomenology, and dramaturgical analysis are examples of metatheories. Unit theories are theories that are more specific and testable, in part or totally. Unit theories frequently take the form of "If A, then B." Whereas metatheories are general orientations or orienting frameworks that sensitize us to features of a phenomenon, such as deviant conduct, unit theories are derived from a metatheory and serve as specific explanations of observable phenomena, such as crime, problem drinking, mental disorders, and so on.

Historically, virtually any kind of explanation of social phenomena has been considered some form of sociological theory. These explanations, such as the sweeping conceptions of societal development and change found in the works of Durkheim and Weber, are best conceived as metatheories. Theory within a positivisitic tradition is unit theory and is found in hypothesized conditonal relationships. A unit theory may be considered a statement about a set of facts in their invariant relationship to another set of facts. Such a statement may take the following form: For any X, if X is A, then X is B. This form may be simplified as follows: For X, if A, then B. The "if" clause is called the antecedent; the "then" clause is called the consequent. Metatheories marked the early development of sociology and are found in the work of Durkheim, Marx, and Weber. Unit theories in sociology have been stressed more than metatheories in this century because of the distinct advantage they offer: they can be tested. Without testable theories, the ideas of sociologists on social phenomena differ little from those of philosophers, priests, and journalists.

Problems of Developing Unit Theory in Deviance

While there are many issues in developing deviance theory, there are two that deserve special mention here. First, the connection between metatheory and unit theory in the study of deviance has often been obscure. Labeling theory, for example, which might reasonably be considered an example of a metatheory, has been criticized for its inability to develop testable unit theories (Gibbs 1966). Yet within labeling theory, a unit theory has developed (i.e., the theory of secondary deviation; see Lemert 1951), and that theory can be held accountable to empirical test. It is inappropriate, however, to condemn the metatheory of labeling perspective by confusing it with unit theory.

A second problem in the development of deviance theory is that adequate unit theory cannot develop without metatheory. No existing metatheory of deviance recognizes that several core concepts in the field—deviance, social control, and social problem—are closely related and that a general theory could conceivably incorporate them all into the same theoretical framework. In turn, the development of such a theoretical framework requires a foundation of conceptual development where the concepts of norm, rule, sanction, power, and social control are all recognized as essential to an understanding of deviance theory. Statements of relationships among concepts do not constitute a theoretical integration but are necessary components in the development of theory. It is, in short, necessary to return to a basic understanding of concepts, their meaning and interrelationships, and their utility in constructing larger theoretical schemes. For this reason, theoretical development in the sociology of deviance is more likely to be fruitful if a "theoretical methods" approach is adopted rather than one that debates the merits and demerits of various substantive theories (Meier 1985).

A Micro/Macro Perspective on Deviance

Deviance theory is sometimes thought to exist apart from other bodies of theory. This impression is fostered by accounts of deviance theory that disassociate it substantively from sociological theory (e.g., Shoemaker 1984). Yet, if deviance is in some sense a core concept in sociology, as some have argued (DeFleur and Meier, 1988), theorizing about deviance should be significantly related to theorizing about other social processes. One way to deal with the disjunction between deviance theory and sociological theory is to link deviance theory with wider concerns in sociological theory. For example, there is a close relationship between the nature of social inequality and social deviance (for a brief statement on this relationship, see Clinard and Meier 1985, pp. 324–325; a slightly more extended discussion can be found in DeFleur and

Meier forthcoming.) The connection can be seen by comparing the meaning of social differentiation, social stratification, and social deviance.

Social Differentiation and Social Stratification

Social differentiation is a core concept in sociology. It refers to distinctions among social units (Svalastoga 1965). It resides at the center of recent macro-theoretical attempts to explain the structure and process of modern industrial societies, and its centrality is reflected in its usefulness to functional and evolutionary (Parsons 1971), structural (e.g., Blau 1977), and conflict (e.g., Collins 1975) theorists. And the importance of the concept of social differentiation to classical social theorists such as Durkheim, Comte, Adam Smith, and Herbert Spencer can hardly be denied. As sociological theorists use the term, social differentiation refers to the diversity of status and roles in a society, to differences among people based on socially relevant dimensions (e.g., sex, occupation, level of education).

Actually, social differentiation is a process of making people different, recognizing differences among people, and presupposing or asserting the social significance of differences among people. People can be differentiated not only on characteristics they may possess but also upon characteristics they are imputed to possess. As Catton (1978) has pointed out:

> Our distinction-making habits which separate the sexes, age categories, and more combine with an equally persistent tendency to assign value to differences between us. So differentiation leads to ranking. Populations become stratified—differentiated "vertically" as well as "horizontally." (p. 697)

Social stratification is thus a subset of social differentiation. Stratification refers to the *ranked* differences among social positions, and those ranks are determined by social definitions and judgments. These definitions may be based on ascribed characteristics (e.g., age, sex, or race) or achieved characteristics (e.g., wealth and occupational prestige). There is no theoretical consensus on whether such invidious distinctions are universal in time and space (Haug 1977) or whether they are perpetuated because of functional consensus (Davis and Moore 1945), group conflict (Dahrendorf 1959), or competition for scarce resources.

There appears to be greater consensus that social strata, at least in industrialized societies, are based on three dimensions: class, status, and power. Class has an economic referent, status a social referent, and power a political referent. While different theorists have emphasized each of these dimensions (e.g., Marx emphasized class, Durkheim status, and Weber power), there is general agreement that these three dimensions are closely related both conceptually and empirically (Jackson 1968; Runciman 1968). In the past two decades, one group of sociologists, following Blau and Duncan's (1967) lead, have concentrated on occupation as a single indicator of a person's relative standing on all three dimensions. These status attainment researchers conceive of stratification as an intergenerational process where background conditions (e.g., respondent's father's occupation) help explain outcome statuses (e.g., respondent's occupational prestige). Other theorists view the stratification system as a structural phenomenon not reducible to individual-level observation and measurement (Wright 1977). By virtue of agreement on measurement and analysis techniques, one scholar was able to claim that ". . . the subdiscipline of sociology known as 'social stratification and mobility' has made greater progress toward cumulative social science than any other branch of sociological research" (Featherman 1981, p. 79).

Social Deviance

At the most general level, deviance refers to differentness. For this reason, the concept of deviance would have no meaning in an undifferentiated society. Since, however, such a society does not and cannot exist (Durkheim 1982 [1895]), deviance is ubiquitous. But deviance is hardly static or constant. What varies is the forms deviance takes and the degree of disapproval it elicits. What makes the concept of deviance unique is its application to human but not other animal communities. The reason for this uniqueness is that deviance has a moral dimension. That dimension is not found in evaluating other differences among people, such as size, age, skin color, and so on, nor in differences among members of a non-human population.

Conceptually, deviance has been defined both as a violation of social norms (Clinard and Meier, 1985) and as any behavior that is reacted against by a social audience (Becker, 1963). While these definitions may be irreconcilable, each conception—the normative and the reactivist respectively—agrees that deviance refers to disvalued conduct and conditions (see also Sagarin 1975). Some behavior is thought to represent conduct that 'ought not' to occur; similarly, some conditions (e.g., being a homosexual or mental patient) are negatively evaluated. The meaning of deviance is found in the process by which social definitions of behavior and conditions as undesirable are generated.

Disvalued statuses are the result of social definitions and judgments. Those definitions may be based on ascribed characteristics (e.g., sexual preference, physical disabilities) or achieved characteristics (e.g., criminal behavior, suicide). There is no consensus on how the degree of disvaluement should be measured, although the severity of a sanction attached to the behavior or condition is a good indication. Thus if a deviant act draws a mild sanction, chances are it is disvalued relatively little; if an act attracts a strong sanction, it is disvalued a great deal.

Regardless of how it is measured, the concept of deviance explicitly refers to ranked positions created from social judgments that assign persons to particular statuses. We can thus conceive of a distribution of acts or actors ranging from more to less condemned or disvalued. The distribution of deviant statuses based on the degree of disvaluement is analogous to a distribution of occupations based on prestige scores or classes based on relationship to the means of production. In each case, however, social judgments produce the ranking as to whether those judgments are based on economic, social, or moral criteria.

Differentiation and Deviance

The conditions that promote social differentiation also promote deviance. Consider the following argument: Those conditions that increase differentiation are likely to increase the degree and range of social stratification by increasing the number of ways in which people can be compared among one another.[3] Those comparisons are often invidious, with some characteristics being more highly valued than others. To the extent that the bases on which persons are stratified increases, so too does the range of conditions that are disvalued or not as highly ranked (Cohen 1974).

If this argument is correct, we should expect that the range of statuses ranked to form a stratification system should have roughly the same range from top to bottom as the range of ranked negative statuses that comprise a structure of deviance. A more highly differentiated society should have a greater number of ranked statuses, while a less differentiated society should have a smaller number of ranked statuses. Similarly, a more stratified society should have a greater number of negatively ranked statuses than a less stratified society; just as the number of bases on which judgments of positive and negative status are made increases, so too should the correspondence between the two systems. A simpler society would then have both a simple structure of social stratification and a simple or narrow structure of deviant statuses.

The Relativity of Deviance. There are at least two implications of this argument. First, the concept of deviance is probably best viewed as a relative one, with some conditions, behavior, and characteristics being more highly valued than others. Reactivist theorists have long argued that what makes something deviant has nothing whatsoever to do with the behavior or condition itself, but with other peoples' opinions of that behavior or condition (Becker 1963). While that argument is not new, its usefulness has been denigrated by observations such as "nothing is inherently deviant" or "deviance, like beauty, is in the eyes of the beholder." While these comments are consistent with the common observation that deviance is a created entity and not a crescive one, such comments all too frequently have been made without conceptual or theoretical development and therefore have not advanced the argument.

However, deviance is relative not because no trait or act is everywhere and for all time deviant, but because the processes of social differentiation and social change produce alterations in social judgments. The key question is how some conditions come to be ranked the way they are (i.e., why are some acts and actors deviant but not others?). This is a question sociologists frequently answer in terms of power—powerful groups expand the range of stratified social phenomena by engaging in a process of definition (Chambliss 1964) and influence (Nuehring and Markle 1974), the outcome of which is socially rewarded conditions and behavior and socially punished conditions and behavior. A generic term for this process is 'norm promotion.' Regardless of the specific answer to the question about how conditions are ranked, it can hardly be denied that social judgments of disvaluement represent a core component of the concept of deviance. This is presumably why Lemert (1982) uses the phrase "moral differentiation" to refer to deviance.

The Sociological Context of Deviance. The second implication of a conception that links the notions of differentiation, stratification, and deviance is that deviant behavior cannot be adequately grasped apart from its social context. While the study of deviance is considered a 'specialty' in sociology, the study of deviance may actually differ little from the study of other social structural phenomena. One cannot understand the dynamics of social deviance without an understanding of political processes, the allocation of scarce economic and environmental resources, the nature of social interaction, and the operation of institutional systems (e.g., family, law, education, occupational structure).

Contemporary sociological formulations emphasize the interrelationships among these social phenomena, so much so that deviance is implicitly a core concept in understanding other social phenomena. Giddens' (1984) structuration theory, for example, attempts to explain the continuity of social structures and the reproduction of social systems with an understanding of processes of differentiation and integration. The social systems in which structure is found comprise the activities of human agents reproduced in space over time. The structures themselves, according to Giddens, are composed of rules and resources. Following Wittgenstein, Giddens views rules as techniques or procedures that continue a series of social actions, a conception that is close to commonly accepted conceptions of norm as a shared understanding of what social action should take place next in a series of actions (Giddens 1984, p. 21).

However, rules themselves are insufficient to explain continued structured social action. Another concept—power—is also needed. Power is the ability to use resources in the course of interaction. Put another way, "resources are media through which power is exercised" (Giddens 1984, p. 16). Power is a routine aspect of all interactions and since all parties in an interaction can have access to resources, there is always the possibility that subordinates can influence the activities of superordinates.

In a similar analysis—but one focused only on the origins of social inequality—Dahrendorf (1968) reduces the nature of social stratification to constituent parts: the creation of norms, the violation of norms, and the exercise of sanctions by persons in positions of power. Thus, it is only by understanding normative expectations and the sanctioning of social behavior that it is possible to understand the nature of inequalities among individuals and positions. Inequality is, according to Dahrendorf, due to processes regarded as of central importance to students of social deviance. Such overlap should be expected since processes of deviance and stratification are conceptually similar.

Strangely, students of stratification have defined their interests to be only in systems that allocate rewards (positive sanctions) while students of social deviance have shown more interest in systems that allocate punishments (negative sanctions). The greater contemporary emphasis in stratification theory and research on social rewards—prestige, status, upward mobility—may represent the most enduring legacy of Davis and Moore's (1945) theory of stratification, not its association with a functionalist ideology. The approach by Lloyd Warner and his associates (1949) was similarly on documenting a "good" lifestyle, as his studies of the living rooms in middle-class communities showed.[4] Today's analysis of stratification systems regard the prediction or explanation of occupational prestige to be the central issue in the study of ranked differences rather than an analysis of systems of punishments (Blau and Duncan 1967).

The existence of norms and their maintenance through the application of sanctions creates systems of stratification. Social differentiation, in this view, is, in the language of measurement, merely a nominal level phenomenon; the results of processes of social stratification are ordinal level phenomena where distinctions of "higher" and "lower" (or "ought" and "ought not") are appropriate depending on the nature of norms and on who has sanctioning power through access to resources. It is within this context that we can see connections among several related concepts: deviance and social control.

If we can think about processes of stratification and deviance in a conceptually similar manner, we should also be able to ask many similar questions about these phenomena. For example: From where do the norms that regulate social behavior come? Under what historical conditions do these norms change? Why must the near-compulsory character of certain norms be enforced by sanctions? Under what conditions does society confer status (or take it away), deference (or disrespect) or other institutional rewards (or institutional punishments)? In what ways are structures of rewards (e.g., occupational systems) and structures of punishments (e.g., criminal justice system) alike?

The importance of behavioral diversity and other forms of differentiation has been the theme of several recent sociological writings. Bellah and colleagues (1985) note the increasing diversity taking place in the United States but decry the reduction in community this increasing differentiation entails. Jones and Gibbons (1987), similarly, note the increasing lifestyle diversity and sketch out some implications for a conception of deviance based on the notion of diversity. They suggest that "the social structure of modern, urban societies . . . produced a population with many and diverse tastes, that is, dispositions and interests directed at various forms of behavior" (Jones and Gibbons 1987, p. 10). Yet diversity itself is not deviance, only differentiation. Only once elements of that diversity are perceived to be "better," "worse," "desirable," or display some other moral connotation can we talk about deviance. The critical sociological question pertains to the conditions under which some elements of diversity are the objects of moral evaluations. On what bases are evaluations of conduct (or norms) derived regarding the diversity? Whose evaluations are they? How are those evaluations shared with others and how successful is that process? How, in essence, does the origin and structure of deviance systems arise and how are they maintained? These are similar questions to those asked by stratification theorists.

Similarly, if like questions can be asked, perhaps there are similar concepts that can be shared by deviance and stratification theorists. Consider, for a moment, the concept of deference. Shils (1970 p. 421) points out that "the granting of deference entails an attribution of superiority (or inferiority) but it is not the same as an attribution of goodness or wickedness." Clearly, though, deference is not to be paid to persons who have not earned it or who do not deserve it. What other characteristics they may have, deviants are not entitled to deference. Instead, they are disvalued persons (e.g., Sagarin 1975). Yet the processes of deference-conferring may be the opposite of deference-reduction; at least, these important processes may have implications for one another.

The connection between the study of deviance and the study of social stratification should not be overstated, but the answers to questions such as those posed above would be helpful in understanding the derivative nature of deviant behavior in various societies, and they would also extend greatly our knowledge about the nature of stratification systems. Clearly, deviants are not only differentiated from nondeviants; they also coexist in a system of stratification.

Related Concepts

Framing the concept of deviance within a context of social differentiation not only helps to further explicate the concept of deviance, it also helps elucidate two related concepts, social problem and social control. The interrelationships among these concepts require extended discussion, but only a few words can be offered here.

Social Problems

Because of the cognitive similarity between disvalued behavior and undesirable social conditions, there is much overlap between questions about the origins of social problems and the origins of specific deviant acts. Studies of the origins of social problems, for example, point to a remarkably similar process to that described here regarding the origin of norms. Gusfield (1963), for one, identifies particular groups who held to norms prohibiting the consumption of alcoholic beverages and the influence of these groups—largely made up of white, middle-class women—on the passage of the Prohibition amendment. These prohibitionists were successful in influencing others to adopt their norms, at least temporarily. It goes beyond this paper, but successful norm promotion also has been implicated in the social creation of many specific social problems (cf. Spector and Kitsuse 1977). Their term, "claims making," is similar to the concept of norm promotion as discussed here. The creation of legal institutions may also follow a similar path of norm promotion. Platt (1969) argues that this type of process is so general it might also account for the creation of legal institutions. He points to groups of moral entrepreneurs, called "child savers," who were very instrumental in the creation and operation of the juvenile court.

Other examples suggest that the general processes by which social problems are identified and those by which forms of deviant behavior are identified are quite similar. These processes highlight the central role of power in norm promotion. The relative power of those promoting the norm vis-a-vis those being influenced is certainly one component that requires greater understanding. In fact, so general are these processes that sociologists have failed thus far to specify the general conditions under which norms are created and successfully promoted.

Social Control

It might be said that social control is something that a superordinate does to a subordinate, often with the motivation of obtaining normative compliance from the subordinate. But the very idea of 'superordinate' and 'subordinate' assumes a system of ranked differences, a system of stratification. This suggests that social control cannot take place between or among equals, and that is indeed the case. Persons may influence one another, but when it is done among those from positions of unequal power this process is called "social control;" when it is done among those from positions of equal power, it is called "social influence," or, perhaps, "peer pressure."

The idea of ranked differences or unequal power is applicable to both individuals and to groups including organizations. We can, for example, speak of subordinate persons or subordinate classes. There are, in other words, different types of stratification and deviance. In each instance, we are speaking of the power to control, to create and maintain norms, and to sanction violations of those norms. As with the notion of power, social control is a routine aspect of all interactions among persons or groups with unequal power; and since all parties in such an interaction can have access to resources, there is always the possibility that subordinates can influence or control the activities of superordinates.[5]

Conclusion

Students of social deviance should not neglect the broader sociological context in which the concept of deviance has meaning. The strategy suggested here advocates more attention to basic sociological concepts and the development of more adequate metatheory and derivative unit theory so that more adequate micro and macro analyses of deviance can be generated. Then, and only then, should the issue of theoretical integration be placed on the intellectual agenda.

Surely, a general theory of the origins of deviance requires a more precise statement than is contained in this paper. In fact, to suggest that the notion of deviance is closely linked with that of power is trite, given theoretical work during the past two decades. Surprisingly few students of deviance look at the work of other sociologists who are interested in social power, and there is much that could be gained there, particularly in the works of sociologists interested in processes of differentiation, integration, and stratification.[6] Most of the excitement in social theory today, it seems to me, is found in work that deals with these core concepts and their meanings for understanding both micro and macro social processes. As for the study of deviance, we must begin slowly, examining basic concepts and then going on to explorations of conceptual interrelationships. From these beginnings, unit and metatheory can develop. In short, what is advocated here is not the development of narrow but more inclusive or generalized theory.

Preliminary theory would recognize the close conceptual relationships among the notions of deviance and social problem and the common basis of norm promotion that links these concepts. Whatever form preliminary theory of deviance and social problem might eventually take, there is the additional consideration that the concept of social control has also often been defined in terms of social influence or norm promotion (see Meier 1982; Gibbs 1981). To the extent that the process of defining social problems and deviance is a process of social control, labeling theorists are clearly correct in their assertion that social control leads to deviance, not the reverse (Lemert 1972, p. ix). As with the more general theory of the creation of social problems and social deviance, whether such insights can be developed more precisely—to permit empirical tests, for example—remains questionable. For whatever reason, labeling theorists, who have grappled with such matters for more than two decades, have been slow to formulate testable propositions; as a result, consequent insights of this perspective have remained undeveloped. Of course, other scholars have been free to develop ideas about the interrelationships among the concepts of deviance, social problems, and social control, but to date no agreed-upon theoretical connections have been proposed.

The path to theoretical development is bound to be fraught with disappointments and pitfalls, but it can be no worse than what we have now—divisive theoretical camps sniping at each other over the claimed superiority of "their" theory of deviance. If, however, the strategy of generalization would eliminate these battles, it also must be admitted that this strategy suggests that a sophisticated theoretical statement would result in a theory of deviance, social problems, *and* social control—and that seems too much to ask even of our brightest social thinkers. Only a sustained collective effort, not disparate work conducted in separate "theory camps," can lead to such a theory.

14

Micro and Macro Structures of Delinquency Causation and a Power-Control Theory of Gender and Delinquency

———John Hagan———

Introduction

Although class and gender are widely studied correlates of juvenile delinquency, little attention is given to their combined role in the explanation of delinquent behaviour. Power-control theory proposes that the class structure of gender relations plays a significant role in explaining the social distribution of delinquent behavior. In doing so, this theory proposes a new etiology of delinquency and combines levels of explanation that characteristically have been kept apart. This paper considers the ways in which micro and macro structures of delinquency causation are linked in power-control theory. However, before presenting the theory itself, we first consider the context from which it emerges.

Old and New Etiologies

We begin by considering briefly the historical background of modern theories of crime and delinquency. Contemporary accounts typically trace such theories to the work of the Italian criminologist Cesear Lombroso. Lombroso is undoubtedly best known for his view that criminals are atavistic throwbacks to primitive beings, and for his hypothesis that 'true criminals' can be identified by observing the physiological characteristics of such beings. This thesis is testable, and Lombroso is today better remembered for embarking on such tests than for the rigor of his research or for the capacity of his thesis to survive such tests, when properly conducted.

Yet if Lombroso left a legacy, it was not only a growing interest in the empirical study of criminality but also a resulting skepticism about the possibilities of determining causes of criminal behavior. It is not difficult to see how this two-edged legacy developed. America at the turn of the century had a better developed physiological than sociological imagination. As a result, the suggestion that criminal behavior had physiological roots was eagerly entertained at the turn of the century in Europe and the United States. However, as evidence mounted that Lombroso's thesis was unsubstantiated, questions also were raised, especially by sociologists, as to the usefulness of studying the etiology of criminal behavior at all. Although sociologists understandably were quicker to accumulate evidence on the absence or weakness of physiological (Lindesmith and Levin 1937) and psychological (Schuessler and Cressey 1950) causes of criminal behavior, the issue ultimately was confronted in terms of social causes as well. Perhaps predictably, it was an historian with sociological interests, Franklin Tannenbaum (1938), who first asked if we might better shift our focus to the study of reactions to such behavior, especially delinquency. In a famous phrase, "the dramatization of evil," Tannenbaum focused new attention on the 'reactors' to crime and delinquency and anticipated a shift in theoretical interest that was to characterize much, if not most, sociological study of crime and delinquency for nearly a half century to follow.

Some of this early work retained an etiological component, attempting to explain 'secondary deviance,' the behavior that followed the responses of the police and other guardians of official morality to what usually were regarded as random or nonproblematic behaviors (Lemert 1967). However, secondary deviance itself often became secondary to a growing interest in the official control agents themselves. Nonetheless, this research tradition established that both actors and reactors, actions and reactions, are important in the study of crime and delinquency. A result is that there are now new opportunities to achieve a better balance in crime and delinquency research.

A renewed interest in the role of gender in the study of crime and delinquency is part of such an opportunity. The correlation of gender with criminal and delinquent behavior is one of the few findings from the beginnings of criminological research that, although questioned, has never been doubted seriously. The addition of victim (Hindelang 1971) and self-report (Smith and Vischer 1980) data sources to the traditional official tabulations (Steffensmeier 1978; 1980) increases the assurance of a gender-based behavioral reality. Perhaps only age is better known for the consistency of its correlation with criminality, however measured. The question therefore endures (Simon 1975; Adler 1975; Harris 1977): can gender differences in criminal and delinquent behavior be explained?

Feminist scholars have done the sociological study of crime and delinquency a service by refocusing attention on this important question. The effect is to suggest alternative paths that the development of the causal explanation of criminal and delinquent behavior might usefully have taken much earlier. Although the path originally chosen by Lombroso and those who followed his lead was fundamentally wrong, it was nonetheless instructive in unintended ways.

Confronted with the observed facts that women were less criminal than men, Lombroso might of been expected to argue that this was so because they were less atavistic than men. Instead, Lombroso (1895, p. 107) insisted woman was "atavistically nearer to her origin than the male," and that her lesser criminality was explained by "piety, maternity, want of passion, sexual coldness, weakness and an undeveloped intelligence" (p. 151). It may well be that Lombroso's theory of female criminality gained currency because it both asserted women's biological inferiority and warned of the dangers of arousing her passions or developing her intelligence. In any case, Lombroso's arguments are today more easily seen as justifications for paternalistic social policies than as causal explanations of gender differences in criminality. Again, if these were the kinds of pathways to be traveled in the development of the causal explanation of gender differences in criminality, it is easy to see why few sociologists were interested in traveling them.

However, alternative possibilities were available, even at the turn of the century when American scholars chose to embrace the works of Lombroso. Most notable, perhaps, were some of the early thoughts of Willem Bonger. Bonger (1916) recognized the importance of the connection between gender and criminality and gathered cross-national data to test explanations of this correlation. Sociology, not physiology, was at the core of Bonger's thinking. He argued that "the smaller criminality of woman is not to be sought in innate qualities, but rather in the social environment" (Bonger, p. 477). Bonger reasoned that if the gender-crime connection was social as well or more than physical, then the strength of this connection should vary across social conditions. Specifically, he argued that the correlation between gender and criminality should weaken as the social circumstances that confronted women as well as men declined. That is, the strength of the correlation between gender and crime should vary directly with social class.

Bonger's cross-national data admittedly allowed only a weak test of his thesis, but the results were nonetheless encouraging, and this is reason for further dismay that Lombroso's work attracted the greater attention during the formative years of American criminology. Indeed, Bonger received almost no attention at all. Note, nonetheless, that in this early work Bonger was bringing together the concepts of class and gender (see Hagan et al. 1985). Bonger's approach to these issues was somewhat different than our own, and we will argue below that a missing component in Bonger's preliminary efforts was a consideration of the reproductive role of patriarchal family structure. Still, the point seems easily made that most sociologists would have found Bonger's framework a more congenial start than was Lombroso's for the etiological study of gender differences in criminal behavior. That Lombroso was the early focal point perhaps does much, then, to explain a long hiatus in the etiological study of gender and crime and of etiological theory more generally. Our suggestion is that a new etiology that assigns primacy to gender relations can effectively point the way to an important new beginning in the development of a sociological explanation of criminal and delinquent behavior.

This new beginning receives encouragement from feminist scholars such as Catherine MacKinnon (1982), who argue that an exclusive attention to official control agents and the state misses a rather fundamental aspect of the situation that confronts women, particularly those who are victims of crimes by men. As MacKinnon notes, whether some sexual crimes of men against women are called assault or rape and whether they are dealt with in a court system whose functionaries are men or women, the behaviors themselves remain much the same and largely unexplained. This point does not, of course, diminish the importance of arguments about language and the elimination of sexual discrimination in the hiring of police and court officials. Rather, the point is to reassert that there is an underlying behavioral reality involving male criminality, often directed against women, that requires further explanation. MacKinnon's arguments return us to fundamental behavioral questions, and to the source of these behaviors in the social organization of gender relations.

But feminist scholars not only bring us back to fundamental questions about the causal explanation of criminal and delinquent behavior, they also redirect our attention to the role of the state, and especially to family structure, in the explanation of these behaviors. Wilkinson (1974) has noted that the family has not consistently sustained the interest of sociologists, including those who have remained concerned with the explanation of criminality. However, feminist scholarship assigns renewed importance to the family and to variations in its structure. In particular, it brings attention to the role of patriarchal family relations in developing, perpetuating, and thereby reproducing gender differences in behavior. Much of this discussion focuses on issues of power and control, concepts that are also, of course, central to the classical theories of delinquency. These concepts of power and control are central to the ways in which we will tie together our interest in class and gender. They are the conceptual cornerstones of our theory of class, gender, and delinquency.

Power, Patriarchy, and Delinquency

The concepts of power and control typically are treated as being, respectively, macro and micro-structural in content. The macro-micro distinction may or may not be one of simple aggregation, as—for example—when classes are thought of as all persons found in common social relations of production, or as also sharing views of these conditions that result in group-based actions organized and carried out in ways that go beyond the simple summation of individual preferences. In either event, conceptual and empirical considerations of power typically occur at higher levels of aggregation and abstraction than do discussions of control, and therefore are characteristically kept separate. Considerations of power and control nonetheless have important features in common: for example, they are both relational in content. For example, power theories in sociology often focus on relations of production in the workplace, while control theories frequently focus on relations of domination in the family. We do both here. Essential to the conceptualization and measurement in both areas of theory construction is the effort to capture a relational component of social structure. In power theories of the workplace, the relational structure may be that between owner and worker or between supervisor and supervisee. In control theories of the family, the relational structure may be that between parent and child or between parents themselves. In both cases, however, it is a sociological concern with relational and hierarchical structure that drives the conceptualization and measurement (see also Hagan 1988a).

Power-control theory brings together these relational concerns in a multi-level framework. In doing so, this theory highlights another concern that the power and control traditions share. This common concern is with the conditions under which actors are free to deviate from social norms. Both the presence of power and the absence of control contribute to these conditions. A particular concern of power-control theory is to identify intersections of class and family relations that increase freedom for adolescent deviation. Power-control theory assumes that the concept of patriarchy is of fundamental importance in identifying such intersections.

Curtis (1986, p. 171) persuasively argues that patriarchy should not be seen as a theoretical concept with a standard definition but as a generalization about social relations that calls for sociological investigation and explication. This generalization involves the propensity of males to create hierarchal structures through which they dominate others. It is important to emphasize here that these others may be male as well as female. The study of patriarchy, therefore, includes within it the analysis of structures through which men exercise hierarchal domination over both males and females—for example, including children of both genders in the family. Curtis goes on to point out that patriarchy is extremely widespread, including structures of the state (such as police, courts, and correctional agencies) as well as the workplace and the family. The *source* of patriarchy, nonetheless, is assumed to be the family. Millett (1970, p. 33) calls the family patriarchy's "chief institution," suggesting that the family is the fundamental instrument and the foundation unit of patriarchal society, and that the family and its roles are prototypical.

We are now in a position to begin sketching the outlines of a power-control theory of delinquency. We begin with the three levels of the theory, as illustrated in Figure 14.1. These include, in order of level of abstraction, *social-psychological processes* involving the adolescents whose behaviors we wish to explain, *social positions* consisting of the gender and delinquency roles in which these adolescents are located, and the *class structures* by which families are socially organized. Five kinds of links, described further below, bring together the social positions and social-psychological processes that are the core of power-control theory.

We begin with the connections between the social positions and social-psychological processes identified in Figure 14.1. Link 1 is the correlation between gender and state-defined delinquency that criminologists long have observed. We need only note here that gender and delinquency both constitute ascribed positions that are socially designated and legally identified. Our interest is in establishing the family class structures and social-psychological processes that account for these social positions being joined in the correlations that criminologists so consistently have recorded. Note that the interest of power-control theory is in individuals only insofar as they are located as occupants of these positions, and not therefore in these individuals per se. By virtue of the premises noted above, the question power-control theory inevitably asks is: how and why are individuals located in male adolescent positions freer to deviate in ways defined by the state as delinquent than are individuals located in female adolescent positions?

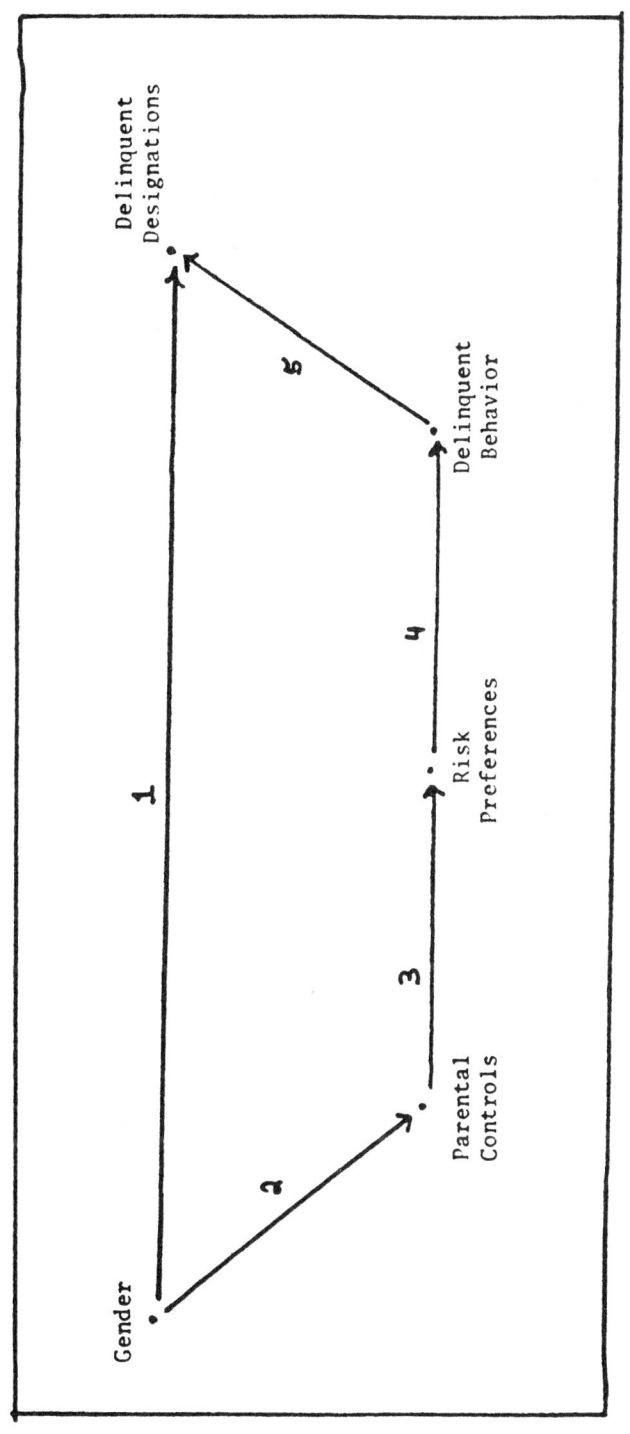

Figure 14.1. A power-control theory of gender and delinquency.

Note that the reference to state definition above indicates that the connection between officially defined delinquency and delinquent behavior is not assumed. Nor is a consensus assumed about what is to be called delinquent behavior. Indeed, it is assumed that police practices sometimes operate to inflate the gender-delinquency correlation. As we will discuss further below, the effect of this inflation is to reinforce a sexual stratification of family and work activities, with females ascripted disproportionately for the former and males appropriated disproportionately for the latter. Nonetheless, a sufficient consistency is hypothesized between police processing and delinquent behavior to make the above question relevant in behavioral terms.

Note also that while the above question makes no value judgments as to the 'goodness' or 'badness' of delinquency, it does nonetheless imply that there is a pleasurable or enjoyable aspect of delinquency. Indeed, power-control theory assumes that delinquency can be fun, if not liberating, as well as in other ways rewarding. Said differently, delinquency may involve a spirit of liberation, the opportunity to take risks, and a chance to pursue publicly some of the pleasures that are symbolic of adult male status outside the family. One reason why delinquency is fun, then, is because it anticipates a range of activities, some criminal and some more conventional, that are more open to men than women. The interests of power-control theory is in how a sense of this sexually stratified world of licit and illicit adult pleasures, and restrictions of access to them, is communicated and reproduced across generations through gender relations.

Link 2 takes the first step in addressing such issues by explicating a connection between gender positions and the parental control of children. This link first calls attention to the proposition that parental controls are imposed selectively: that is, daughters are controlled more extensively than sons. Conceptually we represent this by noting that parents are characteristically the instruments of familial controls, while children are the objects; most significantly, *daughters* are disproportionately the objects of this socially structured domination. The instrument—object relationship established between parents and children is thus applied more selectively and extensively to daughters than sons. Beyond this, within patriarchal family structures mothers are particularly likely to be placed in the primary position of implementing this instrument-object relationship.

Of course, control can be established through ties of affiliation as well as through subordination. Indeed, it might well be argued that a lot of affiliation and a little subordination is the most effective basis of social domination. Again, however, power-control theory predicts that ties of affiliation will be applied, selectively and more extensively, to daughters than to sons. We will refer to these affiliative ties as relational controls, as contrasted with more instrumental kinds of controls involving supervision and surveillance (see Hagan, 1988b). However, it is again the sexual asymmetry that is of greatest importance here, with power-control theory predicting that the larger burden of these controls is imposed on daughters than sons. Furthermore, it is mothers more than fathers that the patriarchal family holds responsible for the everyday imposition of these controls.

Links 3, 4, and 5 in our theoretical framework lead us to a consideration of the consequences of this sexual stratification of social control. In link 3 the focus is on the risk preferences of adolescents. Risk-taking can be regarded as an expression of freedom, an expression that power-control theory predicts will be allowed selectively and more extensively to males than females. Delinquency can be regarded as an adolescent form of risk-taking (hence links 4 and 5) that we have argued above can carry with it an element of pleasure, excitement, and therefore fun. The interest of power-control theory is in how a taste for such risk-taking is channeled along sexually stratified lines.

Link 3 in our theoretical framework predicts that gender differences in risk preferences will be observed and that they are mediated by the structures of parental control introduced above. That is, parents control their daughters more than their sons, and in so doing diminish the preferences of daughters to take risks. The logical links in this theory therefore predict that daughters will be more risk averse than sons, and that therefore daughters will be less delinquent in their behavior than sons. In an important sense, then, what a power-control theory of delinquency is saying is that the higher likelihood of delinquency among boys than girls, and ultimately the higher likelihood of crime among men than women, is an expression of gender differences in risk preferences, which in turn are a product of the different patterns of parental control imposed on daughters compared to sons. In a still more ultimate sense, however, power-control theory goes beyond this to locate the source of such gender differences in a patriarchal connection between the family and the world of work outside it. We turn next, then, to an explication of this connection between work and family.

Class, State, and Household

We have made recurring references to the role of the patriarchal family in reproducing the five links presented in Figure 14.1 as the core of power-control theory. In this section we will argue that the patriarchal family is one distinct type of family class structure. Power-control theory predicts that the links identified in Figure 14.1 are strongest within this family class relation and that therefore this type of family structure plays a central role in accounting for a strong connection between gender and crime. Because patriarchal family structures historically have played such a prominent role in the development of western capitalist societies, the effects of this family structure may be seen throughout our society, even within families that seek to reduce or eliminate patriarchy. We live, in short, in a patriarchal society. Nonetheless, if power-control theory is correct, it should be possible to identify variations in the effects of patriarchy across family class structures. Our recent empirical work reported elsewhere (e.g., Hagan et al. 1987) is devoted to undertaking such tests of our theory. Here, however, we consider the historical roots of the patriarchal family structure to which we attach so much importance, and the place of this family structure in the theory we propose.

Power–control theory focuses on the social organization of gender relations. It is concerned with the ways in which gender relations are established, maintained, perpetuated, or otherwise reproduced. The social reproduction of gender relations occurs across generations, and adolescence thus provides a crucial context in which to address such issues. Meanwhile, societies vary in the social organization and reproduction of their gender relations, so it is highly significant that our development of power-control theory occurs within an industrial capitalist society. Indeed, the question we must initially confront is: What is it about the macro-level development of industrial capitalist societies that accounts for the way in which they reproduce gender relations?

Weber (1947) begins to answer this question by noting that an important juncture in the development of modern capitalism involved the separation of the workplace from the home. Two distinct spheres, which Weber regarded as crucial to the rationalization of an industrial capitalist economy, resulted from this separation: the first was populated by women and focused on domestic labor and consumption and the second was populated by men and centered around labor power and direct production. Weber referred to these respectively as the consumption and production spheres.

The differentiation of the consumption and production spheres is significant for the social reproduction of gender relations. The reproduction of gender relations occurs in both spheres. The state (through police, courts, and correctional agencies) assumes responsibility for reproductive functions in the production sphere, while the family assumes reproductive functions in the consumption sphere. These reproductive functions are inversely related and sexually stratified.

The inverse relationship derives from the fact that as the reproductive activities of the family and kinship groups decline, the reproductive activities of state agencies increase. So, for example, we have elsewhere tested and found evidence (Hagan et al. 1979) to support the following kind of proposition: as informal social controls of family and kinship groups decrease, contact with state agencies such as the police increase. This inverse relationship between state and family-based systems of social control is discussed in greater detail by Donald Black (1976) and Andrew Scull (1976). The important point here is that this differentiation of state and family reproductive functions and the inverse relationship between them also have their source in the separation of the workplace from the home that accompanied the emergence of western capitalist societies. Therefore, the separation of the workplace from the home brought a change in production relations that in turn resulted in changes in reproductive relations, both of which had profound implications for gender relations. Among the most significant of the new gender relations was an intensification of the sexual stratification of social reproduction.

The sexual stratification of reproductive functions in the production and consumption spheres inheres in the fact that while females are disproportionately the instruments and objects of the informal social control activities of the family, males are disproportionately the instruments and objects of formal social control agencies of the state, such as the police. The overall effect of the sexual stratification of these reproductive functions is to perpetuate a gender division in the production and consumption spheres, with females restricted to the home-based consumption sphere and males appropriated to the production sphere, where, among other things, males are more liable to police contact.

The reproductive structures of both the production and consumption spheres are patriarchal in form. However, we have argued that the family is the primary source of patriarchal relations; as a result, in this theoretical statement we give greater attention to the reproductive activities of the family than the state. Nonetheless, we do elsewhere (see Hagan 1988b, chapter 6) address at greater length the role of the state in the reproduction of gender relations. Meanwhile, our attention turns now to the role of the patriarchal family in reproducing the separation of the production and consumption spheres and to recent evidence of change in these arrangements.

The new family that emerged from the separation of work and home assumed responsibility for reproducing (Vogel 1983) the gender division of the production and consumption spheres. This family was patriarchal in form and created a "cult of domesticity" around women (Welter 1966). Today, however, Coser (1985) notes that there is a declining division of the consumption and production spheres, which is reflected in the increased participation of women in the labor force. Coser goes on to note that as women have joined the labor force, they have gained new power in the family, particularly in the upper classes. The result is considerable variation in family class structure, which we model in greater detail elsewhere (Hagan et al. 1987). For the moment, we consider a highly abridged version of this model of family class structure, noting that these family structures vary between two extreme family class relations that form real-life counterparts to two ideal-type families.

The first of these ideal types is largely a residue from an earlier period in which the consumption and production spheres were more strictly divided by gender. To reflect this legacy, we will call this the patriarchal family. Of the family class relations we have identified in our empirical work, the one that should most closely correspond to the ideal-type patriarchal family consists of a husband who is employed in a position with authority over others and a wife who is not employed outside the home. Power-control theory predicts that patriarchal families will tend to reproduce daughters who focus their futures around domestic labor and consumption, as contrasted with sons, who are prepared for participation in direct production. We say more about how this happens below. Here we simply repeat that Weber regarded this process of social reproduction, and implicitly the social reproduction of gender relations, as crucial to the rationalization of industrial capitalism.

At the other extreme is an ideal type we call the egalitarian family, in which the consumption and production spheres are undivided by gender. Of the family class relations we have identified in our empirical work, the one that should most closely correspond to the ideal type egalitarian family includes a mother and father who both are employed in positions with authority over others outside the home. Power-control theory predicts that egalitarian families tend to socially reproduce daughters who are prepared along with sons to join the production sphere. Such families are therefore a part of an overlapping of the consumption and production spheres, which a post-industrial society no longer so clearly keeps apart; such families are a part as well as a product of changing economic relations.

So the patriarchal family perpetuates a gender division in the consumption and production spheres, whereas the egalitarian family facilitates an overlapping of these spheres. The question is how this occurs.

How does this happen and what are its consequences? Power-control theory answers these questions by joining a class analysis of the family with an analysis of the division of parental social control labor discussed above. The link is that parents socially reproduce their own power relationships through the control of their children. The key process involves the instrument-object relationship described under link 2 of Figure 14.1, which is assumed to be at its extreme in the patriarchal family. Here fathers and especially mothers (i.e., as instruments of social control) are expected to control their daughters more than their sons (i.e., as objects of social control). In regard to mothers, we should emphasize that our point is not that they are, in any ultimate causal sense, more important than fathers in the control of daughters, but rather that mothers in patriarchal families are assigned a key instrumental role that involves them more in the day-to-day control of their children, especially their daughters. This imbalanced instrument-object relationship is a product of a division in domestic social control labor and it is a distinguishing feature of the control of daughters in patriarchal families. This instrument-object relationship is a key part of the way in which partriarchal families socially reproduce a gender division in the spheres of consumption and production.

Alternatively, it is through the diminution of this relationship that egalitarian families can generationally reproduce an overlap of the production and consumption spheres. This does not mean that fathers will become as involved as mothers are in the parental control of children; indeed, evidence mounts that this is not the case (e.g., Huber 1976). What it does mean is that parents in egalitarian families will redistribute their control efforts so that daughters are subjected to controls more like those imposed on sons. In other words, in egalitarian families, as mothers gain power relative to husbands, daughters gain freedom relative to sons. In terms of the social reproduction of gender relations, the presence of the imbalanced instrument object relationship helps perpetuate patriarchy, and its absence facilitates equality.

Our final task at this stage is to link this discussion of ideal-type families and the instrument-object relationship with predicted gender differences in common delinquent behavior. This final intervening connection involves the attitudes toward risk-taking involved in the discussion of links 3 and 4 in Figure 14.1. At one extreme, the patriarchal family and its acute instrument-object relationship between parents and daughters engenders a lower preference for risk-taking among daughters. Risk-taking is the antithesis of the passivity that distinguishes the "cult of domesticity." In patriarchal families, then, daughters are taught by their parents to be risk averse, while in egalitarian families, daughters and sons alike are encouraged to be more open to risk-taking. In part, this accommodation of risk is an anticipation of its role in the entrepreneurial and other activities associated with the production sphere, for which daughters and sons are similarly prepared in egalitarian families.

Control theories often regard delinquency as a form of risk-taking (Thrasher 1937; Hirschi 1969), sometimes as an unanticipated consequence of a rewarded willingness to take risks. The result is a parallel in delinquent and entrepreneurial orientations that is reflected in Veblen's frequently quoted observation that "the ideal pecuniary man is like the ideal delinquent in his unscrupulous conversion of goods and persons to his own ends and in a callous disregard of [i.e., freedom from] the feelings and wishes of others or the remoter effects of his actions"(Veblen 1934, p. 237). Power-control theory does not regard this parallel as simple irony but as an unintended consequence of a patriarchal social structure that is valued for its capacity to foster entrepreneurial, risk-taking orientations. With this in mind, power-control theory predicts that patriarchal families will be characterized by large gender differences in common delinquent behavior, while egalitarian families will be characterized by smaller gender differences in delinquency. In egalitarian families, daughters become more like sons in their involvement in such forms of risk-taking as delinquency.

We will go no further here in developing the model of family class relations that we use in further exploring and testing power-control theory. It is sufficient to note that a range of households beyond the forms we have yet considered can be analyzed. The extreme forms of patriarchal and egalitarian family structures discussed so far simply provide a set of scope conditions that may facilitate the application and test of power-control theory. We have set the groundwork for the development and test of this theory.

Some Tentative Conclusions

The statement of power-control theory outlined above is partial, and open to the revision and elaboration that subsequent empirical tests should bring. It deals primarily with links between work and the family and with the connection of these experiences to the reproduction of gender relations that are expressed, in part, in gender differences in involvement in common forms of juvenile delinquency. We have only noted in passing the implications of this theoretical formulation for an understanding of the role of the state in gender relations and delinquency. However, enough has been said to make explicit a basic premise of power-control theory: the idea that linkages between micro and macro levels of explanation are important to the understanding of delinquency causation. Indeed, a central point of power-control theory is that it is only when the macro and micro levels of work and family experience are connected that we begin to see the important ways in which class and gender interact in producing gender differences in delinquency. Gender differences in delinquent and criminal behavior are among the most consistently observed social facts of our discipline. They are neglected starting points for a new etiology of delinquent and criminal behavior.

15

Strategies for Cross-Level Theorizing: Comments on the Meier and Hagan Papers

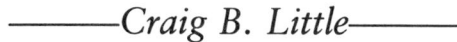
Craig B. Little

My comments on the Meier and Hagan papers will address two issues. First, and most briefly, I will discuss what the papers have to say about cross-level integration as a mode of theorizing, and then I will examine what they offer substantively to the possibilities for cross-level theoretical integration. In this second section, I will relate the papers to one another and look at the contributions and problems posed by each.

Cross-Level Theoretical Integration: Is Now the Time?

While acknowledging the lure of integration, Meier is skeptical of its utility—particularly at present. He claims that prudence might dictate ignoring the issue of integrating micro and macro-level perspectives for now. There are at least three reasons: (1) theorizing is not yet adequate on either level, and therefore we might better concentrate on intra-level theorizing; (2) to date, integrative efforts have not been satisfactory; and (3) such efforts are likely to be unsuccessful even with adequate micro and macro-level theories.

He then presents us with an hypothesis and a conclusion that follows if the hypothesis is correct: ". . . integrations are most pursued when there is little else to do theoretically. In much the same ways that typologies usually signal the failure of theory, so too does the appearance of theoretical integrations." Contained in this hypothesis is an implication that attempts at theoretical integration are borne mostly of theoretical desperation. The evidence from Hagan's work suggests that the hypothesis has some merit.

Hagan takes the value of cross-level theorizing to be self-evident. On his way to outlining the historical background of his power-control theory of gender differences in delinquency rates, he argues that for a time labeling theory disposed of tricky etiological questions about deviance simply by ignoring them. He urges a return to etiological theory and sees the roots of his own growing out of encouragement by feminist scholars (e.g., MacKinnon 1982) to pursue etiological questions—particularly as they pertain to the "underlying behavioral reality involving male criminality," i.e., men commit more crime, especially violent crime, than women.

The search for reasons leads immediately to consideration of gender relations in the family. However, asks Hagan, what theory of the family's relationship to delinquency holds promise? To be sure, the role of the family, particularly its 'breakdown,' had been considered by previous criminologists with confusing, even conflicting, results (Wilkinson 1974). Moreover, "the family has not consistently sustained the interest of sociologists, including those who have remained concerned with the explanation of criminality." In this climate of disarray, possibly with "little else to do theoretically," Hagan proceeds to erect his own cross-level theory.

Now Hagan might agree with my abridged account of his theoretical odyssey, and Meier might agree that Hagan's experience is generally the sort of thing he had in mind when he proposed his hypothesis, but does the hypothesis, provisionally supported by the Hagan case, add anything significant to our insight into cross-level theorizing? Does the hypothesis differ substantially from the observation that when present theories are inadequate, theorists will simply try to construct new ones?[1]

To me, at least, *how* theorizing is done is more important than *when*. The Hagan and Meier papers, taken in comparison, are especially instructive in respect to modes of theorizing, because they advocate different strategies to resume stalled theoretical development. Hagan attempts to *link* theories at different levels of analysis, freely acknowledging (while attempting to accommodate) their conceptual differences. Meier, in contrast, concentrates on erasing conceptual differences by searching for generalizing concepts that *encompass* different theoretical levels. Thus, the Hagan and Meier papers, respectively, represent two distinct cross-level theoretical strategies.

Cross-Level Theoretical Integration: What Is the Payoff?

Without question, the centrality of concepts related to stratification is the most striking similarity in these two papers. Meier, in light of his misgivings about the fruitfulness of cross-level integration, calls for more attention to basic sociological concepts, metatheory, unit theory, and intra-level theories. If I understand him correctly, he predicts failure when trying to stick micro-level theories to macro-level ones without an adequately formulated glue, compatible with both levels to be joined. The glue of theory is concepts, and he suggests that we construct more generalized theories by generalizing the application of our concepts—by creating a more universally compatible glue. "One way to deal with the disjunction between deviance theory and sociological theory is to explicitly link deviance theory with wider concerns in sociological theory." Stratification theory is the domain in which he chooses his initial attempt.

Hagan also borrows heavily from stratification theory, employing the concept of *power* at the macro-structural level of relations in the workplace and *control* in the micro-structural environment of the family to explain gender differences in delinquency rates. In neither case, Meier's conceptual generalizing or Hagan's cross-level theoretical linking, should we find the centrality of concepts from stratification theory surprising. Social differentiation, class, status, and power are certainly among sociology's most widely used concepts. A plausible case could probably be made that they are the most important demarcators of the field.

Social Inequality and Deviance

Meier begins by noting that deviance, whether defined normatively or in terms of audience reaction, depends upon the process of social differentiation. Deviance designation, however, goes beyond mere social differentiation to include a moral dimension. Common to both the normative and societal reaction modes of definition, he argues, is agreement that "deviance refers to disvalued conduct and conditions." He goes on to note that "the concept of deviance explicitly refers to ranked positions created from social judgments that assign persons to particular statuses." The result is a distribution of acts or actors ranging along a continuum from more to less condemned or disvalued—analogous to a distribution of occupations. Thus, we can conceive of parallel stratification systems for nondeviant and deviant statuses in which the former are more likely to be highly valued than the latter. Figure 15.1 makes the point schematically.

Taking the model a step further, Meier argues that we normally conceive of nondeviant stratification systems in terms of rewards such as prestige and deviant ones in relation to punishments. Indeed, one of the presumed punishments for being deviant, he claims, is not being entitled to deference. This is the case, however, depending entirely on our definition of deviance, for there are occasions when deference is a *reward* for rule-breaking. Leaders of delinquent gangs, pimps, and organized crime

Figure 15.1. Types of Status

Social Value	Nondeviant Status	Deviant Status
Highly Valued	A	
.	B	
.	C	
.	.	
.	.	A
.	.	B
.	.	C
.	.	.
.		.
.		.
Disvalued		.

bosses all may have their statuses enhanced and deference toward them increased by their reputations for illegal exploits, actual or fabricated.

Contradictions about the relationship between deviance and deference stem partly from Meier's failure to be clear about what he means by deviance, a not-infrequent shortcoming. At the outset, he implies that crime and deviance are the same. This entails a *normative* definition of deviance.[2] Subsequently, he defines deviance in *reactivist* terms, saying that "deviance refers to differentness." In fact, most of his argument applies best to the marginal deviance most amenable to a reactivist definition (e.g., mental illness, homosexual behavior, unconventional lifestyles, and ascribed conditions such as stuttering or unusual physical appearance), as opposed to 'hard core' deviance consisting of serious rule-breaking, about which there is a great deal of normative consensus reflected in the law (e.g., murder, robbery, or assault).

Nor do the normative and reactivist approaches exhaust the definitional possibilities. There is a third alternative, the statistical, first suggested by Durkheim's discussion of the normal and the pathological. Durkheim defined 'normal' as the average (typical) condition or behavior, with 'pathological' being defined in terms of deviation from the norm. For example, intelligence, operationalized as performance on the Stanford-Binet, ranges along a continuum with the exceptional individuals at both ends representing wide deviations from the norm. According to this definition, both the idiot and the genius are deviants by virtue of their IQs relative to the norm. One advantage of this conception is that it suggests how deviance *and nondeviance* can be conceived along the same dimension of differentiation. In addition, of course, it does not limit the designation of deviant only to the negatively valued. I would submit that such an approach to the definition of deviance adds to Meier's well-taken suggestion that we search for points of conceptual integration between stratification and deviance theory.

Actually, we might even go farther by scrapping the language of deviance theories in favor of the more general language of stratification. Thus, we could think in terms of socially relevant dimensions of differentiation, each of which ranges from valued to disvalued. The selected examples in Figure 15.2 suggest application of this conceptual integration to our analysis of work, gender studies, race, and ethnicity, as well as the inclusion of categories typically subsumed under the study of deviance.

Given the dependence of deviance upon differentiation, Meier suggests that conditions that promote the latter will also promote the former. Thus, he seems to be saying that the more homogeneous a society (i.e., the fewer the dimensions of differentiation), the lower its amount of deviance and the more heterogeneous a society, the greater its amount of deviance. This strikes me simply to follow by definition from his suggested conceptual integration. However, note from Figure 15.2 that the amount of deviance depends not *only* on the number of dimensions of differentiation, but also (often primarily) on people's capability to evaluate positively or negatively along those dimensions. The reduction of the amount of deviance could follow from the elimination of dimensions of differentiation as socially relevant and/*or* reduction of the tendency to evaluate along them. It strikes me that the hidden (though sometimes explicit) agenda of many articles, monographs, and undergraduate sociology courses, including those specifically concerning deviant behavior, is to temper the tendency to apply these socially acquired predispositions to evaluate, especially to evaluate negatively. This is a laudable goal in reference to certain kinds of marginal deviants, such as mental patients or gays. It is a less compelling one in regard to rapists, murderers, or thieves.

Deviance, Differentiation, and Boundary Maintenance

Meier argues that "social judgments of disvaluement represent a core component of the concept of deviance."[3] He observes that social disvaluement also has its place in systems of stratification. I agree. The demand for deference is actually a social control technique used by su-

Figure 15.2. Socially Relevant Dimensions of Differentiation

Social Value	Occupational Prestige	Type of Work (Gender)	Race/ Ethnicity	Height	IQ	Sexuality
Highly Valued	A	"Men's"	WASP	Med./Tall	High	Hetero Sexual
.	.	.	.	.	.	.
.	.	.	.	.	.	.
.	.	.	.	.	.	.
.	.	.	.	.	.	.
Disvalued	Z	"Women's"	Nonwhite/Non European	Short	Low	Homo-sexual

perordinates to enforce a system of stratification on subordinates. Witness the role of deference in perpetuating segregation, America's apartheid, as described in John Dollard's mid-1930s study of *Caste and Class in a Southern Town* (1937). The successful impositon of demands for deference, of course, has implications for subordinates' self-esteem, and at least one previous sociologist, John Hewitt in his book *Social Stratification and Deviant Behavior* (1970), has attempted to set out systematically the implications of stratification for deviant behavior using self-esteem as the pivotal linking concept. Simply put, those who are denied equal opportunities to participate and succeed in the dominant system of stratification will suffer the injury of lowered self-esteem. Many will passively suffer this injury and its attendant anguish; others will more agressively seek status attainment and higher self-esteem in alternative spheres—e.g., delinquent subcultures or gang delinquency.[4]

Taking Meier's lead, I would like to suggest an additional concept, fairly well developed in respect to deviance theory, that also seems to be relevant to a consideration of stratification—the concept of boundary maintenance. Kai Erickson made excellent use of it in his study *Wayward Puritans* (1966) to suggest that deviance designation is an essential part of community definition. A community is only meaningful as such if its members can distinguish themselves (insiders) from others (outsiders). Likewise, it seems to me, stratification systems depend upon boundary maintenance between strata. In stratification systems, higher-level participants establish boundaries between themselves and lower-level participants through a combination of structured exclusion and demands for deference. Threats to the institutions that maintain the boundaries between strata are threats to the system of stratification itself. Superordinates know this very well and, therefore, will go to great lengths to protect the institutions of boundary maintenance. Such institutions range from laws or rules that segregate by social category (sex, race, age) to less formal customs, such as pressures or prohibitions against marrying outside one's ethnic group.

Both communities and stratification systems rely upon boundary maintenance, a fact that reinforces and extends Meier's observation that the processes of deviance creation and the reproduction of classes are similar in important ways. The similarity also points to a paradox, however. Being somewhat left-leaning and egalitarian in their politics, most sociologists today would regard stratification as bad, to be ameliorated, and a legitimate prime target for activists seeking social change. I count myself among them. Sociologists are sometimes seen as mildly threatening by elites, as they often attack the very boundary-maintaining institutions that insure the differentiation between members of classes. At the same time, however, these same sociologists are apt to bemoan the loss of civility, mutuality, and community in contemporary society. Many sociologists, it seems, would ideally like to see less stratification and greater community.

The paradox is that the characteristics we often admire about communities—close-knit, caring, mutually responsible attitudes and social relations supported by customs or institutions that promote solidarity—depend heavily on the process of establishing community identity. And community identity, in turn, inevitably involves establishing and maintaining normative boundaries. We care especially about those in *our* community—whether defined by residence, race, religion, or ethnicity—because we share their insider status. Community identity entails boundary maintenance, and boundary maintenance entails identification of insiders versus outsiders. The negative aspects of boundary maintaining—institutions of exclusion, in-groups, prejudice against outsiders, and the like—are readily decried in the case of stratification. But how are we to resolve the positive elements of community with the exclusivity so much a part of its establishment and maintenance? Considering the convergence of stratification and deviance theory could help us to frame and confront this question more forthrightly than we have heretofore.

Power-Control Theory

Three questions will be considered: What is power-control theory? In particular, is it really cross-level theorizing? Is it important? What are its alternatives?[5]

What Is It?

The essence of Hagan's theory is that differences in rates of delinquency by gender can be accounted for by differences in the amount of control exercised over boys versus girls in families. The greater the control, the greater the aversion to risk and the lower the delinquency. Generally, girls are subject to more control; thus their lower rates of delinquency. More specifically, girls in patriarchal families are subject to more control than girls in egalitarian ones. Thus, the theory predicts that the delinquency rate differences between boys and girls will be *greater* in patriarchal families than in egalitarian families. The distinction between patriarchal and egalitarian families takes us outside the internal structure and dynamics of the family to include the role of each parent in relation to the workplace. In this sense the theory could be considered cross-level theorizing, dealing with the micro-environment of the family and the macro-environment of economic production and class relations.

Thus, the 'power' side of the theory Hagan claims to be the macro dimension, while the 'control' side is micro. Frankly, I do not agree that "conceptual and empirical considerations of power typically occur at higher levels of aggregation and abstraction than do discussions of control, and therefore characteristically are kept separate." I find the attempted distinction forced and unconvincing. The concept of power has been employed usefully in the analysis of families (Straus et al. 1980; Allen and Straus 1980) and the concept of control certainly could be used in analyses of international relations.[6]

To be sure, Hagan's theory does link the family, a smaller unit of analysis, with the societal economy, a larger one. The theory is indeed 'cross-level' if simply linking small units of analysis to large ones is what is meant by such theorizing. My own preference is shared by Meier, who states that micro theories identify social psychological properties of individual actors and employ concepts such as socialization, motivation, and identification, while macro theories concentrate on features of social structure and tend to use concepts such as class, power, and anomie. According to these definitions, Hagan's formulation is primarily a *structural* theory. It focuses on how the social class structure influences the structure of families and, in turn, how family structure shapes gender socialization. For this and other reasons, the theory might be better named "A Structural Theory of Class, Family Control, and Gender Socialization."[7]

Is the Theory Important?

You will notice that my proposed name for the theory omits a reference to delinquency. In other statements and tests of the theory (Hagan, Gillis, and Simpson 1985; Hagan, Simpson and Gillis 1987) the dependent variable has been "common delinquency." As operationally defined, this type of delinquency tends to be relatively frequent, minor in severity, and therefore, fairly common amongst adolescents. Though unquestionably illegal, these types of adolescent activities tend mostly to be annoying and transitory. The vast majority of those who commit common offenses as teenagers do not, then, lead lives of street crime as adults. However, when expressing concern about delinquency, most people are worried about hard core violent street crime often associated with gang violence and habitual drug use; that is, violent acts that are perceived as dangerous to the public and have a high potential for marking the onset of an adult, recidivist criminal career, including multiple and extended encounters with the criminal justice system.

Common delinquency, as a dependent variable, does have the virtue of being operationally clear and measurable for an empirical test of the theory. Moreover, it is activity at this low level of severity that is probably most amenable to explanation by control theory. Hagan states that his theory intends to address two questions: "how and why are individuals located in male adolescent positions *freer to deviate* in ways defined by the state as delinquent than are individuals located in female adolescent positions?" Deviant activity, given the freedom to engage in it, is assumed.[8] I find this assumption easier to accept in reference to common offenses than for hardcore ones. Thus, certain status offenses, such as underage drinking, marijuana smoking, fighting, and joyriding can be fun and, in Hagan's words, represent "a range of activities, some criminal and some more conventional, that are more open to men than women."[9] Assault with a weapon, muggling, or armed robbery are probably beyond what can be characterized as the kind of enjoyable, pleasurable, or liberating activities that almost anyone would engage in merely if he or she dared. Put bluntly, Hagan's theory may be appropriate to explain some amount of the gender differences in respect to some common status offenses; it is probably not adequate to explain as much variance in the more serious ones. And the type of delinquency (and crime, for that matter) that people generally most fear is street crime, especially that involving violence.[10]

Therefore, I think that Hagan's theory is less important as a theory of delinquency than as a more general structural theory of gender socialization. It probably does explain some of the gender variance in common delinquency, but it has even more extensive implications in reference to gender differences in risk taking. Hagan, of course, alludes to this through Veblen's words: "the ideal pecuniary man is like the ideal delinquent . . . in a callous disregard of the feelings and wishes of others. . ." Thus being a 'good' well-behaved adolescent in American society may not be the most effective preparation for later adult success. The daring, even mildly illegal, aggressive behavior more common to male than female adolescents may be most important for what it tells us about the gender biases in American standards for success and who is best socially equipped to meet them.[11]

The theory states that gender differences in risk aversion depend upon different patterns of parental control imposed on daughters as compared to sons. In patriarchal families, those in which father works outside the home while mother does not, much more control is imposed on daughters than on sons. In egalitarian families where both parents work, "parents . . . will redistribute their control efforts so that daughters are subjected to controls more like those imposed on sons. In other words, in egalitarian families, as mothers gain power relative to husbands, daughters gain freedom relative to sons." Of course, one reason that egalitarian families' daughters, and presumably also sons, gain more freedom is simply the *time* that is devoted to control. In a patriarchal family a full-time 'controller' (mother) is permanently on duty. Not so in dual-career or single-parent families, where 'latchkey' children and adolescents are common.

The ideal types of the theory's independent variable—intact, nuclear patriarchal, or egalitarian families—may better reflect the past than the future, at least in America.[12] Moynihan (1986) has summarized Census Bureau figures.

> In overall terms by the end of the century we project that about three-quarters of American families will be of the "traditional" sort, whereas in 1960 nearly nine of ten families could be so described. In less than two generations the proportion of families headed by single persons will have doubled. Again, we can assume a good deal of churning, with children more and more likely to spend some portion of their childhood in single-parent households.
>
> In the final two decades of the century we project that the number of families will increase from 59.5 million to 72.5 million, which is to say a net of 13 million families. But of these additional households, only 5.9 million are expected to be "traditional" husband-wife families. Female-headed families will account for 5.8 million of the net increase, and male-headed families for 1.3 million. Put another way, in the period 1980–2000 the number of female-headed families will increase at more than five times the rate of husband-wife families. Family households headed by males with no wife present will increase at some six times the rate of the traditional sort. (p. 147)

The Hagan theory refers to an intact nuclear family, which continues to be less archetypical in the United States. Furthermore, the single-parent family varies in frequency and form—certainly by race and probably by class. In 1984, amongst families with children under 18 in the United States, 80 percent of white families had both parents in residence while 41 percent of black families did. Fifty-six percent of black families were maintained by the mother alone, compared to 17 percent of white families. Hagan notes that a range of household types beyond the patriarchal and egalitarian forms remain to be incorporated in the theory. Inferences for family class relations between these two polar ideal types are not straightforward. We must surely know a great deal more than we do about the dynamics of two-parent versus single-parent households before the theory's implications for the latter become apparent.

What Are the Alternatives?

The predictions of the theory are clear: ". . . patriarchal families will tend to reproduce daughters who focus their future around domestic labor and consumption, as contrasted with sons who are prepared for participation in direct production. . . . (E)galitarian families will tend to socially reproduce daughters who are prepared along with sons to join the production sphere." The reason is the *structure* of control relations in the family. Greater control leads to greater risk aversion; greater risk aversion means greater passivity (this distinguishes the "cult of domesticity") and poorer preparatiion for roles in the entrepreneurial and production sphere.

But why is the control variable necessary at all? Why not turn directly to a micro-level theoretical concept—role modeling? Thus, in both patriarchal and egalitarian families, sons model their behavior on fathers and daughters on mothers. Sons in patriarchal families are more oriented toward work outside the family and daughters less so simply because that is the reality of their own family experience in which they learn about the socially approved behavior for each gender role. In egalitarian families where fathers and mothers are more alike in relationship to the work sphere, sons and daughters will learn to be more alike on a whole range of attitudes and behaviors, including risk-taking and participation in illegal activity.

Put simply, the effects of control and role modeling are difficult, if not impossible, to disentangle theoretically or empirically. Stated in its purest form, control theory is *not* a motivational explanation. The goal is to explain why people do *not* engage in deviant acts as opposed to why they do. It is assumed that they will if left uncontrolled. Likewise, in Hagan's theory, control is used to explain risk aversion (i.e., why people do *not* engage in risk-taking activity) by incorporating the assumption that when left uncontrolled, people will become risk takers. It is risk aversion that requires an explanation. His explanation is found in the application of control. Less control leads to greater *freedom* to be what one will be naturally, a risk taker; greater control leads to less *freedom* to be a risk taker and, therefore, to patterns of risk-averse behavior.[13] In contrast, the language of role modeling, a motivational theory concept, is the language of 'learning to become' as opposed to 'freedom to become.'

Note how Hagan himself incorporates the language of socialization into his theory. ". . . In patriarchal families daughters are *taught* by their parents to be risk averse. Alternatively, in egalitarian families, daughters and sons alike are *encouraged* to be more open to risk-taking" [italics added]. We must ask in respect to Hagan's theory: Are daughters in egalitarian families proposed to be *left free* to become greater risk-takers or are they *taught* to be so? And presuming the answer is that the theory emphasizes the freedom over the teaching, what kind of research design could provide the evidence to choose conclusively between the alternatives? Now, of course, it is possibly true that both extent of control and role modeling contribute to the variation in risk aversion. The research task then would be to sort out the amount of variance accounted for by each.

Conclusion

Meier and Hagan have provided us with alternative strategies for attaining cross-level theoretical integration. Meier, doubtful of the utility (to say nothing about the motivation) of such theorizing, opts for conceptual generalization at the metatheoretical level. The result is fruitful, in my judgment, simply because it encourages one to play creatively with concepts. The danger is that the playfulness can be deceptively satisfying and even deter us from trying to sort out our metatheoretical insights in terms of unit theoretical analyses.

Hagan's work, as a unit theory, makes specific predictions in propositional form. Thus it is more vulnerable to a detailed attack on its concepts and falsifiability. Whether Hagan's theory is actually a case of cross-level theorizing is less important than the issues it raises in reference to differential gender socialization.

16

Exploring Integration of Theoretical Levels of Explanation: Notes on Gang Delinquency

——————James F. Short, Jr.——————

The goals of this paper are modest and straightforward: (1) to suggest a rationale for integrating levels of explanation; (2) to suggest alternatives to simplifying assumptions which ignore well established knowledge; (3) to identify relationships between levels of explanation which might foster their integration.[1]

Levels of explanation refer to what is to be explained as well as to how it is to be explained. As I will use these terms, the *individual* level seeks to explain behaviors of individuals, while the *macrosocial* level focuses on rates and types of behavior. Explanation at the individual level is in terms of characteristics of individuals, while at the macro level it is on social and cultural system differences. The *microsocial* level directs attention to behavioral outcomes of ongoing behavioral events, and seeks explanation in terms of the interaction processes characteristic of such events (see Short 1985a; Cohen and Short 1976). The relevance of each level of explanation to the other levels is what theoretical integration is about.

The rationale is simple. Theoretical and empirical advance, as well as effective social policy, require knowledge that transcends the limitations of levels of explanation standing alone. Yet scholarly disciplines and practitioners in juvenile justice remain by and large locked in departments, research units, and programs which, if not mutually exclusive, tend to be compartmentalized and insular. Nevertheless, it is clear that there is much overlap among disciplines, and between disciplines and practitioners, in the nature of their interests in delinquency and delinquents.

Simplifying Assumptions and Gray Areas of Knowledge

The fact that one cannot say everything at once forces decisions as to how to organize theory and research. We do so clumsily, often by the use of simplifying assumptions. Simplifying assumptions are useful, indeed necessary, but they often become little more than easy ways out of the difficult task of critical examination and use of knowledge from other disciplines or research traditions.[2] Thus, for example, the assumption that there is *a* human nature or that human nature is *either* fixed and antisocial *or* malleable and developing is untenable and unnecessary. As knowledge of genetic limitations and potentialities has grown, it has become clear that biology and experience interact, and that physiological conditions *in combination* with social processes and conditions shape human development.

Similarly, the manner in which individual compositional features of social and cultural systems affect those systems, as well as the outcomes of events within them, is critical to macro- and microsocial levels of explanation. Recent research on crime and communities, for example, suggests that communities, as well as individuals, have "careers in crime" (see Reiss and Tonry 1986). The manner in which these careers relate to the sorts of individuals who compromise communities must be neither assumed nor ignored.

The discovery that involvement in minor delinquencies is virtually universal has led some to assume that it is unnecessary to inquire as to why young people commit delinquent acts. It is important only to know why they sometimes do not do so. Increasingly, that question is being posed as "Why don't they commit *serious* crimes?" That is the more popular (and troubling) question (see Blumstein et al. 1986; cf. Gottfredson and Hirschi 1986). Most criminal involvement also is varied and widespread, rather than esoteric, specialized, or confined to a small minority. In view of these facts it makes little sense to ask what distinguishes delinquents from nondelinquents. Nor is it sufficient to limit inquiry to why young people do or do not commit delinquent behaviors. Etiologically relevant questions must concern the processes and mechanisms of motivation *and* control, in different social systems and subcultures that account for variations in behavior.

A very large number of adolescent (and preadolescent) behaviors are of sufficient concern to adults to have been legally proscribed. Many of these change over time and circumstances. Motivations of 'reactors' to such behaviors vary, as do those of offenders.[3] Finally, those who engage in acts defined as delinquent do so only occasionally. Even the most seriously delinquent boy or girl does not spend much of his or her time committing delinquent acts; in addition, most youngsters in even the highest 'delinquency areas' do not become seriously delinquent. It is in 'gray areas,' such as that between 'normal' adolescent behaviors and those that stretch the bonds and the boundaries of control beyond toleration levels in families and communities, that different levels of explanation become critical. Subcultures and related group processes help to explain both why some individuals do and others do not commit proscribed behaviors, and perhaps the circumstances in which some individuals will or will not do so. The strength of 'mainstream' cultural norms varies, as do local community toleration levels. When either of these is weak or ambiguous, the push needed to encourage participation in law breaking is lessened. The ambiguity of general American norms concerning erosion of income tax, 'sharp' business dealings, macho images and the use of violence to settle disputes lends support to those who would commit both property and person offenses (see Matza and Sykes 1961). In some communities, 'hustling' is regarded as 'hard work' and a way of life (Valentine 1978). When opportunities for illegal gain exist and when community or group norms support illegal behavior, or when group processes lead in that direction, legal proscriptions may lack force. Research at the microsocial level is necessary for more precise understanding of the situations or circumstances under which group processes supersede conventional norms and the mechanisms by which individual decisionmaking leads to delinquent v. nondelinquent behavior choices.

Such broadly sketched parameters leave many questions unanswered—e.g., which boys and girls make which choices, or have such choices made for them by others; why delinquency episodes occur when and where they do; what sorts of occasions give rise to delinquency on the part of what sorts of youngsters. Still another gray area thus concerns the processes, mechanisms, and types of life events which trigger delinquent episodes, lead to greater individual commitment to deviant identities, or both.

Delinquency as Collective Behavior

The remainder of this paper focuses on relationships between levels of explanation of individual and group behaviors among members of delinquent gangs. Observations are drawn chiefly, but not exclusively, from studies conducted in Chicago during the period 1959 through the early 1970s (see Short and Strodtbeck 1965; Short and Moland 1976).

The research is embedded in the following widely accepted theoretical principles regarding subcultural formation: (1) "social separation produces cultural differentiation" (Glaser 1971); (2) available alternative choices for action are socially structured, (see Merton 1957; also Stinchcombe, 1975); and (3) "the crucial condition for the emergence of new cultural forms is the existence, *in effective interaction with one another, of a number of actors with similar problems of adjustment*" (Cohen, 1955, p. 59).[4]

The gangs we studied fit the following defining criteria: (1) recurrent congregation outside the home; (2) self-defined inclusion and exclusion criteria and continuity of affiliation; (3) a territorial basis consisting of customary hanging and ranging areas, including self-defined use and occupancy rights; (4) a versatile activity repertoire; and (5) organizational differentiation—e.g., by authority, roles, prestige, friendship, or special interest cliques.[5]

Macrosocial Observations

All of the gang communities (where the lower-class gang and nongang groups were located) were characterized by lower socioeconomic status indicators. There were, however, marked differences between the black and white gang areas, e.g., income levels and overcrowded living conditions—no white gang community studied was as disadvantaged as the least disadvantaged black gang community. The latter were also more disadvantaged with respect to family stability and other institutional measures. In sum, members of the black gangs lived in communities consisting of the "unstable poor," while the white gangs resided in working-class communities among the "stable poor" (Miller 1964).[6]

Youth groups from the black and white middle-class communities were better off than any of the gang communities, but the white middle-class community, as well as the white middle-class boys studied, were more affluent than the black middle-class boys and their local community (see Short and Strodtbeck 1965; also Cartwright et al. 1975).

Life in the white gang areas revolved around conventional institutions such as the Catholic church, local political organizations, and 'improvement associations' (a euphemism in some instances for keeping blacks from moving into white neighborhoods). Ethnic organizations and extended kinship groups, unions and other job relationships, and formally organized recreational patterns (e.g., bowling leagues) were important sources of community stability for both adults and young people. Neighborhood taverns, often with a distinct ethnic clientele, were the exclusive domain of neighborhood adults.

Life in the black gang communities was characterized by informal neighboring from the vantage of front-door steps or stair landings, and by socializing in local taverns and pool halls and other quasi-public settings such as 'quarter parties.' There was a great deal of mingling of young people and adults, which sometimes resulted in delinquent episodes such as the following observation of a 'quarter party':

> This woman who is called "Ma" was giving the party. There was a lot of drinking—inside, outside in the cars, in the alleys, everywhere. There were Rattlers (the gang to which the worker was assigned) and a bunch of boys from the (housing) projects. They had two rooms, neither of them very large. There was some friction going on when I got there—boys bumping each other, and stuff like this. There were a lot of girls there. Must have been about fifty to seventy-five people in these two rooms, plus another twenty or twenty-five outside. There were some older fellows there, too—mainly to try and grab one of these younger girls. The girls were doing a lot of drinking—young girls, twelve- and thirteen-year olds. The age group in this party must have been from about eleven to the thirties. There were girls there as young as eleven, but no boys younger than about fifteen. The girls are there as a sex attraction, and with the older boys and men around, you know the younger boys aren't going to do any good.
>
> We had one real fight. One of David's sisters was talking to one of these boys from the projects. I guess she promised to go out to the car with him. To get outside you had to go out this door and down this hall, and then out on the porch and down the stairs. She went as far as the porch. As she got out there, I guess she changed her mind. By this time the guy wasn't standing for any "changing the mind" business, and he started to pull on her. She yelled for David, and he came running out. All he could see was his sister and a guy he didn't know pulling on her. David plowed right into the guy. I guess he hit him about fifteen times and knocked him down and across the street, and by the time I got there the guy was lying in the gutter. I took David off to the side and told Gary to get the guy out of there.
>
> Duke, Red, and Mac were standing eight or ten feet away, sort of watching these project boys. This one boy goes up the street on the other side and comes up *behind* David and me. We don't see him. All of a sudden Duke runs right past me and he plows into this guy. Duke said, "Well look, man, the guy was sneaking up behind you and I wasn't gonna have him hit you from behind! I did it to protect you."
>
> I got the guy up and he said, "I wasn't going to hit you. I just wanted to see what was going on." But Duke says, "Let's run all these project guys out." I talked them out of it. I said, "Look, don't you think you've done enough? The police aren't here yet, but if you start anything else somebody is bound to call them. The party is still going on so why don't we all just go back inside. No sense in breaking up a

good thing. You paid your quarter." (Adapted from Short and Strodtbeck 1965, pp. 110–111)

In contrast to the relationships between black gang members and local adults, white gang boys more often found themselves openly at odds with proprietors of local hangouts and other adults and adult institutions, particularly concerning drinking (which was virtually universal), drug use (which was rare among most of these boys), sexual delinquency, and general rowdyism. Stealing was tacitly condoned by adult 'fences' and other purchasers of stolen goods but deeply resented by those local residents who had been victimized, and feared by others. In communities undergoing racial transition (during the period of study this included most lower-class white communities in Chicago), the rowdyism complained of was at times turned to advantage and encouraged by local adults. An apposite case is the following:

> At approximately 12:30 at night, I was hanging with a group of fifteen to twenty members of the Amboys, Bengals, Sharks, and a few Mafia, at the corner of the park. The group was a mixed one of boys and girls ranging in age from sixteen to twenty. For the most part, they were sitting or reclining in the park, talking, drinking beer, or wrestling with the girls. They were not unusually loud or boisterous because a policeman on a three-wheeler had been by a half-hour earlier and had warned them of the lateness of the hour.
>
> I noticed a solitary teenage figure ambling along on the sidewalk heading toward the Avenue, but paid no particular heed. As the figure neared the group, he made no effort to swerve over and join the group but continued by. This was an oddity, so I watched the youth as he neared the curb where I was sitting. I suddenly realized that the boy was black, and in danger if detected. I did not dare do or say anything for fear of alerting the kids, and for a few minutes I thought he could pass by without detection. However, a Bengal who had been drinking beer spotted him and immediately asked, "Am I drunk or is that a Nigger?" The attention of the entire group was then focused on the black youth, who by this time had stepped off the curb and was walking in the center of the street.
>
> Behind him, however, consternation and anger arose spontaneously like a mushroom cloud. I heard muttered threats, "Let's kill the bastard," "Get the motherfucker," "Come on, let's get going." Even the girls agreed.
>
> Within seconds, about a dozen of the kids began running after the black youth. Realizing that I was unable to stem the tide, I yelled out

"Hey man, look alive." The boy heard me in midstride, but did not turn around. Again I found it necessary to shout a warning as the white teen-agers were rapidly overtaking him. At my second outcry, the black youth turned around and saw the white kids closing in on him. Without hesitation, he took off at full speed with the white mob at his heels yelling shouts of "Kill the bastard—don't let him get away."

I remained standing by my car, joined by three Amboys who did not participate in the chase. The president of the Amboys shook his head, stating that his guys reacted like a bunch of kids whenever they saw a colored guy, and openly expressed his wish that the boy would get away. Another Amboy, in an alibi tone, excused his non-participation by explaining that he couldn't run fast enough to catch anybody. Harry merely stated that the black kid didn't bother him, so why should he be tossed in jail for assaulting a stranger.

We could hear the progress of the chase from the next block. There were shouts and outcries as the pursued ran down the street and his whereabouts were echoed by the bedlam created by his pursuers. Finally, there was silence and we waited for approximately fifteen minutes before the guys began to straggle back. As they returned, each recited his share of the chase. Barney laughingly related that Guy had hurdled a parked car in an effort to tackle the kid, who had swerved out into the street. He said he had entered a coal yard, looking around to find where the boy had hidden, when an adult from a second floor back porch warned that he had better get out of there as the coal yard was protected by a large and vicious Great Dane.

The black youth apparently had decided that he couldn't outrun his tormenters and had gone in and out of back yards until he was able to find a hiding place. His pursuers began to make a systematic search of the alleys, garages, back yards, corridors, etc. *The boys were spurred on to greater efforts by the adults of the area who offered advice and encouragement.* One youth laughingly related that a woman, from her bedroom window, kept pointing out probable hiding places in her back yard so that he would not overlook any sanctuary. Other youths related similar experiences. Glen related that as the youths turned onto X street, he began to shout to the people ahead in the block that "a Nigger was coming" so that someone ahead might catch or head off the boy. (Adapted from Short and Strodtbeck 1964, pp. 112–114)

This scene was typical of late evening gatherings of boys and girls at 'their' park in a neighborhood that was unsuccessfully resisting invasion by black families. In both of these field reports, macro-level phenomena (the ecological setting, normative properties of the community, and the general structure of relationships between young people and adults) set the stage for events that resulted in delinquent behavior. In both, the action is a function of the ongoing interaction of parties involved in the events. There is, of course, much we do not and cannot know about these events—their outcomes and other possible outcomes—but it is clear that the behavior observed cannot be understood without reference to both macro- and micro-level phenomena.

Because of the racial ecology of Chicago, black and white gangs did not fight with one another. Black gangs were deeply embedded in lower-class cultural and community settings. In contrast, many black families in the vanguard of invasion of white residential areas were able to do so as a result of relative economic affluence (see Bursik 1986).

The Individual Level of Explanation. Direct evidence of "common crime" role models in the black gang areas is found in field observations:

> That poolroom down there is nothing but hustlers—the worst type of people in the area—prostitutes dressed kind of flashy, and their pimps. There was one guy, a dope addict, wears his shades, one of the regulars. He was shooting pool, and he recognized me and spoke to me and to the fellows.
>
> The three of us started shooting a game on the back table. There was a conversation that the older fellows were having on one of the front tables about some kind of robbery that they had just pulled. They had been busted. They were all teasing one of the guys that was shooting, about the fact that he was caught. The police had him chained around a lamp post. He got his hand out of one of the cuffs, but he still had one of the cuffs on. He couldn't get it off, and they were teasing him. Everyone in the poolroom was aware of what was going on. (Adapted from Short and Strodtbeck 1965, p. 108)

The "business as usual" nature of criminal behavior in the black gang communities is further illustrated by another detached worker's report that a street dealer in marijuana was enclosing a note with her new address in each bag she sold. Customers were thanked for their business and asked to continue their patronage in her new location.

Such crime as existed in the white gang communities was more covert. The white gangs themselves were also less visible in their communities, to younger children as well as to adults, than was the case in the black communities. Field observations confirmed these differences. While attending an evening of boxing matches between members of two black gangs, I was seated at ringside with the leader of one of the gangs. Several pre-teen boys were seated immediately back of us. One of these boys, aged nine or ten, whispered loudly (and admiringly) to another, "That's Buck, president of the Cobras." Pre-teens also were much in evidence at other social occasions involving gang members, far more so than in comparable gatherings in the white gang areas.

These observations were confirmed by interview responses of boys in each of our six research design strata (black and white lower-class gang and non-gang, and black and white middle-class) concerning their perceptions of legitimate and criminal opportunities (see Cloward and Ohlin 1960; Short, Rivera, and Tennyson 1965). Legitimate educational and occupational opportunities tended strongly to be perceived as more open by whites than by blacks, by middle-class than by lower-class boys, and by nongang than by gang boys. Perceptions of adult clout and helpfulness to young people followed this same pattern. Responses indicative of integration of the carriers of criminal and noncriminal values, criminal learning structures, and visibility of criminal careers were precisely the opposite.

A consistent picture emerged also from interviews with boys and with adults whom they had nominated as those with whom they had the most contact (see Rivera and Short 1967a). Gang members were more isolated from the conventional adult world, more embedded in the lower-class milieu, and less likely to receive assistance from adults than were nongang boys from the same communities. Middle-class boys were more favored in each respect. The contrast was especially notable among the black youngsters studied and among their 'significant adults.' Gang members, compared to their nongang counterparts, had little reason to believe that adults were willing or able to help them in substantial ways. Analysis of the boys' evaluations of adult roles suggested that detached workers played a compensating, albeit quite limited, role for gang boys vis-a-vis the adult world (see Short, Rivera, and Marshall 1964). Study of the occupational choices of the boys found *social relationships with adults* to be more influential than were the boys' perceptions of the mobility chances of neighborhood peers, again highlighting the importance of adult relationships, again to the detriment of the gang boys (see Rivera and Short 1967b).

All of these observations suggest that adult-world macro-level influences are 'translated' by means of conventional socialization processes, such as those specified in social learning theory (Akers 1977) and social cognitive theory (Bandura 1986).

The Social Disability Hypothesis. Very early in the research, field observations indicated that lower-class boys and girls lacked social assurance and possessed few social skills. Detached workers frequently reported that members of their gangs did not feel comfortable when outside 'the area' and that they were ill at ease in many social situations. The following excerpt from a detached worker's report is apposite, and suggests as well that members of the gang under observation had a low degree of mutual obligation to one another outside of the gang context. The worker is describing events prior to and during the annual banquet of the YMCA of Metropolitan Chicago, a very large, 'dressy' affair attended by many of the city's political, business, and philanthropy leaders.

> I talked it over with Duke. Duke wanted me to get him a date with one of the YMCA girls from the downtown office. I told him I thought maybe he'd be better to take Elaine because she's never been to a downtown affair. Elaine has a baby girl who is a year old and one that's three. Duke's never taken her to a real nice place. I had an extra ticket and I said, "Well, Duke, seeing that you and Butch get along real well, maybe Butch would go."
>
> Duke said, "No, no, we don't want to take Butch because he doesn't know how to eat out in company."
>
> I smiled and said, "Crisake, he knows just as much as you do."
>
> "No, he just don't know how to eat out in company." Then he went back to the time I took them to the Prudential Building. I suggested that we go in and get a cup of coffee, but Butch said, "No, we'd better go back to the area and get a hot dog or Polish [sausage]." And Duke was all for it, too, because he didn't want to go in there either. They're real shy about going into a strange place that's real nice. Earlier in the summer I took Duke, Butch, and Harry out to Lake Meadows, and they were real shy. They didn't want to go in because they felt they weren't dressed good enough. Anyway, Duke didn't feel Butch was qualified. So I said, "Okay, how about Harry?"
>
> "Hell no. Harry hasn't got enough clothes to go."
>
> On the way to the banquet I told them approximately what was going to go on, about the main speaker being President Eisenhower's doctor. When we got to the amphitheater, I dropped Elaine and Alice [Duke's aunt and the worker's date for the evening], and Duke and I went to park the car. I told him to go in and check the coats. He look around and finally came back because he didn't know where they were supposed to go. Then I found the tables and I put Duke and Elaine together.
>
> Overall, he had a real good time. Elaine complained because Duke insulted her. Duke was trying to show her how to cut the meat. He said Elaine didn't know which hand to hold the knife in. She was real hungry and she ate everything but the meat, because Duke was rapping on

her so much. She felt real bad for not having eaten the meat. She didn't know whether it would have been appropriate to have Duke cut her meat or not. (Adapted from Short and Strodtbeck 1965, pp. 219–220)

The boys' lack of social skills was advanced as a possible explanation for aggressive behavior both within the gang and in relations between gangs (see Short and Strodtbeck 1965; Gordon, 1967). In the absence of social skills, verbal aggression, body punching, wrestling, and aggressive posturing serve as a sort of least common denominator for interpersonal relationships. Boys who possess more advanced social skills are often rewarded with leadership positions. However, the gang provides no encouragement for (and often discourages) the development or exercise of skills necessary to function in such conventional settings as school, work, or marriage. Again, a field report is illustrative:

Fuzzhead, a member of the Chiefs, approached the detached worker in a pool hall hangout and began to talk very seriously about his plans to get and keep a job so that he could provide for the girl he wanted to marry. The worker probed Fuzzhead and, finding him deadly in earnest, encouraged the boy in these ambitions and indicated his willingness to help him secure a steady job. In the midst of the conversation other Chiefs entered the pool hall and came over to where the worker and Fuzzhead were conversing. Upon discovering the topic of conversation they began ridiculing Fuzzhead's ambitions. Fuzzhead abruptly discontinued this discussion and withdrew from the conversation. (Adapted from Short and Strodtbeck 1965, p. 222)

Participation in the gang does little to prepare young people for conventional adult roles. Being 'streetwise' is not an asset in most available low-level jobs. Toughness and physical and verbal aggression are often counterproductive on the job, as is the casual attitude toward time displayed in hanging activities. Demands for punctuality, perseverance, and quality performance are likewise alien to gang culture. As a socializing context, the gang runs counter to many requirements of modern civilization (see Inkeles 1966).

Systematic Testing of Individual Gang Boys

Several more systematic and rigorous individual-level measures also differentiated among our samples. Gang boys made the lowest scores on six measures of intelligence, designed specifically so as not to be biased against lower-class and gang subjects (see Cartwright et al. 1980). Gang members were followed in these measures by lower class nongang and middle-class nongang boys, in that order. In each class-by-gang-status category, black youngsters scored lower than did their white counterparts.

From the same set of testing routines, Desmond Cartwright and his colleagues also found that the gang boys differed from the nongang boys on several personality factors. The data suggest that gang boys tended to be more uncertain of themselves, more self-critical and self-questioning, and to have a poor regard for self. The tests also provided evidence that the gang boys were less decisive and more suggestible, and that they had more difficulty in task concentration. They had poor immediate memory, were slower in making judgments, and were less effective on performance tests. The gang boys appeared to be more cautious, more easily distracted, and more concerned with how they were doing relative to their peers than were the other boys.

Early Socialization, Normative Ambiguity, and Delinquent Behavior. Trutz Trotha (1974) has explored the linkage between macrosocial, microsocial, and individual levels of explanation, based largely on the research literature from the United States. Trotha's analysis is based on a proposition drawn from role theory, viz. that socialization is a process of learning the *predictability of the behavior of others*. Conversely, one's own responses to the behavior of others are expected to be predictable in order that social interaction and normal community life may be facilitated. In this way much human behavior acquires a 'taken for granted' quality.

Trotha notes that many inner-city communities are characterized by normative ambiguity and by inconsistency in the observation of conventional norms and sanctioning behavior. There is ample evidence of normative ambiguity in other segments of society, but it is among the ghetto underclass that ambiguity with respect to crime and delinquency is most evident (see Valentine 1978; Liebow 1967; Anderson 1978; Wilson 1987). Petty crime, police activity, welfare workers, and government bureaucracies are a constant presence in many slum communities, yet law enforcement and the bureaucracies of government and business often seem more a part of the problems than of the solution to individual and community ills. One result of this combination of circumstances is a 'hustling' orientation to life. These factors combine to reduce the predictability of behavior and of life in general.

An inability to tolerate ambiguity has been found to be associated with a large number of personal characteristics, including the need for social approval, anxiety, and a negative self-concept (see Farrell, this volume). Ambiguity and unpredictability on the scale found in many urban ghetto communities may strain even those who have a high tolerance for ambiguity. A causal mechanism, one which regrettably cannot be documented from this research, thus may exist between life conditions among the urban underclass, intolerance of ambiguity, and the social disabilities of gang boys.[7]

Trotha attributes the polarities found in Walter Miller's "focal concerns of the lower class" to a combination of reduced behavioral predictability, normative ambiguity, and inconsistency in sanctioning (see Miller 1958). Thus, for example, belief that luck or 'fate' largely determines one's life chances is enhanced by conditions of disadvantage that are beyond one's control, and by the necessity to hustle as a means of economic survival. Universal dependency needs heighten the need for autonomy under such circumstances.

Trotha's focus on the predictability of behavior is relevant, as well, to the role of the unsocialized aggressive adolescent in the gang. Given the highly aggressive nature of much interpersonal interaction within the gang, one might expect such behavior to be approved, perhaps even rewarded. While systematic evidence is lacking, this appears not to be the case. The phenomenon was so rare in the gangs we studied that the one such case which clearly fit the category was noteworthy. The young man in question was a member of perhaps the most feared conflict gang in the city. His frequent outbursts of temper and assaults on others, within and outside the gang, led the boys to regard him as 'crazy' and undependable, and he was actively shunned by many. He often behaved aggressively in situations in which aggression was inappropriate, even by gang standards. His presence made the group more vulnerable to police intervention, and his low status in the gang was related to this fact as well.

The Microsocial Level of Explanation: An Integrative Perspective

As is suggested from the field observations, microsocial processes may be helpful in explaining the proximate causes of behavior and in linking macro- and individual-level theories. In this respect, our research focused particularly on the group process mechanisms involved in precipitating delinquent behavior or in decisions to 'join the action' once started. These included (1) the reactions of gang leaders to status threats; (2) the reactions of gangs (or segments of gangs) to status threats; and (3) a utility-risk paradigm of individual decisionmaking in situations involving the group (see Short and Strodtbeck 1965, chapters 2, 8, 9, and 11).

Our attention was first drawn to the reactions of gang leaders to status threats by an apparently dramatic reversal of behavior on the part of Duke, a strong gang leader, following his return from a brief period of jail detention. Duke was a very cool leader of a tough, conflict-oriented gang of black teenagers. More socially skilled than the others, he maintained his position by cultivating nurturant relationships with other members of the gang and by negotiating with other leaders in intergang councils.

Upon his return from detention, Duke began acting very unusually, provoking conflict with rival gangs. The boys responded enthusiastically to Duke's aggressive behavior, but he soon returned to being cool. It appeared that, for a brief period, Duke simply catered to the most broadly held normative characteristics of the group. Following reestablishment of his leadership role and with the support of the detached worker, he was able to resume his customary mode of relating to the group.

As similar cases came to our attention, we were able to formulate what we believe to be the general mechanism at work. Abstracting the basic theoretical elements of this mechanism facilitates empirical and theoretical exploration of its generality and the possible integration of levels of explanation. A fundamental individual-level principle, common to the behavioral sciences, holds that behavior is adaptive or problem-solving—i.e., reactive. The nature of any particular adaptation depends heavily on the nature of the problem to which the behavior is a response. The definition of any condition or situation as problematic is, in turn, in large part determined by social and cultural factors—e.g., culturally or socially defined desiderata (or, conversely, things to be avoided).[8]

In the adolescent gang world we studied in Chicago and apparently in other adolescent social worlds, status vis-a-vis one's peers was a major problem. The saliency of status and the intensity with which related problems were experienced (e.g., the perception of status threat) varied a great deal in different situations and for boys occupying different roles in the group. Solutions to status problems were deeply embedded in normative properties and processes of the group.

The extent to which this principle applies to group behavior is not clear, though our research suggests that it does. We found evidence of the operation of the status threat mechanism, for example, in group behavior, as when rival gangs confronted one another 'accidentally' on the street, or in public settings, such as attendance at a professional basketball game.

Incidents such as these provided grist for the mill of individual and group status among fighting gangs, and they served to perpetuate the investment of these boys in their gang 'rep.' They also served the image of these boys as street warriors whose group norms required their participation in conflict with rival gangs. Without the detailed accounting of the incidents available through the field research, such an interpretation would seem reasonable. The normative explanation is inadequate on several grounds, however. In nearly all cases, fights were quickly and easily stopped. In none of the cases observed did all of the boys participate in the fighting or related delinquent behaviors.

Careful review of many incidents suggests that those most centrally involved were gang leaders and boys striving for leadership, as well as other core members. Membership roles and personal investment in the gang are variable among both groups and individuals, and such variation influences the likelihood of involvement in the give and take of such incidence.

The influence of normative properties of the group on most gang members thus appears to be tenuous and largely situational. The Chicago gangs were characterized by loose criteria of membership, frequently changing membership, and relatively low cohesion except under special circumstances that drew members together. Members of the gangs came and went for days or weeks at a time; unless they occupied particularly strong leadership, or other roles central to the group, most were hardly missed.

Situational Factors, Group Solidarity, and Behavior

The reaction of groups to situations in which group status is threatened, or in which status may be enhanced, supports observations made by others concerning the importance of the *group qua group* to the behavior of group members. Miller et al.'s (1961) documentation of the occurrence of physically and verbally aggressive behaviors among members of a Boston gang found that the great majority of these acts were directed toward other members of the gang. Most served group purposes—e.g., demonstrating personal characteristics related to group acceptance and prestige.

The gang thus may be seen as an arena for status achievement, maintenance, and defense among young men who lack both skills and opportunities for status outside of this context. Violent exchanges within the gang and delinquent responses to status threats are often the result of reliance upon the lowest common denominator of skills and understandings with broad appeal within the group. The greater social skills possessed by gang leaders and their generally supportive and nurturant style of leadership confirms the value of group membership to gang members. Ironically, the leaders often were exposed as a result to situations in which there was a high risk of delinquency involvement.

Together with observations by Klein and Crawford (1967) concerning gang solidarity, these findings suggest that gang delinquency is a function of a combination of individual characteristics of members, internal group dynamics, and external pressures. Other field observers also have documented the importance of internal group processes and relationships with the external environment in gang formation and behavior (see Yablonsky 1962; Jansyn 1966; and Brymmer 1967).

The Importance of Cultural Differences

Group processes are circumscribed by cultural differences. Differences between group and individual fighting reported by the Cambridge (England) Study in Delinquent Development are instructive in this respect. David Farrington and his colleagues (1981) report that the nature of aggressive incidents depended heavily on whether they were group fights or simply altercations between individuals. Individual fights more often involved "hostile aggression" and feelings of anger, while group fights were more *instrumental* in character (e.g., coming to the aid of a friend or to gain status). Group fights occurred most frequently in pubs and streets, often in both. Compared to individual fights, they more frequently involved weapons and resulted in serious injuries. The young men who took part in group fighting were more likely than individual combatants to belong to "anti-social groups." Case studies suggest that group fighting was a matter largely of life style, rather than of participation in conflict gangs.

Conclusion

This chapter does little more than lay the groundwork for more formal integration of levels of explanation for collective (in this case, gang) delinquency. The microsocial level of explanation appears to be useful in linking the macrosocial and individual levels, as well as in its own right. While the microsocial level is the least understood of the levels of explanation, it bears on important and neglected issues. Understanding of this level may, for example, offer a way out of sociology's chronic difficulties with the concept of *norm* and our failure to explain the circumstances in which normative properties of groups become manifest in behavior, are modified, or ignored.

Perhaps, as Gibbs (1981) suggests, the explanatory power of 'group norms' has been overemphasized. The manner in which 'normative properties' of groups are manifest in attitudes and in behavior varies a great deal between and among individuals and in different types of situations. This chapter suggests some of the microsocial processes and mechanisms that 'translate' normative properties of groups into individual and group behavior.

Bridging concepts are needed between social psychological and social structural explanations. The *gang* appears to be such a concept for understanding juvenile delinquency (see Finestone 1976). Concepts alone are insufficient, however. The microsocial level of explanation, implying methods, data, and theory, is likely to be a necessary part of the bridging and integrating task.

17

Confronting Control Theory's Negative Cases[1]

────Peggy C. Giordano────

This paper focuses on control theory's negative cases as a way of critically evaluating that theory and of integrating it with other theoretical traditions. Our methodology is also integrative. Both quantitative and qualitative data are utilized, although we place heavier emphasis on the qualitative data. The ability to move freely between these two types of data offers an opportunity to 'get underneath' the scale scores that form the core of our knowledge about what causes delinquency. This is particularly important in relation to control theory, where the survey approach has predominated.

This study differs from typical qualitative analyses, in that in-depth interviews are conducted not with a small homogeneous group (e.g., a delinquent gang) but with subjects who were chosen on the basis of standard survey sampling techniques. The contextual data derived from these interviews are the point of departure from which we will argue the following: Control theory needs greater refinement, and in some cases revision of its basic tenets. The theory *can* be useful as an explanation of forms of deviation in addition to delinquency, and indeed may actually be more useful in understanding outcomes other than criminal involvement. However, while the so-called 'integrated model' makes a great deal of intuitive sense, it outlines only one path to delinquency, one that may not be the dominant or most common route. Finally, the pure forms of other theoretical traditions, some currently out of favor, are actually embedded in our samples, reflected in the life circumstances of individual actors. These traditional forms should be resurrected and allowed to stand on their own, rather than necessarily tacked onto or integrated with another theory (i.e., control theory).

Defining Negative Cases

By negative cases, we mean those subjects in our research whose pattern of responses do not fit neatly with our hypotheses. We have focused specifically on the role of parental attachment because we believe that this goes to the conceptual heart of control theory (Hirschi 1969). Attachment has been called the most important element of the bond, and among the types of attachment, ties of affection and respect for parents are thought to be most pivotal. Obviously, this approach does not do justice to the other elements of the bond. What we are attempting to do is to highlight the complexity surrounding the concept of attachment and the way in which it operates. The same procedure could be followed with the other components important to control theory. We do, however, recognize that this represents a simplification of the theory. For our purposes in this paper, then, the negative cases for control theory would be of two kinds: (1) those youths with low levels of attachment to parents who are not delinquent and (2) those youths with high levels of attachment who are delinquent nevertheless.

Methodology

The original purpose of this study was to examine the role of social supports (primarily peer and family attachments) in adolescence in greater detail than has been characteristic of previous research, including our own. In 1982 we conducted personal interviews with a sample ($N = 942$) of all youth 12–19 years of age living in private households in a large north central SMSA. These interviews contained extensive data regarding the qualities of family and peer relationships of the respondents and included as assessment of their levels of delinquency involvement, using a revised version of Elliott and Ageton's self-reported delinquency scale. Nevertheless, we were frustrated by the limitations of the highly structured scale score approach, and vowed to personally re-interview as many of these youths (four years older now) as possible.

In the spring and summer of 1986, we attempted to re-interview all youths who had been fourteen or fifteen at the time of the first wave. Of 302 eligible respondents, we were able to locate and interview 197, or approximately 65%, of these youths (who are now eighteen or nineteen). This paper is an analysis of the second wave data. Our follow-up interview contained family and peer relationship items identical to those used in the first wave, as well as new items developed largely from the social support literature. We were attempting to create items and scales that reflected the complexity of the concept of attachment and indexed the multiple functions served by intimate relations. Both of these kinds of items were highly structured; we also included an open-ended section that focused on the changes in the life circumstances of our respondents since the time when they had first been interviewed. Again we wanted to understand more about the role of intimate networks, both in general and as they relate to actors' involvement in deviant behavior.

Specific topics covered in the open-ended section include the following:

Friendship and Family Relations. We reminded subjects who they had indicated they were friends with at age fourteen or fifteen, and discussed whether they had remained friends with these same people. If not, we explored their perceptions regarding the reasons for such changes. Relationships with family members and changes over time were also discussed.

Stressful Life Events. Questionnaire items such as "I respect my family/friends' opinions about the important things in life" (Hirschi 1969) provide a somewhat abstract assessment of family quality. We asked respondents to talk about the "three most distressing" things (as well as the three best things) that had happened to them since they were last interviewed, as a way of eliciting more concrete responses. The focus here was not so much on the degree to which they had experienced particular life events as on their perceptions of parent and peer support during those times.

Delinquency Involvement. Respondents were asked whether the overall amount they were "involved in things that could get them in trouble with the law was the same/more/or less" than when they filled out the survey before. They were also asked to talk about whether parents or peers had any role in their delinquency involvement, and about their supportiveness if they had been in trouble. A 30-item self-reported delinquency scale was also administered as a more objective indicator (Elliott, Huizinga, and Ageton 1982).

Other Problem Behaviors. Respondents were also asked open-ended questions and short scales indexing depression, loneliness, eating disorders, and pregnancy histories. Interviewers probed for information about the role of parents and peers in relation to each of these kinds of problems.

Why Examine the Negative Cases?

The primary reason for examining more closely control theory's negative cases is that we uncovered so many of them. Although this perspective has emphasized that strong bonds to family and other institutions deter youth from delinquency involvement, we were struck by the number of youths who expressed low levels of attachment (sometimes downright hostility) and who had experienced a variety of distressing or alienating family circumstances but who were nevertheless extremely conforming in their behavior. In addition, many of our most delinquent youth expressed high attachment or bonding to family members.

We decided to analyze more closely these seemingly negative cases by focusing on the other kinds of qualitative data we had gathered about them and on the interrelationship between their closed and open-ended responses. The unit of analysis became the life circumstances of a case, taken as a whole, rather than response to one item or scale. The determination of whether a case was characterized by high or low attachment was essentially a subjective task, and involved examining both types of data. Classifying youths as low or high on delinquency was somewhat easier because of the self-reported delinquency scale; however, as we will see, there were interesting discrepancies between the closed and open-ended data on delinquency involvement. Once cases had been classified on the basis of attachment and delinquency, we began the process of conceptual sorting. This resulted in the development of several conceptual categories that we believe provide some insights about the concept of attachment, both in general and as it relates to delinquency.

Negative Cases

Youth Who Should Be Delinquent But Are Not

Other Forms of Deviance. In most delinquency research, our dependent variables are limited to the items comprising a standardized self-reported delinquency scale. Although we recognize that we have not captured all the deviant behavior of our respondents, we tend to bracket off other outcomes and then proceed to act as if those who score at the low end of our delinquency scales are the conformists in our sample. In those studies where other problem outcomes have been examined, the emphasis is generally placed on the degree to which such problems tend to cluster. The syndrome approach (Clayton 1984; Jessor, Chase, and Donovan 1980) emphasizes that individuals committing criminal acts are more likely to engage in early intercourse, to be more psychologically maladjusted, and so forth. The striking category of youth in our sample, however were *not* such multiple problem youth. Rather, there were a considerable number of respondents who were extremely conforming in relation to delinquent behavior but could be considered deviant in some other way. For example, at age nineteen, one of our "low family attachment" respondents had already experienced four pregnancies.

Although it is often criticized for being descriptive and atheoretical, hypotheses within the teen pregnancy literature are entirely consistent with the logic of control theory. These behaviors need to be examined within the same study in order to determine whether the same kinds of processes lead to these different outcomes, to compare multiple problem youths with those who have experienced only one sort of problem, and to examine the sequencing of the problem behaviors. For example, several respondents reported cutting down on cocaine or marijuana use "for the baby" and pointed to their increased responsibilities as mothers when asked to explain their decreasing involvement in other illegal activities.

An unwanted pregnancy was by far the most common "deviant behavior" that would not be captured using standard self-report instruments. Nevertheless, we also uncovered other personally distressing outcomes. One negative case (low attachment, low delinquency) told us:

> I'm more depressed now. I mean, I've been through a lot. I always thought I was fat. I would eat, but not much. I guess I wasn't getting enough food to my brain or something and I would hallucinate sometimes. That's why I had to go to the hospital. When I did eat, I forced myself to throw up. Now when I eat I still throw it up, if I eat a lot. Not like a sandwich, but sometimes I throw those up too. My mom just goes on like nothing's wrong.

Both pregnancy and bulimia or anorexia are problem behaviors. However, we would suggest the importance of casting an even wider net to include those youths experiencing high degrees of loneliness, sadness, or depression, even in the absence of overt deviant behaviors:

> Lynn was never very close to her father, and when he died her mom poured all her time and energy into Bingo, which reduced opportunities for any closeness. Lynn feels her mother is addicted to Bingo, and that is all she cares about. Overall she is an unhappier person than when interviewed before, and has more times when she feels down or depressed.

The non-delinquent deviants, then, are not, strictly speaking, negative cases for control theory at all. They fit its logic precisely. Calls for integration usually refer to the combination of independent variables from two or more theoretical traditions. Here we are arguing for greater attention to integration at the level of our *dependent* variables. To the degree that control theory is applied to these other arenas, its overall explanatory power will be increased. Ultimately, similarities and differences in the types of attachment processes relating to these separate outcomes could be specified. This kind of 'integration' is particularly important if we are to understand the role of gender in the etiology of problem behaviors. Thus, while females' involvement in delinquent acts is usually lower than that of their male counterparts, the consequences of an unwanted pregnancy are more directly experienced by females; females are also much more likely to suffer from eating disorders and the like.

Commitment Without Attachment. A second conceptual category of negative cases is also, in a way, consistent with control theory, although not in its pure form. According to Hirschi, the elements of the bond are related, so that youths who develop strong affective ties to parents should be more committed to conforming lines of activity, have a larger stake in the future, and so forth (e.g., high commitment). However, we discovered a type of youth who had weak ties to parents but who especially strong commitment to some goal—it was this commitment that served as a salient identity hook or anchor, as an insulator against delinquency.

> Daren (a nineteen-year-old black male) described a difficult relationship with his father. His dad constantly encouraged him to fight and "Be a real man" and to play football. Daren would much rather work on his art, and plans to attend art school next year in Pittsburgh. He proudly showed the interviewer his work.
>
> Mary (a nineteen-year-old black female), in describing her relationship with her family, said she couldn't talk about her problems with them. "They've always felt that girls should do certain things and act certain ways. They weren't too happy about me getting into the military. They never have liked a girl to be independent, and the military has given that to me. Before the military I felt overshadowed by my parents. My parents wanted me to get married by age 20 like my sisters. They didn't think I'd make it through basic training." She did and now feels "more optimistic, more self-confident, more goal-oriented, more disciplined," and continued "I have more control now. I know who I am now."

Compensating Attachments. In the second conceptual category, we placed youths who lacked strong family bonds but who nevertheless had a talent or interest that gave them a strong goal orientation and sense of identity. In these cases, commitment may have served as a compensation for a lack of attachment rather than as a logical extension of it. Our third category consists of youths who have low levels of attachment to parents but strong substitute attachments through their friendships. This category represents a departure from the logic of control theory (Hirschi argues that youths who possess strong bonds to parents will also be more strongly attached to peers, and further that both of these factors will inhibit delinquency involvement). It also suggests that the integrated models (emphasizing high attachment to *delinquent* peers combined with low family bonding) sketch out only one of several possible linkages between peer and family relations. Ron, an eighteen-year-old black male, scored extremely low on the structured family attachment scales. He described the most distressing and the best things that had happened since he was fourteen:

> One was the death of my grandparents whom I really loved and cared about. My friends were there to support me by hanging out with me to take my mind off of it. My family members gave me no support at all. The other thing was going to jail for ten days. When I got in a little trouble, my friends stuck by me and tried to steer me in the right direction. The best thing was playing basketball in high school. I was a power forward. My friends were really great. They came to see me play often. I guess my family wanted me to do good, but they never did come to see me play. Getting a job was also something that happened. I do a lot of painting and yardwork. The money is pretty good. My friends seemed to be glad for me but my family said "so what."

Rodney, a nineteen-year-old black male, describes his family relationships in a way which challenges the stereotypic notion of the family as prosocial and peers as antisocial influences:

> There are more fights because his parents are always telling him what to do. They don't want him to go to college, think is wasting his time. Right now he is not enrolled in school, but he goes to classes with his best friend Marcus at B.G.S.U. (He is very close with his friend Marcus).

The Silver Lining Effect. One of the more serious problems with traditional surveys is that they provide a static conception of what may be a fluid and changing set of relationships. In our fourth category, then, we place those youths who may score relatively low on various indices of attachment *but* who believe that progress is being made. The belief that things are improving may be more powerful than the objective conditions (such as the actual level of communication) within the family. This kind of case is exemplified by the statement of one youth about his improved family relations:

Donny said his relationship with his parents has changed since the last interview. *His parents beat him less than before,* and they have fewer arguments.

Shawna is an eighteen-year-old white female who, by traditional survey indices, would be classified as having seriously deficient family relationships:

She sees her father rarely, but "doesn't like to spend time with him because he is an alcoholic and very moody. It is hard to be around him." Her mother is also an alcoholic, but her stepfather helped her mother get involved with a clinic. *She describes herself as much happier now that the problems with her mother's drinking are getting under control.* Shawna has no delinquency involvement, was voted Homecoming Queen, cheerleader all four years, student council, got the lead in the school play, and has been on the honor roll. She plans to attend UT, where she will major in accounting.

Non-Intimate Attachments. The fourth type of negative cases are a set of youths who scored low on communication and intimacy but who nevertheless should be considered bonded to parents. This group simply requires a slight redefinition of attachment as necessarily involving close ties of affection and respect. Lori described her family relationships:

They have these set values—you know what I mean. I'm Lebanese. I'm not allowed to date boys, they have a lot of pressure to get good grades—you know. I hate it. I guess it's for my own good, but sometimes I feel so stupid around my friends who are going out and partying. My parents are so traditional.

Lewis, nineteen, another non-delinquent male, said that "his parents' pressure to remain good" has been important in his lack of involvement, even as he described them as "becoming senile in their old age."

Physical, Mental or Emotional Barriers to Delinquency. A final category of negative cases consists of the youths who possess personal characteristics which, even in the absence of strong attachments, make delinquency involvement unlikely:

Karyn had an abusive and alcoholic mother, and scored very low on attachment; however the fact that she had been born with cerebral palsy made goals such as improved walking and gaining job skills her first priorities.

Jason was mildly retarded. He scored low on family attachment and argued constantly with his mother. A closer examination of his friendship networks underscores that the absence of attachment in itself is not sufficient to produce delinquent patterns. His "best friends" in 1982 were two little boys he babysat and played with at that time. Current best friends included a middle-aged neighbor and his wife and a sixty-five-year-old woman.

The Problem of Reverse Causal Order. In the above section, we examined situations where youths with low familial attachments refrain from delinquency involvement. Before turning to the second class of negative cases ('attached' youths who are delinquent) we point to another category that lies in the grey area between the larger classes of negative cases. Strictly speaking, these youths are not negative cases; their family relationships are good or at least improving, and their delinquency level is low. However, they point up the complexity of establishing the links between attachment and delinquency. For such youths, the major reason for discord and fighting in their families was their delinquency involvement, not the reverse. The problem of establishing causal order is widely recognized in the literature and then often ignored. These cases underscore the need for research which effectively handles causal direction:

> Angie states that she now fights less with her parents because *she was a very rebellious youngster* and she really didn't care what they thought of her. She has done a complete turnaround since then. Her relationship with her parents and family is very close.
>
> Mike's relationship with his family has changed a great deal. He is grown up and less rebellious now. He *"was such a smartass"* when he was younger and feels he was *"probably going through a stage."*
>
> James' relationship with family has gotten better: *He thinks it is because "I used to be a troublemaker" and they fought a lot over that.*
>
> Joe says that he is close to his parents and that they can talk together about most things. *His relationship with family has changed drastically since the time of the last interview because he has gotten off drugs.*

Youths Who Should Not Be Delinquent But Are

The largest class of negative cases is the category we discussed above—youths with low levels of attachment who nevertheless avoid delinquency. We outlined several new categories which summarize the kinds of life circumstances that may account for their lack of involvement. The following section describes the second type of negative case—youths who score high on family attachment even as they admit their involvement in criminal behavior.

Economic Marginality. The first conceptual category consists of youths who express great regard for family members and yet engage in delinquency largely for utilitarian purposes. Cohen's (1955) notion that most delinquency is non-utilitarian notwithstanding, the situations of several respondents (particularly those who sell drugs) must be understood from this perspective. Although we do not have a large enough empirical base to substantiate this, we hypothesize that economic motivations play a larger role in the involvement of black in contrast to white youth. Put another way, control theory appears a more powerful explanation—on its own—in explaining the delinquency of whites. The examples below show that some kinds of delinquency are a way of getting by, either alone (as in selling drugs) or in combination with legitimate jobs (as in the case of the youth whose truck was used for his hauling job and as a way to cart around stolen goods).

> Terrance, a nineteen-year-old black male, is from a family of five children. He described his family relationships as very open, and scored high on family attachment. Terrance was one of the most delinquent youth in our sample. When asked about his involvement in illegal activity he responded: "I hustle on the side!" He deals drugs every day in school. His friends don't participate in the dealing but they don't condemn him for it; they look out for him. His mother doesn't really know about it. *Terrance said that he started working as a dishwasher and once he had money he wanted more and more. That's why he says he has this "odd job." He want more.*

Neither differential association theory ("My friends don't participate") nor control theory are consistent with Terrance's account for his involvement in deviant behavior.

Another example which appeared most consistent with an economic marginality explanation is provided by Vernon, a nineteen-year-old black male. A pattern of illegal activity was documented both by Vernon's self-reported delinquency score and by the fact that we had to wait until he got out of jail to interview him. Vernon also scored high on family attachment:

> His family is closer now. He said that his parents have always been very supportive of him when he's been in trouble. They give him a lecture on what he did and help him. His parents just recently got him

out of jail and he said that they have done so much for him. He also said he does a lot with his parents [involvement?]. His cousin is the one that got him started selling drugs, and his mom knows about his cousin's 'work' because he doesn't have any kind of job, yet his cousin always has a wad of money in his pocket and is always buying new things. When asked if he smoked pot, Vernon said, *"No way. I'd rather drink. You wouldn't make a profit if you did that stuff too."* He told us that when he got the car, he paid $2000 in cash for a down payment right away. Before he got arrested, he worked at Ponderosa 8 hours a week, got paid $3.35 an hour, and made $150 a week (He added in what he makes selling drugs).

Luke, a nineteen-year-old black male, had high attachment scores, which reflect primarily an excellent relationship with his mother. Luke was very proud of his 3.91 GPA (pre-law) at T.U., his 161 IQ, his place on the all-State Track Team, and his high score on a military examination. Both his self-reported delinquency scores and open-ended comments reflect extensive delinquent activity. "I need money bad and now I would do anything to get it." His need for money is centered on the baby *(Luke, Jr. age 1), his education, his need for a car, and his desire to move out of his parents' house.*

William described himself as a happy person and says he has always been that way. Its just an overall attitude he got from his family. He likes smiling, having friends and being a positive person. He says he is a good person all the way through. If he were to get down, his parents and friends would try to joke and cheer him up. William is involved in hiding and selling stolen goods (stereos, TVs, appliances) and also deals drugs. Family is sheltered from illegal activities but they have a good idea what he does since he doesn't have a steady job. He has been doing it for as long as he can remember. *Feels it's just a way of survival*—he *"does what he has to do."*

While such accounts are consistent with strain theory, we have avoided this label because strain arguments emphasize the actor's perception of blocked opportunities, depicting him or her as alienated. As the above statements reveal, such youths may not reject 'legitimate means' (e.g., Terrance is still in school, Vernon works at Ponderosa, Luke is keeping up his G.P.A. at T.U.) but are merely diversifying their financial portfolios through deviant activities.

Cultural Transmission

The next four categories involve considerable conceptual overlap in that they all illustrate the importance of social learning in developing delinquent behavior patterns. The first category are cases where family members appear to be involved in the direct transmission of deviant lines of activity. Hirschi (1969, p. 108) contends that this is not likely to occur:

"It seems clear, then, that the lower-class parent, even if he is himself committing criminal acts, does not publicize this fact to his children. Since he is as likely to express allegiance to the substantive norms of conventional society as is the middle-class parent, he operates to foster obedience to a system of norms to which he himself may not conform."

The following examples illustrate that we can not always equate 'family' and 'prosocial influence':

> His sisters moved out when they were fourteen years old, but he never felt like he could leave his mother that way. They are able to talk about his bisexuality openly and she is very supportive. In fact, *when he was seventeen he says his mother got him started dressing as a woman. She let him use her clothes.* He is involved in more illegal activity now. He smokes reefer daily and has sold reefer. *His friends and his mother smoke, too.* He shoplifts anywhere from $200 to $300 in clothing each week. *No one but his cousin knows that he shoplifts, and she goes with him and shoplifts also.*
>
> Troy really feels that his relationship with his folks has not changed in any way since he was in the ninth grade. He is still comfortable talking to them and they are still just as close with him. Troy is more involved in illegal activity in that he smokes dope regularly. He says that although his friends also smoke a lot of dope they do not encourage or discourage his dope smoking. *His parents are involved. His parents also smoke dope and he is allowed to smoke at home. He does on occasion smoke dope with his parents.*

Differential Association. The above examples illustrate that family members do not always present conforming norms to their children. Nevertheless we agree with Hirschi that the number of parents who specifically *teach* their children to be criminals is likely to be small. The more common setting for learning about delinquency is the wider milieu—the neighborhood, the high school, and especially the friendship network of the adolescent. (An example of the wider milieu is provided by Darla, whose first exposure to marijuana occurred when the woman she was babysitting for left her a joint). More typically, respondents attribute delinquent influence to their peers. While we previously discussed how peers can act as a strong and positive support network in the absence of family attachment (compensating attachments), we also encountered several other categories: youths whose pattern of responses were most consistent with an 'integrated' approach (i.e., low attachment and strong bonds to delinquent peers), adolescents who attributed little or no causal significance to their associations, and the following type of negative case—youths who *do* attribute a criminogenic influence to peers even in the presence of strong family attachment:

> Kevin is involved with things that could get him in trouble with the law more than when he was interviewed before. "It is not that I was brought up wrong, we've just done a lot more things." When he and his friends are together they "go crazy." In the summer, when they are bored, they walk around to see what they can get into.
>
> Evette's illegal activity has increased. She smokes reefer and drinks. She also has a friend who sells dope and is sometimes around while sales are happening. Her friends influence her because they smoke reefer, too, and "I be around them a lot."
>
> Dave's friends do have something to do with his trouble—he drinks with them and he is usually drunk when he gets into trouble. His mother was very "pissed" when he was in jail. His friends thought that it was "cool"—another notch in his belt.

The Subculture of Violence: The Clustering of Violent Offenses. Our third category are youths who have relatively high attachment to parents and are basically non-delinquent except in the areas of simple and aggravated assault, carrying a weapon, and, rarely, rape. This type of respondent did not have a delinquent identity, and would be very conforming except for this cluster of violent offenses. Studies of the patterning of responses on self-report surveys emphasize the high degree of intercorrelation between types of offenses. This is similar to the emphasis on the 'clustering' of problems generally (e.g., depression and delinquency) as discussed above. This emphasis has the effect of obscuring subgroups within our samples which do *not* fit this generalization (i.e. the depressed-only, the sexually active-only, and in this case the "violent-only" groups). The following examples illustrate youths who claim good girl or good boy status, except in the area of fighting and weapons:

> Robert said his mom listens to him and is a good person. They often talk about school work and preventing pregnancy. She advises, "Don't put your thing into a girl you don't want to marry." Robert says he is involved less with illegal activities "cause I understand it more. I've got my own car and I wouldn't want someone throwing a rock through my car window." He does have a history of fighting—he doesn't start the fights and would prefer to talk them out. But he carries a stick in his car just in case. "People just don't fight fair anymore,

so you must have a weapon for defense." He did bust someone in the head with it because the guy messed with his sister: "I don't like fighting but if it comes down to it I will." Robert's self-report scale reflected no delinquency involvement, except carrying a weapon, attacking someone with the idea of seriously hurting them, and hitting or threatening to hit someone.

This violence cluster is not limited to male respondents:

> Marla was very certain that she does fewer things now that could get her in trouble with the law. She did, however assault a girl in school between classes—the girl pulled a knife on her and she "beat the shit out of her." During the court proceedings all her friends, and especially her family were supportive of her.

Delinquents With A Non-Delinquent Identity. There is considerable conceptual overlap between the above category (the violent cluster) and what we call 'delinquents with a non-delinquent identity.' Both types reveal the utility of moving back and forth freely between the closed and open-ended responses. Such youths were consistent with control theory's basic tenets, in their love and respect for parents and in their desire to avoid delinquency involvement. In the open-ended interviews they described themselves as 'straight' and talked about how 'they were brought up right.' All that kept them from emerging as a perfect case for control theory was their self-reported delinquency involvement:

> Marcus is happier than he was when he was fourteen. He says this is because he's involved in a lot of activities. For example he is on the diving team at school, enjoys roller skating a lot, and he enjoys his jobs. He said he was never very involved in things that were against the law so he would have to say that he is involved the same amount as the last time he filled out the survey. (Self-report survey revealed selling stolen goods, property damage, carrying a hidden weapon, cheating in school, and marijuana sales, as well as selling hard drugs).
>
> Jimmy says he has fewer opportunities to break the law because of working and his attitude toward the law. His family and peers steer him away from engaging in unlawful activity. (Self-report scale reveals damaging property, major theft, stolen goods, carrying a weapon, aggravated assault, gang fights, selling marijuana, simple assault, rape, strong arm methods, medium-level theft, drug and alcohol use).
>
> Jana said, "I never really got into trouble—me and my friends are straight. My family would be very upset." Jana also has good family relations and considers herself non-delinquent. (She checked stolen

goods, runaway, selling marijuana, assault, auto theft, disorderly conduct, drunk in a public place, alcohol and drug use).

Dennis has a very close family relationship and feels more comfortable talking about things now than before. Dennis indicated less delinquency involvement now because now he is older and the penalties are tougher. Friends have been taken "downtown" and the "way they talk about it, I wouldn't like to go." (Self report checklist includes selling marijuana, assault, and gang fights).

Stephen feels a little closer to his parents now than at fourteen, mostly because they've been through more together. They are able to talk more (both parents and Stephen) now. He said he had "No involvement with the law except for traffic violations." (Delinquency scale reveals major and medium theft, bought stolen goods, gang fights, simple and aggravated assault, auto theft, robbery, breaking and entering, and drugs).

Marvin feels that he is less involved overall in things that could get him in trouble with the law overall than when he filled out the survey before. He thinks it is due to the fact that he has never been in jail or acquired a police record. This makes it an incentive to keep things this way. Also the fact that his friends keep out of trouble plays a part. (Delinquency includes carrying a concealed weapon, attacking someone with the idea of seriously hurting them, frequent drug selling, gang fights, and breaking and entering.)

This extraordinary set of responses can be interpreted in a number of ways. The most straightforward explanation is that there are simply subcultural differences in the definitions of what is normative and what is delinquent. Recreational use of marijuana and occasionally selling some to a friend or getting in a fight are not viewed as serious business, even if they are technically law violations. Another possibility (which also points to subcultural differences) is that these respondents are setting up *contrasts*. They may have mental images of truly 'bad' actors they know—in the neighborhood, in their high school, perhaps even in their family—who have much more extensive involvement with crime than they do (e.g., the friends who were sent 'downtown'). Another kind of contrast is in relation to their own earlier behavior, which may have also been more deviant than it is now.

Conclusions

The point of departure for this paper has been that "it is in control theory . . . that attachment to parents becomes a central variable." (Hirschi, 1969, p. 86). Regardless of the class or racial status of the parent, "the closer the boys' ties to him, the less likely he is to commit delinquent acts" (p. 97). We would agree that there is an association between family factors and delinquency involvement, but our data show stronger effects for white in contrast to black respondents (Cernkovich and Giordano 1987). We argue further that while this has been a kind of conceptual anchor for control theory, many cases do not square with the attachment–delinquency hypothesis. We examined two general classes of these negative cases: youths who evidence low attachment to parents and nevertheless refrained from delinquency and youths who admitted delinquency involvement in the face of high levels of family bonding. Our first conceptual category pointed up the necessity of avoiding what Cassell has called the "fallacy of etiological specificity," the tendency of researchers to assume a direct one-to-one link between a certain independent variable and one specific kind of outcome.

Youths who were not delinquent but who evidenced other problem behaviors such as pregnancy, depression, or bulimia comprised our largest category of negative cases. This group of youths do not, then, represent negative cases for control theory at all—they suggest, instead, the need for extending its reach.

The second category of negative cases was also largely consistent with control theory. While attachment is thought to foster commitment to conventional lines of activity, we encountered youths whose commitment to important goals served as an effective compensation for a lack of bonding (commitment without attachment). Our third category (compensating attachments) pointed up that peer networks can be a source of social support and control, even in the absence of parental closeness. This represents a departure from the logic of control theory, which assumes that parental and peer intimacy are highly correlated.

Our fourth category, non-intimate attachments, suggests the need to broaden the concept of attachment itself. We encountered a type of youth who considered her or his parents hopelessly "out of it" and who did not have the kind of intimacy and ease of communication we generally associate with effective bonding. Nevertheless control was exercised, and such youths appeared to take the perspective of parents into account as they refrained from involvement in delinquent activity.

Another kind of negative case suggested the importance of viewing attachments as fluid and changing. Youths who saw hope or improvement even in what might be objectively bad circumstances (the silver lining effect) were often conforming in their behavior. The fifth type of negative case focused attention on the individual level of analysis. There were youths with physical, mental, or emotional characteristics that made adopting delinquent patterns of behavior extremely unlikely, even in the context of low levels of parental bonding.

Standing midway between our two larger classes of negative cases was a set of youths who were not at all negative cases, in that they showed high attachment and low delinquency. But there is evidence that a primary source of their earlier lack of intimacy and closeness and high levels of familial conflict was their involvement in delinquency, and not the reverse. This group's statements are included primarily to make us all more nervous about the well known problem of establishing causal order.

We agree with control theorists that strong bonding is important as an explanation of non-delinquency, but the situations of those in our sample who adapted delinquent patterns point to processes more complex than merely the absence of such bonds. Both structural (economic) and social psychological (group process) factors play a role, either in combination with a lack of bonding (the integrated model) or even in the presence of high attachment. Indeed, our second class of negative cases (high attachment, high delinquency youths) suggests that the situations of many youths seem more consistent with the logic of other theoretical traditions than with either control theory or an integrated model. We encountered youths with high attachment whose pattern of involvement and whose accounts of their own involvement comes closest to strain theories (economic marginality). We also documented life circumstances of youths (e.g., those who smoked marijuana with their parents) consistent with the idea of cultural transmission, and found high attachment youths who located the sources of delinquent influence with their intimate friendships (differential association). The presence of subcultural differences and social learning was further shown by two categories of youths who had high attachment and did not consider themselves delinquent—in spite of their overall self-reported delinquency scores (delinquents with a non-delinquent identity) or a clustering of violent offenses (the subculture of violence). These kinds of youths either do not regard certain kinds of offenses as deviant (even if they are coded in that fashion by delinquency researchers) or they recognize them to be delinquent acts but believe that their infractions are petty and inconsequential in contrast to those of others with whom they are familiar. Either explanation points to neighborhood or community effects that transcend the level of family bonding.

The negative cases we have outlined have implications for future research. For example, scales could be devised even for cross-sectional surveys, which index the degree to which respondents perceive that their family relationships are improving (the silver lining effect). Short checklists of problem behaviors (other forms of deviance) should be included, even where our primary interest is delinquency involvement.

Every theory has negative cases. Rather than ignore them, analyzing their characteristics in more detail offers a useful mechanism for refining and extending a given perspective.

18

The Challenge and Promise of Theoretical Integration in Criminology

Roland Chilton

An important aspect of the papers by James Short (1987) and Peggy Giordano (1987) is their illustration of theoretical issues through the use of data drawn from the authors' own research. Professor Giordano uses in-depth interviews in combination with new and older survey results to examine one aspect of control theory—the suggestion that some children are less delinquent than others, in part, because of their attachment to their parents. Among other findings, Professor Giordano's examination of the answers to some fairly direct questions suggests that influences outside of the individual child and independent of the child's attitude toward his or her parents appear to be necessary to explain some of the conduct reported.

Professor Short relies on information obtained from detached workers and others involved in direct observation of black and white gangs in Chicago to illustrate the potential importance of social interaction and cultural influences in the production of some kinds of crime and delinquency.

Although I have reservations about the possibilities for distortion and inconsistency in the use of loosely structured interviews conducted by students as well as in the use of reports of detached workers and other observers, these techniques have distinct advantages over simple survey procedures. Survey approaches severely limit the possibilities for identifying cultural and structural influences and do not permit observation of social interaction. Perhaps one of the advantages of theories developed to work with more than one level of explanation would be that they would require the use of a variety of research strategies. This would move us away from the heavy reliance on the research strategies currently associated with specific levels of explanation—surveys and experiments for individual-level explanations, the use of census materials and other available data for structural explanations, and observational techniques for studies of social interaction and social process.

The empirical emphasis of the Short and Giordano papers is also important because it avoids a longstanding impediment to the development of convincing theory—the reluctance of criminologists to struggle with both theory and data simultaneously. It is not that this has not been done but that it has not been done often enough. Too frequently, the absence of sustained efforts to relate theoretical propositions and research results is presented as a limitation of social research. We have been trained to believe, and are constantly being told, that our research must be theoretically informed. However, it should be obvious that it is equally important that our theory be empirically informed. This is often not the case. In fact, much theoretical work in criminology can be seen as reactions to and modifications of earlier theory, variations developed without any substantial empirical test of the theories being revised. Important examples of this would be the use of notions from Sutherland and Merton by Cohen (1955) and the subsequent extension of this work by Cloward and Ohlin (1960).

Professor Short works to keep delinquency theorists empirically informed when he presents a set of results from his studies of gang delinquency which require explanations that go beyond a focus on individual characteristics. Some of these results include the following findings: (1) that gang members were quite isolated from the adult world, (2) that the communities in which gangs were found were essentially low-income communities, (3) that there were marked differences between black and white gang neighborhoods, with the black areas being more economically disadvantaged, (4) that the relationships between adults and juveniles were quite different in the black and white neighborhoods, (5) that drug dealing and other forms of crime were less visible in the white communities, and (6) that legitimate opportunities were probably more open to middle class kids than to lower class kids, to white children rather than black children, and to non-gang members rather than to gang members.

Theories of delinquency must be developed or modified to explain these and other facts coming out of such studies—or the findings must be shown to be empirically false. It seems unlikely that theories focused on individual characteristics alone will be very useful in explaining these aspects of gang delinquency. In fact, the importance of income in the production of gang delinquency and the impact of race on the types and amounts of crime suggested by these findings clearly implies the need for integrating at least two and probably three of the levels of explanation described by Professor Short.

Peggy Giordano presents another set of facts that require explanations that go beyond an emphasis on individual characteristics. She finds that friendship networks and relationships with other juveniles can produce both delinquent and conforming conduct, regardless of the juvenile's attachment to his or her parents. She finds that stressful life events, such as pregnancy or illness, may have more impact on the behavior of some children than parental attachment, and that the family may not always be a good influence.

Professor Giordano's analysis of the comments of self-reported delinquent children who would not be expected to be delinquent if attachment to parents were a sufficient deterrent for delinquency contains several challenging facts. She found that some children report engaging in delinquent activity for economic reasons. They described their delinquent acts as "a way to get by." She also found that economic motivation appeared to play a larger role in the delinquent involvement of black children than white children. These findings argue strongly for explanations that go beyond the individual level. Her general suggestion that control theory appears to explain delinquency by white children better than it explains the delinquency of black children is important for just this reason. Her findings may also reflect the fact that the best-known control theory was developed using the responses of white boys (Hirschi 1969).

Professor Giordano's finding that some young people involved in relatively frequent assaultive behavior believe that their parents and friends approve of it presents another important problem for theories limited to explanations at the level of the individual. The responses she presents from children who report considerable delinquent involvement but who consider themselves non-delinquent also raises important questions for theories that ignore cultural and subcultural influences. To the extent that the facts she presents suggest that economic factors and interaction process are important in the production of some juvenile delinquency, theories focused on individual characteristics will be incomplete and probably misleading.

In addition to the facts presented by Short and Giordano, facts produced by examinations of the characteristics of persons arrested or incarcerated in the United States also suggest the inadequacy of individual-level explanations. Recent attention to the racial composition of adult and juvenile prisons in the United States, for example, reminds us that crime and delinquency is not distributed evenly across all segments of the population (Blumstein, 1982; Chilton and Galvin, 1985; Langan, 1985). We know that arrest and incarceration rates are high for identifiable subsets of the U.S. population—males, blacks, young people—and that the arrest rates for young black men are higher than the rates for any other segment of the population.

In a recent paper, Krisberg and others (1986) call attention to the large and apparently increasing overrepresentation of black and Hispanic young people in juvenile correctional institutions. They might also have expanded the discussion to adult institutions, where a similar overrepresentation is apparent. These facts, the gap between the 11 percent black representation in the U.S. adult population and the 50 percent black representation among persons in state prisons, and the gap between the percentage of black children in the U.S. population and the percentage of such children in custody require explanations that go beyond a focus on individual characteristics—unless one argues that, as individuals, black men and boys are more likely than white men and boys to be crime prone.

Peggy Giordano's data, James Short's data, and U.S. census data all point to persistent and sizeable differences in the economic circumstances of black Americans—especially those most likely to be involved in delinquent or gang activity. Census data also tell us that large segments of the black population are increasingly isolated in large urban ghettos. These facts are virtually undiscussed in theories of crime and delinquency that focus on individual characteristics. Yet they are facts with which any theorist of crime must come to grips if his or her theory is to be empirically informed.

My own belief is that the facts require the development of explanations of crime that move beyond individual characteristics. Theories of crime must bring together 'structural' factors, 'interaction process,' *and* individual characteristics. This is the challenge of cross-level theoretical integration.

The promise of such an approach is important because it suggests that there may be ways to integrate the results of two or three different kinds of research. One kind is focused on attempts to answer the questions that Short presents on an individual level of explanation—why some young people resist the social control efforts of other people. Another kind of research is suggested by Short's 'macrosocial' level of explanation. This kind of research attempts to answer a different set of questions, questions about the existence of social organizational pressures toward resistance to social control. This kind of research also asks if social organizational pressures increase the probability of rule violation by persons in specific situations or social categories.

Short's 'microsocial' level of explanation is also important. His suggestion that a focus on interaction process raises a slightly different set of questions and provides a different kind of explanation than that provided by a purely individual focus or a macrosocial focus is probably essential to an understanding of many forms of crime and delinquency.

Neither the individual characteristics and beliefs of young people in the kinds of street groups he describes nor social organizational pressures alone will explain why some of them become more involved than others and why some become involved when many do not. As Cohen suggested over 30 years ago (1955), some rule violations are at least in part the product of a process of interaction that produces a course of action that only one or two—or perhaps none—of the participants have in mind in the beginning. For these events, the individual characteristics of those involved will be less important than the specific situations and settings in which they find themselves.

Regardless of the promise of what we are calling cross-level theoretical integration, there are major obstacles in the way of such developments. As I see it, the major impediments to the development of integrated theories are linguistic and ideological. Taking the linguistic impediment first, sociologist talk of values, economists of tastes. Some sociologists talk of social organization, others of social structure, and others of social systems. Some talk of social institutions and culture; others talk of subcultures, cultures of violence, and cultures of poverty. Some talk of social interaction, others of symbolic interaction, and still others of interaction process. Some talk of psychological mechanisms and learning, others talk of labeling and societal response. The possibilities for theoretical integration are probably limited by what can only be described as linguistic confusion, because different people use many of these same terms to mean slightly different things.

Working from Short's early discussion, for example, if crime rates are high for an identifiable subset of the population, is this subset a separate social system? Does it have a distinct culture? Do its members interpret the general culture in ways that differ from those not in the subset? Is this what is meant by subculture?

A similar set of questions is raised by variations in the use of social structure and structural. Do we mean to imply that some social arrangements, especially economic arrangements, are so rigid that they can be described as if they were a physical structure? Are the arrangements being described primarily or entirely economic? We will need greater agreement on the meaning of these terms and the ways in which structures and cultures are related to notions of socialization, learning, belief, and conduct if we are to debate and test explanations of crime that are broader and more integrated than those now in vogue.

Giordano cuts through this linguistic confusion to some extent by focusing on what young people say in response to some straightforward questions. If young people explain some of their delinquent conduct as a way to supplement their income, we may not need to describe this as 'strain' or as 'opportunity,' as 'learned' or as the result of 'attachment' to parents. If we find that a sizeable segment of the population engages in crime as a gainful activity and that the same segment is systematically disadvantaged in their access to other ways to make a living, do we need 'anomie' or 'attachment' to explain this conduct?

In addition to this linguistic confusion, a major obstacle to theoretical integration is professional ideology. I include under this heading strongly held professional and methodological beliefs that are not dictated by logic or empirical observation. These ideological commitments are essentially value positions—notions of what the good problems are and how they should be studied. They grow out of each individual's experience and socialization. They include beliefs about the nature of the subject matter of criminology and almost resolute commitments to self-report approaches or to regression analysis or to observational techniques as *the* most appropriate way to study social life. These commitments frequently remain unexamined and are rarely acknowledged. Nevertheless, I believe they have enormous influence over the theoretical perspectives we find attractive, our reaction to facts, and our notions of convincing explanation.

In their mildest academic form, these commitments represent a trained incapacity to see beyond our own fields. In their most impressive form, they are ways of looking at the world that rule out some kinds of explanation. If an individual believes that everyone is crime prone and that what needs to be explained is why some do not engage in criminal conduct, it is unlikely that he or she would develop a theory suggesting that an individual's social location and economic circumstances produce some kinds of crime and delinquency. It might even seem that the only way to study the problem is through the use of self-report surveys of individual children. If an individual comes to believe that people act to maximize pleasure and minimize pain, it is unlikely that he or she would develop a theory focused on structural pressures and social interaction. I believe that it is in this way that professional ideologies influence the research programs and the theoretical orientations of almost all criminologists.

Over and above our professional and methodological ideologies, our political ideologies and our unwillingness to recognize them for what they are create an enormous impediment to theoretical integration. Perhaps one of the best examples of an unwillingness to examine or consider some possible explanations of crime and delinquency is the widespread reluctance of criminologists to examine differences in crime rates by race. The political and moral justifications for this constraint on inquiry are not always identified, although some criminologists are willing to say that they believe that theory and research focused on racial differences in criminal involvement is inappropriate.

Some criminologists believe that even citing current arrest rates or describing the racial composition of U.S. prisons is unacceptable—unless rather standard disclaimers are presented. For the past 25 to 30 years, academic attempts to understand the ways in which the various systems of justice in the United States operate have focused on discriminatory practices as the primary explanation for the statistics showing minority overrepresentation. Only a few recent studies have departed from this pattern. I believe that this continuing focus on a search for discriminatory practices in the criminal justice system, despite the meager results it has produced, is driven by a widespread ideological commitment that makes other explanations of the situations in our courts and prisons unacceptable. I am not suggesting that there is no discrimination in the system. I am suggesting instead that a focus on discrimination alone is too narrow and that the persistence of this narrow focus is an indication of our unwillingness to recognize the impact of unexamined political ideology on research and theory in the field.

Moving beyond this narrow example, I think we need to expand the characterizations of individual and structural theories attributed to LaMar Empey by Professor Short (1987). Empey relates control theories to a pessimistic view of human nature, one that sees people as essentially antisocial. He relates structural theories to an optimistic view—one that sees people as malleable, neither essentially good or evil. I think we can expand these characterizations with little danger of distortion and suggest that some theories and some theoretical perspectives are more convenient to those whose political convictions can be described as conservative (meaning, those who are reasonably satisfied with our current economic and social arrangements) and that other theoretical perspectives are more convenient to those with political convictions that can be described as liberal (those who are more receptive to change).

A little reflection suggests that individual-level explanations are convenient to political and policy orientations that call for little in the way of changes in social and economic arrangements. Even theories emphasizing symbolic interaction and learning theory put the burden for crime reduction on individuals. Individuals must either change themselves or be changed; in any case, individuals must adjust to the system if crime is to be reduced.

Theories and perspectives with an organizational or structural focus, on the other hand, are more convenient to those who believe that current economic procedures and programs need to be improved. To those committed to this view, theories of crime that are focused on individuals are more likely to seem misdirected or irrelevant. Another set of criminologists, those who believe that nothing short of fundamental change in our society will produce cooperation and something approximating social justice, will also be attracted to theories of crime that focus on social arrangements rather than individual predilection.

This suggestion of an important link between political ideology and criminological theory will probably be repugnant to almost all criminologists, most of whom would maintain that they have no political ideology or that they are able to rise above it to achieve more or less complete objectivity. Even many radical criminologists, who can be credited with bringing values back into criminology, sometimes reject the suggestion that their approach is moralistic. Nevertheless, I believe it is, in part, the impact of professional ideology, political ideology, and the reluctance to recognize the role of such values in our field that has impeded theoretical development. I believe that this is why there have been so few attempts to develop theories that would link micro-level and macro-level explanations of crime.

If the suggestion that individual theories of crime are frequently a reflection of a conservative approach to crime while structural theories are often a reflection of a liberal approach to crime is even roughly accurate, it describes one of the ways in which unstated political ideologies may have impeded the development of cross-level theoretical integration in criminology. To the extent that such a relationship exists, the development of integrated cross-level approaches to crime will require a willingness on the part of criminological theorists to examine the extent to which their theories are related to deeply held political and economic convictions. Even if there is no patterned link between specific political ideologies and commitment to a particular level of explanation, we may still have to have greater recognition of the impact of professional and political ideology on criminological theory and research before we achieve much success in the development of theories of crime that link individual, interactional, and structural levels of explanation.

I believe the papers by James Short and Peggy Giordano move in this direction. In their willingness to use types of data frequently linked with different levels of explanation and their willingness to struggle with theory and data simultaneously, they may be harbingers of a break in the traditions that have isolated criminologists on different levels of explanation for so long. An explicit recognition of the professional and political values involved in theories being proposed or tested would provide added impetus to this trend.

List of Contributors

Ronald L. Akers is currently Professor of Sociology and Senior Research Associate of the Center for Studies in Criminology and Law at the University of Florida. He is former head of the department at Florida and at the University of Iowa, and former President (and Vice-President) of the American Society of Criminology. He is also former Chairman of the Section on Criminology of the American Sociological Association, and has served on the Executive Committee of the Southern Sociological Society.

He is one of the leading theorists of crime and deviance today and is author of *Deviant Behavior: A Social Learning Approach*, as well as many articles on crime and deviance. He received the American Society of Criminology's Edwin H. Sutherland Award in 1988.

Thomas J. Bernard received his Ph.D. in criminal justice from SUNY-Albany in 1981, and is currently Associate Professor of Administration of Justice at Penn State. He is coauthor, with George Vold, of *Theoretical Criminology*, and the author of *The Consensus-Conflict Debate: Form and Content in Social Theories*.

Robert J. Bursik, Jr. is Associate Professor of Sociology at the University of Oklahoma. He is currently involved in a two year study of Oklahoma City that integrates the social disorganization perspective with the concerns of deterrence theory. Professor Bursik is a member of the Editorial Boards of the American Journal of Sociology, Criminology, and Social Forces and has served on the peer review panels of the National Institute of Justice and the Bureau of Justice Statistics.

Roland Chilton is Professor of Sociology at the University of Massachusetts at Amherst, where he has taught since 1970. He served on the Assessment Staff of the President's Commission on Law Enforcement and Administration of Justice in 1966 and as a Visiting Fellow at the Social Science Research Council's Center for the Coordination of Research on Social Indicators in 1976. He has published articles in a variety of criminal justice and social science journals, including the American Sociological Review and the Journal of Criminal Law and Criminology. His current research program is focused on urban crime trends, with specific emphasis on the age, race and gender of persons accused or convicted of criminal activity.

Margaret Farnworth is an Assistant Professor in the School of Criminal Justice, State University of New York at Albany. Professor Farnworth's research and professional publications center on the implications of social stratification for delinquency, crime and criminal processing. She is currently a co-Principal Investigator with Terence P. Thornberry and Alan J. Lizotte on a five-year panel study of delinquency, funded by the National Institute of Juvenile Justice and Delinquency Prevention. She has also served as associate editor of the Journal of Research in Crime and Delinquency since 1984.

Ronald A. Farrell is Professor and Head of the Department of Sociology and Anthropology at New Mexico State University. His research has dealt with the development and empirical exploration of causal models of deviance, the effects of criminal conceptions in the legal process, and changing definitions of corporate criminal liability. His published works include *Murder, Inequality and the Law; Deviance and Social Control;* several edited volumes; and articles in areas of deviance and the sociology of law.

Jack P. Gibbs is Centennial Professor of Sociology at Vanderbilt University. He has received a number of scholastic honors, including a Guggenheim Fellowship, election as a fellow of the American Society of Criminology, and recipient of the 1983 Edwin Sutherland Award from the American Society of Criminology. His vita lists 150 publications in the professional literature. He is author of the highly influential books *Sociological Theory Construction* (Dryden Press), *Crime, Punishment, and Deterrence* (Elsevier), and *Norms, Deviance and Social Control: Conceptual Matters* (Elsevier).

Peggy C. Giordano received her Ph.D. in 1974 from the University of Minnesota. She is currently a Professor of Sociology at Bowling Green State University. She has published widely, including articles in the American Journal of Sociology, The Journal of Criminal Law and Criminology, Criminology, Social Problems, Sociological Quarterly and the Administrative Science Quarterly; and she is widely known for her work on gender and crime.

Walter R. Gove is a Professor of Sociology at Vanderbilt University. He is the author or editor of seven books and over sixty articles. His work has consistently appeared in the top sociological journals and his 1979 article on overcrowding in the home won the *Reuben Hill Award* for the most outstanding paper on the family in terms of theory and research. Professor Gove has contributed to the research literature in the areas of crime, deviance, gender and marital roles, aging and household relations, and he is best known for his work in the area of the sociology of mental illness. In addition to research in these areas he is trying to develop a general model of human motivation that combines social psychological and biological processes.

John Hagan is Professor of Sociology and Law at the University of Toronto. He is a Fellow of the Royal Society of Canada, the Canadian Institute of Advanced Research, Statistics Canada, and the American Society of Criminology. He has served as an associated editor of 11 different journals, including the American Sociological Review and the American Journal of Sociology. He has published widely, including six books, over 60 journal articles and 25 book chapters. He is well known for his critical empirical tests and evaluations of criminological theory and is today one of the leading scholars in criminology.

Travis Hirschi is currently Professor of Sociology and Management and Policy at the University of Arizona. He is author or editor of six books. His 1969 book, *Causes of Delinquency,* continues to have a significant impact on criminological theory and research. His *Delinquency Research: An Appraisal of Analytic Methods* won the C. Wright Mills Award of the Society for the Study of Social Problems in 1968. He was the 1986 recipient of the Edwin H. Sutherland Award of the American Society of Criminology, and is also a past President of that Society.

Michael Hughes, Associate Professor of Sociology at Virginia Polytechnic Institute and State University, received his Ph.D. in sociology from Vanderbilt University in 1979. Since then he has published more than 30 research articles, comments, and book chapters. He is also coauthor, with Walter R. Gove, of the monograph: *Overcrowding in the Household* (1983). His major work focuses on micro-environmental determinants of mental health and well-being. In recent work he has examined self-evaluation, ethnic identity, and psychological well-being among black Americans. Currently, he is finishing a monograph on living alone.

Marvin D. Krohn is Professor of Sociology at the State University of New York of Albany. His research has focused on theoretical explanations of juvenile delinquency and adolescent substance use. He is a co-author of *Delinquent Behavior,* 4th Edition with Don Gibbons and has published extensively in sociological and criminological journals. He is currently examining the viability of a theoretical explanation of drug use based on social network principles.

Allen E. Liska received his Ph.D. from the University of Wisconsin-Madison in 1974, and he is presently Professor of Sociology at the State University of New York at Albany. His research has focused both on social psychology, studying the impact of attitudes on behavior, and on social deviance, studying interpersonal theories of deviance and macro theories of social control. He has served on the editorial boards of the Social Psychology Quarterly and Criminology. Recently, he has examined how broad patterns of social control and the fear of crime are shaped and structured by the social composition of macro social units. This work has appeared in the leading journals of sociology and is presently being integrated into a book.

Craig B. Little received his Ph.D. in 1973 from the University of New Hampshire. He is currently Professor of Sociology and Chair of the Department of Sociology and Anthropology at the State University of New York, Cortland. His published journal articles include those in the Sociological Quarterly and the American Sociological Review. He is coeditor of *Theories of Deviance* (Peacock) and author of *Deviance and Control: Theory, Research, and Social Policy* (Peacock). He is well known for his studies of social control in England and the United States.

Robert F. Meier is Professor of Sociology at Washington State University. He is the author or editor of six books, not including revisions, and numerous articles dealing with various aspects of processes of deviance and social control. His specific areas of interest are in criminological and social deviance theory, white-collar crime, and sanction-behavior relationships, such as deterrence.

Steven F. Messner received his Ph.D. from Princeton University in 1978, and he is currently Associate Professor of Sociology at the State University of New York at Albany. His research has examined the relationship between features of social organization and rates of violent crime, with particular concentration on homicide. The results of this research have been published in the leading sociological and criminological journals.

James F. Short, Jr. received his Ph.D. in 1951 from the University of Chicago. He is currently a Professor of Sociology at Washington State University and has served as the president of the American Sociological Association and as editor of the American Sociological Review. Throughout his career, he has published prodigiously and is well known for his research on social processes underlying juvenile delinquency.

Victoria Lynn Swigert is Professor of Sociology at the College of the Holy Cross. She is best known for her efforts to develop the labeling perspective and her studies of the legal treatment of homicide cases. Her major publications include the following books, co-authored with Ronald Farrell: *Social Deviance* (Wadsworth), *Murder, Inequality, and the Law* (Lexington Books), *The Substance of Deviance* (Mayfield Publishing Company), and *Deviance and Social Control* (Random House). She is also the author of *Law and the Legal Process*, published by Sage in cooperation with the American Society of Criminology.

Terence P. Thornberry is Professor of Criminal Justice at the State University of New York at Albany and a former Dean of the University's School of Criminal Justice. He is the co-author of four books including *The Criminally Insane*, which won the Gavel Award from the American Bar Association, and the recently published *From Boy to Man—From Delinquency to Crime*. He has also written articles which appear in the leading sociological and criminological journals. Dr. Thornberry is currently interested in developing and testing an interactional theory of delinquency and is principal investigator of the Rochester Youth Development Study which is designed to test that model.

Charles R. Tittle is Professor of Sociology at Washington State University. He is best known for his work on deterrence and on the relationship between social class and criminality. He is the author of *Sanctions and Social Deviance: The Question of Deterrence* (Praeger) and *Society of Subordinates: Inmate Organization in a Narcotic Hospital* (Indiana University Press), and his work has been extensively published in the major sociological and criminological journals.

Professor *Charles F. Wellford* has been Director of the Institute of Criminal Justice and Criminology at the University of Maryland since 1981. He serves on numerous state and federal advisory boards and commissions and is Executive Secretary of the American Society of Criminology. From 1976–81 Dr. Wellford served in the Office of the United States Attorney General where he directed the Federal Justice

Research Program. During that time he directed research on federal sentencing and prosecution policies and on the state of civil justice in America. The author of numerous publications on criminal justice issues, Dr. Wellford's most recent research has focused on the determinants of sentencing, the factors accounting for changes in levels of imprisonment, and the development of comparative crime data systems. Currently he directs a study on the measurement of white collar crime.

Notes

Chapter 4

1. We would like to thank Laurie Alioto for her special effort in typing this paper.

Chapter 5

1. The author wishes to acknowledge the very helpful comments and suggestions from Carole Case and Christine Kray.

2. Two important exceptions to the purely sociological approaches to theoretical integration are Jeffrey's (1965) and Burgess and Akers' (1968) psychological elaborations of differential association theory. These efforts proposed reformulations of Sutherland's (1947) arguments in terms of the more recent developments occurring in learning theory at the time. While not addressing the mediating effects of basic personality structure, they do point to the significance of individual and social influences in deviance causation.

3. The major propositions of this model have been applied to data pertaining to male homosexuality (Farrell and Nelson 1976) and delinquency (Farrell and Nelson 1978). In both instances, log-linear analysis provided support for the theoretical assumptions from which it was derived.

4. From this standpoint, the social response to deviance would of course, also depend on the cognitive organization of reacting others. Those intolerant of ambiguity would be expected to rely more heavily on the dissonance-reducing mechanisms of the labeling process. While such a supposition is consistent with major conceptual developments from an interactionist perspective and therefore deserving of further theoretical and empirical consideration, it is the personality of those labeled as deviant that is of primary concern in the present work.

5. Some might argue that the ambiguity intolerant individual would be more receptive to the influences of a reference group from which he perceived acceptance on the basis of his nondeviant attributes and behavior. Such a position might appear logical in light of the parallel argument that the intolerant individual is more receptive to the influences of perceived acceptance on the basis of the deviation. However, because acceptance in terms of nondeviant attributes and behavior is at variance with the more salient dominant social

definition and reaction, receptivity to the former acceptances would seem to be facilitated by a personality that could tolerate the contradiction.

6. Analysis of data from a sample of male homosexuals provides support for this argument. The findings showed that individuals who perceived stereotypical imputations of homosexuality tended to reconstruct their past in accordance with the popular definition. Such reinterpretation, in its turn, resulted in identification of oneself as exclusively homosexual (Farrell 1984).

7. One analysis of data on male homosexuals has provided some support for the effects of ambiguity tolerance in an earlier formulation of the model (Janicki 1983).

Chapter 6

1. For a trenchant discussion of the difference between theory and its component parts (propositions and concepts), see Kaplan (1964).

2. I draw in this paper on the standards for integration outlined in the opening pages of Elliott et al. (1985). For problems those authors encountered in realization of their own integration goals, see Hirschi's (1987) review.

3. I realize that my definition is subject to rejection by those with opposing views about the essential nature of theory integration. One topic for further consideration in the ongoing controversy about integration is the fundamental question of its definition.

4. One of the problems I encountered in reviewing both these papers as theory integration is that neither is very clear in specifying (1) what established theory or theories have been selected for integration; and (2) whether indeed the object is to accomplish theory integration. For purposes of discussion, I made some assumptions and conclusions based on my own interpretations, and reiterate the message in footnote 3 (*supra*).

Chapter 7

1. This research was supported in part by Grant # 84–IJ–CX–0017 awarded by the National Institute of Justice. The author would like to thank Mitchell Chamlin, Harold Grasmick, and Jennifer Sedat for their comments and criticism of an earlier draft.

Chapter 8

1. It is commonly accepted that explanations of individual-level variation in criminal behavior will be different from explanations of aggregate variation. For

reasons that will become clear later, this distinction is not important for this discussion. The use of the phrase "theories of criminal behavior" should be understood in this paper as including both individual and aggregate levels.

2. Obviously, resistance to interdisciplinary approaches is based in part on factors independent of empirical or logical demonstrations of its value. For a discussion of the concept of interdisciplinary work and the structural sources of resistance to interdisciplinary theory, see Kockelmans (1979).

3. While I cannot develop it further in this paper, it is important to note that recent advances in the physical and, especially, biological sciences have involved interdisciplinary models of the type described in this paper.

Chapter 10

1. This is distinguished from "terminological" integration, which assumes that the theories make conflicting causal arguments that all can be expressed in a common language (e.g., Pearson and Weiner 1985).

2. "Integrated" theory is distinguished from "general" theory, which attempts to validly explain a wide range of criminal behavior (cf. Braithwaite 1987; Hirschi and Gottfredson 1987; Gottfredson and Hirschi 1988).

3. I use the term 'micro' in its more conventional meaning. Cohen and Short (1976) use the term 'individual' to refer to these theories, and attach the term 'micro' to group process type theories.

4. The issue here is theoretical, not empirical: to simultaneously conceptualize variations in criminal acts and variations in the enactment and enforcement of criminal laws in a single theory of crime as a social phenomenon. Criminologists generally argue that one of the two variables is dependent on the other: some criminologists argue that variations in the enactment and enforcement of criminal laws are explained by variations in the seriousness of the criminal acts, while others argue that variations in the seriousness of criminal actions is explained by variations in the enactment and enforcement of criminal laws (e.g., Black 1979). In Gestalt terms, criminologists have a strong tendency to see one aspect as "figure" and the other aspect as "ground" (Perls et al. 1951, pp. 25–29).

5. Macro theories in general explain both rates and distributions, but the theory of crime primarily explains distributions, not rates. This is because the component theories from which it is derived primarily explain distributions, not rates. As discussed below, Merton's (1968) cultural argument is an exception—it explains the overall rate of crime in American society. Other factors influencing rates would be antecedent to the theory of crime developed here.

6. Criminology theories are largely discursive, and since this paper focuses on the integration of those theories, it is also largely discursive. However, I use

some aspects of the formal mode of theory construction (Gibbs 1972, 1985). Specifically, I identify constructs, issue partial definitions of those constructs, and state the theoretical arguments as axioms defining relations among constructs.

7. The meaning of this relation is best understood by considering the various criminology theories from which it is derived. See below.

8. This is similar to Cullen's (1983) 'structuring' argument. Cullen assumes that special social conditions motivate or predispose people to violate norms, and he focuses on the "structuring" conditions that account for the specific form the deviant response takes. In contrast, I assume that the actions of all people in society are 'structured' in terms of available choices and the costs and benefits of those choices. Both deviant and legal actions emerge from that structuring.

9. Commitment includes two aspects unrelated to structure: subjective perceptions of interests (e.g., 1969, pp. 162–86) and people's efforts to shape their own interests (e.g., 1969, p. 20). Neither of these is tied to structure, so neither can be aggregated into a macro prediction (Bernard, 1987c).

10. The meaning of this relation is best understood by considering the theories from which it is derived. See below.

11. In discussing adolescent subcultures, Short (1985) comments: "It has been said that one of sociology's more important generalizations is that social separation produces cultural differentiation. Perhaps a corollary should be added: all socially and culturally differentiated groups organize status relations in what they perceive to be their own interests."

12. This issue is related to the broader issue in sociology about the relationship between culture and structure (see Wallace, 1986). I think the issue is clearer when applied to "criminal" values. Specifically, I think Kornhauser (1978) is right in arguing that crime is never truly "valued" in any independent sense, and with the possible exception of Sellin's theory I do not believe any criminology theories describe it as such. To that extent, criminal "values" are always structurally derived.

13. This aggregate prediction is not contradicted by individual "celebrated cases" in which wealthy and powerful people are processed (Friedman and Percival, 1981; Walker, 1985). Despite the enormous pubicity, these cases generally receive less processing at each decision point than would have occurred had the defendant been poor and powerless.

Chapter 12

1. All comments on Bernard and Tittle pertain to the last version of their papers examined prior to the Conference.

Chapter 13

1. Since the theoretical development of sociological criminology is very close to that of social deviance, examples and references to crime are used to illustrate these ideas.

2. There is no agreed-upon method of theoretical integration; that is, there is no agree-upon procedure by which components of one theory can be combined with parts of other theories. This may reflect simple naivete, due to the primitive state of integrative work, or it may reflect a confusion about the nature of theoretical integration. In any case, it goes without saying that statements asserting that one theoretical perspective is generally consistent with another do not constitute integrations (e.g., Hirschi 1986 on the similarities of rational choice theory and control theory).

3. A convenient, if inefficient, division of labor has been created in sociology, with social theorists concentrating on theories of social order and deviance theorists concentrating on theories of deviance. Yet we have never really identified the relationship between theories of social order and theories of deviance. As Gibbs (1981) has pointed out, "Despite the preoccupation of sociologists with social order, there are many more theories of deviance than theories of social order. It could be argued that there is no real distinction between the two (p. 2)." However accurate that observation may be, sociologists have clearly treated the two areas as distinct. A work such as Mizruchi's (1987) book on the self-regulating mechanism of abeyance speaks to both bodies of literature, but it might be recognized as being neither a book on "deviance" nor "social order."

4. Warner's approach to the study of stratification in middle America was remarkably similar to that of the Chicago sociologists in studying social phenomena, including many forms of deviance—an observational approach that maintained the "integrity" of the phenomena and reflected appropriate "appreciation" (see Matza 1969). While Warner concentrated on the cultural artifacts found in American homes, the Chicago theorists examined the culture of disorganized communities.

5. Social control, like other forms of control, is never complete or total. This is why relatively small bands of terrorists can influence the behavior of larger, and presumably more powerful aggregates, such as nation states.

6. A notable exception is the work of Hagan and Palloni (1986), who advocate a "structural" approach to the study of crime. According to Hagan and Palloni (1986), "structural criminology is distinguished by its attention to power relations and by the priority it assigns them in addressing criminological issues" (p. 432). They go on to discuss various criminological inequalities, such as those found in differential crime rates by social class, in criminal sentencing, and the relationship between gender and crime.

Chapter 15

1. From a Kuhnian (1970) viewpoint, this may forever be the lot of social scientists whose disciplines have not attained the paradigmatic stage of 'normal science,' and may never do so.

2. Meier rightly notes that the theoretical development of sociological criminology and the study of social deviance are closely related.

3. As I have pointed out above, this claim is most defensible when deviance is defined in reactivist terms.

4. Others on whose work Hewitt draws include Matza (1964), Short and Strodtbeck (1965) and, in part, Cohen (1955). Traditionally (in a trend that continues today) females in American culture have been more apt to endure inequities and their injuries passively than are males, thus probably accounting for a portion of the lower delinquency rates among females.

5. I must confess to a minor dilemma. As an evolving theory with an associated program of research, power–control theory has appeared in print both before and since the paper here under review. Indeed, in several respects the version presented in the 1987 *American Journal of Sociology* is more thoroughly developed. I will, however, be focusing my attention on the present paper with only limited reference to the recent *AJS* piece.

6. For a highly generalized treatment of the concept of power, see Emerson (1962).

7. It is unlikely, of course, that my suggestion will be implemented. The theory has already appeared numerous times in print as "Power–Control Theory" and one does not undertake a label change lightly, whether the wares are commercial or sociological.

8. Hirschi's (1969) statement of this assumption is bold and clear. "In the end, then, control theory remains what it has always been: a theory in which deviation is not problematic. The question 'Why do they do it?' is simply not the question the theory is designed to answer. The question is, 'Why don't we do it?' There is much evidence that we would if we dared" (34).

9. On the other hand, small-scale larceny, especially shoplifting, is a delinquent activity more or less equally open to men and women. And, indeed, there is fairly consistent evidence that females, both adolescent and adult, shoplift at least as frequently as men (Meier 1983).

10. The term 'delinquency,' like many others in the study of deviance such as 'mental disorders,' 'drug abuse,' or 'crime,' has been operationalized in numerous ways. While we, as researchers, are (or should be) sensitive to the importance of operationalization and measurement for the interpretation of our findings, the press and public are usually not. The resulting misunderstanding

can be pernicious. For example, if several studies call their dependent variable 'delinquency' but measure it very differently, they are likely to yield what appear to be conflicting results. The impression of inconsistency and inconclusiveness erodes public confidence in social research, possibly unnecessarily. The addition of adjectives helps in this regard. Thus, the title of articles and abstracts might refer to delinquency as 'common,' 'self-reported,' 'street-gang,' 'adjudicated,' or 'violent,' as appropriate.

11. For example, note that no woman has been implicated in the current Wall Street insider–trading scandal. Stein (1987) lists the male-oriented characteristics of the Wall Street culture that probably contribute to women's exclusion from this kind of activity. This observation, taken together with the fact that women shoplift at least as frequently as men and probably more so (see above), lends weight to theories that emphasize criminal opportunity structure.

12. Hagan and his colleagues work in Canada, and they have so far used Canadian data in tests of the theory.

13. Note again Hagan's statement that "... in egalitarian families, as mothers gain power relative to husbands, daughters gain *freedom* relative to sons."

Chapter 16

1. I use as an exemplar my own research and that of others on gang delinquency. See Short and Strodtbeck 1965 (the 1974 edition included a new introduction and a list of papers published subsequent to the earlier edition); also Short 1974, 1985a, 1985b, and forthcoming.

2. See, also, Swigert, this volume. The subject matter of simplifying assumptions of one discipline are, of course, often of primary interest to other disciplines.

3. Gibbs (1985) notes that the absence of 'reactive' variables in major theories of the etiology of crime and delinquency "may have led criminologists to shift their attention from these ... to labelling theory" (p. 48).

4. The impact on young people of policies and practices of local institutions, as well as that of events in local communities, is critical (see Schwartz 1987). Even the most thorough studies of the historical macro-level forces that have shaped contemporary youth cultures (e.g., Schwendinger and Schwendinger 1985) are weakened by the absence of information concerning the socialization experiences of young people in families and community institutions and the mechanisms by which they influence individual and group behavior (see Short 1985b).

5. These are adapted from Miller (1981). I omit Miller's specification of the centrality of four types of activity (hanging out, relations with the opposite sex, illegal activities, and recreational-athletic activities) on the grounds that it is be-

havior that we wish to explain. Miller's types and subtypes of law-violating youth groups may also be viewed as dependent variables. The specific nature of the subcultures and related behavior of the gangs we studied is discussed in Short and Strodtbeck (1965) and Short (1985b).

Consistent with the importance accorded group definition of gang status, the basic design of the research compared gangs with adult-sponsored groups comprised of the same or similar age, race, and gender peers from the gang neighborhoods. Youth groups from middle-class neighborhoods also were studied, but we did not systematically interview youth workers with nongang groups, nor did we place field observers with these groups. Timing and the shifting nature of the field situation made it impossible always to use the several methods of data collection utilized in the study with precisely the same boys. Group membership changed over time, while our police record checks, interviews, and assessments occurred periodically or at a single point in time. Although field observations of the gangs extended over an initial period of approximately five years, gangs were added to the study over that period. The follow-up study, conducted a dozen years after the beginning of the project, involved approximately two years of data collection (see Short and Molland 1976).

6. Use of the term 'unstable poor,' to describe the families and communities of black gang members is not intended to be evaluative; the term is simply indicative of the instability of circumstances in their lives. (See Liebow 1967; Hannerz 1969; Valentine 1978; Anderson 1978.)

7. The ghetto urban underclass had not yet been 'discovered' when our studies were being conducted. Its rapid consolidation since that time has been documented by William Julius Wilson (1987) and others. The black gangs we studied were, in any case, 'truly disadvantaged' in the same ways as the present-day ghetto underclass.

8. Some problems may, of course, be rooted in biological imperatives or limitations (see Pollack et al. 1983). Even so, such problems are likely to be mediated by macro- and perhaps microsocial definitions, perceptions, and interactive effects.

Chapter 17

1. The research reported here was a part of a larger study conducted with H. Theodore Groat and supported by a grant from the Ohio Board of Regents' Research Challenge Program. The author would like to thank Ted Groat and Charles H. McCaghy for their helpful comments on this manuscript.

References

Introduction

Burgess, Robert L. and Ronald L. Akers. 1966. "Differential Association-Reinforcement Theory of Criminal Behavior." *Social Problems* 14:128–146.

Clinard, Marshall B. and Richard Quinney. 1973. *Criminal Behavior Systems*. New York: Holt, Rinehart and Winston.

Cloward, Richard A. and Lloyd E. Ohlin. 1964. *Delinquency and Opportunity*. New York: Free Press.

Cole, Stephen. 1975. "The Growth of Scientific Knowledge." In *The Idea of Social Structure: Papers in Honor of Robert K. Merton*, edited by Lewis A. Coser (pp. 175–220). New York: Harcourt Brace Jovanovich.

Collins, Randall. 1986. "Is 1980's Sociology in the Doldrums?" *American Journal of Sociology* 91:1336–1355.

Colvin, Mark and John Pauly. 1983. "A Critique of Criminology: Toward an Integrated Structural-Marxist Theory of Delinquency Production." *American Journal of Sociology* 89:513–551.

Elliott, Delbert. 1985. "The Assumption That Theories Can Be Combined With Increased Explanatory Power: Theoretical Integrations." In *Theoretical Methods in Criminology*, edited by Robert F. Meier (pp. 123–149). Beverly Hills, CA: Sage.

Elliott, D. S., S. S. Ageton and R. J. Cantor. 1979. "An Integrated Theoretical Perspective on Delinquent Behavior." *Journal of Research in Crime and Delinquency* 16:3–27.

Elliott, Delbert, David Huizinga, and Suzanne Ageton. 1985. *Explaining Delinquency and Drug Use*. Beverly Hills, CA: Sage.

Gibbons, Don C. 1985. "The Assumption of the Efficacy of Middle-Range Explanation: Typologies." In *Theoretical Methods in Criminology*, edited by Robert F. Meier (pp. 151–174). Beverly Hills, CA: Sage.

Gibbs, Jack. 1972. *Sociological Theory Construction*. Hinsdale, IL: Dryden.

Hempel, Carl. 1966. *Philosophy of Natural Science*. Englewood Cliffs, NJ: Prentice-Hall.

Hirschi, Travis. 1979. "Separate and Unequal is Better." *Journal of Research in Crime and Delinquency* 16:34–37.

———. 1986. "On the Compatibility of Rational Choice and Social Control Theories of Crime." In *The Reasoning Criminal: Rational Choice Perspectives on Offending*, edited by D. B. Cornish and R. V. Clarke (pp. 105–118). New York: Springer-Verlag.

Jensen, Gary and David Brownfield. 1983. "Parents and Drugs: Specifying the Consequences of Attachment." *Criminology* 21:543–554.

Jessor, R. and S. Jessor. 1973. "The Perceived Environment in Behavioral Science: Some Conceptual Issues and Some Illustrative Data." *American Behavioral Scientist* 16:801–828.

Johnson, Richard E. 1979. *Juvenile Delinquency and Its Origins: An Integrated Theoretical Approach*. Cambridge: Cambridge University Press.

Massey, J. L. and M. D. Krohn. 1986. "A Longitudinal Examination of an Integrated Social Process Model of Deviant Behavior." *Social Forces* 65:106–34.

Merton, Robert K. 1987. "Three Fragments From a Sociologist's Notebooks." *Annual Review of Sociology* 13:1–28.

Myers, Martha A. and Susette M. Talarico. 1987. *The Social Contexts of Criminal Sentencing*. New York: Springer-Verlag.

Nagel, Ernest. 1961. *The Structure of Science*. New York: Harcourt, Brace & World.

Pearson, Frank S. and Neil Alan Weiner. 1985. "Toward an Integration of Criminological Theories." *Criminology* 76:116–150.

Sampson, Robert J. 1986. "Effects of Socioeconomic Context on Official Reaction to Juvenile Delinquency." *American Sociological Review* 51:876–885.

Sherman, Lawrence W. and Richard A. Berk 1984. "The Specific Deterrent Effects of Arrest for Domestic Assault." *American Sociological Review* 49:261–272.

Stinchcombe, Arthur. 1968. *Constructing Social Theories*. New York: Harcourt, Brace and World.

Taylor, Ian and Paul Walton, Jock Young. 1973. *The New Criminology: For A Social Theory of Deviance*. New York: Harper and Row.

Tittle, Charles R. 1975. "Deterrents or Labelling?" *Social Forces* 53:399–410.

Wagner, David and Joseph Berger. 1985. "Do Sociological Theories Grow?" *American Journal of Sociology* 90:697–728.

Chapter 1

Agnew, Robert. 1985. "A Revised Strain Theory of Delinquency." *Social Forces* 64:151–167.

Akers, Ronald L. 1968. "Problems in the Sociology of Deviance: Social Definitions and Behavior." *Social Forces* 46:455–65.

_____. 1973. *Deviant Behavior: A Social Learning Approach* Belmont, CA: Wadsworth.

_____. 1977. *Deviant Behavior: A Social Learning Approach* (2nd edition). Belmont, CA: Wadsworth.

_____. 1985. *Deviant Behavior: A Social Learning Approach* (3rd edition). Belmont, CA: Wadsworth.

Akers, Ronald L. and John K. Cochran. 1985. "Adolescent Marijuana Use: A Test of Three Theories of Deviant Behavior." *Deviant Behavior* 6:323–46.

Alexander, Jeffrey C., Bernhard Giesen, Richard Munch, Neil J. Smelser, eds. 1987. *The Micro-Macro Link*. Berkeley, CA: University of California Press.

Baldwin, John D. 1981. "George Herbert Mead and Modern Behaviorism." *Pacific Sociological Review* 24:411–40.

Bandura, Albert. 1986. *Social Foundations of Thought and Action: A Social Cognitive Theory*. Englewood Cliffs, NJ: Prentice-Hall.

Burgess, Robert L. and Ronald L. Akers. 1966. "A Differential Association-Reinforcement Theory of Criminal Behavior." *Social Problems* 14:128–47.

Braukman, C. J., N. Goodman, F. Ambellan, and J. Revenson. 1980. "Group Home Treatment Research: Social Learning and Social Control Perspectives." In *Understanding Crime* edited by Travis Hirschi and Michael Gottfredson (pp. 117–130). Beverly Hills, CA: Sage.

Cloward, Richard and Lloyd Ohlin. 1959. "Illegitimate Means, Anomie, and Deviant Behavior," *American Sociological Review* 24:164–177.

_____. 1960. *Delinquency and Opportunity: A Theory of Delinquent Gangs* Glencoe: The Free Press.

Cohen, Albert K. 1955. *Delinquent Boys: The Structure of the Gang*. Glencoe, IL: The Free Press.

Conger, Rand. 1976. "Social Control and Social Learning Models of Delinquency: a Synthesis." *Criminology* 14:17–40.

———. 1980. "Juvenile Delinquency: Behavior Restraint or Behavior Facilitation?" In *Understanding Crime*, edited by Travis Hirschi and Michael Gottfredson (pp. 131–192). Beverly Hills, CA: Sage.

Cressey, Donald R. 1960. "Epidemiology and Individual Conduct: A Case From Criminology." *Pacific Sociological Review* 3:47–58.

Elliott, Delbert S. 1966. "Delinquency and Perceived Opportunity." *Sociological Quarterly* 32:216–227.

Elliott, Delbert S., David Huizinga, and Suzanne S. Ageton. 1985. *Explaining Delinquency and Drug Use*. Beverly Hills, CA: Sage.

Gibbs, Jack P. 1982. "Status Integration and Suicide Rates." *American Sociological Review* 47:227–37.

Gibbs, Jack P. and Walter T. Martin. 1964. *Status Integration and Suicide*. Eugene, OR: University of Oregon Press.

Gove, Walter R., and G. Russell Carpenter, eds. 1982. *The Fundamental Connection Between Nature and Nurture*. Lexington, MA: Lexington Books.

Hirschi, Travis. 1969. *Causes of Delinquency*. Berkeley, CA: University of California Press.

———. 1979. "Separate and Unequal Is Better." *Journal of Research in Crime and Delinquency* 16:34–38.

Hirschi, Travis and Michael Gottfredson (eds) 1980. *Understanding Crime: Current Theory and Research*. Beverly Hills, CA: Sage.

Johnson, Richard E. 1979. *Juvenile Delinquency and Its Origins: An Integrated Theoretical Approach*. Cambridge: Cambridge University Press.

Krohn, Marvin D., Lonn Lanza-Kaduce, and Ronald L. Akers. 1984. "Community Context and Theories of Deviant Behavior: An Examination of Social Learning and Social Bonding Theories." *Sociological Quarterly* 25:353–71.

Liska, Allen E. 1971. "Aspirations, Expectations, and Delinquency: Stress and Additive Models." *Sociological Quarterly* 12:99–107.

———. 1986. *Perspectives on Deviance* (2nd edition). Englewood Cliffs, NJ: Prentice-Hall.

Mednick, Sarnoff and Giora Shoham, eds. 1979. *New Paths in Criminology*. Lexington, MA: Lexington Books.

Merton, Robert K. 1938. "Social Structure and Anomie." *American Sociological Review* 3: 672–82.

Nettler, Gwyn. 1984. *Explaining Crime* (3rd edition). New York: McGraw-Hill.

Orcutt, James D. 1983. *Analyzing Deviance*. Homewood, IL: Dorsey.

Pearson, Frank S. and Neil Alan Weiner. 1985. "Toward an Integration of Criminological Theories." *Journal of Criminal Law and Criminology* 76:116–50.

Quinney, Richard. 1980a. *Class, State, and Crime* (2nd ed). New York: Longman's.

———. 1980b. *Providence*. New York: Longman's.

Short, James F. 1964. "Gang Delinquency and Anomie," In *Anomie and Deviant Behavior* edited by M. D. Clinard (pp. 98–127). New York: Free Press.

Simmons, Ronald L., Martin G. Miller, and Stephen M. Aigner. 1980. "Contemporary Theories of Deviance and Female Delinquency: An Empirical Test." *Journal of Research in Crime and Delinquency* 17:42–57.

Sutherland, Edwin H. 1947. *Principles of Criminology* (4th Edition). Philadelphia, PA: J. B. Lippincott.

Taylor, Ian, Paul Walton, and Jock Young. 1973. *The New Criminology*. New York: Harper & Row.

Vold, George B. 1986. *Theoretical Criminology* (3rd edition). Prepared by Thomas J. Bernard. New York: Oxford University Press.

Weis, Joseph G. and J. David Hawkins. 1981. "Preventing Delinquency." Reports of the National Juvenile Justice Assessment Centers. National Institute for Juvenile Justice and Delinquency Prevention. Washington, D.C.

Chapter 2

Akers, Ronald L. and John K. Cochran. 1985. "Adolescent Marijuana Use: A Test of Three Theories of Deviant Behavior." *Deviant Behavior* 6:323–346.

Cohen, Lawrence E. and Marcus Felson. 1979. "Social Change and Crime Rate Trends: A Routine Activity Approach." *American Sociological Review* 44: 588–608.

Cornish, Derek B. and Ronald V. Clarke. 1986. *The Reasoning Criminal*. New York: Springer-Verlag.

Elliott, Delbert. 1985. "The Assumption That Theories Can Be Combined With Increased Explanatory Power." In *Theoretical Methods in Criminology*, edited by Robert F. Meier (pp. 123–149). Beverly Hills, CA: Sage.

Elliott, Delbert, David Huizinga and Suzanne S. Ageton. 1985. *Explaining Delinquency and Drug Use*. Beverly Hills, CA: Sage.

Felson, Marcus. 1986. "Linking Criminal Choices, Routine Activities, Informal Control, and Criminal Outcomes." In *The Reasoning Criminal*, edited by Derek Cornish and Ronald Clarke (pp. 119–128). New York: Springer-Verlag.

Glueck, Sheldon and Eleanor Glueck. 1950. *Unraveling Juvenile Delinquency.* Cambridge, MA: Harvard University Press.

Gottfredson, Michael and Travis Hirschi. 1986. "The True Value of Lambda Would Appear to Be Zero." *Criminology* 24:213–234.

———. 1987. "The Methodological Adequacy of Longitudinal Research on Crime." *Criminology* 25:581–614.

———. 1988. "A Propensity-Event Theory of Crime." *Advances in Criminological Theory* Vol. 1.

Hirschi, Travis. 1969. *Causes of Delinquency.* Berkeley, CA: University of California Press.

———. 1979. "Separate and Unequal Is Better." *Journal of Research in Crime and Delinquency* 16: 34–38.

———. 1986. "On the Compatibility of Rational Choice and Social Control Theories of Crime." In *The Reasoning Criminal*, edited by Derek Cornish and Ronald Clarke (pp. 105–118). New York: Springer-Verlag.

Hirschi, Travis and Michael Gottfredson. 1987. "Causes of White Collar Crime." *Criminology* 25: 949–974.

Johnson, Richard E. 1979. *Juvenile Delinquency and Its Origins.* Cambridge: Cambridge University Press.

Klein, Malcolm. 1971. *Street Gangs and Street Workers.* Englewood Cliffs, NJ: Prentice-Hall.

Kornhauser, Ruth. 1978. *Social Sources of Delinquency.* Chicago, IL: University of Chicago Press.

Lasley, James. 1987. "Toward a Control Theory of White-collar Offending." Unpublished manuscript, Department of Criminal Justice, Claremont Graduate School, Claremont, CA.

Short, James F. and Fred L. Strodtbeck. 1965. *Group Process and Gang Delinquency.* Chicago, IL: University of Chicago Press.

Suttles, Gerald. 1968. *The Social Order of the Slum.* Chicago, IL: University of Chicago Press.

Tittle, Charles. 1985. "The Assumption That General Theories Are Not Possible." In *Theoretical Methods in Criminology*, edited by Robert F. Meier (pp. 93–121). Beverly Hills, CA: Sage.

Wilson, James Q. and Richard Herrnstein. 1985. *Crime and Human Nature.* New York: Simon & Schuster.

Wolfgang, Marvin, Robert Figlio, and Thorsten Sellin. 1972. *Delinquency in a Birth Cohort.* Chicago, IL: University of Chicago Press.

Chapter 3

Akers, Ronald. 1977. *Deviant Behavior: A Social Learning Perspective.* Belmont: Wadsworth.

Akers, Ronald. 1987. "A Social Behaviorist's Perspective on Integration of Theories of Crime and Deviance." Paper presented at the Albany Conference on Theoretical Integration in the Study of Crime and Deviance.

Blalock, Hubert M. 1969. *Theory Construction.* Englewood Cliffs, NJ: Prentice-Hall.

Cloward, Richard and Lloyd E. Ohlin. 1960. *Delinquency and Opportunity: A Theory of Delinquent Gangs.* Glencoe, IL: Free Press.

Elliott, Delbert. 1985. "The Assumption That Theories Can Be Combined With Increased Explanatory Power: Theoretical Integrations." In *Theoretical Methods in Criminology,* edited by Robert F. Meier (pp. 123–150). Beverly Hills, CA: Sage.

Elliott, Delbert, S. S. Ageton, and R. J. Canter. 1979. "An Integrated Theoretical Perspective on Delinquent Behavior." *Journal of Research on Crime and Delinquency* 16:3–27.

Elliott, Delbert, D. Huizinga, and S. S. Ageton. 1985. *Explaining Delinquency and Drug Use.* Beverly Hills, CA: Sage.

Hirschi, Travis. 1969. *Causes of Delinquency.* Berkeley, CA: University of California Press.

Hirschi, Travis. 1979. "Separate and Unequal Is Better." *Journal of Research in Crime and Delinquency* 16:34–38.

Hirschi, Travis. 1987. "Exploring Alternatives To Integrated Theories." Paper presented at the Albany Conference on Theoretical Integration in the Study of Deviance and Crime.

Liska, Allen and Mark Reed. 1985. "Ties to Conventional Institutions and Delinquency." *American Sociological Review* 50: 547–560.

Pearson, Frank, and Neil Alan Weiner. 1985. "Toward an Integration of Criminological Theories." *Journal of Criminal Law and Criminology* 76: 116–150.

Short, James F. 1979. "On the Etiology of Delinquent Behavior." *Journal of Research on Crime and Delinquency* 16: 28–33.

Sztompka, Piotr. 1979. *Sociological Dilemmas: Toward a Dialectic Paradigm.* New York: Academic Press.

Thornberry, Terence P. 1987. "Toward an Interactional Theory of Delinquency." *Criminology* 25:863–892.

Thornberry, Terence P. and R. L. Christenson. 1984. "Unemployment and Criminal Involvement: An Investigation of Reciprocal Causal Structures." *American Sociological Review* 49: 398–411.

Chapter 4

American Psychiatric Association. 1980. *Diagnostic and Statistical Manual of Mental Disorders* (Third Edition). Washington, DC: American Psychiatric Association.

Bateson, Gregory, D. Jackson, D. Haley, and J. Workland. 1956. "Toward a Theory of Schizophrenia." *Behavioral Science* 1:251–264.

Berger, Phillip. 1978. "Medical Treatment of Mental Illness: Pharmacotherapies Revolutionize Psychiatric Care and Present Scientific and Ethical Challenges to Society." *Science* 200:974–981.

Blake, R. and J. Mouton. 1961. "Conformity, Resistance and Conversion." In *Conformity and Deviation*, edited by I. Berg and B. Biss (pp. 1–37). New York: Harper.

Bliss, E., L. Clark, and C. West. 1969. "Studies of Sleep Deprivation—Relationship to Schizophrenia." *Archives of Neurology and Psychiatry* 81:384–395.

Cooley, Charles Horton. 1902. *Human Nature and the Social Order.* New York: Charles Scribner's Sons.

Frank, Jerome. 1961. *Persuasion and Healing.* Baltimore, MD: Johns Hopkins University Press.

Goffman, Erving. 1961. *Asylums*: Garden City, NY: Anchor.

———. 1971. *Relations in Public: Micro Studies of the Public Order.* New York: Harper and Row.

Gove, Walter R. 1968. "A Theory of Mental Illness: An Analysis of the Relationship between Symptoms, Personal Attributes and Social Situations." Ph.D. dissertation, University of Washington.

———. 1970. "Sleep Deprivation: A Cause of Psychotic Disorganization." *American Journal of Sociology* 75:782–799.

———. 1980. "Labelling and Mental Illness: A Critique." In *The Labelling of Deviance: Evaluating a Perspective*, edited by Walter R. Gove (pp. 53–110). Beverly Hills, CA: Sage.

Klerman, Gerald. 1982. "The Psychiatric Revolution of the Past Twenty-five Years." In *Deviance and Mental Illness*, edited by Walter R. Gove (pp. 177–198). Beverly Hills, CA: Sage.

Maury, A. 1848. "Des hallucinations hypnagogiques ou des erreurs de sens dans l'etat intermediaire entre le sommeil et veille." *Annales Medico-psychologigues* 11:404.

Morris, G. O., H. Williams, and A. Lubin. 1960. "Misperception and Disorientation During Sleep Deprivation." *Archives of General Psychiatry* 2:247–54.

Scheff, Thomas. 1984. *Being Mentally Ill: A Sociological Theory*. New York: Aldine.

Smith, M., G. Glass. 1977. "Meta-analysis of Psychotherapy Outcome Studies." *American Psychologist*. 31:752–760.

Tyler, D. 1955. "Psychological Changes during Experimental Sleep Deprivation." *Diseases of the Nervous System* 16:293–99.

West, Louis. 1967. "Psychopathology Produced by Sleep Deprivation." In *Sleep and Altered States of Consciousness*, edited by S. Kety (pp. 535–538). Baltimore, MD: Williams and Wilkins.

Chapter 5

Adler, Alfred. 1937. "Significance of Early Recollections." *International Journal of Individual Psychology* 3:283–287.

———. 1956. *The Individual Psychology of Alfred Adler*. H. L. Ansbacher and R. R. Ansbacher, editors. New York: Basic Books.

Adorno, T. W., Else Frenkel-Brunswick, D. Levinson, and R. N. Sanford. 1950. *The Authoritarian Personality*. New York: Norton.

Akers, Ronald L., Marvin D. Krohn, Lonn Lanza-Kaduce, and Marcia Radosevich. 1979. "Social Learning and Deviant Behavior: A Specific Test of a General Theory." *American Sociological Review* 44:636–655.

Ansbacher, Heinz L. 1973. "Adler's Interpretation of Early Recollections: Historical Account." *Journal of Individual Psychology* 29:135–45.

Ball-Rokeach, Sandra. 1973. "From Pervasive Ambiguity to a Definition of the Situation." *Sociometry* 36:378–389.

Becker, Howard S. 1963. *Outsiders*. New York: Free Press.

Berscheid, E., E. Graziano, T. Monson, and M. Dermer. 1976. "Outcome Dependency: Attention, Attribution, and Attraction." *Journal of Personality and Social Psychology* 34:978–989.

Budner, Stanley. 1962. "Intolerance of Ambiguity as a Personality Variable." *Journal of Personality* 30:29–50.

Burgess, Robert L., and Ronald L. Akers. 1968. "A Differential Association-Reinforcement Theory of Criminal Behavior." *Social Problems* 14:128–147.

Chabassol, David J., and David Thomas. 1975. "Needs for Structure, Tolerance of Ambiguity and Dogmatism in Adolescents." *Psychological Reports* 37:507–510.

Clayson, Dennis E., and Taggart F. Frost. 1984. "Impact of Stress and Locus of Control on the Concept of Self." *Psychological Reports* 55:919–926.

Cloward, Richard A., and Lloyd E. Ohlin. 1960. *Delinquency and Opportunity: A Theory of Delinquent Gangs*. New York: Free Press.

Cohen, Albert K. 1959. "The Study of Social Disorganization and Deviant Behavior." In *Sociology Today*, edited by Robert K. Merton, Leonard Broom, and Leonard S. Cottrell, Jr. (pp. 461–484). New York: Basic Books.

Cooley, Charles Horton. 1902. *Human Nature and the Social Order*. New York: Charles Scribner's Sons.

di Cindio, Linda A., H. Hugh Floyd, Jerry Wilcox, and Dennis R. McSeveney. 1983. "Race Effects in a Model of Parent-Peer Orientation." *Adolescence* 18:369–379.

Elliott, Delbert S., Suzanne S. Ageton, and Rachelle J. Canter. 1979. "An Integrated Theoretical Perspective on Delinquent Behavior." *Journal of Research in Crime and Delinquency* 16:3–27.

English, R. William. 1971. "Correlates of Stigma Towards Physically Disabled Persons." *Rehabilitation Research and Practice Review* 2:1–17.

Farrell, Ronald A. 1984. "Deviance Imputations, Early Recollections, and the Reconstruction of Self." *Social Psychiatry* 30:189–200.

Farrell, Ronald A., and Thomas J. Morrione. 1974. "Social Interaction and Stereotypic Responses to Homosexuals." *Archives of Sexual Behavior* 3:425–442.

Farrell, Ronald A., and James F. Nelson. 1976. "A Causal Model of Secondary Deviance: The Case of Homosexuality." *The Sociological Quarterly* 17:109–120.

———. 1978. "A Sequential Analysis of Delinquency." *International Journal of Criminology and Penology* 6:255–268.

Farrell, Ronald A., and Victoria L. Swigert. 1982. *Deviance and Social Control*. New York: Random House.

———. 1988. *Social Deviance*, Third Edition. Belmont, CA: Wadsworth.

Feather, N. T. 1967. "Evaluation of Religious and Neutral Arguments in Religious and Atheist Student Groups." *Australian Journal of Psychology* 19:3–12.

Festinger, Leon. 1957. *A Theory of Cognitive Dissonance*. Stanford, CA: Stanford University Press.

———. 1964. *Conflict, Decision and Dissonance*. Stanford, CA: Stanford University Press.

Frenkel-Brunswick, Else. 1949. "Intolerance of Ambiguity as an Emotional and Perceptual Personality Variable." *Journal of Personality* 18:108–143.

Galbreath, Judith, and Lawrence B. Feinberg. 1973. "Ambiguity and Attitudes Toward Employment of the Disabled: A Multidimensional Study." *Rehabilitation Psychology* 20:165–174.

Garfinkel, Harold. 1956. "Conditions of Successful Degradation Ceremonies." *American Journal of Sociology* 61:420–424.

Glaser, Daniel. 1956. "Criminality Theories and Behavioral Images." *American Journal of Sociology* 61:433–444.

Goffman, Erving. 1963. *Stigma: Notes on the Management of Spoiled Identity*. Englewood Cliffs, NJ: Prentice-Hall.

Goldsmith, Ronald E. 1984. "Some Personality Correlates of Open Processing." *The Journal of Psychology* 116:59–66.

Hackler, James C. 1971. "A Developmental Theory of Delinquency." *The Canadian Review of Sociology and Anthropology* 8:61–75.

Hassan, M. K., and A. Khalique. 1981. "Religiosity and Its Correlates in College Students." *Journal of Psychological Researches* 25:129–136.

Hirschi, Travis. 1969. *Causes of Delinquency*. Los Angeles, CA: University of California Press.

Ickes, W. J., and R. D. Barnes. 1977. "The Role of Sex and Self-Monitoring in Unstructured Dyadic Interactions." *Journal of Personality and Social Psychology* 35:315–330.

Ilardo, Joseph. 1973. "Ambiguity Tolerance and Disordered Communication: Therapeutic Aspects." *Journal of Communication* 23:371–391.

Janicki, Barbara L. 1983. "Ambiguity Tolerance and its Relationship to the Process of Secondary Deviance among Male Homosexuals." Masters Thesis, Dept. of Sociology, SUNYA, Albany, New York.

REFERENCES

Jeffrey, Clarence Ray. 1965. "Criminal Behavior and Learning Theory." *Journal of Criminal Law, Criminology, and Police Science* 56:294–300.

Jellison, Jerald M., and Jane Green. 1981. "A Self-Presentation Approach to the Fundamental Attribution Error: The Norm of Internality." *Journal of Personality and Social Psychology* 40:643–649.

Keenan, A., and G. D. McBain. 1979. "Effects of Type A Behavior, Intolerance of Ambiguity, and Locus of Control on the Relationship between Role Stress and Work-Related Outcomes." *Journal of Occupational Psychology* 52:277–285.

Kitsuse, John. 1962. "Societal Reaction to Deviant Behavior: Problems of Theory and Method." *Social Problems* 9:247–256.

Lemert, Edwin M. 1951. *Social Pathology: A Systematic Approach to the Theory of Sociopathic Behavior.* New York: McGraw-Hill.

———. 1962. "Paranoia and the Dynamics of Exclusion." *Sociometry* 25:2–20.

———. 1967. *Human Deviance, Social Problems and Social Control.* Englewood Cliffs, NJ: Prentice-Hall.

Linden, Eric, and James C. Hackler. 1973. "Affective Ties and Delinquency." *Pacific Sociological Review* 16:27–46.

Lippa, R. 1978. "Expressive Control, Expressive Consistency, and the Correspondence Between Expressive Behavior and Personality." *Journal of Personality* 46:438–461.

MacDonald, A. P., and Richard G. Games. 1974. "Some Characteristics of Those Who Hold Positive and Negative Attitudes Toward Homosexuals." *Journal of Homosexuality* 1:9–27.

Matthijssen, Mathieu. 1973. "The Socio-Genesis of Personality Structures: An Interpretation of the Socialization Theory." *Sociologia Neerlandica* 9:88–110.

Matza, David. 1969. *Becoming Deviant.* Englewood Cliffs, NJ: Prentice-Hall.

Merton, Robert K. 1938. "Social Structure and Anomie." *American Sociological Review* 3:672–682.

Parsons, Talcott. 1951. *The Social System.* New York: Free Press.

Pawlicki, Robert E., and Carol Almquist. 1973. "Authoritarianism, Locus of Control, and Tolerance of Ambiguity as Reflected in Membership and Nonmembership in a Women's Liberation Group." *Psychological Reports* 32:1331–1337.

Posner, Barry Z. and Alan W. Randolph. 1980. "Moderators of Role Stress Among Hospital Personnel." *Journal of Psychology* 105:215–224.

Quinney, Richard. 1970. *The Social Reality of Crime*. Boston, MA: Little, Brown.

Rotter, Julian B. 1966. "Generalized Expectations for Internal Versus External Control of Reinforcement." *Psychological Monographs: General and Applied* 80:1–28.

Rotter, Naomi G., and Agnes N. O'Connell. 1982. "The Relationships Among Sex-Role Orientation, Cognitive Complexity, and Tolerance for Ambiguity." *Sex Roles* 8:1209–1220.

Sampson, E. E. 1978. "Personality and the Location of Identity." *Journal of Personality* 46:552–568.

Sandler, Irwin N., and Brian Lakey. 1982. "Locus of Control as a Stress Moderator: The Role of Control Perceptions and Social Support." *American Journal of Community Psychology* 10:65–80.

Scheff, Thomas J. 1984. *Being Mentally Ill*. Chicago, IL: Aldine.

Schmitt, J. Patrick, and Lawrence A. Kurdek. 1984. "Correlates of Social Anxiety in College Students and Homosexuals." *Journal of Personality Assessment* 48:403–409.

Schrecker, Paul. 1973. "Significance of First Childhood Recollections." *Journal of Individual Psychology* 29:146–156.

Schur, Edwin M. 1971. *Labeling Deviant Behavior: Its Sociological Implications*. New York: Harper & Row.

Scott, Marvin B., and Stanford M. Lyman. 1968. "Paranoia, Homosexuality and Game Theory." *Journal of Health and Social Behavior* 9:179–187.

Scott, Robert A. 1969. *The Making of Blind Men*. New York: Russell Sage.

Scully, Diana, and Joseph Morolla. 1984. "Convicted Rapists' Vocabulary of Motive: Excuses and Justifications." *Social Problems* 31:530–544.

Simmons, J. L. 1965. "Public Stereotypes of Deviants." *Social Problems* 13:223–232.

Snyder, M., and T. C. Monson. 1975. "Persons, Situations, and the Control of Social Behavior." *Journal of Personality and Social Psychology* 32:637–644.

Snyder, Mark. 1974. "The Self-Monitoring of Expressive Behavior." *Journal of Personality and Social Psychology* 30:26–537.

──────. 1979a. "Cognitive, Behavioral, and Interpersonal Consequences of Self-Monitoring." In *Advances in the Study of Communication and Affect*, Vol. 5, *Perception Emotion of Self and Others*, edited by P. Pliner, K. R. Blankstein, and I. M. Spigel. New York: Plenum.

———. 1979b. "Self-Monitoring Processes." In *Advances in Experimental Social Psychology*, Vol. 12, edited by L. Berkowitz. New York: Academic Press.

Sutherland, Edwin H. 1947. *Principles of Criminology*. Philadelphia, PA: Lippincott.

Sykes, Gresham, and David Matza. 1957. "Techniques of Neutralization: A Theory of Delinquency." *American Sociological Review* 22:664–670.

Tannenbaum, Frank. 1938. *Crime and the Community*. New York: Columbia University Press.

Tatzel, Miriam. 1980. "Tolerance for Ambiguity in Adult College Students." *Psychological Reports* 47:377–378.

Trow, Donald B. 1977. "Status Equilibration: Fueled by Uncertainty, Frustration, or Anxiety." *Human Relations* 30:721–736.

Wilkins, Leslie, T. 1965. *Social Deviance*. Englewood Cliffs, NJ: Prentice-Hall.

Chapter 6

Akers, Ronald L. 1973. *Deviant Behavior: A Social Learning Approach*. Belmont, CA: Wadsworth.

———. 1987. "A Social Behaviorist's Perspective on Integration of Theories of Crime and Delinquency." Paper presented at the Albany Conference (May), Albany, NY.

Akers, Ronald L., Marvin D. Krohn, Lonn Lanza-Kaduce, and Marcia Radosevich. 1979. "Social Learning and Deviant Behavior: A Specific Test of a General Theory." *American Sociological Review* 44:636–655.

Blalock, Hubert M., Jr. 1969. *Theory Construction: From Verbal to Mathematical Formulations*. Englewood Cliffs, NJ: Prentice-Hall, Inc.

Burgess, Robert L. and Ronald L. Akers. 1966. "A Differential Association-Reinforcement Theory of Criminal Behavior." *Social Problems* 14:128–147.

Cernkovich, Stephen A. 1978. "Evaluating Two Models of Delinquency Causation: Structural Theory and Control Theory." *Criminology* 26, 3:335–352.

Elliott, Delbert, Suzanne Ageton and R. Cantor. 1979. "An Integrated Theoretical Perspective on Delinquent Behavior." *Journal of Research in Crime and Delinquency* 16:3–27.

Elliott, Delbert, David Huizinga, and Suzanne S. Ageton. 1985. *Explaining Delinquency and Drug Use*. Beverly Hills, CA: Sage.

Farrell, Ronald A. 1987. "Psychological Dimensions to an Elaboration of Deviance Theory." Paper presented at the Albany Conference (May), Albany, NY.

Farrell, Ronald A. and James F. Nelson. 1976. "A Causal Model of Secondary Deviance: The Case of Homosexuality." *The Sociological Quarterly* 17:109–120.

_____. 1978. "A Sequential Analysis of Delinquency." *International Journal of Criminology and Penology* 6:255–268.

Gove, Walter R. and Michael Hughes. 1987. "A Theory of Mental Illness: An Attempted Integration of Biological, Psychological, and Social Variables." Paper presented at the Albany Conference (May), Albany, NY.

Hanson, N. R. 1958. *Patterns of Discovery*. Cambridge, England: Cambridge University Press.

Hirschi, Travis. 1969. *Causes of Delinquency*. Beverly Hills, CA: Sage.

_____. 1987. "Review of Elliott et al., Explaining Delinquency (1985)." *Criminology* 25,1:193–201.

Johnson, Richard. 1979. *Juvenile Delinquency and its Origins: An Integrated Theoretical Approach*. Cambridge: Cambridge University Press.

Kaplan, Abraham. 1964. *The Conduct of Inquiry*. San Francisco, CA: Chandler.

Kuhn, Thomas. 1970. *The Structure of Scientific Revolutions*. Chicago, IL: University of Chicago Press.

Pearson, Frank S. and Neil Alan Weiner. 1985. "Toward an Integration of Criminological Theories." *The Journal of Criminal Law and Criminology* 76:116–150.

Popper, Karl. 1959. *The Logic of Scientific Inquiry*. New York: Harper & Row.

Schur, Edwin M. 1971. *Labeling Deviant Behavior*. New York: Harper & Row.

Simons, Ronald L., Martin G. Miller, and Stephen M. Aigner. 1980. "Contemporary Theories of Deviance and Female Delinquency: An Empirical Test." *Journal of Research in Crime and Delinquency* 17:42–57.

Sutherland, E. H. 1939. *Principles of Criminology*. Philadelphia, PA: Lippincott.

Chapter 7

Allihan, M. 1938. *Social Ecology: A Critical Analysis*. New York: Columbia University Press.

Baldwin, J. 1979. "Ecological and Areal Studies in Great Britain and the United States." In *Crime and Justice: An Annual Review of Research*, edited by N. Morris and M. Tonry (pp. 29–66). Chicago: University of Chicago Press.

Berry, B. J. L., and J. D. Kasarda. 1977. *Contemporary Urban Ecology*. New York: Macmillan.

Bottoms, A. E., and P. Wiles. 1986. "Housing Tenure and Residential Crime Careers in Britain." In *Communities and Crime*, edited by A. J. Reiss, Jr. and M. Tonry (pp. 101–162). Chicago, IL: University of Chicago Press.

Burgess, E. W. 1925. "The Growth of the City." In *The City*, edited by R. E. Park, E. W. Burgess and R. D. McKenzie (pp. 47–62), Chicago, IL: University of Chicago Press.

Bursik, R. J., Jr., and J. Webb. 1982. "Community Change and Ecological Studies of Delinquency." *American Journal of Sociology* 88:24–42.

Bursik, R. J., Jr. 1984. "Urban Dynamics and Ecological Studies of Delinquency." *Social Forces* 63: 393–413.

———. 1986. "Ecological Stability and the Dynamics of Delinquency." In *Communities and Crime*, edited by A. J. Reiss, Jr. and M. Tonry (pp. 35–66). Chicago, IL: University of Chicago Press.

Clark, T. N. 1981. "Fiscal Strain and American Cities: Six Basic Processes." In *Urban Political Economy*, edited by K. Newton (pp. 137–155). New York: St. Martin's Press.

Clarke, W. A. V., and E. G. Moore. 1980. "The Policy Context for Mobility Research." In *Residential Mobility and Public Policy*, edited by M. A. V. Clark and E. G. Moore (pp. 1–15). Beverly Hills, CA: Sage.

Finestone, H. 1976. *Victims of Change: Juvenile Delinquents in American Society*. Westport, CT: Greenwood Press.

Foley, D. L. 1973. "Institutional and Contextual Factors Affecting the Housing Choices of Minority Residents." In *Segregation in Residential Area*, edited by A. H. Hawley and V. P. Rock (pp. 85–147). Washington, DC: National Academy of Sciences.

Guest, A. M. 1984. "They City." In *Sociological Human Ecology*, edited by M. Micklin and H. M. Choldin (pp. 277–322). Boulder, CO: Western Press.

Heitgerd, J. L., and R. J. Bursik, Jr. 1987. "Extra-Community Dynamics and the Ecology of Delinquency." *American Journal of Sociology* 92:775–87.

Hirsch, A. R. 1977. "Race and Housing: Violence and Communal Protest in Chicago, 1940–1960." In *the Ethnic Frontier*, edited by M. G. Holli and P. d'A. Jones (pp. 331–368). Grand Rapids, MI: Eerdmans.

———. 1983. *Making the Second Ghetto: Race and Housing in Chicago 1940–1960*. Cambridge: Cambridge University Press.

Janowitz, M. 1967. *The Community Press in an Urban Setting*. Second Edition. Chicago, IL: University of Chicago Press.

———. 1976. *Social Control of the Welfare State*. Chicago, IL: University of Chicago Press.

Kornhauser, R. R. 1978. *Social Sources of Delinquency*. Chicago, IL: University of Chicago Press.

Liska, A. E., M. B. Chamlin, and M. D. Reed. 1985. "Testing the Economic Production and Conflict Models of Crime Control." *Social Forces* 64: 119–138.

Park, R. E., and E. W. Burgess. 1924. *Introduction to the Science of Sociology*. Second Edition. Chicago, IL: University of Chicago Press.

Rossi, P. H., E. Waite, C. E. Bose, and R. E. Berk. 1974. "The Seriousness of Crimes: Normative Structure and Individual Differences." *American Sociological Review* 39:224–237.

Schuerman, L. A., and S. Kobrin. 1983. "Crime and Urban Ecological Processes: Implications for Public Policy." A paper presented to the Annual Meetings of the *American Society of Criminology*, Denver, CO.

Sellin, T., and M. E. Wolfgang. 1964. *The Measurement of Delinquency*. New York: Wiley.

Shaw, C. R., F. M. Zorbaugh, H. D. McKay, and L. S. Cottrell. 1929. *Delinquency Areas*. Chicago, IL: University of Chicago Press.

Shaw, C. R., and H. D. McKay. 1942. *Juvenile Delinquency and Urban Areas*. Chicago, IL: University of Chicago Press.

Snodgrass, J. 1976. "Clifford R. Shaw and Henry D. McKay: Chicago Criminologists." *British Journal of Criminology* 16: 1–19.

Spergel, I. A., and J. Korbelik. 1979. *The Local Community Service System and ISOS: An Interorganizational Analysis*. Executive Report submitted to the Illinois Law Enforcement Commission.

Suttles, G. D. 1972. *The Social Construction of Communities*. Chicago, IL: University of Chicago Press.

Thomas, W. I., and F. Znaniecki. 1920. *The Polish Peasant in Europe and America*. Volume IV. Boston, MA: Gorham Press.

Tittle, C. R. 1983. "Social Class and Criminal Behavior: A Critique of the Theoretical Foundation." *Social Forces* 62:334–358.

Weicher, J. C. 1980. *Housing: Federal Policies and Programs*. Washington, DC.: American Enterprise Institute.

Chapter 8

Cohen, Albert K. 1951. Multiple Factor Approaches. In *Sociology of Crime and Delinquency* (second edition), edited by Marvin Wolfgang, Leonard Savitz, and Norman Johnston (pp. 123–126). New York: Wiley.

Cohen, Albert K. 1987. "Review of Crime and Human Nature." *Contemporary Sociology* 16:92–97.

Edel, Abraham. 1959. "The Concept of Levels in Social Theory." In *Symposium on Sociological Theory*, edited by Llewllyn Gross (pp. 167–195). Evanston, IL: Row, Peterson and Co.

Ferdinand, Theodore. 1967. *Typologies of Delinquency*. New York: Free Press.

Ferri, Enrico. 1917. *Criminal Sociology*. Boston, MA: Little, Brown.

Garofalo, Raffaele. 1914. *Criminology*. Boston: Little, Brown.

Glueck, Sheldon and Eleanor Glueck. 1950. *Unraveling Juvenile Delinquency*. Cambridge, MA: Harvard University Press.

Kockelmans, Joseph J. (ed.). 1979. *Interdisciplinarity and Higher Education*. University Park: Pennsylvania State University Press.

Lombroso, Ceseare. 1912. *Crime: Its Causes and Remedies*. Boston, MA: Little, Brown.

Parsons, Talcott. 1961. "Outline of the Social System." In *Theories of Society*, edited by Talcott Parsons, Edward Shils, Kaspar D. Naegele, and Jesse R. Pitts (pp. 30–79). New York: Free Press.

Rieff, Philip. n.d. *Class Roles*. Class taught at University of Pennsylvania.

Torgerson, Warren. 1958. *Theory and Methods of Scaling*. New York: Wiley.

Vold, George. 1979. *Theoretical Criminology*. New York: Oxford University Press.

Williams, Frank. 1984. "The Demise of the Criminological Imagination: A Critique of Recent Criminology." *Justice* 1:91–106.

Wilson, James Q. and Richard J. Herrnstein. 1985. *Crime and Human Nature*. New York: Simon and Schuster.

Chapter 9

Bell, Alan P., Martin S. Weinberg, and Sue Kiefer Hammersmith. 1981. *Sexual Preference: Its Development in Men and Women*. Bloomington, IN: Indiana University Press.

References

Ben-Yehuda, Nachman. 1985. *Deviance and Moral Boundaries: Witchcraft, the Occult, Science Fiction, Deviant Sciences and Scientists.* Chicago, IL: University of Chicago Press.

Burgess, Robert L. and Ronald A. Akers. 1968. "A Differential Association-Reinforcement Theory of Criminal Behavior." *Social Problems* 14:128–147.

Cloward, Richard A. and Lloyd E. Ohlin. 1960. *Delinquency and Opportunity: A Theory of Delinquent Groups.* New York: Free Press.

Davies, Christie. 1982. "Sexual Taboos and Social Boundaries." *American Journal of Sociology* 87: 1032–1063.

Dentler, Robert A. and Kai T. Erikson. 1959. "The Functions of Deviance in Groups." *Social Problems* 7: 98–107.

Durkheim, Emile. 1904. *The Rules of Sociological Method.* S. A. Solovay and J. H. Mueller, trans. George E. G. Catlin, ed. New York: Macmillan, 1938.

Hirschi, Travis. 1969. *Causes of Delinquency.* Los Angeles, CA: University of California Press.

Jones, David A. 1986. *History of Criminology: A Philosophical Perspective.* New York: Greenwood Press.

Lauderdale, Pat. 1976. "Deviance and Moral Boundaries." *American Sociological Review* 41:660–676.

Luckenbill, David F. 1977. "Criminal Homicide as a Situated Transaction." *Social Problems* 25:176–186.

Masters, William H. and Virginia Johnson. 1979. *Homosexuality in Perspective.* Boston, MA: Little, Brown.

Mead, George H. 1918. "The Psychology of Punitive Justice." *American Journal of Sociology* 23: 577–602.

Merton, Robert K. 1938. "Social Structure and Anomie." *American Sociological Review* 3: 672–682.

———. 1968. *Social Theory and Social Structure.* New York: Free Press.

Rennie, Ysabel. 1978. *The Search for Criminal Man.* Lexington, MA: Lexington Books.

Schur, Edwin M. 1971. *Labeling Deviant Behavior: Its Sociological Implications.* New York: Harper & Row.

Shaw, Clifford R. and Henry D. McKay. 1942. *Juvenile Delinquency in Urban Areas.* Chicago, IL: University of Chicago Press.

Chapter 10

Akers, Ronald L. 1985. *Deviant Behavior.* Belmont, CA: Wadsworth.

Bernard, Thomas J. 1987a. "Testing Structural Strain Theories." *Journal of Research in Crime and Delinquency* 24:262–80.

———. 1987b. "Reply to Agnew." *Journal of Research in Crime and Delinquency* 24:287–90.

———. 1987c. "Structure and Control." *Justice Quarterly* 4:409–24.

———. 1985. "Criminal Justice in a Hobbesian World: A Starting Point for Criminology." Paper presented at annual meeting of the American Society of Criminology.

———. 1984. "Violence and Conflict Criminology." Paper presented at annual meeting of American Society of Criminology.

Black, Donald. 1979. "Common Sense in the Sociology of Law." *American Sociological Review* 44:18–27.

Blalock, Hubert M., Jr. 1984. *Basic Dilemmas in the Social Sciences.* Beverly Hills, CA: Sage.

Blau, Peter M. 1977. *Inequality and Heterogeneity.* New York: Free Press.

Braithwaite, John. 1987. "The State of Criminology." Paper presented at annual meeting of American Society of Criminology.

Briar, Scott and Irving Piliavin. 1965. "Delinquency, Situational Inducements, and Commitment to Conformity." *Social Problems* 13:35–45.

Burgess, Robert L. and Ronald L. Akers. 1966. "Are Operant Principles Tautological?" *Psychological Record* 16:305–12.

Cloward, Richard A. 1959. "Illegitimate Means, Anomie, and Deviant Behavior." *American Sociological Review* 24:164–76.

——— and Lloyd Ohlin. 1960. *Delinquency and Opportunity.* New York: Free Press.

Cohen, Albert. 1955. *Delinquent Boys.* New York: Free Press.

——— and James Short. 1976. "Crime and Juvenile Delinquency." In *Contemporary Social Problems,* edited by Robert K. Merton and Robert Nisbit (pp. 47–100). New York: Harcourt Brace Jovanovich.

Cohen, Lawrence E. and Marcus Felson. 1979. "Social Change and Crime Rate Trends: A Routine Activities Approach." *American Sociological Review* 44:588–608.

Cornish, Derek B. and Ronald V. Clarke. 1986. *The Reasoning Criminal*. New York: Springer-Verlag.

———. 1987. "Understanding Crime Displacement: An Application of Rational Choice Theory." *Criminology* 25:933–47.

Cullen, Francis T. 1983. *Rethinking Crime and Deviance Theory*. Totowa, NJ: Rowman and Allenheld.

Curtis, Lynn A. 1975. *Violence, Race, and Culture*. Lexington, MA: D.C. Heath.

Dahrendorf, Ralf. 1979. *Life Chances*. London: Weidenfeld and Nicolson.

———. 1959. *Class and Class Conflict in Industrial Society*. Stanford, CA: Stanford University Press.

Durkheim, Emile. 1951. *Suicide*. New York: Free Press.

Elliott, Delbert S. 1985. "The Assumption that Theories Can Be Combined with Increased Explanatory Power: Theoretical Integrations." In *Theoretical Methods in Criminology*, edited by Robert F. Meier (pp. 123–149). Beverly Hills, CA: Sage.

———, David Huizinga and Suzanne G. Ageton. 1985. *Explaining Delinquency and Drug Use*. Beverly Hills, CA: Sage.

Etzioni, Amatai. 1987. "How Rational We?" *Sociological Forum* 2:1–20.

Frank, Robert H. 1987. "Shrewdly Irrational." *Sociological Forum* 2:21–41.

Foucault, Michel. 1977. *Discipline and Punish*. New York: Pantheon.

Friedman, Lawrence M. and Robert V. Percival. 1981. *The Roots of Justice*. Chapel Hill, NC: University of North Carolina Press.

Gibbs, Jack P. 1985. "The Methodology of Theory Construction in Criminology." In *Theoretical Methods in Criminology*, edited by Robert F. Meier (pp. 23–50). Beverly Hills, CA: Sage.

———. 1981. *Norms, Deviance, and Social Control*. New York: Elsevier.

———. 1972. *Sociological Theory Construction*. Hinsdale, IL: Dryden.

Gottfredson, Michael and Travis Hirschi. 1988. "A Propensity-Event Theory of Crime." In *Advances in Criminological Theory*, Vol. 1, edited by Freda Adler and William Laufer. New Brunswick, NJ: Transaction Books.

Hirschi, Travis. 1979. "Separate but Equal is Better." *Journal of Research in Crime and Delinquency* 16:34–38.

———. 1969. *Causes of Delinquency*. Berkeley, CA: University of California Press.

———. and Michael Gottfredson. 1987. "Toward a General Theory of Crime." In *Explaining Crime*, edited by Wouter Buikhuisen and Sarnoff Mednick (pp. 8–26). Leiden: Brill

———. and Michael Hindelang. 1977. "Intelligence and Delinquency." *American Sociological Review* 42:572–87.

Kitsuse, John I. and Aaron V. Cicourel. 1963. "A Note on the Uses of Official Statistics." *Social Problems* 11:131–39.

Kornhauser, Ruth R. 1978. *Social Sources of Delinquency*. Chicago, IL: University of Chicago Press.

Kuhn, Thomas S. 1970. *The Structure of Scientific Revolutions*. Chicago, IL: University of Chicago Press.

Lemert, Edwin. 1964. "Social Structure, Social Control, and Deviation." In *Anomie and Deviant Behavior*, edited by Marshall Clinard (pp. 57–97). New York: Free Press.

Liebow, Elliott. 1967. *Tally's Corner*. Boston, MA: Little, Brown.

Merton, Robert K. 1957. *Social Theory and Social Structure*. New York: Free Press.

Nettler, Gwynn. 1984. *Explaining Crime*. New York: McGraw-Hill.

Parsons, Talcott. 1951. *Toward a General Theory in Action*. New York: Harper & Row.

Pearson, Frank S. and Neil Alan Weiner. 1985. "Towards an Integration of Criminological Theories." *Journal of Criminal Law and Criminology*, 76: 116–150.

———. 1937. *The Structure of Social Action*. New York: McGraw-Hill.

Perls, Frederick, R. E. Hefferline, and Paul Goodman. 1951. *Gestalt Therapy*. New York: Dell.

Robinson, W. S. 1950. "Ecological Correlations and the Behavior of Individuals." *American Sociological Review* 15:351–57.

Sellin, Thorsten. 1938. *Culture Conflict and Crime*. New York: Social Science Research Council.

Shaw, Clifford R. and Henry D. McKay. 1942. *Juvenile Delinquency and Urban Areas*. Chicago, IL: University of Chicago Press.

Short, James F. 1985. "Review Essay." *Criminology* 23:189.

Stinchcombe, Arthur L. 1975. "Merton's Theory of Social Structure." In *The Idea of Social Structure*, edited by Lewis Coser (pp. 11–33). New York: Harcourt Brace Jovanovich.

Sutherland, Edwin H. and Donald R. Cressey. 1978. *Criminology.* Philadelphia: Lippincott.

Sykes, Gresham M. and David Matza. 1957. "Techniques of Neutralization: A Theory of Delinquency." *American Sociological Review* 22: 667–70.

Tittle, Charles R., Wayne J. Villemez, and Douglas A. Smith. 1978. "The Myth of Social Class and Criminality." *American Sociological Review* 43:643–56.

Toby, Jackson. 1957. "Social Disorganization and Stake in Conformity." *Journal of Criminal Law, Criminology, and Police Science* 43:12–17.

Vold, George B. and Thomas J. Bernard. 1986. *Theoretical Criminology.* New York: Oxford University Press.

Walker, Samuel. 1985. *Sense and Nonsense About Crime.* Monterey, CA: Brooks/Cole.

Wallace, Walter L. 1986. "Social Structural and Cultural Structural Variables in Sociology." *Sociological Focus* 19:125–38.

Wilson, James Q. 1978. *The Investigators.* New York: Basic Books.

Wolfgang Marvin E. and Franco Ferracuti. 1981. *The Subculture of Violence.* Beverly Hills, CA: Sage.

Chapter 11

Angell, Robert C. 1974. "The Moral Integration of American Cities: II." *American Journal of Sociology* 80:607–629.

Bennett, Richard B. 1980. "Constructing Cross-Cultural Theories in Criminology: Application of the Generative Approach." *Criminology* 18:252–268.

Bernard, Thomas J. 1986. "A Structural Interpretation of Strain Theory." Presented at the Convention of the American Society of Criminology, Atlanta.

Blalock, Hubert M. 1969. *Theory Construction: From Verbal to Mathematical Formulations.* Englewood Cliffs, NJ: Prentice-Hall.

Bohm, Robert M. 1982. "Radical Criminology: An Explication." *Criminology* 19:565–589.

Bonger, Willem. 1969. *Criminality and Economic Conditions.* Edited by Austin T. Turk. Bloomington, IN: Indiana University Press.

Braithwaite, R. B. 1960. *Scientific Explanation.* New York: Harper & Row.

Clinard, Marshall B. and Robert F. Meier. 1979. *Sociology of Deviant Behavior*, Fifth Edition. New York: Holt, Rinehart and Winston.

Cohen, Lawrence E. and Marcus Felson. 1979. "Social Change and Crime Rate Trends: A Routine Activities Approach." *American Sociological Review* 44:588–608.

Crutchfield, Robert D., Michael R. Geerken, and Walter R. Gove. 1982. "Crime Rate and Social Integration: The Impact of Metropolitan Mobility." *Criminology* 20:467–478.

Cullen, Francis T. 1984. *Rethinking Crime and Deviance Theory: The Emergence of a Structuring Tradition*. Totowa, NJ: Rowman and Allanheld.

Durkheim, Emile. 1933. *The Division of Labor in Society*. New York: The Free Press. (Orig. 1893).

———. 1951. *Suicide*. Glencoe, IL: The Free Press. (Orig. 1897).

Elliott, Delbert S. 1985. "The Assumption That Theories Can Be Combined with Increased Explanatory Power: Theoretical Integrations." In *Theoretical Methods in Criminology*, edited by Robert F. Meier (pp. 123–149). Beverly Hills, CA: Sage.

———. 1984. *The Urban Experience*, Second Edition. Atlanta, GA: Harcourt Brace Jovanovich.

Fischer, Claude S. 1975. "Toward a Subcultural Theory of Urbanism." *American Journal of Sociology* 80:1319–1341.

Freese, Lee. 1972a. "Cumulative Sociological Knowledge." *American Sociological Review* 37:472–482.

———. 1972b. "Cumulative Sociological Knowledge: An Addendum." *American Sociological Review* 37:486–487.

Friday, Paul C. and Jerald Hage. 1976. "Youth Crime in Postindustrial Societies: An Integrated Perspective." *Criminology* 14:347–368.

Gibbs, Jack P. 1964. *Status Integration and Suicide: A Sociological Study*. Eugene: University of Oregon Books.

———. 1972. *Sociological Theory Construction*. Hinsdale, IL: Dryden.

———. 1985. "The Methodology of Theory Construction in Criminology." In *Theoretical Methods in Criminology*, edited by Robert F. Meier (pp. 25–30). Beverly Hills, CA: Sage.

Glaser, Daniel. 1980. "The Interplay of Theory, Issues, Policy, and Data." In *Handbook of Criminal Justice Evaluation*, edited by Malcolm W. Klein and Katherine S. Teilman (pp. 123–142). Beverly Hills, CA: Sage.

Greenberg, David F. 1981. *Crime and Capitalism: Readings in Marxist Criminology.* Palo Alto, CA: Mayfield.

Hage, Jerald. 1972. *Techniques and Problems of Theory Construction in Sociology.* New York: Wiley.

Hirschi, Travis. 1969. *Causes of Delinquency.* Berkeley, CA: University of California Press.

Kitsuse, John I. 1980. "The 'New Conception of Deviance' and Its Critics." In *The Labelling of Deviance: Evaluating a Perspective,* Second Edition, edited by Walter R. Gove (pp. 381–392). Beverly Hills, CA: Sage.

Liska, Allen E. 1987. *Perspectives on Deviance,* Second Edition. Englewood Cliffs, NJ: Prentice-Hall.

Lyerly, Robert R. and James K. Skipper, Jr. 1981. "Differential Rates of Rural-Urban Delinquency: A Social Control Approach." *Criminology* 19:385–399.

McGahey, R. M. 1980. "Dr Ehrlich's Magic Bullet: Econometric Theory, Econometrics, and the Death Penalty." *Crime and Delinquency* 26:485–502.

Merton, Robert K. 1968. *Social Theory and Social Structure.* Glencoe, IL: The Free Press.

Park, Robert. 1969. "The City: Suggestions for the Investigation of Human Behavior in the Urban Environment." Pp. 91–130 In *Classic Esays on the Culture of Cities,* edited by Richard Sennett. New York: Appleton-Century-Crofts. (Orig. 1916)

Shaw, Clifford R. and Henry D. McKay. 1969. *Juvenile Delinquency and Urban Areas,* Revised Edition. Chicago: University of Chicago Press.

Shevky, Eshref and Wendell Bell. 1955. *Social Area Analysis.* Stanford, CA: Stanford University Press.

Simmel, Georg. 1969. "The Metropolis and Mental Life." In *Classic Essays on the Culture of Cities,* edited by Richard Sennett (pp. 47–60). New York: Appleton-Century-Crofts. (Orig. 1903).

Tittle, Charles R. 1985. "The Assumption That General Theories Are Not Possible." In *Theoretical Methods in Criminology,* edited by Robert F. Meier (pp. 93–121). Beverly Hills, CA: Sage.

Vold, George B. and Thomas J. Bernard. 1986. *Theoretical Criminology,* Third Edition. New York: Oxford University Press.

Wagner, David G. and Joseph Berger. 1985. "Do Sociological Theories Grow?" *American Journal of Sociology* 90:697–728.

Walker, Henry A. and Bernard P., Cohen. 1985. "Scope Statements: Imperatives for Evaluating Theory." *American Sociological Review* 50:288–301.

Willer, David and Murray Webster, Jr. 1970. "Theoretical Concepts and Observables." *American Sociological Review* 35:748–757.

Wilson, James Q. and Richard J. Herrnstein. 1985. *Crime and Human Nature*. New York: Simon and Schuster.

Wirth, Louis. 1938. "Urbanism As a Way of Life." *American Journal of Sociology* 44:1–24.

Wolfgang, Marvin E. (ed.) 1968. *Crime and Culture*. New York: Wiley.

Chapter 12

Clinard, Marshall B., ed. 1964. *Anomie and Deviant Behavior*. New York: Free Press.

Dubin, Robert. 1978. *Theory Building*. rev. ed. New York: Free Press.

Elliott, Delbert S. 1985. "The Assumption that Theories Can Be Combined with Increased Explanatory Power. In *Theoretical Methods in Criminology*, edited by Robert F. Meier (pp. 123–149). Beverly Hills, CA: Sage.

Gibbons, Don C. 1982. *Society, Crime, and Criminal Behavior*, 4th ed. Englewood Cliffs, NJ: Prentice-Hall.

Gibbs, Jack P. 1972. *Sociological Theory Construction*. Hinsdale, IL: Dryden.

———. 1981a. *Norms, Deviance, and Social Control*. New York: Elsevier.

———. 1981b. "The Sociology of Deviance and Social Control." In *Social Psychology*, edited by Morris Rosenberg and Ralph H. Turner (pp. 483–522). New York: Basic Books.

———. 1982. "Evidence of Causation." *Current Perspectives in Social Theory* 3:93–127.

———. 1985. "The Methodology of Theory Construction in Criminology." In *Theoretical Methods in Criminology*, edited by Robert F. Meier (pp. 23–50). Beverly Hills, CA: Sage.

Gouldner, Alvin W. 1970. *The Coming Crisis of Western Sociology*. New York: Basic Books.

Hempel, Carl G. 1965. *Aspects of Scientific Explanation*. New York: Free Press.

Hirschi, Travis. 1979. "Separate and Unequal is Better." *Journal of Research in Crime and Delinquency* 16:34–38.

Homans, George C. 1974. *Social Behavior*, rev. ed. New York: Harcourt Brace Jovanovich.

Jencks, Christopher. 1987. "Genes and Crime." *New York Review of Books* 34, August 17:33–41.

Kuhn, Thomas S. 1970. *The Structure of Scientific Revolutions*, 2nd ed. Chicago, IL: University of Chicago Press.

Masterman, Margaret. 1970. "The Nature of a Paradigm." In *Criticism and The Growth of Knowledge*, edited by Imre Lakatos and Alan Musgrave (pp. 59–89). London: Cambridge University Press.

Merton, Robert K. 1957. *Social Theory and Social Structure*. New York: Free Press.

Messner, Steven F. and Kenneth Tardiff. 1986. "Economic Inequality and Levels of Homicide." *Criminology* 24:297–317.

Quinney, Richard. 1976. "Book Review." *Contemporary Sociology* 5:414–416.

Salmon, Merilee H. and Wesley C. Salmon. 1979. "Alternative Models of Scientific Explanation." *American Anthropologist* 81:61–74.

Sutherland, Edwin H. and Donald R. Cressey. 1974. *Criminology*. Philadelphia, PA: Lippincott.

Turner, Jonathan H. and Leonard Beeghley. 1981. *The Emergence of Sociological Theory*. Homewood, IL: Dorsey.

Chapter 13

Alexander, Jeffrey C. 1982–84. *Theoretical Logic in Sociology*. Berkeley, CA: University of California Press.

Becker, Howard S. 1963. *Outsiders: Studies in the Sociology of Deviance*. New York: Free Press.

Bellah, Robert N., Richard Madsen, William B. Sullivan, Ann Swidler, and Steven M. Tipton. 1985. *Habits of the Heart*. New York: Harper & Row.

Blau, Peter M. and Otis Dudley Duncan. 1967. *The American Occupational Structure*. New York: Wiley.

Blau, Peter M. 1977. *Inequality and Heterogeneity: A Primitive Theory of Social Structure*. New York: Free Press.

Breault, Kevin D. 1986. "Suicide in America: A Test of Durkheim's Theory of Religious and Family Integration, 1933–1980." *American Journal of Sociology*, 92:628–656.

Catton, William R., Jr.. 1978. "Understanding Social Differentiation." *Contemporary Sociology*, 7:695–698.

Chambliss, William J. 1964. "A Sociological Analysis of the Law of Vagrancy." *Social Problems*, 11:67–77.

Clinard, Marshall B. and Robert F. Meier. 1985. *Sociology of Deviant Behavior*, 6th ed. New York: Holt, Rinehart and Winston.

Cohen, Albert K. 1974. *The Elasticity of Evil: Changes in the Social Definition of Deviance*. Oxford, England: Oxford University Penal Research Unit Basil Blackwell.

Collins, Randall. 1975. *Conflict Sociology: Toward an Explanatory Science*. New York: Academic Press.

Colvin, Mark and J. Pauley. 1983. "A Critique of Criminology: Toward an Integrated Structural-Marxist Theory of Delinquency Production." *American Journal of Sociology*, 89:513–551.

Davis, Kingsley and Wilbert Moore. 1945. "Some Principles of Stratification." *American Sociological Review*, 10:242–249.

Dahrendorf, Ralf. 1959. *Class and Class Conflict in Industrial Society*. Stanford, CA: Stanford University Press.

_____. 1968. *Essays in the Theory of Society*. Stanford, CA: Stanford University Press.

DeFleur, Lois and Robert F. Meier. 1988. "Deviance and Social Control: Revisiting Our Intellectual Heritage." In Edgar F. Borgatta and Karen S. Cook (eds), *The Future of Sociology*. Newbury Park, CA: Sage Publications.

Durkheim, Emile. 1983 [1895]. *The Rules of Sociological Method*, edited with an introduction by Steven Lukes. New York: Free Press.

Elliott, Delbert S., Suzanne S. Ageton, and R. J. Canter. 1979. "An Integrated Theoretical Perspective on Delinquent Behavior." *Journal of Research in Crime and Delinquency*. 16:3–27.

Elliott, Delbert S. 1985. "The Assumption that Theories Can Be Combined With Increased Explanatory Power: Theoretical Integrations." In *Theoretical Methods in Criminology*, edited by Robert F. Meier (pp. 123–150). Beverly Hills, CA: Sage.

Featherman, David L. 1981. "Stratification and Social Mobility: Two Decades of Cumulative Social Science." In *The State of Sociology: Problems and Prospects*, edited by James F. Short, Jr. (pp. 79–100). Beverly Hills, CA: Sage.

Gibbs, Jack P. 1966. "Conceptions of Deviant Behavior: The Old and the New." *Pacific Sociological Review*, 9:9–14.

_____. 1981. *Norms, Deviance, and Social Control: Conceptual Matters.* New York: Elsevier.

Giddens, Anthony. 1984. *The Constitution of Society: Outline of the Theory of Structuration.* Berkeley, CA: University of California Press.

Gusfield, Joseph R. 1963. *Symbolic Crusade.* Champaign, IL: University of Illinois Press.

Hagan, John and Alberto Palloni. 1986. "Toward a Structural Criminology: Method and Theory in Criminological Research." *Annual Review of Sociology,* 12:431–449.

Haug, Marie R. 1977. "Measurement in Social Stratification." *Annual Review of Sociology,* 3:51–77.

Hirschi, Travis. 1979. "Separate and Unequal is Better." *Journal of Research in Crime and Delinquency,* 16:34–38.

_____. 1986. "On the Compatibility of Rational Choice and Social Control Theories of Crime." In *The Reasoning Criminal: Rational Choice Perspectives on Offending,* edited by Derek B. Cornish and Ronald V. Clarke (pp. 105–118). New York: Springer-Verlag.

Jackson, J. A. 1968. "Editorial Introduction." In *Social Stratification,* edited by J. A. Jackson (pp. 1–13). Cambridge: Cambridge University Press.

Jones Joseph F. and Don C. Gibbons. 1987. "Deviance and Diversity: Notes on an Emerging Perspective." Paper presented at the annual meeting of the Pacific Sociological Association, Eugene, Oregon.

Kornhauser, Ruth Rosner. 1978. *Social Sources of Delinquency.* Chicago, IL: University of Chicago Press.

Lemert, Edwin M. 1951. *Social Pathology.* New York: McGraw-Hill.

_____. 1972. *Social Problems, Human Deviance and Social Control.* Englewood Cliffs, NJ: Prentice-Hall.

_____. 1982. "Issues in the Study of Deviance." In *The Sociology of Deviance,* edited by M. Michael Rosenberg, Robert A. Stebbins, and Allan Turowetz (pp. 233–257). New York: St. Martin's.

Matza, David. 1969. *Becoming Deviant.* Englewood Cliffs, NJ: Prentice-Hall.

Meier, Robert F. 1982. "Perspectives on the Concept of Social Control." *Annual Review of Sociology,* 8:35–65.

_____. 1985. "Introduction." In *Theoretical Perspectives in Criminology,* edited by Robert F. Meier (pp. 11–19). Beverly Hills, CA: Sage.

Mizruchi, Ephraim H. 1987. [1983] *Regulating Society: Beguines, Bohemians, and Other Marginals.* Chicago: University of Chicago Press.

Nuehring, Elane and Gerald E. Markle. 1974. "Nicotine and Norms: The Reemergence of a Deviant Behavior." *Social Problems*, 21:513–526.

Parsons, Talcott. 1971. *The System of Modern Societies*. Englewood Cliffs, NJ: Prentice-Hall.

Pearson, Frank S. and Neil Alan Weiner. 1985. "Toward an Integration of Criminological Theories." *Journal of Criminal Law and Criminology*, 76:116–150.

Platt, Anthony. 1969. *The Child Savers*. Chicago, IL: University of Chicago Press.

Runciman, W. G. 1968. "Class, Status and Power." In *Social Stratification: Sociological Studies*, edited by J. Jackson (pp. 25–64). Cambridge, England: Cambridge University Press.

Sagarin, Edward. 1975. *Deviants and Deviance: An Introduction to the Study of Disvalued People and Behavior*. New York: Holt, Rinehart and Winston.

Shils, Edward A. 1970. "Deference." In *The Logic of Social Hierarchies*. edited by Edward O. Laumann, Paul M. Seigel, and Robert W. Hodge (pp. 420–448). Chicago, IL: Markham.

Shoemaker, Donald J. 1984. *Theories of Delinquency: An Examination of Explanations of Delinquent Behavior*. New York: Oxford University Press.

Short, James F., Jr. 1979. "On the Etiology of Delinquent Behavior." *Journal of Research in Crime and Delinquency*. 16:28–33.

———. 1985. "The Level of Explanation Problem in Criminology." In *Theoretical Methods in Criminology*, edited by Robert F. Meier (pp. 51–78). Beverly Hills, CA: Sage.

Spector, Malcolm and John I. Kitsuse. 1977. *Constructing Social Problems*. Menlo Park, CA: Cummings.

Svalastoga, Karl. 1965. *Social Differentiation*. New York: McKay.

Wagner, David G. 1984. *The Growth of Sociological Theories*. Beverly Hills, CA: Sage.

Warner, Lloyd, Marchia Meeker, and Kenneth Eells. 1949. *Social Class in America*. New York: Harper & Row.

Wright, Eric Ohlin. 1977. "Marxist Class Categories and Income Inequality." *American Sociological Review*, 42:32–55.

Chapter 14

Adler, Freda. 1975. *Sisters in Crime*. New York: McGraw-Hill.

Black, Donald. 1976. *The Behavior of Law.* New York: Academic.

Bonger, Willem. 1916. *Criminality and Economic Conditions.* Boston, MA: Little, Brown.

Coser, Rose. 1985. "Power Lost and Status Gained: The American Middle Class Husband." Paper presented at the American Sociological Association meeting, Washington, DC.

Curtis, Richard. 1986. "Household and Family in Theory on Equality." *American Sociological Review* 51:168–83.

Hagan, John. 1988a. *Structural Criminology.* Cambridge, England: Polity Press.

———. 1988b. "Feminist Scholarship, Relational and Instrumental Control, and a Power-Control Theory of Gender and Delinquency." *British Journal of Sociology.*

Hagan, John, John Simpson, and A. R. Gillis. 1979. "The Sexual Stratification of Social Control: A Gender-Based Perspective on Crime and Delinquency." *British Journal of Sociology* 30:25–38.

———. 1985. "The Class Structure of Gender and Delinquency: Toward a Power-Control Theory of Gender and Delinquency." *American Journal of Sociology* 90:1151–78.

———. 1987. "Class in the Household: A Power–Control Theory of Gender and Delinquency." *American Journal of Sociology* 92:788–816.

Harris, Anthony, 1977. "Sex and Theories of Deviance: Toward a Functional Theory of Deviant Type-Scripts." *American Sociological Review* 42:3–16.

Hindelang, Michael. 1971. "Age, Sex and Versatility of Delinquency Involvement." *Social Problems* 18:522–35.

Hirschi, Travis. 1969. *Causes of Delinquency.* Berkeley, CA: University of California Press.

Huber, Joan. 1976. "Toward a Socio-Technological Theory of the Women's Movement." *Social Problems* 23:371–88.

Lemert, Edwin. 1967. *Human Deviance, Social Problems and Social Control.* Englewood Cliffs, NJ: Prentice-Hall.

Lindesmith, Alfred and Y. Levin. 1937. "The Lombrosian Myth in Criminology." *American Journal of Sociology* 42:653–71.

Lombroso, Cesear. 1895. *The Female Offender.* New York: Fisher Unwin.

MacKinnon, Catherine. 1982. "Feminism, Marxism, Method and the State: Toward Feminist Jurisprudence." *Signs* 8:185–208.

Millett, Kate. 1970. *Sexual Politics*. Garden City, NY: Doubleday.

Schuessler, Karl and Donald Cressey. 1950. "Personality Characteristics of Criminals." *American Journal of Sociology* 55:476–84.

Scull, Andrew. 1976. "Madness and Segregative Controls: The Rise of the Insane Asylum." *Social Problems* 24:337–51.

Simon, Rita. 1975. *Women and Crime*. Lexington, MA: Lexington Books.

Smith, Douglas and Christy Visher. 1980. "Sex and Involvement in Deviance/Crime: A Quantitative Review of the Empirical Literature." *American Sociological Review* 45:691–701.

Steffensmeier, Darrel. 1978. "Crime and the Contemporary Woman: An Analysis of Changing Levels of Female Property Crime, 1969–1975." *Social Forces* 57:566–84.

———. 1980. "Sex Differences in Patterns of Adult Crimes, 1965–1977: A Review and Assessment." *Social Forces* 58:1080–1108.

Tannenbaum, Franklin. 1938. *Crime and Community*. Boston, MA: Ginn.

Thrasher, Frederick. 1937. *The Gang*. Chicago, IL: University of Chicago Press.

Veblen, Thorstein. 1934. *The Theory of the Leisure Class*. New York: Mentor.

Vogel, Lise. 1983. *Marxism and Oppression of Women: Toward a Unitary Theory*. New Brunswick, NJ: Rutgers University Press.

Weber, Max. 1947. *The Theory of Social and Economic Organizations*, translated by Talcot Parsons and A. M. Henderson. New York: Free Press.

Welter, Barbara. 1966. "The Cult of Womanhood, 1820–1860." *American Quarterly* 18:151–74.

Wilkinson, Karen. 1974. "The Broken Family and Juvenile Delinquency: Scientific Explanation or Ideology?" *Social Problems* 21:726–39.

Chapter 15

Allen, Craig M., and Murray A. Straus. 1980. "Resources, Power and Husband-Wife Violence," In *The Social Causes of Husband-Wife Violence*, edited by Murray A. Straus and Gerald T. Hotaling (pp. 188–208). Minneapolis, MN: University of Minnesota Press.

Cohen, Albert K. 1955. *Delinquent Boys*. Glencoe, IL: Free Press.

Dollard, John. 1937. *Caste and Class in a Southern Town*. New Haven, CT: Yale University Press.

Durkheim, Emile. 1966. (1938). *The Rules of Sociological Method*, translated by Sarah A. Solavay and John H. Mueller, edited by George E. G. Catlin. New York: Free Press.

Emerson, Richard M. 1962. "Power-Dependency Relations," *American Sociological Review* 27:31–40.

Erikson, Kai T. 1966. *Wayward Puritans: A Study in the Sociology of Deviance*. New York: Wiley.

Hagan, John, A. R. Gillis, and John Simpson. 1985. "The Class Structure of Gender and Delinquency: Toward a Power–Control Theory of Common Delinquent Behavior," *American Journal of Sociology*. 90:1151–1178.

Hagan, John, John Simpson, and A. R. Gillis. 1987. "Class in the Household: A Power-Control Theory of Gender and Delinquency," *American Journal of Sociology* 92:788–816.

Hewitt, John P. 1970. *Social Stratification and Deviant Behavior*. New York: Random House.

Hirschi, Travis. 1969. *Causes of Delinquency*. Berkeley, CA: University of California Press.

Kuhn, Thomas S. 1970. *The Structure of Scientific Revolutions*. 2nd edition. Chicago, IL: University of Chicago Press.

MacKinnon, Catherine. 1982. "Femininism, Marxism, Method and the State: Toward Feminist Jurisprudence." *Signs* 8:185–208.

Matza, David. 1964. *Delinquency and Drift*. New York: Wiley.

Meier, Robert F. 1983. "Shoplifting: Behavioral and Economic Aspects," In *Encyclopedia of Crime and Justice*, Volume 4. edited by Sanford H. Kadish (pp. 1497–1500). New York: Free Press.

Moynihan, Daniel Patrick. 1986. *Family and Nation*. New York: Harcourt Brace Jovanovich.

Short, James, Jr. and Fred L. Strodtbeck. 1965. *Group Processes and Gang Delinquency*. Chicago, IL: University of Chicago Press.

Stein, Benjamin J. 1987. *Barrons* February 23:16

Straus, Murray A., Richard J. Gelles and Suzanne Steinmetz. 1980. *Behind Closed Doors:* Violence in the American Family. Garden City, NY: Anchor.

Wilkinson, Karen. 1974. "The Broken Family and Juvenile Delinquency: Scientific Explanation or Ideology?" *Social Problems* 21:726–739.

Chapter 16

Akers, Ronald L. 1977. *Deviant Behavior: A Social Learning Approach* (2nd ed). Belmont: Wadsworth.

Anderson, Elijah. 1978. *A Place on the Corner.* Chicago, IL: University of Chicago Press.

Bandura, Albert. 1986. *Social Foundations of Thought and Action: A Social Cognitive Theory.* Englewood Cliffs, NJ: Prentice-Hall.

Blumstein, Alfred, Jacqueline Cohen, Jeffrey A. Roth, and Christy A. Visher. 1986. *Criminal Careers and "Career Criminals"*, vol. 1. Panel on Research on Criminal Careers, National Research Council. Washington, DC: National Academy Press.

Brymmer, Richard A. 1967. "Toward a Definition and Theory of Conflict Gangs." Paper presented at the annual meeting of the Society for the Study of Social Problems.

Bursik, Robert J. 1986. "Ecological Stability and The Dynamics of Delinquency." In *Communities and Crime, Crime and Justice,* vol. 8., edited by Albert J. Reiss, Jr. and Michael Tonry (pp. 35–66). Chicago, IL: University of Chicago Press.

Cartwright, Desmond S., Barbara Tomson, and Hershey Schwartz. 1975. *Gang Delinquency.* Monterey, CA: Brooks/Cole.

Cartwright, Desmond S., Kenneth I. Howard, and Nicholas A. Reuterman. 1980. "Multivariate Analysis of Gang Delinquency: IV. Personality Factors in Gangs and Clubs." *Multivariate Behavioral Research* 15:3–22.

Cloward, Richard A. and Lloyd E. Ohlin. 1960. *Delinquency and Opportunity: A Theory of Delinquent Gangs.* Glencoe, IL: Free Press.

Cohen, Albert K. 1955. *Delinquent Boys: The Culture of the Gang.* Glencoe, IL: Free Press.

Cohen, Albert K. and James F. Short, Jr. 1976. "Crime and Juvenile Delinquency." In Contemporary Social Problems, edited by Robert K. Merton and Robert Nisbet (pp. 47–100). *Contemporary Social Problems* (4th ed). New York: Harcourt Brace Jovanovich.

Farrington, David P., Leonard Berkowitz, and Donald J. West. 1981. "Differences Between Individual and Group Fights." *British Journal of Social Psychology* 20:163–71.

Finestone, Harold. 1976. "The Delinquent and Society: The Shaw and McKay Tradition." In *Delinquency, Crime, and Society,* edited by James F. Short, Jr. (pp. 23–49). Chicago, IL: University of Chicago Press.

Gibbs, Jack P. 1981. *Norms, Deviance, and Social Control: Conceptual Matters.* New York: Elsevier-North Holland.

Gibbs, Jack P. 1985. "The Methodology of Theory Construction in Criminology." In *Theoretical Methods in Criminology,* edited by Robert F. Meier (pp. 23–50). Beverly Hills, CA: Sage.

Glaser, Daniel. 1971. *Social Deviance.* Chicago, IL: Markham.

Gordon, Robert A. 1967. "Social Class, Social Disability, and Gang Interaction." *American Journal of Sociology* 73:42–62.

Gottfredson, Michael and Travis Hirschi. 1986. "The True Value of Lambda Would Appear to be Zero: An Essay on Career Criminals, Criminal Careers, Selective Incapacitation, Cohort Studies, and Related Topics." *Criminology* 24:213–234.

Inkeles, Alex. 1966. "Social Structure and the Socialization of Competence." *Harvard Educational Review* 36:265–283.

Jansyn, Leon R. 1966. "Solidarity and Delinquency in a Street Corner Group." *American Sociological Review* 31:265–283.

Klein, Malcolm W. and Lois Y. Crawford. 1967. "Groups, Gangs, and Cohesiveness." *Journal of Research in Crime and Delinquency* 4:63–75.

Liebow, Elliott. 1967. *Tally's Corner.* Boston, MA: Little, Brown.

Matza, David and Gresham Sykes. 1961. "Juvenile Delinquency and Subterranean Values." *American Sociological Review* 26:712–719.

Merton, Robert K. 1957. "Social Structure and Anomie." In *Social Theory and Social Structure,* edited by Robert Merton (pp. 131–194). Glencoe, IL: Free Press.

Miller, S. M. 1964. "The American Lower Class: A Typological Approach." *Social Research.* (Reprinted in the Syracuse University Youth Development Reprint Series).

Miller, Walter B. 1958. "Lower Class Culture as a Generating Milieu of Gang Delinquency."*Journal of Social Issues* 14 (Summer): 5–19.

Miller, Walter B. 1981. "Gangs, Groups, and Serious Youth Crime." In *Critical Issues in Juvenile Delinquency,* edited by David Schichor and Delos H. Kelly (pp. 115–133). Lexington, MA: D.C. Heath.

Miller, Walter B., Hildred S. Geertz, and Henry S. G. Cutter. 1961. "Aggression in a Boys' Street-Corner Group." *Psychiatry* 24:283–98.

Pollack, Vicki, Sarnof Mednick, and William F. Gabrielli, Jr. 1983. "Crime Causation: Biological Theories." In *Encyclopedia of Crime and Justice,* vol. 1 (pp. 308–316). New York: Macmillan.

Reiss, Albert J., Jr. and Michael Tonry. 1986. *Communities and Crime*. Chicago, IL: University of Chicago Press.

Rivera, Ramon and James F. Short, Jr. 1967a. "Significant Adults, Caretakers, and Structures of Opportunity: An Exploratory Study." *Journal of Research in Crime and Delinquency* 4:76–97.

Rivera, Ramon and James F. Short, Jr. 1967b. "Occupational Goals: A Comparative Analysis." In *Juvenile Gangs in Context: Theory, Research, and Action*, edited by Malcolm W. Klein and Barbara C. Meyerhoff (pp. 70–90). Englewood Cliffs, NJ: Prentice-Hall.

Schwartz, Gary. 1987. *Beyond Rebellion or Conformity: Youth and Authority in America*. Chicago, IL: University of Chicago Press.

Schwendinger, Herman and Julia Siegel Schwendinger. 1985. *Adolescent Subcultures and Delinquency*. New York: Praeger.

Short, James F., Jr. 1974. "Youth, Gangs, and Society: Macro- and Micro-Sociological Process." *Sociological Quarterly* 15:20–31.

———. 1985a. "The Level of Explanation Problem in Criminology." In *Theoretical Methods in Criminology*, edited by Robert F. Meier (pp. 51–72). Beverly Hills, CA: Sage.

———. 1985b. "Review Essay: Adolescent Subcultures and Delinquency." *Criminology* 23:181–191.

———. 1987. "Exploring Integration of Theoretical Levels of Explanation: Notes on Juvenile Delinquency Paper Presented at the Albany Conference on Theoretical Integration in the Study of Deviance and Crime, State University of New York at Albany.

———. Forthcoming. *Delinquency and Society*. Englewood Cliffs, NJ: Prentice-Hall.

Short, James F., Jr. and John Moland, Jr. 1976. "Politics and Youth Gangs." *Sociological Quarterly* 17:162–179.

Short, James F., Jr., Ramon Rivera, and Harvey Marshall. 1964. "Adult-Adolescent Relations and Gang Delinquency." *Pacific Sociological Review* 7:59–65.

Short, James F., Jr., Ramon Rivera, and Ray A. Tennyson. 1965. "Perceived Opportunities, Gang Membership, and Delinquency." *American Sociological Review* 30:56–67.

Short, James F., Jr. and Fred L. Strodtbeck. 1965. *Group Process and Gang Delinquency*. Chicago, IL: University of Chicago Press.

Stinchcombe, Arthur L. 1975. "Merton's Theory of Social Structure." In *The Idea of Social Structure: Papers in Honor of Robert K. Merton*, edited by Lewis A. Coser (pp. 11–13). New York: Harcourt Brace Jovanovich.

Trotha, Trutz. 1974. *Jugendliche Bandendelinquenz*. Stuttgart: Verlag.

Valentine, Bettylou. 1978. *Hustling and Other Hard Work: Life Styles in the Ghetto*. New York: Free Press.

Wilson, William Julius. 1987. *The Truly Disadvantaged: The Inner City, the Underclass, and Public Policy*. Chicago, IL: University of Chicago Press.

Yablonsky, L. 1962. *Violent Gang*. New York: Macmillan.

Chapter 17

Cassell, John. 1975. "Social Science in Epidemiology: Psychosocial Processes and 'Stress' Theoretical Formulation." In *Handbook of Evaluation*, edited by Elmer Struening and Marcia Guttentag, (pp. 537–49). Beverly Hills, CA: Sage.

Cernkovich, Stephan A. and Peggy C. Giordano. 1987. *Family Relationships and Delinquency*. Unpublished manuscript.

Clayton, Richard R. 1984. "Multiple Problem Youth—Defining the Problem and Searching for Solutions." Paper presented at the ADAMHA/OJJDP State-of-the-Art Research Conference on Juvenile Offenders with Serious Drug, Alcohol and Mental Health Problems. Washington, DC.

Cohen, Albert K. 1955. *Delinquent Boys: The Culture of the Gang*. Glencoe IL: Free Press.

Elliott, Delbert S., David Huizinga, and Suzanne S. Ageton. 1982. "Explaining Delinquency and Drug Use." The National Youth Survey Project Report No. 21. Boulder, CO: Behavioral Research Institute.

Hirschi, Travis. 1969. *Causes of Delinquency*. Berkeley, CA: University of California Press.

Jessor, R., J. A. Chase, and J. E. Donovan. 1980. "Psychosocial Correlates of Marijuana Use and Problem Drinking in a National Sample of Adolescents." *American Journal of Public Health* 6:604–613.

Chapter 18

Blumstein, Alfred. 1982. "On the Racial Disproportionality of United States' Prison Populations." *Journal of Criminal Law and Criminology* 73:1259.

Chilton, Roland and James Gavin. 1985. "Race, Crime, and Criminal Justice." *Crime and Delinquency* 31:3.

Cloward, Richard and Lloyd Ohlin. 1960. *Delinquency and Opportunity: A Theory of Delinquent Gangs.* New York: Free Press.

Cohen, Albert K. 1955. *Delinquent Boys: The Culture of the Gang.* Glencoe, IL: Free Press.

Giordano, Peggy. 1987. "Confronting Control Theory's Negative Cases." Paper presented at the Albany Conference on Theoretical Integration in the Study of Deviance and Crime, State University of New York at Albany.

Hirschi, Travis. 1964. *The Causes of Delinquency.* Berkeley and Los Angeles, CA: University of California Press.

Krisberg, Barry, Ira Schwartz, Gideon Fishman, Zvi Eisikovits and Edna Guttman. 1986. "The Incarceration of Minority Youth." Paper presented at the Annual Meeting of the American Society of Criminology in Atlanta, Georgia, October.

Langan, Patrick. 1985. "Racism on Trial: New Evidence to Explain the Racial Composition of Prisons in the United States." *Journal of Criminal Law and Criminology* 76:666.

Short, James F. Jr. 1987. "Exploring Integration of Theoretical Levels of Explanation." Paper presented at the Albany Conference on Theoretical Integration in the Study of Deviance and Crime, State University of New York at Albany.

Index

Age and crime, 46–47
Aggregate level of analysis. *See* Level of analysis; macro
Ambiguity tolerance, 22, 77, 82, 90, 95, 293 and gang behavior, 254–5. *See also* Psychological concepts
Anomie Theory. *See* Strain Theory

Biological theories of deviance integrated with sociological theories, 30, 61, 76, 98, 99

Causal image, 138–9
Conceptual issues. *See* Dependent variable; definition of
Crime; acts compared to official reactions, 140; age and, 46–47; and criminality distinguished, 47; definitional issues. *See* Dependent variable: definition of; legal, 133
Conflict theory, 158; and power-control theory, 221–226; and theory of action, 152–155; integrated with consensus theory, 106, 152; integration of concepts with Social Disorganization theory, 101, 105–6
Control Theory. *See* Social Control Theory
Criminal justice system, 153–5; and definition of deviance; *see* Dependent variable definition of; Deviance
Criteria for theory evaluation; crucial tests, 2, 4; empirical testability, 97–98, 187, 194; explained variance, 18, 187; explanatory, 137, 182; generation of research agendas, 18–19, 48; ideology, 179; logical consistency, 18–19, 48; parsimony, 99, 106, 156; predictive power, 3, 18, 52, 99, 103, 137, 156, 161–162, 172, 182–183, 186, 194; range, 187–188; scope, 188; verstehen, 182–3

Data; analysis, 114–6; discipline of criminology as, 129–135; qualitative, 261–263; quantitative, 261–263; relationship to dependent variable, 185; role in theoretical development. *See* Theoretical development: empirical input to
Delinquency; as collective behavior, 245; and Social control theory predictions, 261–2; cross level explanations of, 197, 243; definitional problems. *See* Dependent variable: definition; gang. *See* Gang deviance; measurement of, 112, 263; and power-control theory of delinquency. *See* Power-control theory; rates of and social disorganization variables, 110; relevant questions about, 244–5
Dependent variable in studies of crime and deviance; definition of, 8, 16, 47, 102–3, 121, 132, 155, 183–6, 204, 231, 237–238, 244, 265, 298; implications for integration, 25, 26; integration of, 264–265; measurement of. *See* Measurement; relationship to level of analysis, 138–9; social construction of, 132–35; *See also* Crime; Delinquency; Deviance; Mental illness
Deterrence theory, 156; issues of integration with Labelling Theory, 3, 7–8, 31
Deviance; and social differentiation; and social inequality, 231; and social problems, 209–265; conceptualization of. *See* Dependent variable: definition of; etiological questions about, 183, 244; learning role of, 87. *See also* Mental illness; integrated systems model of, 79–84; primary and secondary, 214; reactive questions about, 181, 244; social, 204; sociological context of, 207–209; typology of, 7
Differential Association theory, 9, 13, 42, 272; as theoretical imperialism, 24; integrated with Social Learning theory,

339

17, 33–34; integrated with Strain theory, 17, 33–34

Ecological theory, 105, 106; community-ecological explanation of delinquency, 163–164; *See also* Social disorganization theory
Elaboration. *See* Theoretical development: elaboration
Explanation; and levels of analysis. *See* Level of analysis; as criteria for assessing theory. *See* Criteria for theory evaluation; biological, 61; distinguished from prediction, 137; distinguished from theory, 162–65; interdisciplinary, 101, 120–21, 244, 259, 277; multiple factor approach to, 101, 119–20; psychological, 61; single factor approaches to, 101, 119–20; systemic reductionism, 101, 119–20; through empirical research, 120, 192, 282

Family relations; and delinquency, 230; *See* Power-control theory of delinquency; Social Control Theory

Gang deviance, 139, 148, 280; and individual variables, 253–254; cross-level explanation of, 245–258; *See also* Subcultural theory
Gender; and delinquency, 214–217, 298; and socialization, 248–251, 254; *See also* Power-control theory of delinquency
General theory; characteristics of, 123; need for, 126, 162; of action, 102, 140–159; of gender socialization, 238; of social integration, 166–172; of mental illness, 61–76; Social Control theory as, 44; Social Learning theory as, 21, 28; *See also* Level of analysis; Theory
Group processes in deviance theory, 257–258, 277

Ideology; and theory, 179–181; as obstacle to integration, 198, 283–286; *See also* Criteria for theory evaluation: ideology

Individual level of explanation. *See* Level of analysis: micro
Integrated systems model of deviance, 78–91; evaluation of, 95–99
Integration of theory; across levels of analysis. *See* Level of analysis; alternatives to, 16, 37, 56, 59, 99. *See also* Theoretical development; bridging concepts and, 299; definition of, 1, 2, 22, 52–53; desirability of, 1, 3, 14, 34, 51, 55, 137, 162, 258–259, 279, 282–283; directions for, 15; oppositional philosophies to, 175–177; preconditions for, 25, 198, 200; problems with, 10, 18, 24, 35–36, 41–43, 48–49, 56, 99; social science compared to natural science, 5, 11–13; terminological, 295n; types of. *See* Types of integration; *See also* Theory; Theoretical development

Labeling Theory, 183–4; and mental illness, 69; and theory of action, 158; elaboration of, 22; integrated across levels, 23; integrated with ambiguity tolerance, 22, 77, 83; integrated with Deterrence Theory, 7–8; integrated with psychological variables, 82–5, 90; primary and secondary deviance, 83, 214
Level of analysis, ix, 5, 8, 13–14, 54, 121–122; and dependent variable, 138–9; and type of explanation, 121, 243; cross level, ix, 5, 26–27, 197, 213, 227, 241, 243, 258; *See also* Type of integration: cross-level; macro, ix, 5, 101, 138–9, 163, 197, 199–200, 243, 282; micro, ix, 5, 21, 138–9, 199–200, 243, 282; typology, 26

Measurement, 4, 26; implications for integration, 26, 55, 126–7; in theory testing, 111–112; operationalization of variables. *See* Dependent variable: definition of
Mental illness; and biological attributes, 61, 76, 98; and labelling theory, 69–76; as developmental process, 62, 65, 70–76; cross-disciplinary perspective, 61–76; classification of, 61–62, 70, 74;

Index

interaction with personality attributes, 69; lack of theory, 61–62; theory of, 61–76

Norms, 245, 257–8

Personality attributes, 90, 92; and mental illness, 69; *See also* Ambiguity tolerance; Integration: cross-disciplinary
Philosophy of science, 2, 11–12, 17, 102, 126–127, 161, 173, 175, 181. *See also* Theory
Power-control theory of delinquency, 213–227, 298; evaluation of, 236–241
Psychological concepts; ambiguity tolerance. *See* Ambiguity tolerance; locus of control, 90–91, 294n; risk taking, 221, 225; self monitoring, 90–91; role modeling, 240–241; symptoms, 62; personality attributes, 62, 69

Race; and gang delinquency, 246–251, 300; and deviance, 270, 280, 281–282, 284–285
Rational choice theory, 44; and theory of action, 158
Research strategies; bias in, 279; mixed, 261–279; observation, 243–253, 300; survey, 46, 262–3; theory development and, 44; *See also* Theory: tests of; Data; Measurement
Routine activities theory, 44; and theory of action, 158

Social control, 210; *See also* Social Control theory; Power control theory of delinquency
Social Control Theory, 3, 9, 21; as general theory, 44; assumptions of, 107; comparison with Strain and Social Learning Theory, 28–29, 30–32, 45, 141–151; elaboration of, 57; evaluation of, 261–278; integration with action theory, 151–152; integration with Differential Association Theory, 9; integration with Social Learning Theory, 28–29, 30–32, 45; integration with structural and group process factors, 262–277; negative cases of, 198, 261; predictions of, 3; verification of, 3
Social differentiation and stratification, 86, 203–204, 230–235, 270–271, 279; and economic marginality, 270–271; class and, 146–47; social disability hypothesis, 251; social inequality and, 251; sexual stratification and, 223
Social Disorganization Theory; assumptions of, 107; integrated with Conflict Theory variables, 106, 108–110, 117; measurement issues in, 111–114; *See also* Ecological theory
Social integration, theory of, 167–172
Societal Reaction Theory. *See* Labeling Theory
Social Learning Theory; as general theory, 21, 28; compared with Strain and Control Theory, 141–145; integrated with action theory, 151–152; integrated with Differential Association Theory, 13, 27–28; integrated with other theories over levels of analysis, 21, 27–28, 34; integrated with Strain Theory, 32–34; predictions of, 3; verification of, 3
Social policy; influence of research on, 127
Social structure and crime, 141, 217, 296n; and theory of action, 151–160; theories of and integration across levels, 28–29; *See also* social differentiation and social stratification; structural approaches, 297n
Strain theory; compared with Social Control theory, 151–152; compared with Social Learning theory, 13, 32–34, 141–150; integrated into theory of action, 141–151; integrated with Differential Association theory, 17
Subculture theory, 139, 148, 150, 245–255, 271, 273, 299n; and gangs, 148. *See also* Gang deviance; and values, 147; compared with Social control theory, 149; compared with Strain theory, 150; integrated into theory of action, 148–151; integrated with other levels of explanation, 245, 258, 273–275

Theoretical development; by individual theory development, 44–45, 48, 198, 200; by model building, 96–99; empirical input to, 45–46, 48, 119, 127, 130, 147, 172, 174; history of, 37, 119–120, 129, 213; impediments to, 173, 201–2, 280; of power-control theory, 218–226; role of induction and deduction in, 44–45; through theory competition, 2, 3, 4, 24, 37–39, 40–43, 91; through theory elaboration, 10, 16, 21–22, 56–60; through integration; *See* Integration of theory; through links to sociological context, 210–211; *See also* Philosophy of science; Theory construction

Theory; construction of. *See* Theory construction; criteria for evaluation. *See* Criteria for theory evaluation; comparisons between, 141–147; development of. *See* Theory development; distinction from causal image, 138; distinction from explanation, 162–165; definition of, 2; elements of, 54; integration of. *See* Integration of theory; interdisciplinary, 122–125; latent function of, 18; nature of, 126; metatheory, 201–241; role of theory in science. *See* philosophy of science; structure of. *See* Theory construction; unit 201, 241; verification of. *See* Criteria for theory evaluation

Theory construction, 46, 103, 126, 161–162; formal modes of, 190–191, 193, 295–6n; role of induction in, 46–48; stages of, 54

Types of integration; conceptual, 15, 21, 26–27, 30, 34, 35, 51, 53; contextual analysis, 14; cross-level, 13, 27, 55, 197, 227, 229, 241, 243, 255, 258, 277. *See also* Level of analysis; end-to-end, 5–10, 101, 197; interdisciplinary, 22, 30, 61–63, 76, 78, 90, 92, 98, 100, 122, 131, 227; methodological, 261; middle-range, 16–17; multiple causation approach to, 261; propositional, 15, 35, 53; side-by-side, 5, 8, 13; theoretical elaboration. *See* Theoretical development; elaboration; theoretical reduction, 10–14, 120; theoretical synthesis, 10, 13, 102, 162–163; typology of, 5–6; up-and-down, 5, 8, 10, 102

Urbanism; and theory of social integration, 163–167

Values, 147, 159; and theory of action, 148–151, 159

Youth crime; and theory of Friday and Hage, 165–167; and theory of social integration, 166–167